Information, Media and Power Through the Ages

HISTORICAL STUDIES

The Irish Committee of Historical Sciences inaugurated a series of biennial conferences of historians in July 1953. Since then the 'Irish Conference of Historians'
has circulated among the Irish universities and university colleges and the papers
read since 1955 have been published as *Historical Studies*. Since 1975 the
conferences have been devoted to a single theme, the full list being as follows:

T. D. Williams (ed.) *Historical Studies I* (London: Bowes & Bowes 1958)

M. Roberts (ed.) *Historical Studies II* (London: Bowes & Bowes 1959)

J. Hogan (ed.) *Historical Studies III* (London: Bowes & Bowes 1961)

G. A. Hayes-McCoy (ed.) *Historical Studies IV* (London: Bowes & Bowes 1963)

J. L. McCracken (ed.) *Historical Studies V* (London: Bowes & Bowes 1965)

T. W. Moody (ed.) *Historical Studies VI* (London: Routledge & Kegan Paul
1968)

T. D. Williams (ed.) *Historical Studies VIII* (Dublin: Gill & Macmillan 1971)

J. G. Barry (ed.) *Historical Studies IX* (Belfast: Blackstaff Press 1974)

G. A. Hayes-McCoy (ed.) *Historical Studies X* (Dublin: ICHS 1976)

T. W. Moody (ed.) *Nationality and the pursuit of national independence: Historical
Studies XI* (Belfast: Appletree Press 1978)

A. C. Hepburn (ed.) *Minorities in history: Historical Studies XII* (London:
Edward Arnold 1978)

D. W. Harkness and M O'Dowd (ed.) *The town in Ireland: Historical Studies
XIII* (Belfast: Appletree Press 1981)

J. I. McGuire and A. Cosgrove (ed.) *Parliament and community: Historical
Studies XIV* (Belfast: Appletree Press 1981)

P. J. Corish (ed.) *Radicals, rebels and establishments: Historical Studies XV* (Belfast:
Appletree Press 1985)

Tom Dunne (ed.) *The writer as witness: literature as historical evidence: Historical
Studies XVI* (Cork: Cork University Press 1987)

Ciaran Brady (ed.) *Ideology and the historians: Historical Studies XVII* (Dublin:
The Lilliput Press 1991) ·

T.G. Fraser and Keith Jeffery (ed.) *Men, women and war: Historical Studies XVIII*
(Dublin: The Lilliput Press 1993)

Mary O'Dowd and Sabine Wichert (ed.) *Chattel, servant or citizen. Women's
status in church, state and society: Historical Studies XIX* (Belfast: Institute of
Irish Studies, 1995)

Judith Devlin and Ronan Fanning (ed.) *Religion and rebellion: Historical Studies
XX* (Dublin: University College Dublin Press, 1997)

Jacqueline Hill and Colm Lennon (ed.) *Luxury and austerity: Historical Studies
XXI* (Dublin: University College Dublin Press, 1999)

Information,
Media and Power
Through the Ages

edited by
HIRAM MORGAN

Historical Studies XXII

Papers read before the 24th Irish Conference of Historians
held at University College Cork, 20–22 May 1999

University College Dublin Press
Preas Choláiste Ollscoile Bhaile Átha Cliath

First published 2001 by University College Dublin Press,
Newman House, 86 St Stephen's Green, Dublin 2, Ireland
www.ucdpress.ie

ISBN 1 900621 61 4 hardback
1 900621 62 2 paperback

British Library Cataloguing in Publication Data
A catalogue record for this title is available from the British Library

Title page illustration: detail from messenger Donal O'Brien and
Lord Deputy Sir Henry Sidney from John Derrick's
'Image of Ireland' (London, 1581).

Typeset in Garamond by Elaine Shiels, Bantry, Co. Cork
Printed in Ireland by ColourBooks Ltd, Dublin
Index by John Loftus

In memory of John B. O'Brien (1939–99)

Contents

Preface

Hiram Morgan

This is a selection of papers from the 24th Irish Conference of Historians held at University College Cork on 20–22 May 1999. The conference was run by the UCC History Department on behalf of the Irish Committee of Historical Sciences. This committee – a cross-border body *avant la lettre* – was established in 1938 on an all-Ireland basis and in 1953 as part of its participation in *Comité International des Sciences Historiques* inaugurated an international biennial conference. Each of these conferences, held in turn at the various Irish universities, has a theme and almost all have published their proceedings in the *Historical Studies* series.

The theme of the 1999 conference was the history of information. The idea was to examine the collection and dissemination of information from Neolithic cave paintings to the Internet. Forty papers on a wide range of subjects were given, running chronologically from Herodotus to Habermas and geographically from New Zealand to Norway. It had two interrelated themes – the impact of the changing technologies of information and the use of information by individuals companies and governments. 1999 was a propitious time for such a conference. The novelty of the Internet and digital revolutions was at its height. Ireland was playing a significant role in IT development and because of the resulting economic benefits, it had been nicknamed 'the Celtic tiger'. University College Cork (UCC) was a highly appropriate place for conference on information. Its large collection of Ogam stones dating from the fifth century carry in non-alphabetic form the first written version of the Irish language. Furthermore, in the nineteenth century, Cork's first professor of mathematics George Boole devised the algebra which laid the mathematical basis of the modern computing.

The organiser wishes to thank RTÉ, the Higher Education Authority, the Norwegian Government, the British Council, Thomas Crosbie Holdings, *The Irish Times*, the Boole Library, the Irish Centre for Migration Studies, the Arts Faculty and the Department of Computer Science at UCC for their financial assistance in putting on the conference. It is necessary to thank in particular Micheál Martin TD, then minister of education and his aide, Peter MacDonagh. Bob Collins, director-general of RTÉ, and Gerry Reynolds, formerly head of RTÉ Cork, must be credited for their initiative in supporting this conference. Furthermore Antoin O'Callaghan, also of RTÉ Cork, made a splendid introductory video on the theme of the river of knowledge. Other vital local support came from Anthony Dinan of Thomas Crosbie Holdings and Brian Looney of the *Irish Examiner*. At UCC, President Gerry Wrixon, Vice-President Michael O'Sullivan, and Monica Spencer and Marie MacSweeney at the Information Office were of invaluable assistance. Various UCC professors gave their time and advice – Joe Lee, Tom Dunne, Peter Woodman, Keith Sidwell, Arpad Szakolczai and Donnchadh Ó Corráin but special thanks have to go Professor Dermot Keogh of History and Professor Jim Bowen of Computer Science who were enthusiastic backers of the conference from the outset. Geoff Roberts, Damien Bracken, Piaras MacÉinrí, John Fitzgerald and James Fairhead also gave assistance. Margaret Lantry (Ancient Classics) designed an informative conference website, and technical assistance at the conference itself was provided by Peter Flynn (Computer Centre) and Tony Perrot (Audio-Visual). From the special collections held at UCC, Helen Davis of the Boole Library put on an impressive exhibition of books relating to the conference theme. Many history students helped to promote and stage the event, most notably Alan Burke, Clara O'Byrne, James Cronin, Michelle O'Mahony and Gillian Smith. From outside Cork special thanks must go to the Irish Committee of Historians, in particular Mary O'Dowd (Queen's University, Belfast), John Logan (University of Limerick), Nicholas Canny (NUI Galway). Also to Janice Holmes (University of Ulster) and Eoin Magennis (Linen Hall Library) who convened a Young Historians' Forum to showcase emerging talent as a preliminary to the main conference. Tommy Graham, Rod Eley and the staff of the illustrated quarterly magazine *History Ireland* also deserve a mention for their promotional efforts. This book is published with the assistance of a grant from the National University of Ireland. The editor wishes to record his personal thanks to the master and fellows of St Catharine's College, Cambridge. The editor also extends his thanks to Barbara Mennell of UCD Press, to Bill Sweeney of Liverpool John Moores University and especially to Dorothy Convery who saw this project through from start to finish.

Hiram Morgan
Cork, October 2000

massively staffed Soviet intelligence organisations had a different priority and expended a lot of their resources and went to incredible lengths to prevent subversion of the communist system by dissidents at home and abroad. The same preoccupation about domestic spying was confirmed in Arpad Szakolczai's conference paper about information collection in Hungary under the communists.[25]

Naturally the role of the media in modern Ireland was given a good airing and here too a number of the common features came out in this history conference. A good contrast was presented between Daniel O'Connell's use of the media and Charles Stewart Parnell's. Gary Owens rehearsed his published research on how O'Connell used rhetoric, public rallies, visual media and folkloric imagery.[26] This was in a sense the last flourish of a Renaissance or early modern political campaign, though for decidedly populist ends. Alan O'Day's chapter shows how Parnell, barely a generation later, created himself as a national leader from a remote location through telegraphy and press coverage in spite of the fact that his personality was distinctly media unfriendly and his speeches as dry as dust. Moving out of the Parnellite era, Patrick Maume discussed his ongoing research of the *Irish Independent* newspaper and how William Martin Murphy managed to blend commerce and politics in Ireland's first mass-circulation daily. Again by way of contrast we had Donal Ó Drisceoil's paper on state censorship when nationalism fulfilled its ambitions of independence *á outrance* during wartime neutrality. Ó Drisceoil saw this as not only a response to the international crisis but also an extension of the repressive moral censorship which characterised the earliest days of the state as a whole.[27] Falling into the same category is the Irish government's irritation in 1959 with a CBS documentary made by Willard Van Dyke, scripted by Elizabeth Bowen and presented by Walter Cronkite. The state had little control over the final product which presented the American public with a dreadful picture of Ireland in the 1950s.[28] Indeed it was the desire to project a more positive, modern image of Ireland that made the Lemass government so anxious to get a state television service up and running. However, to make its mark and be commercially viable RTÉ had to respond the changing needs of the society in an entertaining fashion. The most famous example of this was Gay Byrne's *Late, Late Show* (1962–99), which reflected and led public opinion towards the ultimate rejection of the moral climate enforced by state and church. This talk show, the world's longest-running example, is a fine case of 'secondary orality' and John Bowman in introducing Finola Doyle O'Neill's paper on the topic described the TV show as turning the whole of Irish society into 'one village hall'.[29] John Horgan presents here his paper on Irish journalists' relationship with government. Historically 'the lobby' had developed into a cosy relationship – far too cosy and reciprocal one might say for a self-respecting Fourth Estate – until P. J. Mara became Haughey's press secretary and a critical distance began to develop. The result is an Irish lobby system more informal and less deferential than its British counterpart. Also featured at the conference was a subversive use of media. The Portuguese scholar Rita Lago demonstrated Sinn Féin's attempt to set an alternative news and political agenda by exploiting the new electronic media of the Internet.[30]

Allen Bass's chapter is on Habermas's ideas on communication and political democracy; similarly at the conference Patrick O'Mahony discussed and updated in the light of technological developments the Habermasian idea of the public sphere. The problem with the Habermasian position on communication (and one also evident in Bass's take on Arendt) is that it is not particularly new. In terms of western political thought the idea that communication is the basis of community is there in Aristotle through Aquinas; Habermas merely supplies a variant for secular, modern democracy. Furthermore, given what is coming out about the totality of communications in society, as most evident from Darnton, it would appear that the origins of the public sphere with its emphasis on newspapers and coffee-houses is a rather artificial, indeed westernised and modernist, construct. O'Mahony was keen to see the democratic potential of Internet exploited, but equally worried in the light of the uneven achievements of the print medium in the last half millennium.[31] Clearly the advent of print has extended, and now the Internet will extend further, participation allowing the same information to reach a wider and wider mass of people but in both cases the greatest beneficiary has been laissez-faire capitalism not only by the means of the standardisation and commodification of knowledge inherent in these media but also in their general marketing potential. Nevertheless printing and IT have both allowed critical masses of scientific knowledge to be assembled and created thereby massively assisting economic expansion not only to sustain a ever-increasing world population and to produce unparalleled wealth. However, this wealth is divided very unequally and a principal reason for it and symptom of it is the denial of communication rights to a large proportion of the world's population. The materially impoverished and physically malnourished are also 'information poor': not only is illiteracy widespread amongst them but access to nineteenth-century technology such as typewriters and telephones is restricted, let alone to the PC and Internet.

Besides the issues of access, the other perennial problems of communication are cultural and ideological; and these interfaces make some of the most compelling and intriguing of historical problems. The conference publicity featured the woodcut drawing of Donal O'Brien in John Derrick's *Image of Irelande* (London, 1581). This Irish messenger is handing over a

There is a reason for this unwillingness to gather information about other states. The one area where we would expect to find documented knowledge of affairs in other states is the preserved speeches of Athenian politicians: if a speaker were advocating a policy of involvement in a foreign sphere, the presentation of accurate and up-to-date knowledge about that area would seem essential. This is one of the aspects of Athenian thinking most difficult to understand from a modern perspective; it seems improbable that those who spoke and proposed policies in the assembly would not wish to demonstrate superior knowledge as a basis for their claim to offer the best advice. An examination of the orators, nevertheless, illustrates the surprising attitude that too much information could leave a speaker open to suspicion. In a striking interchange from 330, Aeschines mocks Demosthenes' knowledge of Athenian forts in Thrace:

This is the man, Athenians, who first discovered Serrion Teichos and Doriskos, and Ergiske and Myrtiske, and Ganos and Ganeia, places whose very names were previously unknown to us.

Aeschines 3.82

and Demosthenes was duly embarrassed.[18] Politicians were expected to be well informed on internal affairs, where information was of course freely available.[19] But to show specialist knowledge of foreign affairs, especially of the internal politics of other states, raised questions about the nature of the speaker's sources. When Demosthenes discussed Macedonian affairs in the 350s and 340s, he denoted his informants in surprisingly vague ways. 'It is reported by those who have lived with him', 'I heard from certain individuals', 'as I heard from a man who had recently been in that place, a man incapable of lying'.[20] Demosthenes had in fact been to Macedonia himself on embassies, and had friends there, yet rather than demonstrate that his policies are based on first-hand experience, he remains deliberately vague. This is because to be well-travelled implied the possession of friendships outside one's own country, which could in turn call one's loyalty into question. Demosthenes tries to conceal such friendships for fear of the capital his political opponents could make of them, the very thing which happened later on.

Athenian relations with other states were complicated by the form taken by embassies; in archaic times relationships of friendship (*xenia*) were formed across state boundaries by members of the elite, and although the state attempted to formalise such arrangements in the fifth century, ambassadors were still chosen for family or ancestral links with specific places.[21] In his very first speech to the Athenian assembly, Demosthenes assures his audience that his pro-Rhodian policy is not motivated by *proxenia* (official state-friendship):

I would never have said these things, if I thought they were for the benefit only of
the Rhodians. For I am not their proxenos, nor do I have a private friendship with
any of them.

Demosthenes 15.15

He was, however, *proxenos* of Thebes, that is, he was a designated Theban
representative at Athens, offering assistance to visitors from that city, and
maintaining contacts.[22] In 343, Aeschines (2.106) accused Demosthenes of
being sympathetic to Thebes, at that time Athens's great rival. The accusation
concerned an embassy to Macedonia three years earlier, when Demosthenes
had resisted Aeschines' proposal that the embassy should influence Philip
against Thebes. We may understand quite easily that *proxenia* was not
policy – Demosthenes thought it a bad idea to approve Philip's interfering
anywhere in Greece – but Aeschines was able to turn this into an accusation
of pro-Theban bias, because Demosthenes' suspiciously close contacts with
Thebes were known. The purpose behind the very vague references to
informants in speeches, then, is to allow the speaker to present himself as
someone whose knowledge is no better than that of any other citizen. If he
confesses to friends and contacts in Macedonia, how can he prove that he
is offering unbiased advice? Conversely, if an orator denies specific knowledge of foreign affairs, there can be no question of his acting for his own
interests because of foreign contacts – all speakers in Athenian oratory
subscribe to the same ideology of limited communication outside the state.

This same motivation influenced the Greeks very strongly against the
establishment of postal systems such as those they observed in Persia. This
was not because the Greeks lacked the technology to create roads suitable
for riders or horse-drawn traffic: these are found with some frequency providing access to major religious sites. Road networks within the territory of
a polis were the responsibility of the magistrates (at Athens the *hodopoioi*, at
Sparta the kings), and could often be fairly complex; it was, significantly,
under the Athenian tyrants in 520–10 that the road network within Attica
was constructed, with milestones centred on the altar of the Twelve Gods
in the Agora.[23] Yet roads between states were neglected, because the implications of the creation of such a system were unwelcome: just as citizens'
concerns were meant to be focused within the state, so the interests of the
state itself in terms of communication were inward-looking. There was no
central organisation to take responsibility for a road system, as in Persia:
only in religion was there an authority drawing all states together.[24] In other
areas, each state retained autonomy within its own territory, and links
between states were never strong. In part this was for reasons of defence: a
road leading from the territory of another polis into one's own might be as
threatening as it was useful. But mainly ideology restrained the creation

of closer links between poleis: states did not see it as their role to facilitate travel for their citizens.

In the face of developing technologies, then, the Athenian state defined itself as one which did not gather information about its own citizens or other states, which chose not to use spies or informers, and which valued free speech and openness. Consequently Athenian writers demonstrate unease when they are called on to define the areas in which an application of government control might be acceptable. Could the free passage of information ever be banned for the good of the state? Two particular issues are at stake here: whether it was ever admissible for politicians to conduct secret negotiations without the knowledge of the citizens, and whether a general had the right to deceive his army for the sake of military advantage.

On the topic of official secrets, we may begin with a comic scene in Aristophanes' play *Knights*. Athens had a council of 500 (the Boule), which carried out most of the everyday running of the state, and Aristophanes depicts the scene inside the council chamber as a particular item of news arrives:

[The Sausage-Seller barges into the council chamber to interrupt his rival]
. . . opening my mouth wide I bawled: 'Members of the council, I bring good news, and wish to be the first to report it to you. Since the war burst upon us, I've never seen sardines cheaper.' . . . And I told them, in strict secrecy, that to be able to buy the sardines at plenty for an obol, they should make haste to impound all the bowls in the potters' shops.
. . . the councillors stood up and made a hubbub about the sardines. He begged them to wait a moment, 'so you can learn what the herald from Sparta says,' he said, 'because he's come to discuss a peace treaty.' But with one voice they all cried, 'A peace treaty now? Oh yes, my good man, now that they've found out that sardines are cheap here! We don't want any treaty; let the war carry on!'. And they shouted for the Prytaneis to dismiss them; they leapt over the railings at every point.

Aristophanes, Knights 641–73

This comic image tells us a lot about the importance of fish to Athenian diners, and about attitudes towards politicians which we may still recognise, but it is also suggestive about the handling of information.[25] The council members, by virtue of their position, have access to specialised knowledge, and the danger is that they will use this inside knowledge to secure an advantage over the rest of the citizens. As part of Aristophanes' satire on government, the passage comments on the issue of secrecy: the councillors can get information first, can withhold it (at least temporarily) from the citizens, and can profit from what they know. At root is the suspicion that secrecy within government might be pursued for personal gain.

But how real a threat was the idea of government secrecy to the ordinary citizen? Classical Athens had no Official Secrets Act: the ideal was that all public business should be transacted openly, with officials held accountable for their policies. Nevertheless, many episodes indicate that secrecy could be found desirable by the authorities at some times. In 396, for instance, Athens was not officially at war, but an Athenian general, Conon, was commanding the Persian fleet in Asia Minor, effectively operating against Sparta. In winter 396 an Athenian commander named Demainetos made a secret agreement with the Boule, and sailed to Asia, to join Conon:

About the same time a trireme sailed out from Athens without the agreement of the people. In charge of it was Demainetos who had, it is said, made a secret agreement with the Council concerning this affair, since some of the citizens supported him. With them he went down to the Piraeus, launched a ship from the ship-sheds, and, putting to sea, was on his way to Conon.

Thereupon there was a great outcry. Those of the Athenians who were well born and cultivated were indignant, saying that they would destroy the city by beginning a war with the Spartans. The councillors were alarmed by the outcry and called the people together, making out that they had no share in the affair. When the people were assembled, the party of . . . Thrasyboulos, Aesimus and Anytus stood up and told them that they risked great danger unless they absolved the city from responsibility.

. . . the majority of the populace, in a state of fear and persuaded by those who advised them, sent envoys to Milon, the [Spartan] governor of Aegina, to tell him how he could punish Demainetos, who had not acted with the city's approval.

Hellenika Oxyrhynchia 6.1–3

The Boule were thus clandestinely supporting a pro-war policy, opposed by the oligarchic faction, who considered open war too dangerous. What is striking is that there was so much public concern over the affair, and a clear recognition that the council had acted wrongly; even in wartime, the right of the people to be consulted was paramount.[26] In fact, the episode is surprisingly modern, with the council trying to dissociate themselves from the venture when the news got out. Sometimes episodes of official secrecy are explicable as emergency measures – when a conspiracy was suspected, for instance, or to gain the advantage of surprise over an enemy.[27] Yet even these episodes cause unease among ancient commentators. For executive decisions to be made by the Boule alone, without the people being informed, was to convert the democracy to an oligarchy. It was not acceptable that power be kept in the hands of an individual or small group. Just as with spies, it is not that the Athenians could not see other states operating with very strong internal secrecy: Sparta was notorious for its valuing of unquestioning obedience to the magistrates, and its use of paranoia and secret murders to keep its resident slave population in terror.[28] But the Athenians endorsed a universally negative opinion of this behaviour.

The Demainetos affair furthermore highlights a particular area in which information can be a problem: military security. Demainetos and his

debates about ideology, about access, and about state control. What a study of classical attitudes demonstrates is that the liberal paradox, the freedom to innovate and to disagree, was being explored even at the very dawn of IT invention: the terms of the debate have hardly changed. Every era has faced questions associated with the progress of information technology, from sixteenth-century messengers to nineteenth-century newspapers. We should not assume that every state welcomes innovation with open arms: in the ancient world the conceptual systems of the Greeks had a braking effect on the introduction of new technologies, and it was a price which all but a few were happy to pay.

NOTES

1 J. F. McMillan, *Times Literary Supplement*, 31 March 2000.
2 Aristotle, *Politics* 1313b 10–15, 32–8.
3 Polyainos 5.2.3.
4 Thucydides 8.66 describes the parallel situation of fear and uncertainty of the Athenians during the short-lived revolution of 411.
5 Herodotus 5.52–4, 8.98; Xenophon, *Cyropaedia* 8.6.17–18.
6 Herodotus 1.123–4; 5.35; 7.239.
7 S. W. Hirsch, *The Friendship of the Barbarians: Xenophon and the Persian Empire* (Hanover and London, 1985), argues that the King's Eye was an entirely Greek invention
8 J. Ober, *Mass and Elite in Democratic Athens* (Princeton, 1989), p. 296.
9 Plutarch *Lykurgus*, 27.3–4, Plato, *Protagoras* 342c, Xenophon, *Lak. Pol.* 14.4. See in general on Sparta M. I. Finley, 'Sparta', in *The Use and Abuse of History* (Harmondsworth, 1975, repr. 1990), ch. 10, and also E. David, 'Laughter in Spartan society', in A. Powell (ed.), *Classical Sparta: Techniques behind Her Success* (London, 1989), pp. 1–25.
10 Plutarch, *Lykurgus* 18–20.
11 A similar episode is recorded after the Spartan disaster at Lechaeum in 390 (*Hell.* 4.5.10).
12 M. Foucault, *Discipline and Punish: The Birth of the Prison* (London, 1977), section 3.1, 'Docile bodies', comments on the parallel rise in the eighteenth century in the use of the body as a locus of control.
13 Plutarch, *Nikias* 30.
14 Lycurgus, *Against Leokrates* 14–15.
15 A. Gerolymatos, *Espionage and Treason: A Study of the Proxenia in Political and Military Intelligence Gathering in Classical Greece* (Amsterdam, 1986) attempted to establish the proxenos in this role. See also F. S. Russell, *Information Gathering in Classical Greece* (Ann Arbor, 2000).
16 Demosthenes 4.18.
17 *IG* ii 2 29, M. N. Tod, *Greek Historical Inscriptions* (Oxford, 1947), no. 116.
18 Aesch. 3.82; compare Dem. 7.37 and 18.27.

19 See Xenophon, *Memorabilia* 3.6, on the would-be politician Glaucon; R. K. Sinclair, *Democracy and Participation at Athens* (Cambridge, 1988), ch. 7.

20 Demosthenes 11.12, 1.22–3, 2.17.

21 See G. Herman, *Ritualised Friendship and the Greek City* (Cambridge, 1987).

22 Aeschines 2.141. and 143.

23 *Hodopoioi*: Aristotle, Ath Pol. 54.1; Sparta: Herodotus 6.57.4; Athenian tyrants: Thucydides 6.54.7, Herodotus 2.7.1.

24 Responsibility of Delphic Amphictyony for roadbuilding: *IG* ii2 1126, 40–4. See further S. Lewis, *News and Society in the Greek Polis* (London, 1996) 29–31.

25 On the significance of fish in Athenian social and political ideologies, see J. Davidson, *Courtesans and Fishcakes: The Consuming Passions of Classical Athens* (London, 1997).

26 I. A. F. Bruce, *A Historical Commentary on the Hellenica Oxyrhynchia* (Cambridge, 1967) refers to Isaeus 11.48 for a similar expedition, but this time with discussion in the assembly.

27 E.g. Andocides 1.12, Diodorus 11.42. See G. E. M. De ste. Croix, 'The alleged secret pact between Athens and Philip II concerning Amphilpolis and Pydna', *Classical Quarterly* 139 (1963), 110–19.

28 Plutarch Lykurgus 28, Thucydides 4.80; J. Ducat, *Les Hilotes, Bulletin de Correspondance Héllenique*, Suppl. 20 (Paris 1990).

29 D. L. Gera, *Xenophon's Cyropaedia: Style, Genre and Literary Technique* (Oxford 1993), pp. 68–9.

30 Herodotus 6.133

31 Aeschines 3.103.

32 *Acts* 17.21: 'For all the Athenians and strangers which were there spent their time in nothing else, but either to tell, or to hear some new thing.'

33 Plato, *Republic* 386c–394d, 595a–608b; 377a–c; *Laws* 950d–53d; *Laws* 780a, 784a. See G. R. Morrow, *Plato's Cretan City: A Historical Interpretation of the Laws* (Princeton, 1993), ch. 7; J. Annas, *An Introduction to Plato's* Republic (Oxford, 1981), ch. 4.

2 News and Information in the Papyri from Greco-Roman Egypt

B. C. McGing

I f asked to say what they associate with Egypt, most people would probably think first of the well-known images of tourism: the pyramids; or the gold of Tutenkhamun; or perhaps the valley of the kings. In the Greco-Roman world, while the pyramids formed the most famous tourist attraction, what invariably caught the attention of outsiders, almost all of it hostile, was the worship of animals.[1] 'Who knows', asked the Roman satirist Juvenal most famously 'what monsters demented Egypt worships?' (*Satire* 15.1–2). In practical terms, however, the most important thing about Egypt was water (or the lack of it); and in particular the Nile. Egypt *was* the Nile. The only cultivable parts, amounting to a total of about 25,000 square kilometres,[2] were the Delta, the valley of the river itself, only a few miles wide at some points, and the Fayum, a depression about 100 kilometres south-west of Cairo, into which a branch of the Nile flowed. The rest was, apart from some oases in the west, very inhospitable desert. Life in Egypt from man's first presence was dictated by the great natural movement, year in year out, of the river. As the fifth century BC Greek historian Herodotus noted, and tried unsuccessfully to explain (2.20–7), it did exactly the opposite of what every other known river did: it began to flood in June/July, reached a peak in September and then began to fall away, leaving a life-giving deposit of silt – one of the greatest natural fertilisers in the world. The Aswan Dam finally put an end to this primevally old process.[3]

I mention the Nile for two reasons. First, the resulting fertility created the single most important economic activity of Egypt – or important at least from the point of view of the government – the production of grain. The excess went a long way to feeding Rome and later Constantinople, making it easy to understand why the exploitation of the land was so closely monitored and controlled.[4] Second, the marshes of the Nile, particularly in the Delta, seem to have been the only place in the Mediterranean world where papyrus, a member of the sedge family, grew, or was grown on a commercial basis. It features in a decorative role in much Pharaonic art, but was also used in a host of other ways, most importantly of course in the production of ancient writing paper (which we also call papyrus). The paper was made from strips of the pith of the plant, laid in a criss-cross pattern, pressed together, dried and smoothed down to an excellent writing surface.[5]

If Egypt was the only place where papyrus was produced it is also virtually the only place it has survived. The hot desert sands are a great preservative. Papyrus is quite a hardy material, but it must be kept dry and out of the light to survive. Egypt is one of the very few places in the Mediterranean world dry enough, and indeed not all of Egypt, only particular localities within it. Alexandria, for instance, although the capital of a huge bureaucratic system, has produced no finds of papyri, as much of the ancient city is under water, and in any case the water table is so high that moisture must have destroyed anything perishable that was thrown out. Outside Egypt the Dead Sea scrolls survived in caves in the Judaean desert; and there have been other discoveries in the sands of the Middle East.[6] In the wetter climes of the northern half of the Mediterranean, only an occasional accident has preserved any papyrus: the wooden tablets (which usually come under the jurisdiction of papyrology) from Vindolanda on Hadrian's Wall, for example, or the carbonised material from Herculaneum, destroyed in the eruption of Vesuvius in AD 79.[7]

We have papyrus used as writing paper from about 3000 BC in the Egyptian language. With the annexation of Egypt by Alexander the Great in 332 BC, and the subsequent founding of the Ptolemaic dynasty, Egypt enters a period of its history in which Greek remains the official language for almost 1000 years – even after the defeat in 31 BC of the last of the Ptolemies, Cleopatra, when Egypt was incorporated as a province of the Roman empire. Egyptian continued, of course, to be spoken and written in its various forms (Hieroglyphs, Hieratic, Demotic and eventually Coptic), but the papyrological documentation that survives is overwhelmingly in Greek. This Greek millennium finally came to an end in AD 641 with the Arab conquest and the arrival of Islam.[8]

The first Greek papyrus from Egypt was published in 1778 (it was a list of village inhabitants dating to AD 192–3), but in spite of the great interest aroused in things Egyptian by Napoleon's expedition,[9] it was not really until the end of the nineteenth century that papyri began to be found in large quantities. Local farmers discovered that soil from ancient rubbish dumps could be used as fertiliser, and that thousands of pieces of ancient papyrus were to be found (and sold to rich foreigners). The British, followed by other Europeans, soon sent out archaeological expeditions to look for papyrus texts. They found them not only in the ground, but also used as a sort of papier maché wrapping paper (called cartonnage) for mummies. As a result, big collections were formed in, for instance, Oxford,

London, Manchester, Berlin, Heidelberg, Vienna, Prague, Florence and a little later in the United States.[10] At the end of the nineteenth century and beginning of the twentieth century, the main hope of Classical scholars in relation to papyrology was that it would reveal great new works of ancient Greek literature. This hope was largely, although not entirely, dashed when it became clear that the vast majority of texts concerned matters of everyday life. Social and economic history was of little interest to the Classical establishment at the time, with the exception of some, like J. P. Mahaffy (later Provost of Trinity College, Dublin) in particular, who had already written a social history of Greece, and had the foresight to recognise the potential of the papyrological material.[11] It is worth stressing just how extraordinary and dramatic papyri are as source material. For writing the history of the Greco-Roman world we have what I think modern historians would regard as very limited sources.[12] The process of selecting historically significant data has, very largely, been done for us. There is a substantial corpus of Greek and Latin literature, written by an almost exclusively male and aristocratic elite. There are inscriptions, thousands of them, more discovered each year, and extremely valuable at times. There are coins, often an important medium for the conveyance of certain types of royal or imperial message (although this is disputed). And there are the material remains – from pots to pyramids, seeds to sarcophagi, bones, mosaics, jewelry, weapons and so on. All of this kind of evidence is available for Egypt, but in addition we have the qualitatively different evidence provided by papyri.[13] Agreements, receipts, wills, personal correspondence, accounts and lists, government papers going to administration officials or to a wider audience, and documents coming from ordinary people to the administration – petitions, complaints, applications, declarations. This all provides an extraordinary depth of detail, a window on the minutiae of everyday life, for the Ptolemaic kingdom and even more so for the Roman province of Egypt, that is not even remotely matched anywhere else in the ancient world.[14] What does this extraordinary written record tell us about the dissemination of news and information, both public and private?[15] In this chapter I want to avoid the vast body of material that relates to taxation (there is simply too much of it): I am thinking more of the voluntary communication of news/information with someone else, rather than of official record-keeping – an enormous operation in Greco-Roman Egypt – and the compulsory inspections and submissions it required.[16]

Before addressing this question, however, we must briefly mention the problem of literacy. Who could write, and who could read, the written word? And what effect does our answer have on the subject of news? Although literacy levels in the ancient world are disputed, and varied from period to period and place to place, probably only a small percentage of the population was literate.[17] With such a large body of written material, so much of it concerning everyday matters, the evidence from Egypt is obviously particularly striking. Especially interesting is the large number of Greek documents which have the formulaic subscription 'I wrote on his/her behalf because he/she does not know letters'.[18] In Ptolemaic Egypt it was mostly officials of the administration, or those associated with it, who were literate; but even in Roman times, when writing began to intrude much more into the lives of ordinary (and illiterate) people, society remained substantially oral. For example, birth and death certificates seem to have been compulsory in Roman Egypt, but there was no difficulty if you could not write: a professional scribe could do it for you.[19] And very few of the people who wanted to qualify for the corn dole in the town of Oxyrhynchus (there was a limit of 4,000) were able to write the application themselves.[20] Even someone with the job of village-scribe (*komogrammateus*) did not have to be fully literate, as is revealed by the famous case of Petaus in the village of Ptolemais Hormou.[21] Clearly if you were not yourself literate, you could easily avail yourself of someone else's literacy.[22] The whole matter of who could read and write, and to what extent, and in which language, and what any of this signified, is brightly illuminated by the evidence from Egypt. It constantly lurks behind all the documents we read, and will be of concern from time to time in what I say, but it is not the central object of this investigation. If news was transmitted by papyrus text, or information stored on paper, the relatively small proportion of people who could read it evidently passed on by word of mouth whatever needed to be known.

Let us start with the central government, in the form of the king, the emperor or the administration officials within Egypt. What sort of news did they feel it necessary to communicate to the people in general? While there was a great deal of information in writing going up and down the chain of command, there was not much that needed to be communicated by general proclamation. Emperors who had just succeeded to the throne wanted this information disseminated as quickly as possible, particularly, as in later Roman times, when there were pretenders staking a contrary claim to the throne. We have a small number of texts announcing the death of an emperor and the accession of his successor. The following one comes from Oxyrhynchus, a town some 350 kilometres south of Alexandria. The governor of Egypt informs the strategi of the nomes (district administrators) that Trajan has died and Hadrian is now emperor; they are to declare celebrations in their area and publish this information (*P. Oxy.* LV 3781):

Rammius Martialis (to the strategi of the underwritten districts?) greetings.

Be it known to you that for the salvation of the whole race of mankind the imperial rule has been taken over from the god his father by Imperator Caesar Traianus Hadrianus Optimus Augustus Germanicus Dacicus Parthicus. Therefore we shall pray to all the gods that his continuance may be preserved to us for ever and shall wear garlands for ten days. This you are to publish to the districts under your charge.

Year 1, Mesore, 2nd intercalary day.

Letopolite, Memphite, Arsinoite, Aphroditopolite, Heracleopolite, Oxyrhynchite, Oasis of the Heptanomia, Cynopolite, Hermopolite.

The order is dated 25 August AD 117, which is only 14 days after Hadrian's proclamation in Antioch. This is fast for news to travel and interestingly the speed confirms the evidence of our literary sources (*HA Hadr.* 5.9–10; Dio 69.2.1) that Hadrian assumed power without consulting the Senate in Rome. That the text was found in Oxyrhynchus also shows that Rammius accepted Hadrian's accession without hesitation and without waiting for confirmation from Rome. Hesitation could prove dangerous: when the governor of Egypt, Valerius Datus, waited to proclaim Macrinus in AD 217 until the Senate confirmed his accession, Valerius was hunted down and killed. On the other hand backing the wrong person could lead to trouble: Avidius Cassius was supported in AD 175 by the Prefect without authority from Rome, but he lasted only three months. [23]

Another Oxyrhynchite example (in the Library of Trinity College, Dublin) concerns the accession of Nero (*P. Sel.* II, 235). It is not addressed to anyone and must be a draft for an official circular or public proclamation:

The Caesar who had to pay his debt to his ancestors, god manifest, has joined them, and the expectation and hope of the world has been declared emperor, the good genius of the world and source of all good things, Nero, has been declared Caesar. Therefore ought we all wearing garlands and with sacrifices of oxen to give thanks to all the gods. The 1st year of the Emperor Nero Claudius Caesar Augustus Germanicus, the 21st of the month Neos Sebastos.

In this case the date is 17 November AD 54, only 35 days after the death of Claudius. Thirty-five days from Rome all the way to Oxyrhynchus is again very fast. There is an urgency about this process. It could be unsettling to have rumour circulating: it is important, from the emperor's point of view, that everyone should know the situation as soon as possible. In other words this written communication probably is the bringer of the news itself – which is not always necessarily the case with written texts.

As we saw in the Hadrianic proclamation, the local officials were required to 'publish' the news. The Greek just says 'make clear'. One way of making something clear was to have criers read the text. On 10 November AD 41, the emperor Claudius sent a famous letter to the people of Alexandria. [24] There had been fierce strife between the Greek citizens and the Jewish community, memorably described by the Jewish philosopher Philo in his work *Against Flaccus*. Philo led an embassy of his fellow Jews to Italy to plead their case before the emperor Caligula (described in his

Embassy to Gaius); but Caligula was uninterested and it was left to his successor Claudius to deal with the problem. In a series of reasonable and equitable instructions to both sides, Claudius was able to restore order and settle the affair. What concerns us for present purposes is the preamble to the emperor's letter:

Proclamation by Lucius Aemilius Rectus. Seeing that all the populace, owing to its numbers, was unable to be present at the reading of the most sacred and most beneficent letter to the city, I have deemed it necessary to display the letter publicly in order that reading it one by one you may admire the majesty of our god Caesar and feel gratitude for his goodwill to the city. Year 2 of Tiberius Claudius Caesar Augustus Germanicus Imperator, the 14th of Neus Sebastus.

So the governor first had it read aloud and then he posted a copy for people to read one by one. We need not take the governor's instructions as an assumption of widespread literacy: he seems only to have put up one copy, and after the violence of the pogrom he surely knew that Claudius's intervention would be big news and would spread rapidly by word of mouth.

We do have, however, instructions to put up public notices in large and clear letters from different periods. In the early third century BC a royal ordinance instructs tax farmers to 'write this document on a white notice-board in large letters and place it outside the agoranomos-office every day' (*P. Hib.* I, 29.9–10). Sometimes the instructions include an order to publish in both Greek and Egyptian (e.g. *P. Rev.* 9.4 [259 BC]): the most famous example (although not written on papyrus) is the Rosetta Stone, a priestly decree of 196 BC honouring Ptolemy V Epiphanes, which contains at the end an order that it be written up in Hieroglyphics, Demotic and Greek.[25] A Roman governor of the first century AD, Cn. Vergilius Capito, orders the publication of his instructions in clear and easy-to-read letters, so that everyone knows exactly what he has ordered (*OGIS* 665.14). In AD 119 Hadrian granted the right to claim possession of their father's property to children born to, and recognised by, Roman soldiers while in service (*BGU* I, 140). It was an important concession. This is the preamble:

Copy of a letter of the emperor, translated . . . which was publicly displayed in the 3rd year of Traianus Hadrianus Augustus, in the consulship of Publius Aelius for the 3rd time and of Rusticus, at Alexandria (?) in the winter camp of legion iii Cyrenaica and legion xxii Deioteriana, on the 4th of August which is the 11th of Mesore, at headquarters.

So this was posted up in the camps of the two legions stationed in Alexandria. Although there is again no very large assumption of literacy here – in the enclosed community of a legion, the news would be conveyed with great ease by literate staff officers down through the ranks – there is an emphasis on the importance of the written version; and, time and again, on the easy legibility of the notice. In AD 198–9 Q. Aemilius Saturninus issues an edict against fortune-tellers, who have been conning people (presumably even more than usual): local officials are to display it 'in public on a whitened board in characters that are clear and easily legible'.[26] A few years later (AD 206) Subatianus Aquila sends a circular to the nome strategi ordering them to publish it in clear letters in the nome capitals and other prominent places of the nome for a period of not less than thirty days (*P. Oxy.* VIII, 100.3–4). Clearly the writing of these notices was not just an empty gesture: there really was an expectation that *some* people would read them. That the number capable of reading them might have been small does not matter: the written text offered an authoritative version of the government decision, thus minimising any possible misunderstandings.

Sometimes the details of the contents are not necessarily the main message. An edict proclaimed by Severus Alexander on his accession in AD 222 granting a tax concession, has the following instruction at the end (*P. Sel.* II, 216):

The governors of the provinces will learn more and more how zealously it behoves them to spare and be considerate for the peoples over whom they have been placed, when they are able to see the emperor also conducting the business of his realm with so much propriety and moderation and self-restraint. Let the magistrates in each city see to it that copies of this edict are set up in public in full view of those who wish to read it.

The impost itself is quite a technical matter, and I do not think we know who was liable for it, but the important thing is the emperor's generosity: this is a propaganda exercise as well as just the communication of information.

The edicts, letters and rescripts (responses to particular petitions or requests) of the emperors came to be a major source of Roman law.[27] As we have seen, some have specific instructions for publication, but even if such instructions are absent it does look as if there was access to the documents. For they get quoted as supporting documentation in petitions filed by individuals in search of legal redress. Even more frequently decisions of former governors of Egypt, or even lower ranking officials, are adduced as support for a petition. In one remarkable Oxyrhynchus document (*P. Oxy.* VI, 899), a woman called Apollonarion claims, on the basis of her sex, exemption from the forced cultivation of certain plots of Crown land. The date is AD 200, but she is able to append local judgements going back over 160 years earlier.

We have a number of edicts preserved on papyrus of the Ptolemaic monarchs which must have been made public, even though the mechanism for doing so is not specified. On one occasion, from the first century BC, a local official dockets a decree of the king and queen to indicate publication (*P. Sel.* II, 209 [50 BC?]):

Decree of the king and queen. No one purchasing wheat or pulse from the nomes above Memphis shall carry it down to the low country or yet carry it up to the Thebaid on any pretext, though all may transport it to Alexandria free of question, on pain of being liable to death if detected. Whoever wishes shall inform the strategus of his nome about contraventions of this order, on the understanding that he shall receive the third part of the property of the person found guilty, or, if he be a slave, shall be freed and in addition receive the sixth part. Year 3, Phaophi 23.

(2nd hand) I, Horus, district scribe, acting through Onias, scribe, have posted up one copy of the foregoing decree. Year 3, Hathur [.]5.

Such posting must be the normal assumption about major decrees, especially in the area of law and order. In 118 BC the reconciliation of Ptolemy VIII and his sister Cleopatra II and niece Cleopatra III was celebrated with a famous amnesty (*P. Sel.* II, 210):

King Ptolemy and Queen Cleopatra the sister and Queen Cleopatra the wife proclaim an amnesty to all their subjects for errors, crimes, accusations, condemnations and offences of all kinds up to the 9th of Pharmouthi of the 52nd year, except to persons guilty of wilful murder or sacrilege.

The details it then presents paint a fascinating picture of the degree of lawlessness in the Ptolemaic kingdom at the end of the second century BC.[28] Criminals and brigands are forgiven and ordered to return to their homes. The Egyptian clergy receives a series of benefactions, grants and reassurances, in a continuing attempt to keep them sweet. Tax arrears are cancelled. Various agricultural failings are forgiven as are corrupt customs and granary officials. Such an important document must have been posted: it was vital for people to know the specifics.

Similarly the Roman government was at times very anxious to make general proclamations on matters of public order. Banditry was a constant reality in the life of more remote parts of the Roman empire, and the desert wastes of Egypt provided good bandit territory.[29] In about AD 210 the governor of Egypt, Baebius Juncinus, sent the following instructions to his subordinates (*P. Oxy.* XII, 1408 [*c.* AD 210–14]):

Baebius Juncinus to the strategi of the Heptanomia and Arsinoite nome, greeting. I have already in a previous letter ordered you to search out robbers with every care, warning you of the peril of neglect, and now I wish to confirm my decision by a decree, in order that all the inhabitants of Egypt may know that I am not treating this duty as an affair of secondary importance, but offer rewards to those of you who cooperate, and on the other hand expose to peril those who choose to disobey. The said decree I desire to be made public in both the capitals and the most important places of the nomes, penalties including personal risk being laid upon you if in the future evil-doers are enabled to use violence without being detected. I hope for your health. The . . . year, Phaophi 28.

Prices were sometimes set at government level. A Ptolemaic example from 111 BC fixes the price of myrrh (*P. Tebt.* I, 35). It is sent to village officials, with the instruction, 'let the subjoined notice be posted up with the concurrence of the village secretary, who shall sign his name below the order along with you'. It is important, apparently, that it is validated with official signatures. Diocletian's famous Prices Edict of AD 301, applying a schedule of maximum prices for goods and services to the whole empire, must have made its way down to local level in Egypt as in the rest of the empire.[30]

Apart from the relatively few communications from the king, emperor, governor or other senior officials to the people of Egypt in general, a great deal of administrative detail must have been passed on orally at the public level. A good example of an instruction coming down the chain of command is provided by an interesting document of AD 278 concerning the vital matter of dyke work and the cleaning of canals (*P. Sel.* II, 225): all adult males had to give five days' labour to this task. One of the financial officers of Egypt, the dioiketes (at this time a man called Ulpius Aurelius) has sent an instruction from Alexandria to the strategi of the relevant nomes; and Aurelius Harpocration, strategus of the Oxyrhynchite nome, now sends a copy of Ulpius's letter on to lower officials of the nome, the *decemprimi*. It is presumably just sent to the local senate, as Aurelius Harpocration writes 'whoever of you first receives this order should pass it on to the others'. The dykes and canals were crucial for the whole agricultural enterprise of the area:

Therefore let it be the care for you, the strategi and *decemprimi*, both to urge all to take in hand this most necessary labour and to see that the overseers usually elected for the purpose are chosen from magistrates or even private individuals, their task being to compel everyone to perform his proper work in person . . . so that the dykes are brought up to the prescribed height and breadth and the breaches filled in, to enable them to withstand the the flood of the most sacred Nile auspiciously approaching, and that the canals are are cleaned to the depth of the so-called standards and the usual width, in order that they may easily absorb the coming influx of water for the irrigation of the fields . . . and that in no case is money extracted from any person instead of work. If anyone dares to attempt such a thing or disregards these orders, let him know that by impairing measures designed for the welfare of the whole of Egypt he will put at risk not only his property but his very life.

The order has come from the dioiketes in Alexandria to the strategus in Oxyrhynchus; he has passed it on to the *decemprimi*, who are to see to it that reliable overseers are appointed; and the overseers must make sure that everyone does the required work and that no one tries to get out of it by paying money instead. The overseers presumably kept, or had access to, a list of all the people liable for this compulsory labour, but the final order to the individuals must have been done by word of mouth (although you did receive a written certificate when you had completed your five days work[31]). The reason for the concern of the dioiketes is well illustrated by an Oxyrhynchus petition of AD 80–1 (*P. Oxy.* XLV, 3264). An accusation has been made that village officials have accepted a bribe of four drachmas from each of 51 individuals who were detailed to do the five-day work-shift on dike maintenance; they are also accused of covering up for nine others who neglected to perform the work. Only 13 men out of the 60 can be found to swear an oath to the strategus that they have not given money to avoid the dike work, and it is easy to imagine that there has been widespread corruption in the avoidance of this unpopular task.

I have been examining some matters where the government com-municates news or information with the public. In the reverse direction almost the only occasion a private person would voluntarily communicate in writing with the government is when he is wronged, or thinks he is wronged, and seeks redress. There are thousands of petitions from indi-viduals to officers of the state complaining about the infringement of a person's rights and resulting loss.[32] By Roman times the population, or parts of it at least, had become highly litigious: the now famous illustration of this is provided by a papyrus which tells us that in three days of assizes at Arsinoe the Prefect Subatianus Aquila received 1,804 petitions (*P. Yale* I, 61 [AD 208–10]). If you could win restitution without recourse to an official petition, that would be the best outcome of your problem; and presumably many local disagreements were sorted out unofficially.[33] If you took the official route, you would be hoping for an immediate judgement in your favour (which happened only rarely); failing that, the idea was to set in motion a legal process that would eventually secure justice for you. Sometimes it could be a lengthy process with the official you petitioned passing on the matter to a higher authority or ordering subordinates to investigate further (there are some impressive examples of 'passing the buck'). Curiously there was no highly organised procedure for petitioning: you simply appealed to whichever official you thought offered the best chance of action. In the Ptolemaic period it was often the king; but in Roman times, while it was possible to appeal to the governor or even the emperor, it was usually more readily accessible officials. In 220 BC Ktesikles complained to the king that he was being wronged by his daughter Nike and her husband Dionysius (*P. Sel.* II, 268):

For though I nurtured her, being my own daughter, and educated her and brought her up to womanhood, when I was stricken with bodily infirmity and my eyesight became enfeebled she would not furnish me with the necessities of life. And when I wished to obtain justice from her in Alexandria . . . she gave me a written oath by the king that she would pay me twenty drachmas every month by means of her own bodily labour . . . Now, however, corrupted by that bugger Dionysius, she is not keeping any of her engagements to me, in contempt of my old age and present infirmity.

This sort of relatively minor family matter represents well one of the two general categories into which disputes fall: those between private individuals; and those between private individuals and the state. The most common difficulties that people had with each other were probably characteristic of human society at any period in history: disagreements about dowry, inheritance and property rights, defaulting on loans (or other contracts), and theft and assault (both considered civil wrongs). Theft and assault were often simple matters, but, inevitably perhaps, family disputes over inheritance, money, land could get very complicated, and were not conducive to easy solution, any more than they are nowadays. Individuals came into dispute with the state for a variety of reasons. Sometimes it was a matter of incorrect entries in official records: you might be incorrectly listed as liable to certain taxes or duties. Senphibis, for instance, complains to the epistrategus that the land register is wrong (*P. Oxy.* III, AD 488 [second/third century AD]): she has one aroura less than she is registered for – which would have serious tax implications for her. The tone of her petition implies that she thinks the official concerned is being deliberately negligent, and there are plenty of examples of corrupt officials engaging in extortion, fraud, forgery. Perhaps the most troublesome area in the relationship between the state and the individual was in the matter of the extensive system of compulsory public services, called liturgies.[34] These had perhaps started out as theoretically a voluntary display of munificence, but developed into a compulsory contribution of money or labour. They were a relentless reality for the inhabitants of Roman Egypt, from the rich right down the social and economic scale: the maintenance of canals and dikes (as we have seen above), the many tasks relating to the functioning of temples and festivals, supervision of building works, delivery of the harvest to the granaries, upkeep of public baths, the collection of certain taxes, and many more. Two main difficulties arise: incorrect or inapplicable nominations, and neglect or corruption in carrying out the duty.

The petitions present a most revealing picture of individuals in dispute with each other and with the state. Although Tacitus claimed that Egypt was 'indifferent to law and ignorant of civil government' (*Hist.* 1.11), in many ways the petitions prove quite the contrary: the large number of complaints implies a basically law-abiding society, which assumes that law, order and civil government are the norm. Seeking redress for wrong done to you is hardly about the communication of news, but it does concern information and, to a certain extent, power. Ordinary people did have access to the Ptolemaic king (no doubt circumscribed) or Roman emperor (even more circumscribed): there were expectations that you could assert your rights through written communication with the authorities. And even if Aurelia Thaisous thought it might impress the governor that she was able to write her own petition (*P. Sel.* II, 305 [AD 263]), there is no evidence to suggest that literacy was any more necessary in this process than in any of the other areas of life which involved writing.

I end, briefly, with the subject of letter writing. Let us start with a definition:[35]

The letter is a written message, which is sent because the corresponding parties are separated spatially. The letter is a written means of keeping oral conversation in motion. Regarding the essential purposes served by letter writing, the maintenance of contact between relatives and friends was sometimes sufficient motivation for writing. But, on most occasions, the sender had a more specific reason for writing; desiring either to disclose/seek information or needing to request/command something of the recipient.

Amongst the literate the letter has always been a source of news. Cicero in exile longed for news of what was happening politically in Rome; and he wrote to his friends telling them what he himself was doing. Following on from him, and the rhetorical study of the letter, there is a long epistolary tradition in European literature. But you did not have to be literate to engage in correspondence: as we have already seen, even in areas where literacy intrudes forcefully into the life of people who do not know letters, and requires a written response, you could easily borrow someone else's literacy. One of the great gifts of the Greek papyri from Egypt is the thousands of personal letters that survive.[36] These are not, on the whole, self-conscious, 'literary' letters, but the ordinary communications of ordinary people. In some ways they resemble more email messages than the sort of letter people wrote in generations gone by. They tend to be short, often containing instructions to do something or queries about what to do, and written mostly in clichéd and formulaic language, and, therefore, somewhat impersonal: this may be to do with the fact they are often dictated by illiterate correspondents. Even among the educated high officials of state they are not really used as a vehicle for discussion of the current situation. If in some ways, then, they can be seen as disappointing, they still offer the most immediate access to the life and thinking of ordinary people that we have from the ancient world.

Sometimes distance creates newsworthiness, and particularly prominent in this regard are letters from soldiers stationed far from home. Here is a letter from a recruit who has gone off to Italy to serve in the army (*P. Sel.* I, 111 [second century AD]):

Apollinarius to Taesis, his mother and lady, many greetings. Before all I pray for your health. I myself am well and make supplication for you before the gods of this place. I wish you to know, mother, that I arrived in Rome in good health on the 25th day of the month Pachon and was posted to Misenum, though I have not yet learned the name of my company; for I had not gone to Misenum at the time of writing this letter. I beg you then, mother, look after yourself and do not worry about me; for I have come to a fine place. Please write me a letter about your welfare and that of my brothers and of all your folk. And whenever I find a messenger I will write to you; never will I be slow to write. My salutations to my brothers and Apollinarius and his children and Karalas and his children. I salute Ptolemaeus and Ptolemais and her children and Heraclous and her children.

Apollinarius' presence in Rome is no big news in Rome, but in the small Egyptian town of Karanis, where his mother lived, it is easy to imagine how she would have spread the word that her son, the soldier, had arrived in Rome, and he says it's a fine place. Similarly Apion writes to his father Epimachos to tell him he has arrived safely at Misenum after a stormy journey (*P. Sel.* I, 112 [second century AD]):

Apion to his father and lord, Epimachos. Before all else I pray that you are well and that you prosper in continual in continual health, together with my sister and her daughter and my brother. I give thanks to Serapis because, when I was endangered at sea, he rescued me immediately. When I arrived at Misenum, I received three gold pieces from Caesar for travelling expenses and I am well. Therefore, I request you, my lord father, write me a letter, telling me first about your welfare, secondly about the welfare of my brother and sister, in order that, thirdly, I may make obeisance before your handwriting, because you trained me well, and I hope by this means to advance quickly, the gods willing. I greet Kapiton warmly and my brother and sister and Serenilla and my friends. I sent my portrait to you through Euktemon. My name [i.e. his military name] is Antonius Maximus, my company the Athenonica.

If the soldier is older than Apion or Apollinarios, he may have his own land and concerns back home to worry about. Here Apollonous writes to her husband who is a soldier (*P. Mich.* VIII, 464 [AD 99]):

I want you to know that since I wrote to you before about my circumstances . . . the total amount of the rent and the seed will turn out okay. And do not worry yourself about the children: they are well and attending a teacher. And about your field, I have reduced your brother's rent by two artabas. Now I receive eight artabas of grain and six artabas of vegetable seed from him. I learned from Thermouthatas that you acquired a pair of belts for yourself, and I was very pleased. And about the olive groves, they are bearing well so far. And the gods willing, if possible, come to us. And I wish you to be well, and your children and all your people greet you.

This sort of family business is very common in the papyri, as well as the disjointed style. Ptolema writes to her husband, Antas, in the same manner (*P. Sel.* II 119 [second century AD]):

You write to Longinus (?) to look out for the Prefect. Well, the Prefect has come upriver. If you extricate yourself successfully, come up quickly before the Prefect so we can have the youngster examined. All the fields are in good condition. The southern basin of the 17 arourae has been sold for the use of the cattle. Your cattle have eaten one aroura and gone off to Pansoue. All the land there has been given over to the cattle. The west of the vegetable plot has been given over for grass-cutting. We have sold the grass in the cleruchies, except the six eastern basins, for 112 drachmas. Grass is exceedingly cheap. Three arouras were bought for you through Vetranius for 130 drachmas for growing grass, and they have been sold again through him for the use of sheep for 68 drachmas. Longinus and Sarapion and all at home salute you. Vibius has gone off to Psenuris to sell the corn. Your people are all well. Farewell.

Failing to write occurs as a complaint quite often. Thonis berates his father Arion (*P. Sel.* II, 133 [third century AD]):

look, this is the fifth time I have written to you, and you haven't written at all except once . . . nor have you come to see me: although you promised me saying 'I am coming' you have not come to see whether the teacher is looking after me or not.

Thonis adds an interesting PS at the end of the letter: 'Don't forget our pigeons'. Mostly the family letters are good humoured, but occasionally frustration surfaces. Isias cannot get her husband Hephaestion to come home (*P. Sel.* II, 97 [168 BC]). He has been doing service in the Temple of Sarapis at Memphis (modern Cairo):

about your coming home, when all the others who had been secluded there have come, I am annoyed, because having piloted myself and your child through such bad times and been driven to every extremity owing to the price of corn I thought that now at last, with you at home, I should enjoy some respite, whereas you have not even thought about coming home nor given any regard to our circumstances, remembering how I was in want of everything while you were still here, not to mention this long lapse of time and these critical days during which you have sent us nothing. As moreover Horus . . . has brought news of your having been released from detention, I am thoroughly displeased. Your mother also happens to be angry so for her sake as well as mine, please return to the city . . .

One can perhaps understand Hephaestion's reluctance.

If these letters strike a note of familiarity down the centuries, you can very quickly find instances to show just how different some aspects of ancient society were from ours. Hilarion writes to his wife, Alis, from Alexandria (*P. Sel.* I, 105 [1 BC]):

Know that we are even still in Alexandria. Don't worry if they all come back and I remain in Alexandria. I beg and entreat you, be concerned about the child, and as soon as we receive our pay I will send it up to you. If by chance you bear a child, if it is a boy, let it be, if it is a girl, expose it. You have said to Aphrodisias [as a message for Hilarion] 'do not forget me'. How can I forget you? I beg you then not to be anxious.

The easy mixture of affection with the nonchalant instruction to expose a female baby is, for us, strikingly and shockingly alien.

I have given just a few examples of family correspondence, but there are other types of letter. For instance, one of the most important collections of material from any period of Greco-Roman Egypt is formed by the remarkable archive of Zenon, the personal agent and estate manager of Apollonios, dioiketes in the mid-third century BC.[37] It contains hundreds of Zenon's business letters, dealing with all aspects of Apollonios' personal, financial and agricultural interests. When perusing the papyrus letters from Egypt, it would be difficult to think of any type of letter written in the modern world that is not illustrated in the papyri.

Our investigations have brought us from proclamations of kings and emperors to the people at large, to complaints of individuals to government officials and lastly to personal correspondence; that is, the communication of news/information, or at least, some examples of it, from government to private individuals, private individuals to government, and private individuals to each other. There is no question that certainly by Roman times the exercise of power and the organisation of people's lives in Egypt was conducted, not entirely but substantially, through writing. Paradoxically, for a largely illiterate society, there was extensive written communication in all areas of life, even of simple family news. Or perhaps it would be more correct to identify the paradox differently: that while a large proportion of individuals in Egypt were illiterate, society itself was in many ways highly literate.

NOTES

1 On animals in Egyptian religion see especially K. A. D. Smelik, E. A. Hamelrijk, '"Who knows what monsters demented Egypt worships?" Opinions on animal worship in antiquity as part of the ancient conception of Egypt', *Aufstieg und Niedergang der Römischen Welt* II, 17 (1984), 1857–2000.
2 K. W. Butzer, *Early Hydraulic Civilisation in Egypt* (London, 1976), p. 82.
3 D. Bonneau, *Le crue du Nil* (Paris, 1963); *Le fisc et le Nil* (Paris, 1971).
4 In general see A. K. Bowman, *Egypt after the Pharaohs 332 BC–AD 642* (London, 1986), pp. 93–4.
5 For general coverage on all matters to do with the papyrus in the ancient world see N. Lewis, *Papyrus in Classical Antiquity* (Oxford, 1974); E. G. Turner, *Greek Papyri: an Introduction* (Oxford, 1980); O. Montevecchi, *La papirologia*, 2nd edn (Milan 1988).
6 For the extent of the material, see H. M. Cotton, W. E. H. Cockle and F. G. B. Millar, 'The Papyrology of the Roman Near East: a survey', *Journal of Roman Studies* 85 (1995), 214–35.
7 A. K. Bowman, J. D. Thomas, *Vindolanda: the Latin Writing-Tablets* (London, 1983); *The Vindolanda Writing-Tablets* (London, 1994); I. Gallo, *Greek and Latin Papyrology* (London, 1986) 36–45 (Herculaneum).

8 H. I. Bell, *Egypt from Alexander the Great to the Arab Conquest* (Oxford 1956) is still a good outline of Egyptian history in this period; and Bowman, *Egypt* is the best modern synthesis.

9 The scholarly results of Napoleon's expedition were published in the famous *Description de l'Egypte* (Paris 1809–12); for the importance of the Napoleonic invasion in forming modern western perceptions of the east, see E. Said, *Orientalism: Western Conceptions of the Orient*, 2nd edn (London 1995), pp. 42–3; 80–2; 94–5.

10 In Ireland Trinity College has a small, but important collection (I am working on some of the remaining unpublished texts), and the Chester Beatty Museum has a famous collection of biblical papyri.

11 J. P. Mahaffy, *Social Life in Greece from Homer to Menander* (1874); B. C. McGing, H. W. Parke, 'Papyri', in P. Fox (ed.), *Treasures of the Library, Trinity College Dublin* (Dublin, 1986), pp. 29–30.

12 M. Crawford, *Sources for Ancient History* (Cambridge, 1983).

13 On the historical use of papyri, see R. S. Bagnall, *Reading Papyri: Writing Ancient History* (London, 1995).

14 This carries its own problems, most centrally perhaps the question to what extent any of this is characteristic of the rest of the Hellenistic or Roman world.

15 For the distinction between news and information see S. Lewis, *News and Society in the Greek Polis* (London, 1996), pp. 3–4.

16 For coverage of the extensive network of record-offices maintained by the Roman government in Egypt, see W. H. C. Cockle, 'State archives in Graeco-Roman Egypt from 30 BC to the reign of Septimius Severus', *Journal of Egyptian Archaeology* 70 (1984), 106–22.

17 The most important general work on the subject is now W. V. Harris, *Ancient Literacy* (Cambridge MA, 1989), pp. 116–46 (Hellenistic Egypt), pp. 276–81, 289–92 (Roman and Byzantine Egypt): for continuation of the debate he raised see A. K. Bowman and G. Woolf, *Literacy and Power in the Ancient World* (Cambridge, 1994). Harris is a minimalist arguing against what he sees as the optimistically high estimates of most predecessors.

18 These documents have attracted careful study: see R. Calderini, 'Gli *agrammatoi* nell' Egitto greco-romano', *Aegyptus* 30 (1950), 17–41, and above all the articles of H. C. Youtie, particularly '*Agrammatos*: an aspect of Greek society in Egypt', *Harvard Studies in Classical Philology* 75 (1971), 161–76; '"Because they do not know letters"', *Zeitschrift für Papyrologie und Epigraphik* 19 (1975), 101–8; '*Hypographeus*: the social impact of illiteracy in Graeco-Roman Egypt', *Zeitschrift für Papyrologie und Epigraphik* 17 (1975), 201–21.

19 R. S. Bagnall, B. W. Frier, *The Demography of Roman Egypt* (Cambridge, 1994), pp. 25–6.

20 See *P. Oxy.* XL, 2892–2922 (3rd century AD). Papyrological texts are abbreviated throughout this paper in the usual manner, as set out by J. F. Oates, R. S. Bagnall *et al.*, *Checklist of Greek and Latin Papyri, Ostraca and Tablets*, 4th edn (Atlanta, 1992).

21 See H. C. Youtie, 'Pétaus, fils de Pétaus, ou le scribe qui ne savait pas écrire', *Chronique d'Egypte* 81 (1966), 127–43.

22 How disadvantageous it was to be illiterate is disputed: see Harris, *Literacy*, pp. 144–6.

23 See *P. Oxy.* XLIII 3092.5 note, and on the whole subject John Rea's introduction to *P. Oxy.* LV 3781.

24 Text and translation in *P. Sel.* II, 212.

25 For a useful edition of the text and translation of all three versions, see S. Quirke and C. Andrews, *The Rosetta Stone* (London, 1988).

26 See N. Lewis, 'The process of promulgation in Rome's eastern provinces', in R. S. Bagnall and W. V. Harris (eds), *Studies in Roman Law in Memory of A. Arthur Schiller* (Leiden, 1986), pp. 127–39.

27 J. H. Oliver, *Greek Constitutions of Early Roman Emperors from Inscriptions and Papyri* (1989).

28 See C. Préaux, 'Esquisse d'une histoire des révolutions égyptiennes sous les Lagides', *Chronique d'Egypte* 11 (1936), 545–7; B. C. McGing, 'Revolt Egyptian style: internal opposition to Ptolemaic rule', *Archiv für Papyrusforschung* 43 (1997), 296.

29 See B. C. McGing, 'Bandits real and imagined in Greco-Roman Egypt', *Bulletin of the American Society of Papyrologists* 35 (1998), 159–83.

30 S. Lauffer, *Diokletians Preisedikt* (Berlin, 1971).

31 P. J. Sijpesteijn, *Penthemeros-certificates in Greco-Roman Egypt* (*P. Lugd. Batav.* XII, Leiden, 1964).

32 There is no very satisfactory general work on petitions. The most thorough study is P. Bureth, 'Recherches sur la plainte écrite en Egypte romaine', unpublished dissertation, Strasbourg 1979. Otherwise, J. L. White, *The Form and Structure of the Official Petition: A Study in Greek Epistolography* (Missoula, 1972).

33 Especially in Byzantine times an arbitration procedure developed, separate from petitioning an official: see J. Modrzejewski, 'Private arbitration in the law of Greco-Roman Egypt', *Journal of Juristic Papyrology* 6 (1952), 235–56.

34 See N. Lewis, *The Compulsory Public Services of Roman Egypt* (Florence, 1982).

35 See J. L. White, 'The Greek documentary letter tradition, third century BC to third century AD', *Semeia* 22, *Studies in Ancient Letter Writing* (1981), 19.

36 They have been studied extensively. Still interesting is J. G. Winter, *Life and Letters in the Papyri* (Ann Arbor, 1933). See too H. Koskenniemi, *Studien zur Idee und Phraseologie des griechischen Briefes bis 400 n. Chr.* (Helsinki, 1956); J. L. White, *The Body of the Greek Letter* (Missoula, 1972); *Light from Ancient Letters* (Philadelphia, 1986).

37 See C. Orrieux, *Les papyrus de Zénon. L'horizon d'un grec en Egypte au IIIe siècle avant J.C.* (Paris, 1983).

3 Monasteries and Manuscripts: The Transmission of Latin Learning in Early Medieval Ireland

Thomas O'Loughlin

Introduction

Several years ago a slim volume entitled *How the Irish Saved Civilization* became a bestseller on both sides of the Atlantic.[1] The book was largely a retelling of late-nineteenth century romantic images of Irish monks bringing learning 'back' to a ravaged and darkened continent in the aftermath of a complete collapse of civilisation caused by the barbarian invasions. Ireland had been spared, it was the safe lodging of the precious information which civilisation needed, and the monks had a mission to return it back to whence it originated. The book's story-line ignored decades of scholarship on the fifth to ninth-century period, while reducing complex processes to the stark alternatives of civilisation / chaos. And, it added some elements to suit our times by claiming it to be an 'untold story'[2] and by replacing the former religious frame of this myth with the notion of a cultural endeavour of sharing the benefits of a civilised way of life. The older mythology saw early Irish monks as latter-day apostles baptising pagans, the newer myth presents them as forerunners of the Peace Corps. However, underlying that book were more serious questions concerning the value placed on knowledge, the processes for information transfer, and power within early medieval societies. If we accept today that 'information is power', then we must ask how it supported the structures of society at different times, what information was valued, how that evaluation expressed itself, and what technologies and attitudes to information affected its availability within a given society. It is these questions that this paper wishes to address in the context of early Irish monasticism.[3]

The task facing the historian in taking up this question is twofold. On the one hand there is obvious, indeed well known, evidence for the transfer of information in monasteries. There are the 'wonders' of early Irish art such as the Book of Kells and other highly decorated manuscripts, and there are the references to monasteries which needed books, and to scholars and students, but there is still *very little evidence*. Hence, judgements are based on what has happened to survive and what can be inferred from those survivals along with deductions about the nature of the institutions involved. For instance, we can legitimately suppose that each monastery had that range of liturgical books necessary for its cult (for we have no instance of a monastery without such possessions), but a complete range of such books does not survive from early Christian Ireland. This overall scarcity of evidence also determines that the question be posed in terms of information valued within an ecclesiastical, and more precisely a monastic, context. So rather than look at information within the society (a task which may be well nigh impossible), we have to examine it in terms of one, albeit significant, group within that society. If we wish to examine the transfer of information in early Ireland we either concentrate on the transfer of information within the church in Latin, or we make guesses on the basis of random scraps of evidence that have survived. Second, there are very few direct references to the movement of information within that society. Hence the historian must draw conclusions from what can be observed to have happened in that culture, rather than from an analysis of the claims of that society about the value it laid on information, its preservation and storage, or its transmission and diffusion. In short, we must try to find out what books a monastery's library possessed, and then seek to establish what that represents in terms of contacts both near and far, rather than attempt a study – as could be done for other parts of Europe at the time – of deliberate efforts at accumulating books by particular abbots, scholars, or keepers of libraries. However, before looking at a library, it is necessary to set the transfer of written information in early medieval Ireland in context, and assess the value placed on the transfer of information within Christian monasticism.

Writing, Latin, and religion

Ireland enters the world of writing with the coming of Christianity. When exactly that took place we do not know; but if the mid-fifth century is the date which best suits our evidence for Patrick's work in Ireland,[4] then by that date there were sizeable communities of Christians[5] in the country and also monastic communities of men and women.[6] We know that these communities were in contact with Christians elsewhere,[7] and that Christians elsewhere – indeed in Rome itself – expressed an interest in, and concern about, the life of the Christian community in Ireland.[8] This presence of Christians, and these contacts, enable us to assert with confidence that books were being imported into Ireland at that time, and that there was already in all probability some reproduction of those texts within Ireland. As to what those books were we can only guess; however, we can make some very informed guesses. First, and obviously, there were the books that make up the Christian scriptures. It would be anachronistic to speak of 'Bibles', or even of 'the Scriptures' collectively. The notion of 'the Bible' lay centuries ahead, and even the notion of a pandect – a single very large manuscript containing all the books in 'the Canon' – was unknown. Equally, the notion of a fixed list of books – the Canon – was relatively new, and no single list had yet gained dominance,[9] and the presence in Ireland (and elsewhere) of so many works now termed 'apocrypha'[10] shows how long it took for one canon to establish itself. So we should think of these manuscripts as containing, for example, either one or, more probably, four gospels. We should then think of other manuscripts which contained the Pauline letters, others the Book of Psalms, and others that had portions of the Old Testament, and in particular the Pentateuch. They would have had all the works in the present Christian canons, and other texts they valued to the same degree, but it would be a collection of codices copied in various places and from different textual traditions rather than any single bound item such as we find from the thirteenth century onwards.

In addition to the books that make up the Christian scriptures there was an obvious need for liturgical books. Although we do not know the precise form of the liturgical books of the west in that period, we do know that such works were being assembled, and that Latin liturgy was developing some of its characteristic forms in the fifth century.[11] We can assume that this transfer of liturgical materials was ongoing; for while as a general rule older forms survive on the periphery of cultural areas, there is little evidence that Ireland lagged behind other places in terms of the development of the liturgy – indeed the reverse is true.[12] Less obvious are the other religious books that must have been present in Ireland from this early period. The strongest case, given the presence of monks, can be made for the presence of monastic writings. Monasticism had emerged in the fourth century in Egypt and Palestine, and the key works in its dissemination were hagiographical. By the fifth century, Athanasius's *Vita Antonii* circulated in Latin, along with the important lives of early monastic figures by Jerome, and the enormously influential *Historia Lausiaca* by Palladius.[13] Given that the values of these works can be found well established in the earliest records we have of Irish monasteries from the later sixth century, we can assume that they were present from the start. But the fifth century also saw the appearance of some of the other great sources of western monasticism in the form of *regulae* (rules), and, more precisely, the works of Cassian (*c.* 360–435).[14] While we cannot determine when his writings reached Ireland, we know that his spirit pervades all the monastic products that we possess from Ireland[15] and that his ideas were exercising an influence on insular monasticism from the sixth century.[16] Hence there is every likelihood that his works were being used in Ireland in the fifth century.

What other religious writings can we assume to have been in Ireland from this early period? Clearly, the church needed instructional / doctrinal works for the formation of clergy. There is a passing reference in Patrick to *testimonia*[17] and this probably points to the presence of apologetic collections of scriptural texts such as that which survives among the works of Cyprian.[18] The form such collections took in Ireland is unknown, but it is most probable that Patrick had access to one. Equally, there must have been collections of homilies and catecheses for already these were an indispensable tool in preaching, and the possession of cycles of homilies for either books of the scriptures or parts of the year was a widespread desire among clergy. However, as with the books of *testimonia*, we have no surviving examples. The fifth century saw the development of the dispute over the inter-relationship of divine and human action in the process of the Christian life (commonly referred to as 'the debate over Pelagianism') that would remain active in western Christianity until modern times – and the debate can be seen hovering in the background of much writing from the period. It is inconceivable that there would not have been contact about the dispute, and so there would have been a transfer of books on the topic.[19] Lastly, the fifth century saw the appearance of the manual as a theological tool (for example the writings of Eucherius of Lyons[20]) and of the first elaborate statements of canon law, so we can assume that these would have been among the first books imported into Ireland by its Christians.[21]

If, as seems likely, the first Irish Christians were groups of slaves,[22] it was not long before Christianity embraced parts of the native population.[23] This posed to the Christians the task not only of teaching a religion that relied on books and writings, but one which relied on books in a foreign language: Latin. It is this relationship to the language of their new religion that sets Ireland apart from the places where Christianity had established itself in the west up until that time, and it anticipated the situation in which Christianity would find itself later in Britain among the Angles and the Saxons, and in German lands on the continent. Recently, Michael Richter has argued that it is this aspect of the Irish experience with Christianity – accepting a religion entails acquiring literacy and a second language – that allows it to be seen as 'harbinger of the middle ages'.[24] Thus, in a very real sense, for Christians in early Ireland, 'the medium was the message': to acquire Christian faith was to put oneself in the sphere of Latin culture, to acquire Latin culture was to be in contact with the Christian culture that stretched throughout the Latin world and beyond. The saying attributed to Patrick sums up this situation with pithy accuracy: 'if you are Christians, you are Romans!'[25] The practical implication of this situation is that there must have been, from the outset, books to provide instruction in Latin, i.e. in literacy, for those who would teach and provide leadership among the Christians. This activity formed the basic teaching agenda within the monasteries, and a recurrent element in Irish saints' lives is that the future saint showed from his earliest days a propensity towards learning the skills of literacy and Latinity.[26]

Christianity presented itself as the religion offering access to divine truth and salvation to whoever would accept it: '[the Saviour] desires all men to be saved and to come to the knowledge of the truth' (1 Tim. 2. 4), and this determined, for its followers, the value that was to be laid on acquiring the information of that religion and justified the efforts needed to obtain that information. Possession of this knowledge was access to a community not just abroad, but to the community that they believed stretched back in time to the apostles. Equally these literary skills were a precondition of their own community's access to the life of Christ. Learning Latin was not just gaining a skill-base in the then dominant international culture, but was the very key to the sacred, and a preliminary to the ultimate survival of one's community.[27] This integration of medium and message in terms of religion *marks off* the expansion of Latinity in the early medieval world from the spread of world languages today, and if we do seek a modern parallel then we should look to the spread of Islam and the value that is given to the acquisition of Arabic in non-Arab societies as a key to the revelation of the Quran. In short, the adoption of Christianity in Ireland required that its adherents adopt a cultural horizon that embraced as its immediate vicinity the Latin west, and beyond that the Greek speaking east, so that this was perceived as a single intellectual area.[28]

Monasticism and book production

The bulk of our evidence for the transmission of written learning in early medieval Ireland comes from a monastic context. Consequently, it is easy to assume that this is simply an index of the role of monasticism within early Irish Christianity where in a non-urban society the monastery provided structures that would have been provided civilly or by diocesan bishops elsewhere. However, the fact that the monasteries do appear to have played a more significant role in structuring Christianity in the islands than on the continent should not obscure the special position that the transmission of learning played within monasticism everywhere. Moreover, while as a self-perpetuating community we can easily see monasteries as places which valued the acquisition of literacy, Latinity, and doctrine, we must not forget that monasteries also valued the technical skills this literacy demanded in terms of the preparation of writing materials (skins, inks, wax tablets), the labour of producing a fresh copy of a work and checking it against its exemplar, and then the skills of binder and the maker of book covers. Lastly, there are the skills of the artists who might be called upon to embellish either the writing or the book's packaging.[29] Thus when Adomnán portrays Columba retiring to his cell on the day of his death to spend his last hours writing a psalter he is not just retelling an anecdote, but showing him as engaged in a work suitable to monks until the very last moment.[30]

The interest in producing books can be found in the earliest monastic documents. 'Antony so closely listened to what he heard read that he missed nothing and remembered everything, because of this memory he had no need of books.'[31] Implicit in this is that every monk less holy than Antony did need books: while the recurring theme of 'unlearned wisdom' is ironically recorded in books whose very existence supposes monastic writing and reading. Books – the Scriptures principally – were at the heart of monastic reflection, prayer, and study. Monks needed books for the liturgy as did all Christians, but especially for the word-based liturgy of the Office. The identity of the monastery was generated in rules, maxims, and the material on the monastic heroes (lives, conferences, admonitions); and even in unscholarly houses these were read as part of the basic routine.[32] The monastery as a school of holiness was, of necessity, a basic school, and so needed books from introductory texts on reading and spelling to works for teaching the next generation of theologians, such as Cassiodorus's massive, annotated bibliography for monastic education, which lists hundreds of works and became a *desiderata*-list for monastic librarians – indeed, we shall note the possibility that it was so used on Iona in the late seventh century.[33] The monastery without a library was inconceivable, and building the library up and caring for it were important tasks.[34] While we readily see this in the case of European medieval libraries (either extant, for example St Gallen,[35] or through catalogues which allow us to see what was valued[36]), it was a trait present from the start: the Nag Hammadi library (probably mid-fourth century) belonged to a Pachomian-type community in Egypt;[37] while the fourth-century 'Codex Sinaiticus' (one of the most important parchment witnesses to the Christian scriptures) is from St Catherine's Monastery in Sinai.[38] Such attention to writings demanded an equal attention to their acquisition which involved the individual production, by hand, of each copy.

In early monasteries book production does not appear to have been a specialist activity of a few monks but a task engaged in by many as one in accord with monastic ideals. Thus Palladius refers to it on several occasions as work suited to monks saying that copying the Scriptures was a particular form of asceticism.[39] In his description of a Pachomian monastery he mentions that the monks knew the Scriptures by heart, but still he notes 'the copyist' among the skills (alongside, for example, bakers, weavers, and shoemakers) needed in the community,[40] and one monk was still at this work aged eighty,[41] while he notes that his own teacher, the great monastic theorist, Evagrius of Pontus earned his food by copying and was famed for his skill.[42] This approach to the copying of texts as an activity where the spiritual and material realms intermingled ensured that book production could not only be seen as a monastic necessity, but, in so far as it communicated the Christian message or enabled the liturgy to be performed, a saintly one. Adomnán describes a founder-saint, Columba, as producing books throughout his life: he was called to check a book made by another monk for errors (which he did miraculously),[43] was interrupted while working,[44] produced many books including psalters and hymnals for the Office,[45] and, as already noted, he continued working until his death.

Jean Leclercq described medieval monastic culture as 'the love of learning and the desire for God',[46] but for the early medieval period we should add that this involved an engagement with the media of communication – obtaining, copying, and disseminating books – as an integral part of that culture. Without this activity their common life could not continue, and so it was labour of the highest value. The practicalities of book production – each item directly dependent on an exemplar – inserted each monastery into a network of dependence not just on monasteries nearby, but religious houses throughout the Latin West. This network was the physical expression of the spiritual bonds that monks themselves acknowledged as existing between them as monks and members of the Church. Books built up the monastery as a successful place of holiness for its inmates, and so as a place of greater wealth and influence to those living in its vicinity, and for all they helped make it a significant, and so a powerful, place. In short, investment in book production within a monastery whether by the monks or secular rulers brought with it the likelihood of future growth and success by whatever measure one might choose.

Moreover, since involvement with the means of communication was intrinsically linked with leading a holy life, this book production not only created a common monastic culture in the west but a common Christian culture whereby the same texts were recognised as authoritative,[47] the same stories created a common memory,[48] and helped establish that potent notion in western thought that there was a common human psychological identity: what Cassian or Augustine had described as a human propensity or spiritual need in the fifth-century Mediterranean world would apply to seventh-century Iona or ninth-century central Europe.

The Library of Iona in the early eighth century.

While we can apply in a general way what is said about western European monasteries to the monasteries of early medieval Ireland, it is a far more difficult task to build up the Irish portion of the larger picture from specifically Irish evidence. This is partly owing to the amount of early monastic material that has survived in comparison with elsewhere, and partly owing to the fact that there is, as yet, no equivalent to projects such as *Sources of Anglo-Saxon Literary Culture* or *Fontes Anglo Saxonici*.[49] What follows is, therefore, a partial view of one monastery, Iona, at the end of the seventh century based from just two works, the *Vita Columbae* and the *De locis sanctis*, by a single author, Adomnán.[50]

1. The Christian Scriptures
The *sine qua non* of any monastic house, and the version in use on Iona was that of Jerome, commonly called 'the Vulgate',[51] which had established itself as the standard Latin text by the seventh century.[52] While much has been made of non-Vulgate readings found in Adomnán's writings, a study of these passages shows that on each occasion he is quoting Scripture within a quotation of an earlier author whose text was non-Vulgate.[53] The significance of this for our study is that we can dispense at once with popular notions that the insular region somehow lagged behind the rest of Latin Christendom at this time.

2. A sacramentary[54]
The only liturgical book actually quoted by Adomnán is a sacramentary.[55] In addition, given the way that the liturgical books for the Eucharist were arranged at the time, they would have needed at least a lectionary or guide to readings[56] and a *libellus missae* containing the ritual directions.[57]

3. Books for the Office
Adomnán refers to both the activity of celebrating the Office[58] and to the production of psalters.[59] But the liturgical *cursus* would have required many other books such as antiphonaries, collections of hymns, and guides to scriptural readings. In addition, there would have been a need for books which contained other prayers for occasional use such as a processional containing litanies, and a martyrology.[60]

4. Calendar materials
The liturgy is organised around the year so a calendar of feasts is another *sine qua non*.[61] However, before one can use such a calendar one needs to know exactly where one is in time, and so determine the date of Easter. We know from Bede that this whole question of Easter dating was a point of

contention on Iona during the abbacy of Adomnán,[62] and so we can be certain that there were many books relating to the *computus* in its library.[63]

5. Athanasius, *Vita Antonii*[64]

It has long been recognised that Adomnán relied on the standard works of hagiography in producing his portrait of Columba as a saint.[65] In this reliance on Athanasius, as translated by Evagrius of Antioch, and the writings on Martin by Sulpicius he was in line with the larger Latin tradition.[66]

6. Augustine, *De ciuitate Dei*

Written in north Africa in the early fifth century it is one of the major sources of the Latin tradition. There was a copy on Iona, and Adomnán used it to formulate his view of the resurrection.[67]

7. Augustine, *De consensu euangelistarum*

This work dealing with the problem of contradictions between the gospels was used by Adomnán[68] as the basis of an attempt to solve the chronology of Jesus's movements prior to the crucifixion.[69]

The presence of these two works on Iona is of major significance for our understanding of the communication links between Ireland and the rest of the Latin world. Both are major works (both intellectually and in physical size) and assume that their readers are fully integrated within a tradition of Christian learning and debate. Moreover, their presence negates two assumptions that have dogged much writing on early Christian Ireland: first, that it was intellectually remote from the standard books of the Latin west – if they could have access to these works then there is no reason why they could not have had any work of Augustine then in circulation; and second, the notion that while they may have been holy monks and austere ascetics that Irish monasteries had little interest in the discipline of theology as such.[70] Neither work could be described as a work of piety, while both assume the formal study of Christianity's beliefs in a formal way; while the *De consensu*, in particular, assumes the setting of a teacher working through the sacred texts with students.

8. Benedict, *Regula*

The monastic life was, in essence, life according to a rule, and so legal texts had a place of special importance. The Andersons noted the influence of Benedict's *Regula* in their study of the *Vita*,[71] yet given the overlaps that occur between various early monastic *regulae*, the precision of this iden- tification should be subjected to further study. There is every possibility that there were copies of several *regulae* on the island which could have been referred to, and read, to provide guidance for the government of the community. However, the significance lies in the fact that any *regula* from the continent was being used on Iona: this was not an isolated and idiosyncratic monasticism out of step with Latin monasticism elsewhere but a community with concrete links with that larger world from which they were receivers, as in the case of these texts, and to whom they were contributors as the success of Adomnán's *De locis sanctis* as a textbook demonstrates.[72] It is against this Europe-wide horizon we should read references to distant places such as Italy and Rome in the *Vita Columbae*.[73]

9. Cassiodorus, *Expositio psalmorum*

This work from sixth-century southern Italy was one of the most extensive and widely used commentaries in western monasticism.[74] Its citation by Adomnán[75] is possibly the earliest evidence we possess for the use of this work[76] and the existence of the copy on Iona shows that they were in touch with the best, specifically monastic, learning available at the time. Moreover, the presence of one work by Cassiodorus shows that there is no intrinsic reason why his more basic work, the *Institutiones* – a guide to monastic learning with specific reference to scriptural exegesis and what books should be consulted on various topics – was not in the library on Iona.

10. Constantius, *Vita Germani*

This work was identified in the *Vita Columbae* by Brüning.[77] Its use shows that the hagiographic holdings of Iona were not limited to the major figures such as Antony and Martin, but extended widely, as the presence of the *uita* of this minor figure demonstrates.

11. Dionysius Exiguus, *Epistola I*

Dionysius, a Scythian monk, lived and worked in Rome in the first half of the sixth century where he was dubbed '*exiguus*' ('the little one') by Cassiodorus on account of his humility. The presence of this letter was identified by Brüning,[78] but its significance lies in the fact that Dionysius was the first great collector of canon law in Latin[79] and if Iona had one work by him, then equally it could have had many of his writings. Dionysius's collection was an important source for the great Irish work of this period, the *Collectio canonum hibernensis*, whose main claim to fame is that it replaced the Dionysius's chronological arrangement of material with a systematic one.[80]

12. Eucherius, *Liber instructionum*

Although forgotten today, Eucherius was one of the standard introductory textbooks throughout the early middle ages and was recommended as such by Cassiodorus.[81] It was used by Adomnán in *De locis sanctis*,[82] and, in addition to raising the possibility that Iona had his other writings, it shows that the basic monastic training there was in line with what was taken as the basic recommended 'syllabus' for monasteries prior to the Carolingian period.[83]

13. [Pseudo]-Eucherius, *De situ Hierusolyma*
This work was just one of a number of writings dealing with the Holy Places that Adomnán says were available on Iona.[84]

14. Gregory the Great, *Dialogi*
In the century after its appearance this work became a mainstay of monasticism in the Latin west, and was even translated into Greek.[85] Adomnán used it in both of his books.[86] And, especially when seen in connection with the presence of Benedict's *Regula*, it shows that the monasticism of Iona was drawing on the same sources as monasticism across the Latin world at the time.

15. 'Hegesippus', *Historiae*
This work, a Latin version of Josephus, was used in both the *Vita Columbae*[87] and the *De locis sanctis*.[88] This work was far from being a common text in the period.[89] Its use on Iona negates any notion that what was available was a 'minimum repertoire of standard texts' and no more; we must envisage a library that was far larger and more diverse than is directly represented in works that can be linked with certainty to Iona.

16. Isidore, *Etymologiae*
Isidore of Seville is too often dismissed as no more that an early medieval copy-editor skilled only in scissors-and-paste. His work as a theologian is significant,[90] and his most famous work, the *Etymologiae*, is a true encyclopaedia[91] which advanced theological enquiry by resolving many problems inherited from earlier illustrious writers.[92] The presence of this work in Ireland by the mid-seventh century has been noted by several scholars,[93] and its use by Adomnán was first suggested by J. N. Hillgarth.[94]

17. Isidore, *De natura rerum*.
This short work was a synopsis of the scripturally based cosmology of the period and was used in the *De locis sanctis*.[95] The presence of two works by Isidore raises the possibility that the community had other items from his extensive *corpus* and shows us that we cannot imagine Iona simply having works derived from some earlier 'period of contact' with the continent, but rather that it was in ongoing contact with the larger intellectual scene of the later seventh century in the West.[96]

18. Jerome, *De situ et locorum.*

19. Jerome, *Liber quaestionum hebraicarum in Genesim.*

20. Jerome, *Commentarii in euangelium Mathaei.*

21. Jerome, *Commentarii in Naum.*

22. Jerome, *Commentarii in Osee.*

23. Jerome, *Commentarii in Hiezechielem*

The presence of these six works of exegesis from the major exegetical figure in the Latin tradition shows that it is not a vain speculation to suggest that there may have been sizeable holdings of several other important patristic authorities.[97] Indeed, Denis Meehan argued that there was evidence for ten or eleven works by Jerome in *De locis sanctis*, but we can only be certain of the six listed here.[98] However, from the *Vita Columbae* we can be certain that there was at least one other work by Jerome on the island:

24. Jerome, *De uiris inlustribus*

This was demonstrated by Brüning,[99] and we should remember that this work played an important role in the period as a guide to what were the '*auctoritates*' within the tradition.[100] It presence, therefore, is further evidence of how Iona and other centres of learning in the West shared a common agenda.

25. Juvencus, *Historia euangelica*

This poetic retelling of the 'story-line' of the Christian gospels was used in both works by Adomnán.[101] Written in the fourth century it was popular throughout the west for its combination of piety with elegant Latinity.

26. Leo the Great, *Sermo XII*

27. Leo the Great, *Sermo L*

The presence of these two sermons, identified by Brüning,[102] must be taken as representative of what must have been a large homiliary collection for use not only in study, but the liturgy.[103]

28. Sulpicius Severus, *Chronicon*[104]

29. Sulpicius Severus, *Vita Martini*[105]

30. Sulpicius Severus, *Dialogi*[106]

31. Sulpicius Severus, *Epistola II*[107]

The presence of this *corpus* of a writer who was then an important influence in Christian schools is further confirmation that the library of Iona could support the standard intellectual endeavours of the time in a way similar to that occurring throughout the West.

32. Virgil, *Aeneid*

33. Virgil, *Georgics*

The presence of both works by Virgil was identified by Brüning.[108] As with Christian authors, there is the possibility that there were other classical writings on Iona.

34. anon, *Actus Siluestri*.
This work was identified by Brüning using the older name '*gesta Siluestri*'[109] and it shows us that apart from hagiographic material, there were possibly several works relating part of the history (or more accurately the pseudo-history) of the Church.

35. anon, *An earlier vita of Columba*.
The evidence for this work was assembled by the Andersons.[110]

In addition, there are several other works which have been suggested over the years as having an influence on either the *Vita Columbae* or the *De locis sanctis*. In some cases these suggestions can be dismissed (for instance, the suggestion that there was a copy of Solinus on Iona[111]), but regarding other works the jury is still out.[112] And the quest is far from over.

In compiling this list I have deliberately refrained from mentioning texts which could be inferred to have been on the island by using other approaches. One could, for example, start with the need to teach Latin and so list the need for grammars and bilingual word-lists. Equally, there was the need to teach theology to those more advanced along the monastic road at both a basic level (the need for manuals and glossaries – we know at least one of Eucherius's works was there) and in a more advanced manner (other books of scriptural exegesis covering other portions of the Scriptures, other reference works or books dealing with technical matters of theology such as the *Liber de ordine creaturarum* – for we have examples of each type of work). Indeed, the nature of the questions addressed in the *De locis sanctis* supposes such an intellectual culture. Another approach would start with other works from Ireland which show evidence of contact with Iona such as *Annals of Ulster*[113] or the *Collectio canonum hibernensis*[114] and argue that what was present in one place could easily be present in many Irish centres given the known contacts between monasteries. Lastly, since few of the standard works of western monasticism are actually exemplified, we could argue that works such as Palladius, Jerome's hagiographical writings, and

Rufinus's *Historia monachorum in Aegypto* must surely have been present given the fact that it was a sophisticated monastic library.

Only when all these approaches have been explored will a detailed picture emerge of the attitude to information, and its retention and diffusion, within early Irish monasticism. However, that will have to await the Irish equivalent of *Fontes Anglo Saxonici*. In the meantime, the limited list of works we know, with certainty, were on Iona allow us to see the community there in contact with the greatest authorities of the past, the more recent authorities such as Gregory the Great and Isidore who framed the early medieval agenda, and lots of other works without which any library of the period would have looked rather sparsely equipped. By seeking out, copying, and using this range of materials we can see Iona as geographically peripheral, but culturally very well connected to, and in the mainstream of, its Latin monastic world. Its library shows us that Iona was not acting as a 'saviour of civilisation,' nor was it 'the last outpost of a civilisation', but actively playing its part in the give-and-take of Latin Christian letters that constituted the intellectual world of the west at the time.

NOTES

1 T. Cahill, *How the Irish Saved Civilization* (London, 1995).

2 *Ibid.*, p. iii (title page): the subtitle reads 'The Untold Story of Ireland's Heroic Role from the Fall of Rome to the Rise of Medieval Europe'.

3 By early Irish monasticism I mean Ireland between the arrival of the first Christians (fourth or fifth centuries) and the end of the eighth century. For a general background to the period, see D. Ó Cróinín, *Early Medieval Ireland: 400–1200* (London, 1995); and on the church, in particular, see C. Etchingham, *Church Organisation in Ireland: AD 650–1000* (Maynooth, 1999).

4 See T. O'Loughlin, *St Patrick: The Man and his Works* (London, 1999), pp. 14–21.

5 Thus Prosper of Aquitaine records that there were communities by 431 large enough to need a bishop; and cf. E. A. Thompson, 'St Patrick and Coroticus', *Journal of Theological Studies* 31 (1980), 12–27.

6 See Patrick, *Confessio* n. 41 and *Epistola*, n.12.

7 We know this from the references to communities abroad in Patrick's writings; cf. T. O'Loughlin, *Celtic Theology: Humanity, World, and God in Early Irish Writings* (London, 2000), pp. 37–8.

8 See T. Charles-Edwards, 'Palladius, Prosper, and Leo the Great: mission and primatial authority', in D.N. Dumville, *et al.* (eds), *Saint Patrick, AD 493–1993* (Woodbridge, 1993), pp. 1–12

9 See J. Barton, *The Spirit and the Letter: Studies in the Biblical Canon* (London, 1997), pp. 1–34.

10 See M. Schneiders, 'On the use of the label *Apocryphon* in recent studies of medieval Irish texts', *Tijdschrift voor filosofie en theologie* 51(1990), 314–23.

11 See E. Palazzo, *A History of Liturgical Books from the Beginning to the Thirteenth Century*, trans. M. Beaumont (Collegeville, 1998), pp. 19–27.

12 See E. Bishop, 'The litany of the saints in the Stowe Missal', in *Liturgica Historica: Papers on the Liturgy and Religious Life of the Western Church* (Oxford, 1918), pp. 137–64; J. Ryan, 'The Mass in the early Irish Church', *Studies* 50 (1961), 371–84; and T. O'Loughlin, 'The Celtic homily: creeds and eschatology', *Milltown Studies* 41 (1998), 99–115.

13 See T. O'Loughlin, 'Hagiography: Christian perspectives', in W. M. Johnston (ed.), *The Encyclopedia of Monasticism* (London, 2000), pp. 564–6.

14 See C. Stewart, *Cassian the Monk* (New York/Oxford, 1998) which outlines how he adapted the monasticism of the desert to the conditions of Gaul, and so produced a monastic guide well adapted to European conditions.

15 Note the significance of Cassian in the earliest penitentials; cf. O'Loughlin, *Celtic Theology*, pp. 48–67.

16 Cf. T. O'Loughlin, 'The Penitentials', in G. R. Evans (ed.), *A History of Pastoral Care in the Middle Ages* (London, 2000).

17 *Epistola*, n. 9: *per totam legem carpere testimonia* – the notion of 'the testimonies of the whole law' is a complex one in patristic theology, for an introduction to the theme, cf. A. Sundberg, 'On testimonies,' *Novum Testamentum* 3 (1959), 268–1.

18 *Ad Quirinum*, ed. R. Weber, *Corpus Christianorum, Series Latina* 3 (Turnhout, 1972).

19 Prosper who mentions Ireland on several occasions (cf. Charles-Edwards, 'Palladius, Prosper, and Leo the Great') was deeply involved in this acrimonious debate.

20 Cf. T. O'Loughlin, 'The symbol gives life: Eucherius of Lyons formula for Exegesis', in T. Finan and V. Twomey (eds), *Scriptural Interpretation in the Fathers: Letter and Spirit* (Dublin, 1995), pp. 221–52; and see below, for at least one of his manuals was used by Adomnán on Iona.

21 See C. Vogel, 'Statuta Ecclesiae Antiqua', *New Catholic Encyclopaedia* (New York, 1967), vol. 13, p. 682

22 Cf. Thompson, 'St Patrick and Coroticus'.

23 This is clear from Patrick's writings.

24 This is a theme in M. Richter, *Ireland and her Neighbours in the Seventh Century* (Dublin, 1999).

25 Cf. A. Gwynn, 'The Problem of the *Dicta Patricii*', *Seanchas Ard Mhacha* 8 (1976), 69–80.

26 See H. I. Marrou, *A History of Education in Antiquity* (London, 1956), pp. 340–9.

27 Cf. C. Mohrmann, *Liturgical Latin: Its Origins and Character* (London, 1959).

28 See T. O'Loughlin, 'The view from Iona: Adomnán's mental maps', *Peritia* 10 (1996), 98–122; and Richter, *Ireland and her Neighbours*, pp. 41–7.

29 Cf. G. Cencetti, 'Scriptoria e scritture nel monachesimo benedettino', in *Il monachesimo nell'alto medioevo e la formazione della civiltà occidentale*, Settimane di studio 4 (Spoleto, 1957), pp. 187–219.

30 *Vita Columbae* III, 23 [128b], ed. A. O. Anderson and M. O. Anderson (London, 1961), p. 524.

31 Athanasius, *Vita Antonii*, ch. 3 (*Patrologia Latina* 73, 128); I cite this from the Latin translation of Evagrius of Antioch for it was in this form that it was known in the West, and, as we shall see below, was read in such places as Iona.

32 See Benedict, *Regula*, ch. 42. English translation: *The Rule of Saint Benedict*, trans. J. McCann (London, 1951), p. 48.

33 *Institutiones*, ed. R. A .B. Mynors (Oxford, 1937); and cf. J. J. O'Donnell, *Cassiodorus* (Berkeley / Los Angeles, 1979); and on its later impact see T. O'Loughlin, *Teachers*

and *Code-Breakers: The Latin Genesis Tradition 430–800* (Turnhout, 1999), pp. 321–4.

34 See P. Riché, *Education and Culture in the Barbarian West from the Sixth through the Ninth Centuries*, trans. J. J. Contreni (Columbia SC, 1976), pp. 100–22.

35 See W. Bershin, 'The medieval culture of penmanship in the Abbey of St Gall', in J. C. King and W. Vogler (eds), *The Culture of the Abbey of St Gall: An Overview* (Zürich, 1990), pp. 69–92; J. Duft, 'Irish Monks and Irish manuscripts in St Gall', *ibid.*, pp. 119–32; and P. Ochsenbein, 'Teaching and learning in the Gallus Monastery,' *ibid.*, 133–44.

36 Cf. G. Becker, *Catalogi bibliothecarum antiqui* (Bonn, 1885).

37 Cf. J. M. Robinson (ed.), *The Nag Hammadi Library* (Leiden, 1978), pp. 10–26.

38 Cf. B. M. Metzger, *Manuscripts of the Greek Bible: An Introduction to Greek Palaeography* (Oxford, 1981), pp. 76–9.

39 *Historia Lausiaca*, ch. 13, 1. English translation: R. T. Meyer (London, 1965), where this passage is on pp. 48–9.

40 *Historia Lausiaca*, ch. 32, 12 (p. 95).

41 *Historia Lausiaca*, ch. 45, 3 (p. 122).

42 *Historia Lausiaca*, ch. 38, 10 (p. 113).

43 *Vita Columbae* I, 23 [28a–b] (p. 256); with the implication that other, lesser, monks would do this task the hard way.

44 *Vita Columbae* II, 29 [76a–b] (p. 390).

45 *Vita Columbae* II, 8–9 [59a–60b] (pp. 342–6).

46 *The Love of Learning and the Desire for God: A Study of Monastic Culture*, trans. C. Misrahi (New York, 1961).

47 This collective common identity is crucial for understanding the role of written authorities in the period; cf. O'Loughlin, *Teachers and Code-Breakers*, pp. 25–72; and also T. O'Loughlin, 'Individual anonymity and collective identity: the enigma of early medieval Latin theologians', *Recherches de théologie et philosophie médiévale* 64 (1997), 291–314.

48 The case of the stories in Gregory the Great's *Dialogi* are a case in point for they became as much part of the imagination of the monks on Iona in the seventh century (see below; and T. O'Loughlin, '"The gates of hell": From metaphor to fact', *Milltown Studies* 38 (1996), 98–114) as they were of monks in Italy (cf. J. M. Petersen, *The Dialogues of Gregory the Great in their Late Antique Cultural Background* (Toronto, 1984), pp. 153–60).

49 These two research projects complement each other and are best introduced by their websites where now much of their research is made available to scholars. The SASLC website is http://www.wmich.edu/medieval/saslc; that of *Fontes* is http://fontes.ox.ac.uk.

50 For a general assessment of Adomnán as a monk and scholar, cf. O'Loughlin, *Celtic Theology*, pp. 68–86.

51 Cf. E .F. Sutcliffe, 'The Name "Vulgate"', *Biblica* 29 (1948), 345–52.

52 See R. Loewe, 'The medieval history of the Latin Vulgate', in G. W. H. Lampe (ed.), *The Cambridge History of the Bible: The West from the Fathers to the Reformation* (Cambridge, 1969), pp. 102–54.

53 See T. O'Loughlin, 'The Latin version of the Scriptures in use on Iona', *Peritia* 8 (1994), 18–26.

54 For the precise significance of this term, often anachronously confused with the term *missale* (missal) as in the case of 'The Stowe missal', cf. Palazzo, *History of Liturgical Books*, p. 21.

55 See T. O'Loughlin, 'The library of Iona in the late seventh century: the evidence from Adomnán's *De Locis Sanctis*', *Ériu* 45 (1994), 37.

56 See Palazzo, *History of Liturgical Books*, pp. 83–106.

57 On the role of these *libelli* in the Western liturgy before the Carolingian period, see R. E. Reynolds, 'Image and text: a Carolingian illustration of modifications in the early Roman eucharistic ordines', *Viator* 14 (1983), 59–75 (p. 62).

58 See R. Sharpe's translation of Adomnán's *Vita Columbae* (*Adomnán of Iona: Life of St Columba* (London, 1995)), p. 323, n. 238.

59 See the reference to the last hours of Columba's life, above.

60 Examples of all these books exist from other monasteries dating from a later period; however, since we know that all these elements were part of the liturgy at the end of the seventh century we can be sure that this range of books would have been present.

61 On this temporal aspect of their liturgy, see O'Loughlin, *Celtic Theology*, pp. 166–84.

62 *Historia ecclesiastica gentis Anglorum*, V, 15, ed. B. Colgrave and R. A. B. Mynors (Oxford, 1969), pp. 504–6.

63 In the last few years a great deal of work has been devoted to the computistics of the period. However, for my purposes here – where I want to relate the topic to the library of Iona – the key work is the edition by M. Walsh and D. Ó Cróinín of *Cummian's Letter De controversia paschali and the De ratione conputandi* (Toronto, 1988), especially pp. 7–15 of their introduction.

64 Works by named authors are arranged here in alphabetical order.

65 See G. Brüning, 'Adamnans Vita Columbae und ihre Ableitungen', *Zeitschrift für Celtische Philologie* 11 (1917), 213–304 (pp. 245–7); and see the comments by Sharpe, in Adomnán's *Vita Columbae*, pp. 5–7.

66 Cf. L. Bieler, 'The Celtic hagiographer', *Studia Patristica* 5 (1962), 243–65; and M. Herbert, *Iona, Kells, and Derry: The History and Hagiography of the Monastic Familia of Columba* (Oxford 1988), p. 137

67 See O'Loughlin, 'The library of Iona', p. 47.

68 The evidence for Adomnán's use is presented in T. O'Loughlin, 'Adomnán's *De Locis Sanctis*: a textual emendation and an additional source identification', *Ériu* 48 (1997), 37–40.

69 See T. O'Loughlin, '*Res, tempus, locus, persona*: Adomnán's exegetical method', *Innes Review* 48 (1997), 95–111.

70 See P. Sims-Williams's insightful comments on this assumption in 'The medieval world of Robin Flower', in M. de Mórdha (ed.), *Bláithín: Flower* (Dingle, 1998), p. 81; and my comments on this attitude in *Celtic Theology*, pp. 203-205.

71 Anderson and Anderson (eds), *Vita Columbae*, p. 25.

72 See T. O'Loughlin, 'Adomnán the illustrious', *Innes Review* 46 (1995), 1–14; and T. O'Loughlin, 'The Diffusion of Adomnán's *De locis sanctis* in the medieval period', *Ériu*, forthcoming.

73 *Vita Columbae*, I, 28 [30a–31a] (pp. 262–4); II, 46 [102b] (pp. 458–60); and III, 22 [135b] (pp. 540–2); and cf. T. O'Loughlin, 'Living in the ocean', in C. Bourke (ed.), *Studies in the Cult of Saint Columba* (Dublin, 1997), pp. 11–23.

74 See M. McNamara, 'Psalter text and psalter study in the early Irish Church', *PRIA*, 73C (1973), 231.

75 See O'Loughlin, 'The library of Iona', p. 47.

76 McNamara, 'Psalter text', noted that 'the first-attested use of it . . . is in Bede'.

77 Brüning, 'Adamnans vita Columbae', p. 252.

78 *Ibid.*, p. 244.

79 See J. Rambaud-Buhot, 'Dionysiana Collectio', in the *New Catholic Encyclopaedia*, vol. 4, p. 876

80 See T. O'Loughlin, 'Marriage and sexuality in the *Hibernensis*', *Peritia* 11 (1997), 188–206.

81 See O'Loughlin, 'The symbol gives life', and O'Loughlin, *Teachers and Code-Breakers*, pp. 181–3.

82 See O'Loughlin, 'The library of Iona,' pp. 43–4.

83 See Cassiodorus, *Institutiones* I, x, 1 (p. 34); and cf. Riché, *Education and Culture*, pp. 163–9; and T. O'Loughlin, 'Cassiodorus', in A. D. Fitzgerald (ed.), *Augustine Through the Ages: An Encyclopedia* (Cambridge, 1999), pp. 143–4.

84 See O'Loughlin, 'The Library of Iona,' pp. 36 (on the 'other books' on the Holy Places) and 44; and cf. O'Loughlin, 'Dating the *De situ Hierusolimae*: the insular evidence', *Revue Bénédictine* 105 (1995), 9–19.

85 See the references above, and cf. C. Straw, *Gregory the Great: Perfection in Imperfection* (London, 1988) for its impact on monasticism.

86 See Brüning, 'Adamnans Vita Columbae', p. 249; and O'Loughlin, 'The library of Iona', p. 41.

87 See Brüning, 'Adamnans Vita Columbae', pp. 242–3.

88 See O'Loughlin, 'The library of Iona,' p. 42; and cf. L. Bieler, 'Adamnan und Hegesipp', *Wiener Studien* 69 (1956), 344–9.

89 Cf. the introduction by V. Ussani to his edition in *Corpus Scriptorum Ecclesiasticorum Latinorum* (Vienna, 1932), vol. 66, 1.

90 Cf. T. O'Loughlin, 'Christ as the focus of Genesis exegesis in Isidore of Seville', in T. Finan and V. Twomey (eds), *Studies in Patristic Christology* (Dublin, 1998), pp. 144–62.

91 Cf. the still unsurpassed analysis by E. Brehaut, *An Encyclopaedist of the Dark Ages: Isidore of Seville* (New York, 1912).

92 Cf. O'Loughlin, *Teachers and Code-Breakers*, pp. 146–8; and cf. pp. 185–94.

93 Cf. J. N. Hillgarth, 'Visigothic Spain and early Christian Ireland', *PRIA* 62C (1962), 167–94; M. Herren, 'On the earliest Irish acquaintance with Isidore of Seville', in E. James (ed.), *Visigothic Spain: New Approaches* (Oxford, 1980), pp. 243–50; and by D. Ó Cróinín, 'A seventh-century Irish computus from the circle of Cummianus', *PRIA* 82C (1982), 423–4.

94 See J. N. Hillgarth, 'Ireland and Spain in the seventh century', *Peritia* 3 (1984), 8, n. 9; and O'Loughlin, 'The library of Iona', pp. 47–9.

95 See O'Loughlin, 'The library of Iona', p. 49.

96 This can be seen from Adomnán's knowledge, albeit very confused, of the situation in Palestine in the period of Mu'áwiyah I (evidence from sometime after 640 when he became governor of Damascus); cf. T. O'Loughlin, 'Palestine in the aftermath of the Arab conquest: the earliest Latin account', in R. N. Swanson (ed.), *Studies in Church History*, forthcoming.

97 See O'Loughlin, 'The library of Iona', pp. 38–41.

98 See O'Loughlin, 'The library of Iona', pp. 34–7 and 52 where the evidence is reviewed.

99 Brüning, 'Adamnans Vita Columbae', p. 253.

100 For an assessment of its importance in the period, and its use in the insular world, see T. O'Loughlin, 'The list of illustrious writers in the Pseudo-Bedan *Collectanea*', in H. Conrad O'Briain, A. M. D'Arcy, and J. Scattergood (eds), *Text and Gloss: Studies in Insular Learning and Literature Presented to Joseph Donovan Pheiffer* (Dublin, 1999), pp. 34–48; T. O'Loughlin, 'Muirchú's *Vita Patricii*: a note on an unidentified source', *Ériu* 47 (1996), 89–93; and O'Loughlin, 'Adomnán the illustrious'.

101 See Brüning, 'Adamnans Vita Columbae', p. 241; and O'Loughlin, 'The library of Iona', p. 41.

102 Brüning, 'Adamnans Vita Columbae', p. 254.

103 On the importance of such homiliaries, see R. Etaix, *Homéliaires patristiques latins: Recueils d'études de manuscrits médiévaux* (Paris, 1994).

104 See O'Loughlin, 'The library of Iona', p. 41.

105 See Brüning, 'Adamnans Vita Columbae', pp. 247–8; and cf. Richter, *Ireland and Her Neighbours*, pp. 225–31.

106 See Brüning, 'Adamnans Vita Columbae', p. 249.

107 *Ibid.*, p. 248.

108 *Ibid.*, p. 241.

109 *Ibid.*, p. 253; and cf. A. Dekkers, *Clavis Patrum Latinorum*, 3rd edn (Steenbrugge, 1995), item 2235.

110 Anderson and Anderson (eds), *Vita Columba*, p. 19.

111 See J. T. Fowler, *Adamnani Vita S. Columbae* (Oxford, 1894), p. 110 (and taken up by the Andersons, *Vita Columbae*, p. 21); but which has been shown to be based on an interpolated portion of text by Sharpe, *Adomnán's Vita Columbae*, p. 339, n. 314.

112 See the list in O'Loughlin, 'The library of Iona', p. 52.

113 Cf. D. N. Dumville, 'Latin and Irish in the Annals of Ulster, AD 431–1050', in D. Whitelock, R. McKitterick and D. Dumville (eds), *Ireland In Early Medieval Europe* (Cambridge, 1982), pp. 320–41.

114 There are, at the very least, extrinsic links between the *Collectio* and Iona, cf. E. W. B. Nicholson, 'The origins of the "Hibernian" collection of canons', *Zeitschrift für Celtische Philologie* 3 (1899), 99–103.

4 Talking to Themselves: Lay Incursion into Official Religion in the Christ and the Doctors Mystery Plays

Anthony G. Corbett

This chapter began as a study of the social and political aspects of the Christ and the Doctors plays, which occur in four analogues in the English cycles of mystery plays of the late Middle Ages. Although it still conforms largely to that specification, the implications of the evidence for the history of theatre and the processes of communication in an age of censorship are more wide-ranging than I had at first realised.

The anthropologist Mary Douglas, in her assertion that religion is a mode of communication between the living, touches on an idea which has been under-explored in relation to mystery plays. She makes the point that in a marginalised group, symbols are the only method of communication. Furthermore, for communication about religion to take place, the symbols must be structured and 'able to express something relevant to the social order'.[1] The plays may, over time and with revision, have had as much to say about relationships in English society as they have about salvific history. The marginalised in this case are the laity, in particular the lay members of the urban trade guilds, whose burgeoning civic and economic importance was not matched by a concomitant role in the affairs of their church. The predominant symbol used in the plays is that of Christ, the eponymous and probably the most familiar icon of Christianity. The figure of Christ had been altered by the Church from the early image of the triumphant conqueror, the Christus Victor, to the obedient, suffering sacrificial Lamb of God in the late middle ages. The Christ-symbol is re-energised in the plays, returning some of the vigour of the earlier Christ who broke the bonds of Hell and Death. Of course, the play cycles also retained Harrowing of Hell plays, long after the apocryphal story itself had ceased to be part of any official Christology.

Social commentary of sorts has been recognised in the context of one or two plays, the Wakefield *Secunda Pastorum* being the most famous. Some work has also been done on the obvious trade symbolism that pervades the scripts,[2] but the larger question has never been asked. If the plays do articulate the social and religious concerns of the laity in the fifteenth and sixteenth centuries, then much work remains to be done, and the implications for both social history and the history of theatre are manifold. It would mean, for example, that the position of the laity in the Church was being interrogated by groups of relatively conservative Catholics, or by the (presumably) minor clerics paid to write or revise the manuscripts, prior to the Reformation. It is probably an overstatement to claim that this is an important step in the laicisation of control over the means of communication, but it certainly serves to indicate the politicisation of religious drama before the blistering Protestant polemic of John Bale.

The quality of the catechesis in English mystery cycles is, generally speaking, uneven. If the intention was to teach, then the catechetical information imparted by the plays is at best sketchy, at worst misleading. Opinion is divided on the issue of whether the plays succeeded in teaching anything, but there is general, if not total, agreement that they were intended to teach. Rosemary Woolf remarks of liturgical drama that it was allowed '*pro augenda fide*' (to increase faith).[3] V. A. Kolve asserted that: 'the dramatists . . . produced a cycle charged with theological meaning – strong, simple and formally coherent'.[4] E. Catherine Dunn is equally certain that: 'accessibility of the Scriptures to the entire people . . . through the annual Corpus Christi plays, served as a source of information and instruction, like a modern catechetical course in Scripture'.[5]

On the other side of the argument, Hans-Jürgen Diller casts doubt upon the ability of the late medieval plays to increase faith, noting that: 'The plays are sometimes even disappointingly neglectful of doctrinal content'.[6] This unevenness of catechesis has led some scholars to assume a high level of religious knowledge among the audience, an ability to manipulate information and compensate for the gaps in the narrative. Meg Twycross's 'Beyond the Picture Theory' is an excellent example of an article on audience response to the imagery of the plays.[7] However, assumptions such as these, on audience knowledge, can never be more than speculative. I wish, in this chapter, to advance another kind of speculation about the audience, and about the covert purpose of this play, and by extension, of this type of drama. I want to suggest that as the plays may have been speaking principally to a select group, the target audience for the plays may have been much smaller than the total audience numbers. I also want to suggest that this select group was composed of the actors in the plays and their families, of their fellow guildsmen, and of members of associated trades and guilds, in roughly that order. Arising from the assumption of a select target audience, I shall examine the Christ and the Doctors plays or episodes for evidence of a specific discourse directed at that group. Far from the perpetuation of a normative religious doctrine, the plays are engaged in a radical social discourse, which places the laity at its centre. There are implications of this for the way in which the laity viewed stereo-types of itself, and the way in which the plays are used to disseminate a politicised image of a dynamic laity.

The Guild as a target audience

It is axiomatic that guilds operated primarily for the good of their members. This was, and is, after all, the *raison d'être* of the guild structure. This is not to say that guild practices were solipsistic; the evidence is very much to the contrary. Many guilds were responsible for maintaining altars or repairing churches or roads. Larger guilds took part in the education of their commu-nities, by operating schools, or by requiring that priests hired by them should have a teaching function. However, their theoretical exclusivity encouraged unity and loyalty among members in a way that larger groupings, such as the parish and the Church, did not.

The concerns of each guild began, then, with its own members and their families, but broadened out to embrace the other guilds, the city, the country and 'alle cristene'.[8] Guilds maintained torches to burn at high mass, wore livery so that they could be recognised by the general public, and prayed for their own souls. Other guilds included the wider community of Christians in their prayers, but in a general way.

In sharp contrast to the lay brotherhood of the guilds, the Mass – the central act of Christian worship – had been over time oriented away from the laity. It was celebrated in Latin, silently, with the priest's back turned, and often concealed behind a rood screen. The spiritual benefits of the Mass were similarly weighted against the laity by late medieval authorities. Duns Scotus, in the fourteenth century, distinguished three ways in which the graces accruing from attendance at Mass were divided:

1. In a most special way it always benefits the person praying if he is in the state of grace. . . . Neither can one reasonably give away this merit of his in favor of another, since he is obliged in charity to love himself more than another. What is more, it might even be that he could not give it to another without sinning.

2. In a most general way prayer benefits the Church as a whole . . .

3. And in some intermediate fashion prayer must benefit the person being prayed for.[9]

It appears from Scotus's analysis that little more grace accrued to one attending Mass than accrued in general to any member of the Church from any Mass, whether s/he attended it or not. Furthermore, whatever the intention for which the Mass was celebrated, it was the priest, the celebrant of the Mass, who benefited most. Moreover, to attempt to give away this benefit, whatever the motive, might be itself a sinful act. One might extrapolate from Scotus's formulation that, in a similar fashion, the principal beneficiaries of any good works done by guilds were the guilds themselves. Even now, participants in modern-day Catholic religious procession, such as that of Corpus Christi, do so principally for the sake of their own souls. It is not difficult to imagine, then, guild members performing public civic works for their own fraternal benefit.

If the guild activities outlined above were performed primarily for the good of the members and the honour of the guild, there is no reason to suppose that guilds which produced plays operated on anything but the same principles. Eleanor Prosser's picture of the Jolibody family bustling about the business of the pageant now appears quaint, but it may have been quite close to actual occurrences.[10] While there is no documentary evidence of family involvement, guild records do contain much evidence of inter-guild co-operation.

The Ten Commandments in the plays

Each of the versions of Christ and the Doctors contains a recital of the Ten Commandments, and each one uses them in a similar but non-traditional manner.[11] In order to highlight this clearly, the status of the Ten Commandments in the Church's mnemonic syllabus for the laity cannot be overstated. The thirteenth-century Statutes of Lincoln (*c.* 1239), issued by Robert Grosseteste, commented that: 'without observation of the decalogue the health of the soul does not endure'.[12] Grosseteste referred to them specifically as 'the ten mandates of the mosaic law', a description repeated by the Statutes of Worcester in 1240.[13] The most famous formulation of the syllabus, Pecham's *Constitutiones* from the Council of Lambeth in 1281 called the commandments 'decem mandata decalogi' (the ten mandates of the decalogue) and clearly distinguished them from the 'duo precepta evangelii' (the two precepts of the gospel), which also form part of the syllabus:[14]

Thou shalt love the Lord thy God with thy whole heart and with thy whole soul and with thy whole mind. This is the greatest and the first commandment. And the second is like to this: *Thou shalt love thy neighbour as thyself.* (Matt. 22. 37–9)

The *Speculum Christiani*, a fifteenth-century manual based on Pecham, preserved this distinction clearly in both its Latin and English versions. Brit. Lib. MS Harley 6580 states that the First Commandment is: 'Thou schalt haue no false godd*es* be-fore me'.[15] Brit. Lib. MS Lansdowne 344 cites the First Commandment (in Latin): 'The first is: Do not have strange gods before me, nor adore them, nor worship them'.[16] It is then glossed with a verse in English, not found in the Harley MS, which uses one of the precepts of the gospel:

> Thou shalt love God with heart entire
> With all thy soul and all thy might
> Another God in no manner
> Thou shalt not have by day nor night.[17]

After dealing in detail with each of the mosaic commandments, both versions make reference to the precepts of the gospel as separate entities: 'These ten co*mm*aundment*es* be contenede in the two p*re*cept*es* of the gospel, *that* ben to loue god and oure euen-cristen'.[18] The expanded gloss on these passages makes clear the continuing separation of mosaic command- ment from Gospel precept found in Pecham nearly two centuries before.[19]

The commandments were required learning for every Christian above the age of reason, usually about six or seven. To be able to recite them at age twelve, as Jesus was at the time of the events dramatised, was hardly a great feat of wisdom. Their appearance here might be construed as intellectual laziness on the part of the playwright, were it not for two facts: they have been moved from their biblical frame of reference, Exodus, and they have been altered in several versions of the plays.

The Towneley and Chester cycles each contain two versions of the decalogue. In the Towneley cycle, one is in Play VII, *Processus Prophetarum*, and another is in Play XI, *The Play of the Doctors*. In the earlier play, Moses recites the commandments to the audience, who, by virtue of being apostro- phised directly as such by the prophet, function as his surrogate 'folk of Israell' (*Towneley* 7, 1). His speech functions as a prologue to the other prophets also, as he makes some general comments on the profession of prophet:

> Therfore will god stir and raise
> A prophet, in some man days,
> Of our brethere kin. . . .

> (*Towneley* 7, 7–9)

Line 9, 'Of our brethere kin' comes directly from Deut. 18. 15, and is quoted twice in Acts 3. 22 and 7. 37. It principally refers to the Jewish nation as the chosen people, but, as the audience are their actual surrogates, it also refers to them.[20] The reverse is also true. If the audience is composed of the citizens of a late medieval city, and the speaker a guildsman, or an actor paid by the guild, then 'oure brethere kyn' is capable of interpretation as a fraternal reference. Guild documents constantly make references to 'the bretheren and sistren'.[21] The prophet will come not just from their race, but from their brethren, and seeing as many of the 'brethren' present are the brethren of the craft guilds, it could be inferred that the prophet will come from their class. As Christ, the ultimate end of the prophecies, was an artisan, a carpenter, these claims must have had resonances for the target audience.

The New Testament version, furthermore, substitutes the precepts of the Gospel for the first two commandments. A. C. Cawley has pointed out that this was not an isolated incident. According to Cawley, works such as *Kepe Wel Christes Comaundement* and John Audelay's fifteenth-century metrical rendering of the commandments make this substitution. He attempts to explain the difference in the first two commandments thus:

the version of the commandments given in the play of Christ and the Doctors in York, Towneley, Coventry and Chester is christianized by the substitution . . . This substitution serves to distinguish the New Testament version of the decalogue in the Doctors' plays from the Old Testament version in the Prophets'.[22]

Myers offers the additional explanation that:

As a teaching device, the cycle simply contrasts the Old Law and the New for the 'lewed' men in the audience. For the more educated, these frequent references suggest a deeper application of the opposition of the two covenants.[23]

If the men [*sic*] in the audience are 'lewed' such a teaching device would only serve to confuse them, given that it is repeated only once a year, and the references within the text can hardly be described as 'frequent'. Even if the commandments were expounded in their parish churches between performances, it is doubtful whether the unglossed discrepancies in the plays would serve any useful didactic purpose. The 'more educated' might well have been able to discern the difference and see in it 'the conflict of the Old Law and the New Law' but the possibility is predicated on a large section of the audience engaging in sophisticated exegetical processes while watching a play.

The only group associated with individual plays whose exposure to the text could have been frequent enough for meditative purposes was that of the performers themselves. Learning lines and repeatedly performing them would undoubtedly lead them to reflect on the plays. One might include their families, who may have listened to the actors reciting their lines. The group can be extended to the guild in general, members of which were responsible for the maintenance of the properties and the pageant wagon, and whose exposure to their guild play, and possibly to others, would have been more frequent than that of a casual spectator. On the fringes of the group are the members of other guilds who may have undertaken repairs or construction tasks before, during or after the performances. If one takes this group into account, and the knowledge they might have developed over time, not just of the text and its orthodox meanings, but of the dramatic and performance texts, and of the embedded secondary meaning, then it might well have been possible for them to garner a deeper, more meditative significance from the dramatic experience, and to become the true target audience for the plays.

There are points of close similarity between four of the five extant versions of *Christ and the Doctors*. It is well established that the York cycle, or an earlier version of it, is the source of much of the Towneley cycle.[24] The Chester play also displays a dependence on either the York or Towneley versions.[25] The *Christ and the Doctors* episode occurs in Chester Play XI from l. 207 to l. 334. In the course of these 128 lines, fifty-seven are almost identical to, or strongly reminiscent of, the York play. Forty-nine lines from the Towneley play correspond to the Chester version, and likewise thirty-five from the Coventry Weavers' pageant.

The recital of the commandments is also similar in structure in the four versions. In each play the commandments are begun, not by Christ, but by one of the Doctors of the Law:

> *I Doctor*   I rede this is is the first bidding
> That Moses taught us here untill:
> To honour God over all thing
> With all thy wit and all thy will. . . .
>
> (*York* XX, 45–8)

The First Commandment is spoken in all versions by a Magister or Doctor, not by Christ. It is not the commandment from the mosaic law, despite the Doctor's comment in the York version, but one of the precepts of the Gospel. Christ takes up the recital from the Doctor, speaking the second precept:

> *Jesus*   He needs no other books to bring,
> But fandis this for to fulfill.
> The second may men prove
> And clearly know, wherby
> Our neighbours shall he love
> As yourself, sikerly.
>
> (*York* XX, 151–6)

Christ affirms that the law is dependent on these two, and whoever keeps them keeps all the others also. When challenged by the Doctor to recite the rest of the decalogue, he continues with the Third Commandment:

> The iij bids whereso he go
> That he shall hallow the holyday;
> Then is the fourth for friend or foe
> That father and mother honour ay.
>
> (*York* XX, 171–4)

The recitation continues until line 192, whereupon the Doctors profess their amazement at the wisdom of 'yon barne'. The first two precepts were, as we have seen, clearly distinguished from the commandments by episcopal decrees and by devotional manuals. It is unlikely, therefore, that a play written for public catechetical purposes would confuse these two distinct doctrinal elements by accident. And yet the same occurs in all extant versions of the play.

In the York, Towneley, Chester and Coventry plays or episodes of Christ and the Doctors, the commandments are begun by one of the Doctors (or Magisters). If the substitution of the two precepts of the Gospel for the first two commandments is in order to 'christianise' the decalogue, why is it left to the representatives of the Old Law to begin? In each case, Christ either challenges them to begin (*Chester* XI, 271–4), or returns their challenge to them (*Towneley* 18, 113–16; *York* XX, 145–8; *Coventry: Weavers'*, 965–70) and in each case he is answered with the New Testament version. Thus, the Doctors of the Old Law are quite familiar with the New, and the idea of 'christianising', as proposed by Cawley, cannot be the full explanation.

The precepts occur at a different stage in Christ's life in the Gospel versions. In Matthew's Gospel, the adult Christ is answering a challenge from a Pharisee lawyer: 'Then one of them, which was a lawyer, asked him a question, tempting him, and saying, "Master, which is the great commandment in the law?"'.[26] Christ's response is to recite the precepts. In Luke's Gospel there is a variant reading. In it a lawyer challenges Christ, who returns the challenge:

And behold a certain lawyer stood up, tempting him and saying, Master, what must I do to possess eternal life?

But he said to him: What is written in the law? How readest thou?

He answering, said: *Thou shalt love the Lord thy God with thy whole heart and with thy whole soul and with all thy strength and with all thy mind: and thy neighbour as thyself.*[27]

This is, without doubt, the ultimate source of the confrontation between Christ and the Doctors in the plays, transposed to an earlier period of Christ's life:

| *I Doctor* | Say, son, which was the first commandment |
| | That was subscribed in Moses' law? |

Iesus	Sith all you masters together be set
	And your books here laid on breyde [open wide].
	Lay forth your reasons and do not let
	How right that ye can rede.

(*Coventry: Weavers'*, 959–64)

The first Doctor approaches Christ in the same tone as the Pharisee in Matthew's Gospel: the opportunity existed in the plays to follow Matthew's version by having Christ recite the precepts of the Gospel, but it was not taken up. The same happens in the York and Towneley versions. In the Chester version, the Doctors' challenge is omitted and Christ demands that they read the Law from their books. Their literacy (and Christ's lack of it) is a very important factor, as will emerge shortly. Interestingly, despite the fact that it is the lawyer who speaks the precepts in Luke, they were still seen in late medieval catechetical tradition as Christ's fulfilment of the Old Law.

The Presentation of the Doctors and of Christ

In all four versions of the play or episode, the Doctors represent official, organised, medieval Catholicism far more than they represent Jewish High Priests. The opening speech of I Magister in the York play is an example of hierarchical pomposity:

> Masters, take to me intent,
> And rede your reasons right on rawe [in sequence],
> And all the people in this present,
> Every-ilke man let see his sawe.
> But wit I would, ere we hence went,
> Be clergy clear if we could knowe
> Yf any lede [uphold] that life has lent
> Would ought allege against our law,
> Other in more or less.
> If we default might feel,
> Duly we shall gar dress [correct it]
> Be dome [judgement] every-ilk a dele [entirely].
>
> (*York* XX, 49–60)

The Doctors look for incidents of unorthodoxy among the people, whether great or little. The law is referred to as 'oure lawe' rather than God's law. There appears to be both an appropriation of authority and an obsession with heresy. II Magister is even more emphatic:

> For masters in this land are we
> And has the laws lelly to lede [truly to expound],
> And doctors also in our degree
> That demyng [judgement] has of ilk a deed.
>
> (*York* XX, 63–6)

This is the discourse of an elite, speaking to themselves, but allowing others to overhear. These others are at once the people of Israel and the late medieval target audience. It is difficult to read these lines without thinking of the juridical Church and its attempts to root out heterodox opinion throughout the Middle Ages. Pomposity and a concern for heterodoxy are charges which could be levelled against the leaders of most organised religions. There is, however, more evidence.

All the cycles refer to the high priests as bishop, prelate, or chief of clergy. Furthermore, their titles, 'maistir' and 'doctour', were the awards of the universities. This is not merely a title of convenience, as the Coventry Weavers' pageant makes clear. The text of the play clearly portrays the Doctors as university men. The third Doctor refers to himself and his fellows as 'gradudis gret of old antequete . . .' (*Coventry: Weavers'*, 1166). The Chester records contain the following information from the Smiths, Cutlers and Plumbers in 1574–5: 'To Io a shawe for lone of a docters gowne & hode for our eldest docter xijd'.[28] Each version of Christ and the Doctors refers to the doctors as 'clerks' or a variant of it. The York version uses the tems 'clargy clere', which appears in the Chester version as 'cleargie cleane' and in Coventry as 'clarge clere' – clear knowledge.[29] Indeed, 'clergy' or 'clerk', appears linked with verbs of knowing twice each in the York, Towneley and Chester versions, and once in the Coventry version. One of the main themes of the play is the knowledge of the Doctors contrasted with the expected knowledge, or lack thereof, of one who is not a cleric. This theme may reflect the early fifteenth-century Oxford debate on the nature of 'vernacular theology and its readers' following Archbishop Arundel's constitutions of 1407–9.[30] In his article on censorship and cultural change, Nicholas Watson points out that Pecham's thirteenth-century syllabus listed the minimum necessary for the laity to know, while after Arundel the same list became the maximum they might 'hear, read or even discuss'.[31] Watson maintains that the debate polarised stereotypes of the laity 'as though this were a homogeneous body'.[32] A clerical fear of lay learning appears to have developed, one contemporary scholar referring to the laity as 'God's enemies'.[33] The fear was, principally, that lay learning would lead to unorthodox opinion and even to heresy. Analogues to these debates are found in all four plays, in the theme of lay learning and clerical law. The real fear, one suspects, was of lay transmission of information without the necessity of clerical intercession or interpretation.

In three of the four Christ and the Doctors plays, the final scene is between Christ, Mary and Joseph as they plan their return to Nazareth. In the Coventry version there is a unique scene between the Doctors, where they discuss the events that have just occurred. The third Doctor, having adjourned their meeting, speaks to the people:

> Where all you, the commonality,
> You may depart on this condition,
> That ye attend at the next monyssion. [ecclesiastical summons]
>
> (*Coventry: Weavers*, 1184–6)

The audience, representing the 'commonality', are imperiously discharged, told when to go and when to come back. These lines underscore the distance between the Doctors and the people. They are also reminiscent of the '*Ite, missa est*' (Go, you are dismissed), the dismissal at the end of Mass, which was frequently used to announce later services or holy days in the same week.[34] This augments the depiction of the Doctors as representations of the Catholic clergy.

There are three elements to the presentation of the figure of Christ in the Christ and the Doctors episodes. He is presented simultaneously as a child, as a non-cleric and as the Word made Flesh. The plays or episodes are framed by contextualising scenes which attempt to set the picture of a child-Christ in the mind of the target audience.[35] In each of these scenes we are reminded that Christ is a child, that he is twelve, and is separated from his parents. The longest of these, in the Coventry Weavers' pageant contains lines in which Mary tells the audience how Jesus has grown and Joseph comments on how obedient he has been to his parents. In the concluding scene of the plays (in Coventry the penultimate scene) Christ is set in his socio-religious context by Joseph's reaction to the Doctors:

> With men of might can I not mell, [mix, associate]
> Then all my travail must I tyne; [waste, lose]
> I can not with them, that wit ye well,
> They are so gay in furs fine.
>
> (*Towneley* 18, 221–4)

The image of Joseph is that of the stereotypical layman, and is used as the dramatic means to separate Christ from the Doctors in socio-economic terms. Joseph, in all of these plays, is the wondering everyman-figure, perplexed and intimidated by the happenings around him. He represents a narrow and pejorative perspective on the medieval laity, which was held, according to Watson, by many leading clergy.[36] The plays exploit the negative stereotype for positive ends, using him as a benchmark against which to measure the status and authority of both the Doctors and Christ.

When Christ approaches the Doctors in the central scene of the plays the text is constructed so as to remind the target audience that Christ is both a child and a non-cleric. His knowledge is continually compared with theirs:

> Certes, son, thou art over-young
> by clergy clean to knowe our laws.
>> (*Chester* XI, 239–42)

> To ken it as a clerk may know.
>> (*York* XX, 124)

> And thou says thou has insight,
> Our laws truly to tell and teach.
>> (*Towneley* 18, 75–6)

> Where noble doctors together are met,
> There children's words are at no charge.
>> (*Coventry: Weavers'* 939–40)

Christ is presented in all versions of the plays as illiterate. Joseph's entry at the end of the play makes explicit the social and educational gulf that exists between his family and the Doctors, and emphasises the fact that Christ transcends mere social and human barriers.

Christ is also presented as the Word made Flesh, which is another reason he does not read the law as the Doctors do; he embodies it. This certainly is the basis of the irony in the Towneley version. It must be borne in mind, however, that, to the audience, the visible 'Word' in the performance text of all versions of the play is clearly a child and a non-cleric, despite the fact that, in Chester at least, he may have had a gilded face. These very clear visual signals would be far more expressive in the minds of a target audience than the more esoteric idea of the Word made Flesh.

Stanzas which appear in all versions

Three stanzas appear in all versions of Christ and the Doctors, even in the Chester version, which is the most divergent of the four. Between ll. 251 and ll. 262 Chester has a unique borrowing from either York or Towneley. These lines do not appear together in the York, Towneley or Coventry versions.[37] They concern, respectively, Christ's authority from God, the Doctors' amazement at his learning, and their fear of his popularity eclipsing their deeds:[38]

Deus	The kingdom of heaven is in me light and hath me annointed as a leech, and given me playne power and might the kingdom of heaven to tell and teach.
Secundus Doctor	Behold how he has learned our laws, and he learned never on book to read. Methinks he says subtle [sawes] and very truth, if you take heed.

Tertius Doctor	Let him wend forth on his ways; for and he dwell, withouten dread, the people full soon will him praise well more than we, for all our deeds.

(Chester XI 251–62)

The first of these stanzas appears in the York play at the point where Christ is making himself known to the Doctors, but before he gives any evidence of his learning. Analogous versions also appear in the Towneley and Coventry plays.

Christ claims to draw his authority not from the official Church, but directly from the Holy Spirit, from God. The York, Towneley and Coventry versions claim that Christ has been given the right to 'preche'. Given that his non-clerical status is emphasised in the play, this is a surprising claim, one not made by the Chester version, which claims only to teach. The *Speculum Christiani* makes the difference clear:

Preaching is in a place where there is a calling together or gathering of people on holy days, in churches or other fixed places and [at] times ordained thereto. And it belongs to those who have been ordained for that purpose, who have jurisdiction and authority, and to no others.[39]

Preaching was forbidden as a lay activity, and as a clerical activity except under licence by Arundel's Constitutions, which were aimed at preventing heterodoxy, in particular Lollardy. Teaching, in the *Speculum Christiani* was considered to be a lower order of activity, and thereby much less contentious, and was acceptable for all Christians in a limited way.[40] It is possible that the lateness of the Chester MSS contributed to its emendation of 'preach' to 'teach'.

All four versions mention the power given to Christ by the Spirit, or by the Kingdom of Heaven. York and Chester expand this to 'pleyne poure'. This phrase is a deliberately provocative one. The term 'pleyn poure', or 'playne power', is almost certainly a translation of the papal phrase *plenitudo potestatis*, variously rendered in modern English as 'the fullness of power', 'the plenitude of power' or 'plenary power'. The phrase had been coined by the fifth-century pope, Leo I, who also formulated the idea of the popes' descent from Peter. By virtue of this descent he was the Church's 'supreme ruler, its supreme teacher, and its supreme judge'.[41] What it meant was that 'the pope's power as head of the Church [was] essentially unlimited, at least in theory'.[42] Practically, it meant that the pope was the earthly controller of the power of God, of the graces and blessings accruing from sacraments and from prayer. The cardinals, bishops and lower clergy had only the *pars solicitudinis*, a share in the responsibilities, while the laity, apparently, had none.[43] The phrase reappeared in *c.* 850 in the Pseudo-Isidorian or 'false' Decretals. These were forged by a Frankish clerk, and aimed again at strengthening the authority of the papacy.[44] The Decretals repeated Leo's phrase in its entirety and attributed it to earlier and later popes, in order to claim a direct descent from apostolic antiquity of the primacy for the See of Peter. In the twelfth century Bernard of Clairvaux advanced the theory further in *De Consideratione*, when he wrote to Pope Eugenius III:

Therefore, according to your canons, others are called to a share in caring, you to the fullness of power. The power of others is confined within determined limits; yours extends also to those who have received power over others. Are you not empowered, should a cause arise, to bar heaven against a bishop, can you not depose him from the episcopal state, indeed, can you not deliver him to Satan? [45]

It was also Bernard who promulgated the assumption that the Church 'properly meant the bishops and above all the pope'.[46]

The theory of *plenitudo potestatis* was exploited to its fullest by Innocent III, whose letters and sermons use the phrase liberally. Innocent reasoned that, whenever sin was involved, papal jurisdiction came into play, and thus extended his sphere of legal influence.[47] In several sermons, he compares the power of the papacy and of the hierarchy in the metaphor of the body:

Just as the plenitude of all the senses are situated in the head, but in the other members there is in some way a part of the plenitude, so others are called to a care in sharing, Peter alone, however, is called to the plenitude of power.[48]

Innocent III also rewrote the imperial coronation rite, requiring the emperor to receive his sword from the pope; a symbolic affirmation of the temporal power's subjection to the spiritual.

In the conciliar fourteenth and fifteenth centuries, the ecumenical councils used the phrase to refer to the absolute power of the pope and of the council itself, as the councils sought to assert supremacy over the pontiff. It is probably no coincidence that the act of Henry VIII, in which he appropriates the power of the Pope to hear appeals which hitherto would have been heard in Rome, describes the king as: 'oon Sup[re]me heede and King . . . beying also institute and furnysshed by the goodnes and sufferaunce of Almyghtie God with plenarie, hoole and intier power'.[49]

The use of the phrase in the plays is complicated. The figure of Christ is claiming power directly from the Holy Ghost to preach and teach the word of God. In making that claim, the text utilises a phrase which is identified with papal claims of authority. The question thus arises of the relationship between the claim and the phrase: is the figure of Christ affirming the power of the pope or interrogating it? In view of the theme of clerical and lay knowledge throughout the plays, I think the play represents a questioning of lay exclusion from the late medieval Church. The questioning is very mild, and could disappear in the performance text, but the evidence stands. Christ is presented as illiterate, the son of a carpenter who has refused to retrieve his son from the Doctors because he is too cowed. The Doctors continually refer to their own knowledge and status. Yet Christ, a member of the laity, a child, an outsider, is claiming, and, from the point of view of any Christian onlooker, deserving of, greater authority and knowledge. The implication of the text is that the descent of *plenitudo potestatis* is not necessarily through the juridical Church. These lines are, in the actual space, spoken by a guildsman on a pageant waggon. There is a subversion at work here, but it is a quiet, orthodox, conservative one. The protest it makes is not a dissent from without, still less a dissent from within designed to destroy the *status quo*. It is an attempt to provide an alternative form of devotion within the framework of the English Church, based on a traditional model, by suggesting a lay spiritual descent from Christ. It strains at Church discipline rather than at Christian dogma.[50]

In the York cycle the second two stanzas appear after the commandments, when the Doctors can express surprise at Christ's display, and foreboding at the consequences for themselves. In the Chester play all three verses appear before the Decalogue, in which position the second two stanzas make little sense. Christ appears to have convinced the Doctors that he has 'learned our laws' without the need to provide any evidence to that effect.

In addition to this textual problem, the order of the commandments themselves is muddled in the Chester version. The First, Second, Third and Fourth are in the correct order. Thereafter the text proceeds with the seventh, eighth, fifth, sixth, ninth, and either the seventh or tenth (*Chester* XI, 288–96).

Without doubt, the section is, as Greg remarks: 'a sad mess'.[51] What is significant about the mess is that although the Chester redactor may have been a poor playwright, and may have had a confused sense of order, he did know what he wanted to include. The borrowed stanzas are of such importance to the Chester text that they have been imported uncritically. Although the Chester redactor makes changes, the stanzas are mostly intact from the source. The carelessness of the Chester redactor may have left a valuable clue to the significance of stanzas which appear in four out of five plays, quite an unusual borrowing.

The first stanza has already been discussed in relation to the York and Towneley cycles. The appearance of the stanza as an importation into the Chester cycle strengthens the evidence for the stanza as a circumvention, an avoidance of priestly power.

The second stanza, were it not out of place in the Chester text, might well have passed unnoticed. The fact that the Doctors have or hold books is emphasised in all versions of the play. They read the law from their books:

> Lay forth our books believe, let see . . .
> As we in scripture read? . . .
> here in this book that written be . . .
> And your books here laid on breyde [laid wide open].
>
> (*York* XX, 67; *Towneley* XVIII, 28;
> *Chester* XI, 250; *Coventry: Weavers'*, 962)

All of the plays have a variation on the line: 'I rede that this is the first bidding'.[52] Similarly, as has been mentioned, in all versions of the play Christ is presented as illiterate: 'and he learned never on book to read'.[53] This is an astute piece of writing. It would be difficult to ascribe illiteracy to the adult Christ, as on several occasions in the Gospels he both reads and writes. In both the apocryphal gospels of Thomas and of pseudo-Matthew and in the *Cursor Mundi*, attempts are made to teach the Christ-child his letters. In each case he confounds the teacher, either by knowing the letters intuitively, or by expounding on a deeper truth behind them.[54] The point of these stories is simply that Christ does not need teaching by any earthly agency, therefore he confronts teachers. In the plays, when Christ confronts Doctors of the Law, the emphasis is different. In the *Cursor Mundi* account, the central point is not the confrontation between Christ and the Doctors. Although all four MSS edited by Morris mention a dispute, the bulk of the narrative is reserved for Mary's reactions, and Christ's words to her. In the plays, the dispute between Christ and the Doctors is the centre of the drama. This is partly to allow a recitation of the commandments, and partly to illustrate the point that knowledge, subtlety and wisdom are possible without literacy, and more importantly, without clerical mediation. Senior churchmen had been for a long time criticising the minor clergy for their ignorance of the basic tenets of the faith, and also for their ignorance of books. The *figura* of the Christ-child is contrasted with those of the Doctors, the hierarchy. They do not recite their initial commandment, they read it. It is Christ who has internalised the word of God, not the churchmen. The letter of the law is being contrasted with the spirit of the law. In this way a wise, subtle, illiterate and authoritative layman confounds the might of the juridical Church. Ironically, it is the figure of Christ who is being appealed to as a subversive, subversive of juridical authority in favour of spiritual awareness. The pun between 'rede', meaning both to interpret, and to read, is also used to its utmost. Christ cannot read, but he can still interpret the Law.

The third stanza in this series concerns the Doctors' dread of the people's adulation of Christ. The Coventry version is the most divergent of these, containing some interesting variations. In all four texts the Doctors worry about Christ's continuing presence. In three they are worried about the consequences if he remains, while the concern in the Coventry text is more acute; it implies that knowledge of Christ will become known whether he stays or goes. All three texts are concerned with praise, the Doctors' own praise compared with Christ's. There is an inference from the context in which the play was staged, that the Doctors are comparing their importance with that of the second person of the Trinity. Whether or not we allow for the operation of dramatic irony here, the target audience cannot have been unaware of the message. The fourth line of the Coventry version makes this clear. While the other texts speak of their 'deeds', Coventry refers to 'clarge', knowledge. Given the transposition of 'clergy' and 'clarge' in the Coventry play (see above) and the association of clergy with knowledge in all of them, this could be an ideologically charged pun.

It is possible that the opposition of the Old Law and the New Law in this play is the opposition of the sacerdotally controlled hierarchical religion and the aspirations of sections of the laity for a share in that control, or at least a share in participation. What is being presented here is a radical Christ, one who is not bound by the disciplines of a bureaucratic Church. It is the opposition of the heroic Christ of Old and early Middle English, the *Christus Victor*, and the post-Anselmiam obedient Christ of the Atonement.[55]

This reading of the Christ and the Doctors plays is, I believe, a coherent one, and one which represents an infinitely small shift in the public utterances of the late medieval urban artisan and commercial class. It is the beginning of the shift which, a generation or so later, allowed laymen like Thomas More the education and authority to pronounce on matters of church and state, and to expect to be listened to. It is, in a sense, one of the stirrings of the English Renaissance.

NOTES

The standard editions of the cycle plays are: Richard Beadle (ed.), *The York Plays* (London, 1982). Martin Stevens and A. C. Cawley (eds), *The Towneley Plays*, I, EETS s.s. 12, (Oxford, 1991, 94); R. M. Lumiansky and David Mills (eds), *The Chester Mystery Cycle*, I, EETS s.s. 3 (London, 1974); Hardin Craig *Two Coventry Corpus Christi Plays*, 2nd edn, EETS e.s. 87, 2nd edn (London, 1957). References to these are given in the main text. With regard to primary text quotations, I have translated, transliterated, or used translations of all but the simplest passages of Latin and Middle English. References to these are to the original language editions where these are accessible. Biblical translations are from the Douai-Rheims version (London, 1914). Other translations are my own unless otherwise specified.

1 Mary Douglas, *Natural Symbols: Explorations in Cosmology* (London, 1973), p. 60.
2 A. D. Justice, 'Trade symbolism in the York cycle', *Theatre Journal* 31 (1979).
3 Rosemary Woolf, *The English Mystery Plays* (Berkeley and Los Angeles, 1972), 80.
4 V. A. Kolve, *The Play Called Corpus Christi* (Stanford, 1966), p. 58.
5 E. Catherine Dunn, 'Popular devotion in the vernacular drama of medieval England', *Medievalia et Humanistica* n.s. 4 (1973), 58.
6 Hans-Jürgen Diller, 'Theological doctrine and popular religion in the mystery plays', in Piero Boitani and Anna Torti (eds), *Religion in the Poetry and Drama of the Late Middle Ages in England* (Cambridge, 1990), p. 201.
7 Meg Twycross, 'Beyond the picture theory: image and activity in medieval drama', *Word and Image* 4 (1988), *passim*.
8 Toulmin Smith (ed.), *English Gilds*, EETS o.s. 40 (London, 1870, repr. 1963), 37.
9 Felix Alluntis, OFM and Allan B Wolter, OFM (eds and trans.), *John Duns Scotus, God and Creatures: The Quodlibetal Questions* (Princeton and London, 1975), 444.
10 Eleanor Prosser, *Drama and Religion in the English Mystery Plays: A Re-Evaluation* (Stanford, 1961), 5.
11 *The N-Town Play*, which was not controlled by crafts guilds, does not contain a recital of the Commandments. There is some uncertainty as to the status of Towneley as a guild cycle. The MS does have some marginal guild ascriptions, but these are in a later hand. Cawley (A. C. Cawley, 'Middle English metrical versions of the Decalogue with reference to the English Corpus Christi plays', *Leeds Studies in English* 8 (1975), 129–45) certainly believed that it was a guild-controlled cycle.
12 F. M. Powicke and C. R. Cheney (eds), *Councils and Synods, With Other Documents Relating to The English Church*, II (Oxford, 1964), p. 268 (translated).
13 *Ibid.*, p. 304.
14 *Ibid.*, p. 901, translated. In point of fact the first of the 'precepts of the Gospel' is mentioned in Deut. 6.5, and the second in Lev. 19.18.
15 Holmstedt, G. (ed.), *Speculum Christiani*, EETS o.s. 182 (London, 1933), 16.
16 *Ibid.*, p. 17 (translated).
17 *Ibid.*, p. 17 (translated).
18 *Ibid.*, p. 38.
19 It is an ironic fact that these precepts, usually attributed to Christ, first appear in the Old Testament.
20 As addressed by a virtual Moses, the audience is a virtual people of Israel; as addressed by an actual guildsman, they are actual members of the audience.
21 Smith, *English Gilds*, 37.
22 A. C. Cawley, 'Middle English metrical versions of the Decalogue with reference to the English Corpus Christi cycles', *Leeds Studies in English* 8 (1975), 129–45 (pp. 133, 139).
23 Walter E. Myers, *A Figure Given: Typology in the Wakefield Plays* (Pittsburgh, 1970), 100. Lauren Lepow follows both Cawley and Myers when she refers to Christ in the Towneley version as 'the fulfilment of the Old Law'. Lauren Lepow, *Enacting the Sacrament: Counter-Lollardy in the Towneley Cycle* (London and Toronto, 1990), p. 96.
24 The earliest exploration of the connection is: Marie C. Lyle, *The Original Identity of the York and Towneley Cycles*, Studies in Language and Literature 6 (Minneapolis, 1919).
25 There is some disagreement as to whether the borrowing was from York directly, or from Towneley. Cawley assumed that it was from York, as do I. David Mills, in an opinion expressed at the 1997 Leeds International Medieval Congress, thought Towneley a more likely source (see below).

26 Matt. 22.35–6.

27 Luke 10.25–7.

28 Lawrence M. Clopper (ed.), *Records of Early English Drama: Chester* (Manchester, 1979), p. 106.

29 The phrase does not appear at all in the Towneley version, suggesting the possibility that the Chester lines were copied from York.

30 Nicholas Watson, 'Censorship and cultural change in late-medieval England: vernacular theology, the Oxford translation debate, and Arundel's constitutions of 1409', *Speculum* 70 (1995), 822–64 (p. 824).

31 *Ibid.*, 828.

32 *Ibid.*, 847.

33 *Ibid.*, 844.

34 W. G. Henderson (ed.), *Missale ad Usum Insignis Ecclesiæ Eboracensis*, I, Surtees Society 59 (Durham, 1874), p. 210.

35 This scene is missing from the Towneley plays. Two leaves are missing from the MS, containing the end of *The Purification of Mary* and the beginning of *Christ and the Doctors*. It is probably safe to assume that the opening scene of the latter play was similar to the other extant versions.

36 Watson, 'Censorship', 841 and *passim*.

37 Hardin Craig favours Towneley as the original of the Coventry Weavers' pageant, but the evidence is slight in any direction.

38 Watson, *Censorship*, 844.

39 Holmstedt, *Speculum Christiani*, 2, translated.

40 *Ibid.*, 2.

41 Thomas Bokenkotter, *A Concise History of the Catholic Church* (New York, 1979), p. 98.

42 Bokenkotter, *Concise History*, p. 98.

43 R. N. Swanson, *Religion and Devotion in Europe c. 1215–c. 1515*, (Cambridge, 1995), p. 47.

44 G. O. Sayles, *The Medieval Foundations of England* (London, 1977), p. 373.

45 Bernard of Clairvaux, *De consideratione ad Eugenium Papam*, ed. Jean Leclercq and Henri Rochais (Rome, 1963), p. 424. I am indebted to Professor Éamonn Ó Carragáin for help with the translation.

46 Colin Morris, *The Papal Monarchy* (Cambridge, 1989), p. 207.

47 Walter Ullmann, *A Short History of the Papacy in the Middle Ages* (London, 1972), p. 224.

48 J. P. Migne (ed.), *Patrologia Latinae* ccxvii, col. 658, translated.

49 24 Henry VIII c. 12 § 1. Alexander Luders, John Raithby and others, *The Statutes of the Realm*, III (London: Record Commission, 1817), 427. The more usual phrase used in the Statutes of Henry VIII to describe the power of the monarch was 'full power & auctorite'.

50 This is the subject of an extended work, provisionally entitled *Orthodoxy and Protest in the English Mystery Plays* (New York, forthcoming).

51 W. W. Greg, 'Bibliographical and textual problems of the English miracle cycles III', *The Library* (3rd series) 5 (1914), 298–305.

52 *Towneley* XVIII, 121. Also *York* XX, 145, *Chester* XI, 275 and *Coventry Weavers'*, 965.

53 *Chester* XI, 265. Also *York* XX, 194; *Towneley* XVIII, 186; *Coventry Weavers'*, 1002.

54 M. R. James, *The Apocryphal New Testament* (Oxford, 1985), pp. 49–65, 73–9.

55 For a comprehensive review of the implications of this change in the figure of Christ, see Gustaf Aulén, *Christus Victor* (London, 1937).

5 The Huguenot Diaspora: Refugee Networks of Power

Charles C. Ludington

More than one hundred and sixty years after the Revocation of the Edict of Nantes – which ended the limited toleration of Protestantism in France – the Irish baronet, Sir Erasmus Borrowes, reflected back with as much imagination as evidence upon the Huguenot army officers and their refugee families who had settled in the Irish midlands village of Portarlington. Life, we are told by Borrowes, was good for the French officers in their Hibernian exile. Their settlement, which straddled a meandering river separating what were then the King's and Queen's counties, was a 'sylvan retreat on the placid waters of the Barrow', and a 'favourite amusement of our interesting foreigners, was to assemble in the cool shade of the primaeval oaks of the O'Demsey's', which had not yet been cleared away from the market place . . . and there they sipped their tea, as a *bonne bouche*, in Lilliputian china cups'.[1] Other nineteenth-century images of the Huguenots in Ireland were equally idyllic and often just as genteel.[2] They were heroic soldiers in King William's victorious army, skilled craftsmen with silver and wood, innovators and organisers of the linen industry, international merchants engaging in *le doux commerce*, and bankers to the Irish aristocracy. Indeed, if any one group in Irish historical imagination could combine a reputation for hard work *and* gentility, thrift *and* luxury, it was the Huguenots.

Late twentieth-century research on the Huguenots has revealed that these contradictory views of the French exiles were also highly romantic. An overwhelming majority of the Huguenots in Ireland were poor refugees living in a poor country, and many moved on within a generation or two, to England, the Protestant nations of the Continent, North America and even South Africa. This is not to deny the validity of Huguenot contributions to Ireland, but it is to say that romantic notions of their communities within Irish historiography have served to obscure both the difficult realities of most refugee lives, as well as the fact that the long Huguenot (and Walloon) diaspora of the early modern period, and especially of the years 1680–1715, was an event of pan-European and even trans-Oceanic consequences. This latter viewpoint was prudently embraced by a conference of historians held in Dublin on the tercentenary of the Revocation in 1985. The resultant book of essays published in 1987, *The Huguenots and Ireland: Anatomy of an Emigration*, has borne fruit at a more popular level. The journals *History Ireland, History Today* and the *Proceedings of the Huguenot Society of Great Britain and Ireland* have all since published articles that both deromanticise the Huguenot settlements in Ireland and help to place them in a broader, European and even Atlantic context. In fact, one such article recently published in the *Proceedings of the Huguenots Society*, suggested that the evidence of anti-Catholicism among Huguenot ministers in Ireland made the Huguenots as a whole, 'manifestly and unapologetically' part of what the author called the English 'imperial project'.[3] This post-colonial approach to the Huguenots in Ireland places them into an extremely wide context indeed, but like earlier nineteenth-century views, it falls prey to a romantic notion of the Huguenots which presumes, but cannot prove, their power. It is one thing to show that some Huguenots – expelled from their own country for their Protestant faith – were anti-Catholic, and philosophically in lockstep Dublin Castle. It is quite another thing to show that Huguenot ranting had any effect on policy makers in Westminster. There were in fact Huguenot initiated plans for a massive resettlement of refugees from Switzerland to Ireland in the 1690s, but the costs and vicissitudes of William's war against Louis XIV meant that the English parliament was reluctant to take the plan seriously, and the poverty of the refugees diminished the incentive of Irish landlords to have the Huguenots as tenants.[4] Given what is actually known about the Huguenot refugees in Ireland, and not what is merely insinuated from the evidence of fiery sermons and nostalgic memoirs of a few self-promoting refugees, it is difficult to discern any broad or powerful involvement in a comprehensive British project, imperial or otherwise.

My dismissal of the aptness of post-colonial theory aside, it is the purpose of this chapter to suggest that by looking at the French Protestant refugees in Europe and its colonies as a whole, the Huguenots did wield power, but not in the ways just described. Rather, Huguenot power, which in any event was limited to a small percentage of their members, derived from the international and trans-oceanic networks they developed throughout the sixteenth, seventeenth and eighteenth centuries. In other words, refugee power as such was more cosmopolitan than local. In fact, their power was derived from their cosmopolitanism, which was partly chosen, but primarily a result of the persecution and proscription of the Calvinist faith within France that sent so many Huguenots into exile. This last point, which might seem self-evident in spite of the historical irony, has been challenged by the Irish historian Louis Cullen in an article on Huguenot involvement in the brandy trade and in his more recent general study of brandy trade during the ancien régime.[5] Cullen uses the existence of, and reasons for Huguenot trading networks prior to and after the Revocation of the Edict of Nantes to conclude: 'It seems hard to relate the origins of Huguenot activity abroad or the success of later Huguenot enterprise in any clear way to the persecution.'[6] While this might be true for the brandy and wine trade of southwestern France – and even here I remain sceptical – by examining a variety of Huguenot commercial and intellectual networks, it becomes clear that there was a link between persecution, exile, international exchange of information, and the development of Huguenot power.

Cullen's study of Huguenot involvement in the brandy trade, and his belief that persecution had little to do with their economic success, takes as its starting point Warren Scoville's meticulously researched book, *The Persecution of the Huguenots and French Economic Development*. In this work, published in 1960, Scoville showed that contrary to previous beliefs, there was no causal connection between the flight of approximately 200,000 Protestants from France (one per cent of the total population) and French economic stagnation in the late seventeenth and early eighteenth centuries. Perpetual war, successive bad harvests at the end of the seventeenth century and the archaic nature of French taxation were primarily to blame. That said, Scoville's work decidedly was not an exoneration of Louis XIV's policy of persecution. He condemned the Revocation as 'a crime against man' because it violated individual freedom and human dignity.[7] It was, however, a corrective to a long-held assumption, which was itself part of the larger debate surrounding the supposed link between Protestantism and capitalism begun so forcefully by Max Weber.[8]

Cullen does not directly enter into this contentious sociological terrain, but his study does attempt to answer why Huguenot families such as Augier, Ranson, Lallemand and Dardillouzes dominated the early stages of the brandy trade. According to Cullen, two important things happened in brandy trade during the first quarter of the eighteenth century. Exports increased enormously, and 'trade was not only handled in the region by Huguenots, but increasingly the houses dealing in it overseas were Huguenot also'.[9] In fact, Cullen maps out an entire network in which Huguenot merchants in France – often officially these were *nouveaux convertis* (new converts to Catholicism), which generally meant discreet Protestants or non-practising religious sceptics – traded with their Huguenot contacts overseas, most notably in Amsterdam, Rotterdam, London and Dublin. When the Huguenot families were joined in the Cognac region by outsiders, it was by merchants like Martell and Le Mesurier, both from the Anglo-

Norman island of Guernsey, and both of Huguenot origin, and as Cullen says, 'this made it easy for them to work up links within the region'.[10]

Cullen concludes that it was the expansion of the demand for brandy and other southwest regional products that 'encouraged the Huguenot merchants whose local demesne had never been encroached on to expand their investment into active disposal of the goods in foreign markets'.[11] While this part of Cullen's argument is convincing, it is difficult to believe that the ability of the Huguenot merchants in France to have or make trustworthy foreign contacts to whom they could send their goods – compared to the same ability of French Catholic merchants in the brandy trade for example – was not greatly facilitated by the strong presence of Huguenot refugees in those foreign port cities. Quite frequently those overseas contacts were friends or relatives who had not abjured their faith. In other instances, *nouveaux convertis* from France would spend some years overseas, learning their trade and practising Protestantism. Thus it seems that the distinctive opportunities for international trade among French merchants from the southwest were not simply a result of the increased demand and supply of wine and brandy, but also a result of the trading links created between Huguenots in France and those in forced exile. This seems particularly true in light of the fact that since 1703, the Methuen Treaty between England and Portugal placed French wine and brandy at a distinct disadvantage with similar Portuguese products. Yet it was precisely in this context that the French brandy trade in England expanded, a fact due as much to the readily established and solid trading networks of Huguenots as to an acquired taste for brandy.[12]

Cullen notes that another reason for the success of the brandy trade was the reliance upon Huguenot banking houses in Paris which were geared to the internal requirements of the kingdom, rather than foreign banks geared to international trade.[13] While this might suggest Huguenot banking was primarily domestic, that decidedly was not the case for Huguenot banks headquartered outside France, especially in Geneva. This point is well illustrated by the Tourton and Guiger family alliance, whose banks in Lyon, Paris, Geneva, London and Amsterdam at the end of the seventeenth century were, according to Herbert Luthy, a 'characteristic product of the "*amalgame lyonnais*"'.[14] The breadth of Huguenot family and banking networks can be found in the peripatetic apprenticeship of Isaac Thelluson, a member of the extended Tourton-Guiger family who was directly descended from a Lyon Calvinist who had fled France for Geneva during the sixteenth-century wars of religion. It is important to point out here, that many historians divide French-speaking Protestant refugees into two waves, the first just as often comprised of Walloon refugees from the Spanish Netherlands as French Huguenots, and the second being those who fled during the reign of Louis XIV. Thelluson's life helps to illustrate that these two waves were not distinct historical phenomena. Rather they ran together, as contacts between the exiles and those who remained in France helped to create what has been called the Calvinist international. Moreover, Huguenot and Walloon refugee churches from the first wave facilitated the settlement and assimilation of refugees from the second, more concentrated wave that climaxed with the Revocation.[15]

When his father died in 1704, the fourteen-year-old Isaac Thelluson left Geneva for Basel, where he stayed for twenty days with a cousin. He then went to Frankfurt, where he was received by a close friend of his father's, a Monsieur Couvreau. After eight days he moved on to Cologne, where he stayed with the brother of his uncle, Monsieur Camp, and then on to Amsterdam and his uncle Isaac Guiger. His next stop was Rotterdam, where he stayed with a Monsieur De la Motte, then to Noortwyk, near Leiden, where he worked in the family bank for two years. In 1706 he crossed the Channel to London (a voyage that took three weeks owing to storms and French pirates), where again he was met by his uncle Isaac Guiger, and his associates Nicolas Tourton and George Tobie Guiger. But learning no English among the French-speaking bankers, Thelluson was sent to one of the bank's business contacts in Exeter, a draper named Hughes Bidwell. This, finally, was Isaac's first non-Huguenot contact in the course of his international apprenticeship. However, after learning passable English and growing tired of Bidwell, Thelluson returned to his cousins in London, moved on to Amsterdam and finally settled in Paris, where he worked in the family bank for fifteen years. He finished his days in Holland, but despite, indeed because of his cosmopolitan existence, he never lived for long outside the tight-knit Huguenot community.[16] Thelluson, it must be acknowledged, was not himself a refugee; he was a cosmopolitan Swiss banker, and therefore part of a well-to-do and well-connected group even in the eighteenth century. Nevertheless, the family banking world in which he operated was full of *nouveaux convertis* within France, Protestant refugees outside, and Huguenots like him, who as citizens of another country could come and go to France and who remained French in language and culture, even if no longer subjects of a Bourbon monarch.

Another good example of the overlap of refugee generations can be found in the early history of the Bank of England. Of the 147 directors of the bank elected during its first fifty years of existence, 24 were Huguenot refugees or the descendants of Walloon and Huguenot refugees. For example, ten early directors belonged to Walloon families settled in England since the days of the 'Spanish Fury' in the late sixteenth century, and three more were connected with this group. The origin of three other directors remains unclear, whether Walloon or Huguenot. Eight directors had undoubted

French roots, and five were first generation immigrants who had fled Louis XIV's persecutions.[17] According to P. G. M. Dickson, 123 Huguenots who had settled in England since 1650 subscribed £104,000 or nine per cent of the Bank's initial capital; 22 of these subscribers came from just five families (Houblon, Lethieullier, Lordell, Du Cane and Chambrelan) and held 5.01 per cent of the initial capital. After the Bank's second subscription in 1697, people of Walloon and Huguenot extraction held almost 15 per cent of the Bank's capital – more than any other 'foreign' group.[18] And yet refugee power should not be exaggerated. Walloons and Huguenots never held enough stock to control decision making by the Bank of England, nor did their financial elite ever constitute more than a tiny minority of the overall refugee population in England at the time (40,000 to 50,000). Nevertheless, these figures are remarkable as they reveal the powerful kinship connections and the economic prowess of the most fortunate Walloon and Huguenot refugees and their descendants.

Many more examples could be cited of the commercial advantages gained by Walloons and Huguenots through inter-generational affiliations and international networks that were often produced by persecution and abetted by exile – one thinks of various cloth industries in particular – but not all such networks were commercially based. Moreover, not all trades for which the Huguenots are remembered constituted a commercial network. To produce fine felt hats, ribbon and quality paper, which Huguenots in England, Holland and Brandenburg did, was not necessarily to operate in a world in which production, distribution and wholesale were controlled by French-speaking co-religionists, although this was often the case within the brandy trade. In fact, while Scoville believed that skilled Huguenot craftsmen did generally help to stimulate the economies of those countries in which they found refuge – England and Holland in particular – and perhaps therefore reduce the dependence of their economies on French luxury goods, he and many other historians have acknowledged that the Huguenot intellectual networks ultimately may have had a more profound effect on their host societies. Certainly these latter networks had a greater impact on the history of France, where the numerous French language journals that were edited and published by Huguenots in Holland circulated clandestinely.[19]

Although cultural influences are much more difficult to prove than economic, it is generally agreed among scholars of the period that the mid-eighteenth century Enlightenment, which had particularly profound effects on France, was made possible by the previously constructed 'Republic of Letters' in which Huguenots of the diaspora played such a prominent role. Indeed, the imaginary and borderless 'Republic' and the Huguenot diaspora were inextricably linked. One need only cite the numerous journals and

their Huguenot refugee authors, editors and contributors to see that this
'Republic' was, more than any other, a Huguenot dominated network.
And one need only examine the international diffusion of these journals to
understand that this network was a powerful cultural force. The most
famous of these journals, which somewhat ironically were based upon the
model of Denis de Sallo's official, French-government sponsored *Journal des
Scavans*, was Pierre Bayle's *Nouvelles de la Republique des Lettres*. And there
were many more, including the various bibliothèques, such as the *Bibliothèque
universelle et historique*, the *Bibliothèque choisie* and *Bibliothèque ancienne et
moderne* of Jean Leclerc. There were also *mercures*, published monthly and
containing contemporary news and comments culled from the more
frequent gazettes. On the more scholarly side of this rapidly evolving field
of journalism, were the annotated bibliographies, such as Henri Basnage de
Beauval's *Histoire des ouvrages des savants*. These texts, often overlapping
in form and function, provided a forum for the international exchange of
ideas. They were the backbone of the Republic of Letters and, in their
content and rules of engagement, they tended to be more dispassionate, sceptical and anti-clerical, than overtly Protestant. Indeed, their form and the
general politeness of their contributors were dictated by a desire to avoid the
kinds of religious controversy that had sent the Huguenots into exile, and
replace it with a more 'rational' exchange of news, insights, ideas and information.[20] Consequently, Huguenot journals were among the few places
that Protestant and Catholic *philosophes* could engage in intellectual debate.

Just as the extent of Huguenot financial networks is nicely illustrated by
the banking voyage of Isaac Thelluson, the importance of Huguenots in
creating a cosmopolitan Republic of Letters is revealed by the literary
voyage of a Berlin-born Huguenot, Charles-Etienne Jordan. Having spent
much of his adult life as a minister to a Huguenot community in provincial
Brandenburg, Jordan's true calling lay elsewhere, in the world of books and
scholarship. Abandoning the ministry when the opportunity arose, he set
out in 1733 to visit the learning centres and learned men of Europe, thereby
hoping to place himself among their members. His voyage from Berlin, to
Halle, Leipzig, Paris, London and Amsterdam quite literally mapped out
the world of European *érudits*. And while his contacts were international
and by no means restricted to fellow French-speaking Protestants, which was
precisely the point of the cosmopolitan Republic of Letters, his *Histoire d'un
voyage littéraire, fait en M.DCC.XXXIII*, published in The Hague in 1735 and
again in 1736, contained a veritable who's who of exiled Huguenot *savants*.[21]

I began by suggesting that the history of the Huguenot refuge in
Ireland, or of Huguenots communities elsewhere for that matter, is best
understood by seeing the refuge as part of one, long international event,
rather than a series of events to be studied within the narrow context of

specific national histories: What did the Huguenots contribute to Ireland? Britain? The Netherlands? Prussia? etc. Having placed the Huguenots at the centre, I would like to end by drawing Ireland back into their world map. Cullen's work on the brandy trade provides by far the best example of Ireland's place within a larger Huguenot-dominated commercial network; however, there is little evidence that Ireland figured prominently in the other type of Huguenot network I have outlined, the intellectual network of the Republic of Letters. True, William Molyneux, who contributed articles for English and Continental learned journals until his early death in 1698, was descended from a Walloon refugee family that had fled to England during the 'Spanish Fury' and then come to Ireland with the Elizabethan administration.[22] But the Molyneux family in Ireland did not maintain a Walloon or immigrant identity. In that sense, Elie Bouhereau from La Rochelle, secretary to Lord Galway (the nominal leader of the Huguenot refugees in Ireland, also known as the Marquis de Ruvigny) and first librarian of Marsh's Library in Dublin, may be the best example of a Protestant refugee in Ireland who also belonged to the international Republic of Letters. As librarian beginning in 1701, Bouhereau purchased the first copy of the *Journal des Scavans*, and attempted to disseminate scholarly news among the library's users. His edition of *Origen* was reviewed in French journals published in Holland, and mentioned by Bayle and Le Clerc.[23] This made Bouhereau a modest, provincial figure in the Republic of Letters, but it did not make Dublin or Ireland a significant location within the Huguenot network of publishers or *savants*.

Perhaps then, the best example of how Huguenot intellectual circles influenced Ireland is to be found, ironically, in the written work of a military officer whose *History of England* inadvertently helped to delegitimise Irish history. I am speaking of Paul de Rapin-Thoyras, who came to Ireland in King William's army, fought at the Boyne, was wounded in the first assault on Limerick, took part in the successful siege of Athlone, and was then stationed for two years at Kinsale. It was there, in the Cork fishing village which has been the scene of so much Irish history, that Rapin had time to reflect on the events in which he had just partaken. When Rapin fled France in 1686, Louis XIV was at the apex of his power, and with his friend James II on the throne of England, Scotland and Ireland, French hegemony seemed certain and Protestant Europe looked doomed. Seen from Kinsale five years later, with James's and Louis's Hiberno-French army having been defeated in Ireland, and Anglo-Dutch power united under William III, Rapin (like many others) believed that he had just witnessed a historical shift in power from court-centred France to the hybrid 'constitutional monarchy' of party-divided England. It was Rapin's desire to understand this powerful island nation, and to explain English history and the English political system to the Continent, especially to his fellow Frenchmen, who he had good reason to believe had suffered (and were suffering) under a Bourbon yoke.[24]

With a timely recommendation from Ruvigny, Rapin left Ireland in 1693 and accepted the job of tutor to Lord Woodstock, eldest son of King William's closest Dutch advisor, Hans Willem Bentinck, now Earl of Portland. This post took Rapin to England and France on occasion, but mostly he lived in The Hague, where he passed his time amongst a coterie of learned Huguenots, including Henri Basnage de Beauval and his brother Jacques Basnage. It was with these men, and Portland's Whig friends, that Rapin began to learn his English history. The *History of England* that Rapin eventually produced was not surprisingly a combination of sixteenth-century Huguenot and seventeenth-century Old Whig ideology. Where François Hotman's *Franco-Gallia* had failed in its bid to help maintain the historic liberties supposedly introduced to Gaul by the Germanic Franks (this had been a critical issue for Huguenots seeking to win constitutional arguments during the French Wars of Religion[25]), Anglo-Saxon liberties in England had never been successfully subverted. Rapin's *History* was published simultaneously in The Hague (French version), and in London (English version) in 1727, and was hailed by Whigs, Tories and Frenchmen alike, as the only objective history of England. In fact, it was the classic exposition of applied Whig theory. It was a story of continuity, of the ancient English constitution with its guarantee of liberty through the separation of powers, and it was to become the paradigmatic interpretation of English history throughout the eighteenth century and beyond.

It was also a teleological interpretation of English history into which the subordinate kingdom of Ireland did not neatly fit. The history of Ireland and the Irish system of government could not be understood as the preservation of immemorial Germanic liberties when in fact England, as Anglo-Saxon, Anglo-Norman or just plain English, had undeniably conquered Ireland and changed the political system there. Darcy's and Molyneux's unsuccessful appeals to the ancient constitution of Ireland during the seventeenth century had already revealed this difficulty, along with the sometimes inconsistent, hypocritical and irrelevant positions that such an appeal forced its authors to take. In short, Irish history could not stand on similar ancient constitutional grounds as England, nor, according to Rapin's teleology, could it be seamlessly woven into English history as part of a comprehensive whole. When Hotman's sixteenth-century French Protestant political theory met with seventeenth-century English Whig political theory in the form of Rapin's *History of England*, it only reinforced the belief that Irish history was an irrelevant afterthought. Historically speaking, all of Ireland was beyond the Pale.

What I have just outlined is admittedly a circuitous connection between the life work of one French refugee who operated within a relatively closed Huguenot intellectual network, and the influence his work had upon the island in which it was first inspired. Nevertheless, I believe that the story of Rapin and his *History of England*, how it was inspired, who influenced it, how it came to be written, published and accepted, and ultimately, how it influenced English, and therefore Irish nation-state building, is a good illustration of the frequently cosmopolitan Huguenot experience, the paradoxical insularity of the refugee community, and the extent of their influence upon European history. That is not to say that there is anything particularly romantic about the Huguenots. They were not, as has sometimes been claimed, endowed with special commercial, intellectual or spiritual gifts. Instead, like many oppressed minority groups they held fast to their faith (for at least a generation or two), they earned their living through those channels that were open to them and they remained weary of grand political schemes that might exclude them. Persecution, forced conversion and exile, did mean the end of a powerful Calvinist political and base within France. However, it did not mean the end of Huguenot power in France or out.

By examining a few of the many international Huguenot networks, I have tried to show how persecution and exile facilitated Huguenot commercial and intellectual power by creating cosmopolitan community of French-speaking, co-religionists. As Herbert Luthy explained about the famous Protestant bankers whose legend fills the close of the ancien régime in France and the beginning of the new era, and was then supplanted by the Jews, 'the problem was to have correspondents in distant places who could accept the papers and advance the money during the time needed for a return transaction, direct or triangular. The difference between a Catholic and a Protestant banker was, to repeat a truism, that the latter tended to have the requisite correspondents, preferably of the same creed and sometimes perhaps the more reliable for it.'[26] The importance of trustworthy contacts can be extended to cover a variety of Huguenot networks, and indeed, to the study of diasporas in general. Contacts alone do not explain the success or failure of a scattered immigrant group, but Armenians within the Byzantine and Ottoman empires, Sephardic and later Ashkenazi Jews in Europe and the Americas, Chinese in Southeast Asia, and as Cullen's work has shown, Irish within the Atlantic trading world all built their networks of power on contacts and trust that were derived from shared language, experience (often in fact historical memory) and frequently religion. Within such an environment, the exchange of information, ideas and capital readily took place for the mutual benefit of everyone. In early modern Europe, as markets for consumer goods and the international exchange of ideas (usually in the form of journals or books) were rapidly expanding in size and distance, the Huguenots, cosmopolitan by force more than choice, had well-placed and reliable correspondents in abundance. These contacts, along with the commercial and intellectual ideas that had been shaped by their experience of persecution and expulsion from France, formed the basis of their mutually beneficial networks. It was upon these networks and the hard work that went into maintaining them, and not their mythic gentility, that Huguenot power ultimately rested.

NOTES

1   E. Borrowes, 'The French settlers in Ireland – Portarlington', *Ulster Journal of Archaeology* 6 (1858), 327, 337.
2   The most influential proponent of this romantic view of the Huguenots was Samuel Smiles, *The Huguenots: Their Settlements, Churches and Industries in England and Ireland*. First published in London and Edinburgh in 1867, the book had a total of eight printings in the UK and one in New York.
3   R. Whelan, 'Persecution and toleration: the changing identities of Ireland's Huguenot refugees', *Proceedings of the Huguenot Society of Great Britain and Ireland*, 27 (1998), p. 33.
4   A. de Chambrier, 'Projet de Colonisation en Irlande, par les réfugiés français, 1692–99', *Proceedings of the Huguenot Society of London*, 6 (1898–1901), 370–432; M. Magdelaine, 'L'Irlande huguenote: utopie ou realité?', in *De L'Humanisme aux Lumières, Bayle et le Protestantisme, Mélanges en l'honneur de Elisabeth Labrousse* (Paris and Oxford, 1996), pp. 273–87.
5   L. M. Cullen, 'The Huguenots from the perspective of the merchant networks of Western Europe (1680–1790): the example of the brandy trade', in C. E. J. Caldicott, H. Gough and J-P Pittion (eds), *The Huguenots and Ireland: Anatomy of an Emigration* (Dun Laoghaire, 1987), pp. 129–49; L. M. Cullen, *The Brandy Trade under the Ancien Régime* (Cambridge, 1998).
6   Cullen, *Brandy Trade*, p. 132.
7   W. Scoville, *The Persecution of the Huguenots and French Economic Development, 1680–1720* (Berkeley, 1960), p. 446.
8   Weber's *Protestantische Ethik und der Geist des Capitalismus* was first published in 1904. Since then it has been translated into many languages and published in English as *The Protestant Ethic and the Spirit of Capitalism*, trans. Talcott Parsons (London, 1930).
9   Cullen, *Brandy Trade*, p. 134.
10 *Ibid.*, p. 135.
11 *Ibid.*, p. 140.
12 C. Ludington, 'The Politics of Wine in Britain and Ireland, 1660–1860', PhD thesis Columbia University (forthcoming), Ch. 3.
13 Cullen, *Brandy Trade*, pp. 146–7.
14 Herbert Luthy, *La Banque Protestante en France, de la Révocation de l'Edit de Nantes à la Révolution*, 2 vols (Paris, 1959–61), I, p. 78.

15 R. Gwynn, *Huguenot Heritage: The History and Contribution of the Huguenots in England* (London, 1985), *passim*.

16 Luthy, *Banque Protestante*, pp. 89–91.

17 François Crouzet, 'Walloons, Huguenots and the Bank of England', *Proceedings of the Huguenot Society of Great Britain and Ireland* 25 (1990), 170.

18 Crouzet, 'Walloons, Huguenots', pp. 173–4. Crouzet's figures come from P. G. M. Dickson, *The Financial Revolution in England: A Study in the Development of Public Credit, 1688–1756* (London, 1967); A.C. Carter, *Getting, Spending and Investing in Early Modern Times: Essays on Dutch, English and Huguenot Economic History* (Assen, 1975); and from his own research at the Bank of England archives. See also, A. C. Carter, 'The Huguenots and the English financial revolution', *Britain, France and International Commerce, from Louis XIV to Victoria* (Aldershot, 1996), pp. 221–66.

19 M. Yardeni, *Le Refuge Protestant* (Paris, 1985), pp. 201–2.

20 Yardeni, *Refuge*, pp. 201–7.

21 A. Goldgar, *Impolite Learning: Conduct and Community in the Republic of Letters, 1680–1750* (New Haven CT, 1995), pp. 1–11 and 219–48.

22 J. G. Simms, *William Molyneux of Dublin*, ed. P. H. Kelly (Blackrock, 1982), pp. 11–17.

23 J-P. Pittion, 'The French Protestants and the Edict of Nantes (1549–1685): a chronology based on material in Marsh's Library, Dublin', in C. E. J. Caldicott, H. Gough and J-P. Pittion (eds), *The Huguenots and Ireland: Anatomy of an Emigration* (Dun Laoghaire, 1987), p. 62.

24 H. Trevor-Roper, 'Our first Whig historian: Paul de Rapin-Thoyras', *From Counter-Reformation to Glorious Revolution* (London, 1992), pp. 249–65.

25 Trevor-Roper, 'Rapin', p. 258; and more generally, see Q. Skinner, *The Foundations of Modern Political Thought*, vol. 2, *The Age of Reformation* (Cambridge, 1978).

26 Herbert Luthy, 'Variations on a theme by Max Weber', in M. Prestwich (ed.), *International Calvinism, 1541–1715* (Oxford, 1985), pp. 389–90.

6 The Men Who Knew Too Much: The Birth of Bureaucracy in Revolutionary France

Ralph Kingston

Paris, Year X of the Republic: a courier arrived at the Ministry of the Interior, hot and sticky from his three-day ride from an outlying province. He was determined to hand his packet to the Minister personally, for the prefect had assured him that it was *urgent* and *very important*. Instead, the uniformed usher showed him to a vestibule, and told him to wait while the Secretary-General was informed of his arrival. Some hours later, after the usher had scoured the nooks and crannies of the former aristocratic *hôtel*, the Secretary-General authorised his Secretariat to take receipt of the courier's burden. They signed it into the register, numbered, dated, and classified its contents for distribution to the appropriate Divisions.[1] The packet was swallowed up by the Ministry; the courier dismissed. He trudged out of the Secretary-General's antechamber, watched curiously by both administrators and petitioners as he crossed the cobblestones of the yard. It became a familiar journey as he returned day after day in expectation of the minister's answer.[2]

The Secretary-General took responsibility for the matters he deemed important, which – in reality – were few. The majority of the prefect's missal made its way to the Division chiefs, who, like the Secretary-General, cherry-picked the few files they thought most significant, and divided it once more for redistribution to the bureaux chiefs. Each time the file was dismembered, a clerk recorded the destination of each piece. All in all, it took over a day for the package's various reports to reach the Ministry's bureaux.[3]

In the Bureau of Agriculture, work was under way on several such reports, on farming in the *départements*, the fortunes of the year's harvest, the number of sheep and the land devoted to them. One *rédacteur*, compiling a notice on pasturage and the dangers of eating alfalfa, had called for information from the prefect a month earlier. When sections of the courier's letter arrived, they were indexed by a *commis d'ordre*, and divided among his colleagues in the room. The report on alfalfa made its way to the *rédacteur*'s desk. He immediately placed it to one side; he would read it when combining it with replies from the other prefectures, the deliberations of the Agricultural Society, and the opinions of his correspondents.[4] The other *rédacteurs* also flipped through their respective papers while the *commis d'ordre* noted the prefect's queries in his work sheet. Drawing a column to suggest what action the ministry should take, he left another empty to register the bureau's eventual reply. Meanwhile, the reports built into portfolios, accompanied by a quick analysis on a single sheet of paper. Both register and portfolio were to be sent with the Division chief, to elicit the minister's approval in their biweekly meeting. If the matter was urgent, the Division chief would have to send it instead through the Secretary-General.[5] These prescribed forms made the minister's burden manageable. He could treat the business of twenty to thirty bureaux with some degree of comprehension. Once the Minister had marked them 'approved', the reports returned to the bureaux where *expéditionnaires* copied them in a firm and legible hand to be sent to the Secretariat for dispatch.

In a single room, the Bureau of Agriculture dismantled and remade dossiers. It pillaged cartons for auxiliary knowledge. Documents were moved from box to box, leaving an impossible trail of destruction. Scraps of paper containing vital information vanished behind heavy writing desks or in between the dusty cartons piled to one side. Though the *commis d'ordre* and the bureau chief both battled valiantly against the paper drift, and kept the official register in minute detail, they still found it impossible to make sense of the clutter and disorder.[6] Ignoring this chaos, the bureau worked all the more furiously, copying out answers, drawing up summaries of the prefects' correspondence for presentation to the minister, comparing and contrasting yields with those of other years and other regions, plucking details of technological advances to be shared with the nation. They passed in and out of the office as they wished, to drop in next door to borrow a document, to discuss problems, or simply to ask help with their workload.[7] The prefect had mixed information on pasturage into a report on abattoirs sent to the Bureau of Commerce.[8] Rules or no rules, the *rédacteur* would retrieve it.[9] The process of analysis in the ministry was a messy one: breaking down the original packet into small pieces to be compared and incorporated in reports was a far from simple task.

Such ordinary scenes in the Bureau of Agriculture had their equivalent in the other central bureaux. One day after another, delivery times and the sheer mass of detail counterbalanced their very usefulness. The telegraph had not yet been invented; the postal system was still rudimentary. Reports passed sluggishly on the 'conveyor-belt' from Secretariat to bureau. The minutely organised breakdown of correspondence through the administrative hierarchy looked good on paper but proved unwieldy in practice. Administrators abandoned the rules as they saw fit, by asking help from the bureau next door, or by supplementing the prefect's letter with the views of private correspondents or societies. In fact, the hierarchy, so carefully detailed in organisational documents, tended to be highly malleable in practice. There was leeway in the offices; and there needed to be, if the administrators were to get their job done.

This useful latitude afforded to employees in the bureaux in Revolutionary France complicates and even contradicts the simple history of bureaucratisation suggested by Max Weber's ideal type, which, nevertheless, has dominated the study of administration.[10] Weber imagined a corporate bureaucracy superior to its non-centralised, non-professional patrimonial and prebendal predecessors. It was defined by its hierarchy and clearly defined regulations, the separation of public office from private ownership, the use of documentary records, and the salaried employment of full-time experts with full-time tenure. Four major historical developments, he believed, had 'caused' bureaucratisation: the emergence of a money economy, the qualitative development of administrative tasks in large states, the expansion in the range of administrative duties and the perceivable technical superiority of bureaucratic organisation.[11] The first three, however, collapsed into the last. The universal process of bureaucratisation was, in his final analysis, the product of society's desire for efficiency. Centralisation of administration occurred as experts gathered effectively in one place to pool their expertise and to establish regular action and authority under the rule of law.

Following Weber's abstract, historians of French administration more often than not have accepted that bureaucracy occurred 'naturally', and have chronologised the insipid development of administration from the eighteenth-century *Fermes Générales* to the sprawling ministries of the mid-nineteenth century.[12] Research on the Revolutionary administration has allied itself with the Tocquevillian argument that the French Revolution was less a point of rupture than the realisation of a process of state consolidation.[13] The most recent major study of revolutionary administration, by Catherine Kawa, however, succeeds in showing the uncomfortable distance between the theoretical ideal type and the prosopographical reality, between what should happen and what actually occurred.[14] As Kawa realised, the Revolution was unsuccessful in creating a Weberian corporate bureaucracy. Post revisionist, Colin Jones suggests the reason for this in 'Bourgeois Revolution Revivified': civic rather than corporate professionalism legitimated the Revolution's attack on privilege. Seeing the people of France as citizens, rather than subjects of a rule of law, serving the public good rather than the will of the king, the administration imagined itself as trans-corporative and open, rather than a disciplined, internalist hierarchy segregated from the wider society.[15]

To understand the development of bureaucracy, therefore, it is important to reappraise historically the construction of an administrative body as an information-gathering network, and to investigate the contemporary 'administrative science'. Much has already been made of the role of the 'Old Boys from Egypt' – the intellectuals and experts in the technical arts who had been with Napoleon in North Africa – who appeared after 18 Brumaire in high-ranking administrative roles under the Consulate and Empire.[16] At more modest levels, however, the Napoleonic administration did not recruit experts. Its strength did not lie in the recruitment of 'whizz kids': entry to the offices was through an unpaid and uncertain 'apprentice-ship' as a *surnuméraire*. The *surnuméraires* had several years to prove his worth while moving from office to office to gain a 'general idea' of admini-stration. An office chief with a post to confer would deem competence for a certain branch of administration less important than knowledge of the practices of the administration as a whole. Montalivet, Minister of the Interior in 1812, tried to regulate the practice, and to set up a *surnumériat* for young men of means.[17] Needless to say, many bright young men were excluded in favour of inferior intellects armed with private fortunes, who could work without indemnities or bonuses. In fact, unique abilities counted for less than the possession of a clear writing hand (for *expéditionnaires*) or a precise prose style (for *rédacteurs*). In the Bureau of Agriculture, promotion depended more on neat script than on a singular knowledge of artificial pastures.[18] Expertise may have been a by-product, but it certainly did not structure bureaucratisation.

One of several administrative guides to appear in the beginning of the nineteenth century, Rémy Fleurigeon's *Code Administratif*, a manual for local and national authorities, explained the priority placed on a 'general idea' of administration. Knowledge of politics, military tactics, or finance, he counselled, would be of little help in negotiating the 'labyrinth of administration'.[19] Fleurigeon wrote as a bureau chief in charge of corres-ponding with 37 *départements*.[20] As one day stretched to a week, and a week became a year, he had perceived a permanence in the administrators' routines, and a solidarity in their acts, scattered though they were, across the country. His code thus described the duties and responsibilities of administrators authoritatively, ensuring that correspondence could make it from one end of the maze to the other. Paper could pass from one office to the next, never with a clear view of its final destination, but secure in the use of prescribed routes and forms. Like Fleurigeon, individual authorities also began to consider themselves part of this 'administration'[21] as the labyrinth became fixed in their habitual relationships. Books like the *Code Administratif* played their own part as they made the order that bound the administration together permanent with a prescribed set of cross-references. Having researched their respective responsibilities, there was no need for the local mayor to be acquainted with the minister for the two of them to belong to the same professional 'corps'. They shared common goals, principles and methods. Thus it was not the speed of paper through the labyrinth, but the routes it took, that formed a 'science of administration'.

This 'science' took on arbitrary theories and hypothetical systems and investigated them with a rigorous experimental method. In the Bureau of Agriculture, the prefect's report on pasturage would be combined with reports from all over France. Not only would the *rédacteur* determine whether alfalfa was dangerous when ingested by beasts, he would also analyse the methods known to produce the best pastures, and would transmit the principles of grazing to the *départements*, with notes on how individual cases might differ owing to climate or topography. The organisation of central administration was built to facilitate such investigations: complex reports were broken down into simple facts as they progressed through the hierarchy.[22] In the bureaux, *rédacteurs* noted and compared. Meticulously, they concocted manuals and codes. The ministry's distance from the beast, they believed, liberated the Bureau of Agriculture and allowed it to make objective, educated judgements. With each report, *rédacteurs* developed new areas of interest and justified new calls for information. Their science of administration could eliminate the bucolic ignorance of the provinces, and replace it with information-gathering and experimental deduction.

The object of 'administrative science' was therefore not merely an analysis of cattle or alfalfa, but of the rules that contrived to bring man and society into concert. It looked for knowledge of particular social relations, so to master the art of regulating them itself.[23] As its keenest proponent, Bonnin, explained, it reapplied the natural order to structure the relationship of citizens in the communal interest.[24] In Bonnin's theory, the administration interfered in production, in consumption and in exchange, as constituting public relationships, but could not enter the realm of personal contracts, of inheritance and ownership.[25] Administrative laws, by ordering the nation's public life, maintained harmony between citizens. Administration was inseparable from the nation: it could neither act independently, nor transgress its responsibilities to the citizens.

In Bonnin's mind, once people and property had been brought into line with the common interest, harmony between their actions and those of the rest of society would be maintained by their participation in an exchange of raw intelligence for considered advice. The natural order, discovered and enforced, would increase the national prosperity, and would be the guarantee of public trust and esteem.[26] The administration's action would before long prove the ongoing benefits of reciprocity in the communes, *arrondissements*, and *départements* of France. Each individual became a member of a great family, linked in an immense chain of dependencies and responsibilities, forged by administrative laws.[27]

The Ministry of the Interior's report on pasturage put theories like Bonnin's into practice. Its report would be transmitted to the prefect, sent to mayors and carried about the countryside in the prefect's annual *tour.* The prefect would interrogate mayors and 'enlightened' citizens on local production and the means by which it could be augmented. He would then compare the methods used against the knowledge aggregated by the central bureaux, and provoke changes by indicating the improvements that could be introduced in the breeding of animals, the organisation of cultivation, and the planting of woodlands. He would demonstrate the advantages of artificial pastures, grazing sheep, and ending the practice of leaving fields fallow.[28] Although routinely faced by 'prejudices', the administrators kept faith that the interests of the individual and society would, by public instruction, be combined to their mutual advantage. The riches of the nation would be augmented by the employment of modern practices. It was not enough to impose improvements from above. Due consideration had to be accorded to the 'honourable profession' of cultivator.[29] The administrator was urged to talk as a father and friend, and not as a master. Accordingly, he instructed the cultivator as an equal, to convince him that the discoveries of administrative science were to *his* benefit as well as to the benefit of society at large.[30]

Being an 'administratee' was not seen as a passive role, then. In aligning the individual's interest with those of the rest of society, administration saw no boundary between the state and the public sphere. Administration existed in the union of citizens: it represented their common interests without recourse to political opinion or election. Sometimes it provided sickles and scythes.[31] More often it shared the fruits of industrial and agricultural progress, of enlightenment and communication, whether it be the movement from a medieval fallow to artificial pasture, or from a jumble of different measurements across France to a rationalised metric system. The administrator encountered the cultivator as a fellow professional, sharing a common conviction about the need for progress. Thus the Ministry was confident that the report on pasturage would not lie in a dusty filing cabinet, forgotten. Equal in the administrative process was the act of transmitting their findings to the people. The interests of the individual were naturally linked to the interest of the nation in the recognition and common enjoyment of the benefits of scientific progress.

Nevertheless, reformers could only give form to administration by objectifying it as a 'moral individual', exercising a decision-making process over and above the agglomerated moral opinion of the people. It could be a father and a friend, looking over the shoulder of its cultivators and giving sage advice; but it also could be a manager, marshalling the action of the administrators and citizens to keep them in constant rapport.[32]

Correspondingly, 'administrative law' aligned the citizens with the development of the common interest, and brought them into harmony with the rest of society, while 'administrative instruction' fed them with the fruits of enlightenment to the benefit of both the individual and the common interest.[33] The state therefore took a corporate form to listen and talk to its citizens, to police the nation and impose a harmony on its parts.

This idea of corporation was as much the product of experimental science as the instructions it offered. It differed greatly from the corporation of the old regime, for the new-regime scientists of society no longer saw the body as a single entity. Theorising that the internal composition of man's body shaped his experiences, a group of 'medical revolutionaries', Pierre-Jean-Georges Cabanis foremost among them, popularised an understanding of bodily functions like reproduction, digestion, or decision making, as the co-operation of one organ with another, in the unity and harmony of the organic body.[34] They called on all branches of science to unite their efforts, to accomplish a 'great regeneration',[35] moving outside their laboratories with this aim in mind.

Canabis, for instance, collaborated with Dominique-Joseph Garat, a Commissioner for Public Instruction, to organise medical education.[36] Also a Commissioner, and involved in that project, was Antoine-François Fourcroy (chair of chemistry in the Jardin des Plantes), who had previously served on the Commission for Arms and Powder, alongside other famous scientists such as Berthollet, Pelletier, Monge, and Chaptal.[37] He was made a Councillor of State in 1800 and Director-General of Public Instruction in 1802.[38] Jean-Antoine-Claude Chaptal also prospered under Napoleon, becoming Minister of the Interior in 1800, and afterwards a member of the Senate. His predecessor as Minister, Lucien Bonaparte, had frequented Cabanis's 'Ideologue' circle in Auteuil.[39] Thus, as fellow professionals, medical and administrative scientists combined to imagine the social body as a chain of action and reaction, design and function, alignment and order.[40]

Dissecting the nation in the administrative 'operating theatre', they depended on the epistemology and anatomy of the time.[41] In particular, the works of John Locke and Etienne Bonnot de Condillac provided their inspiration. Locke's *Essay on Human Understanding* (1689) had seen the human mind at birth as a *tabula rasa*, a blank slate.[42] It was only through the process of perception, through the dissection of complex impressions into simple ideas that this slate was filled.[43] Human memory was thus formed in the accumulation of 'ideas of reflection':[44] sensation provided both the material and the principles by which the mind was formed. In France, Condillac had radicalised the Lockean *tabula rasa* by asserting that man depended absolutely on language. He could not become conscious of other bodies without words, the 'arbitrary sign', to objectify them.[45] Thus, man's command over his imagination, through his command over words, separated him from the beast.[46] Language linked man to his society. Sharing a lexicon allowed communities to pool their experience and to widen their understanding.

To regenerate the nation, reformers ordered the purging of old-regime administration – that suspect functionaries be replaced by proven revolutionaries – to remove the influence of royal form and procedure, and of antique systems of classification. Under the first Brissotin ministry, Dumouriez tore into the heart of the old-regime Ministry of Foreign Affairs.[47] The employees who survived swore oaths to the Constitution and to popular government.[48] A year later, under the new Republic, even those oaths were no longer sufficient. New laws compelled ministry employees to approach their commune for certificates attesting their civic virtue. By the end of the Terror, the ministries had eliminated many of their most experienced personnel to ensure the virtue of their offices. The only administrative experience that counted was to have loved the Republic and to have a proven civic devotion. With each successive reorganisation, a fresh set of faces and minds entered the bureaux, onto which the science of administration could be stamped irrevocably. The new administrators were taught a new lexicon and a new set of rules with which to govern the nation. They were taught new styles of address – *citoyen* replaced *monsieur*[49] – and given a new calendar. Most importantly, clarity and precision were made the watchwords of the administrative profession.[50]

In Condillac's formulation, precise communication was the glue of society: it was imperative that words maintained a constant relationship to one another.[51] Likewise, for the administrative scientists, it was crucial that administrators could be sure of the precise meaning of each missal, to be able to depend on its content, to trust the principles on which the simple facts had been identified and classified. The communication of sensation along the nerves in the living body depended on the combined action of all its parts,[52] their uniformity and a chain of regularised responses and reactions. Administrative science looked to ensure a similar harmony between the action of individuals, of intermediary state organs and, consequently, the entire social body. It clearly defined the functions and duties involved at each juncture of the administrative process. It organised administrative molecules into state organs and shaped them in relationship with one another. The administrative body, like the human body, existed to relay information: the ministry clerk, to compile reports from the aggregate of the nation's experiences, received information from all over France, broke it into manageable chunks, and then remade it through the process of comparison. A hierarchy of communication, stretching from local commune to central bureau, became the spine of the newborn nation.

That is why, on entering the bureaux, the *surnuméraire* was not made to study a particular field or develop a particular expertise. He was instead initiated into his 'profession'. His training made certain that his information could be depended on to travel freely through the hands of a succession of fellow administrators and that it could be trusted for accuracy and clarity of expression. In short, he was initated into a chain of responsibilites that he could not escape. As he gathered experience, he gained a wider appreciation of the part played by his colleagues, his dependence on them, and their dependence on his precision. He became more exact in his *rapports* as he strove to emulate his colleagues and to gain their respect. In theory, each move towards greater precision benefited the administration as a whole; the more the administrator integrated himself in the movement of paper the higher he climbed in the ministry hierarchy.

The appointment of scientific personnel under Napoleon as First Consul cemented the reform of administration by establishing regular channels of communication. Chaptal (chemist, physician and Minister of the Interior) and Fourcroy (chemist and member of the Section of the Interior in the Council of State) both held key positions. Of all the administrators imbued in the sciences, Joseph-Marie De Gérando played and even more crucial role, standing at a key vantage point in the chain of correspondence into and out of the central bureaux of the Ministry of Interior. In Year VIII he had been made a bureau chief and member of the Consultative Bureau for Arts and Manufactures. Thereafter promoted to secretary-general of the Ministry of the Interior (a function he fulfilled between 1804 and 1810), he oversaw the organisation of both the central bureaux and local administrations across France.

De Gérando was – and is – more famous as an epistemologist than as an administrator.[53] He participated in the 1799 debate on the influence of signs on the formation of ideas in the second class of the National Institute, and produced a four-volume work on that same subject a year later. He also dabbled in anthropological investigation but, by and large, continued with his linguistic research, producing two reports for the Institute on a rigidly classified universal language. His major triumph, however, was *De la Génération des connaissances humaines* (1802), winning a prize in the Academy of Berlin, and centring on the idea that 'The secret of the future is in the past'.[54]

De Gérando, with that statement, departed from an epistemology based rigidly on a *tabula rasa*. He broke with the tradition in which the individual philosopher regarded himself as a lone subject, to talk instead of the constant rule of 'our' reason.[55] His work traced the chain of ideas through their historical effect on one another, on separate tables offered to the reader for comparison. He offered a view of man as a species, with an accumulated societal knowledge and understanding.

Developments in epistemology, in this case, lagged behind those in administration.[56] De Gérando's own entry into the bureaux in year VIII already testified to the increased worth attributed to accumulated knowledge in the ministries. 'Shadow' consultative bureaux had been set up in centres of particular complexity and importance for the public good.[57] In particular, they emerged alongside the bureaux of agriculture, the manufacturing arts and commerce. Employees of these consultative bureaux were chosen on the basis of proven experience, whether in terms of a lifetime working in the field, or on the evidence of a long administrative career.[58] The consultative bureaux existed only to advise,[59] to unite the experiences of government inspectors, bureau chiefs and *rédacteurs* in the one room.[60] They took no part in the day-to-day movement of correspondence. Rather, they were a well of knowledge to be mined by the regular bureaux, a collective memory of administrative action.

A rekindled sense of the importance of the administration's collective store of experience underpinned the new emphasis placed on archives in the late 1790s. Cartons of old documents were collected, (re)catalogued and (re)classified to make them useful. The archival depots of the eighteenth century had lain for the most part unused and untouched, remote from the day-to-day work of the bureau.[61] They had been ignored, left to rot in corridors and attics. Under the Directory and the Consulate, however, they were brought into the centre of the administrative process. In the Ministry of the Interior, Chaptal created a new central archive in Year 10.[62] In the Ministry of Foreign Affairs, the archives moved from the depository in Versailles to be lodged inside a new ministry building in Paris between September 1798 and April 1799.[63] Rehoused and reorganised, the papers of the old regime could be used more regularly.

The archivists were eager to reveal how the information of the past could serve the future. Sautereau, an *analyseur* in the Ministry of Foreign Affairs, embarked on an ambitious project to analyse the historical relations of France with other European powers. Beginning his work under the Directory, he made headway, publishing works on the various fluctuations of French political relations with Sweden, Spain and Austria over the course of the eighteenth century.[64] Abeille, a clerk in the Bureau of Commerce, also looked at the principles to be derived from past administrations. He asked for and received permission to produce a detailed history of France's commercial transactions since Colbert.[65] By historicising the administrations of the past, the revolutionaries could safely learn from their experiences, and join them to their own.

The Archives therefore began to be used as a training ground for new recruits in the Ministry of the Interior[66] and in Foreign Affairs, where Caillard, the renowned bibliophile and wine-collector, was put in charge of *surnuméraires'* studies.[67] Future administrators were expected to add to their knowledge of particulars and to gain necessary experience in the art of analysis. Talleyrand, in a letter to his former secretary, Bourjot, recognised this and counselled

Experience and habit are the only way to ensure you act in a firm and sure fashion. It is this experience that it is necessary to acquire, and it is this habit that you must develop. You must also develop the knowledge of a multitude of particulars . . . For that, reading the correspondence, the memoirs and the dossiers contained in the department's archives is a necessity.[68]

The archives were the physical aggregate of the ministry's experience, repositories of the administration's memory, and ensured continuity of practice from generation to generation in piles of papers and boxes of documents. Though revolutionary administration had begun by rejecting past knowledge and purging old regime personnel, it now began to stockpile, distancing themselves from a project of total regeneration. The administrators then looked to the past to discern the principles that governed the interaction of administration with citizens, or the political relations of governments. The administrative 'Corps' constituted itself as a body separate to the nation by turning to accumulated experience and not individual expertise.

Paradoxically, however, the abundance of material that came to the archives did not often clarify the ministries' principles of action. More often it tended only to inflame the harried archivists' disorder. They had continually to explain themselves:

This work is without doubt long and painful. In spite of the intelligence, the zeal and the assiduity of my collaborators which I make it my duty to pay justice to, it is very difficult for us to make any haste in our preparations . . .[69]

Cumulative knowledge swamped the archives, as reports engulfed the other central bureaux. Paperwork was stymied in a flood of statistics and scientific detail. Delays grew longer and longer. The archives became famous for the reply 'we are in the process of classification'.[70] Though the other offices could not so easily be singled out for blame, the central ministries' relationship with its subordinate agencies became increasingly tense. The administration's harmony fell victim to the proliferation of useful knowledge.

As the administration became better at working like a body (as communication speeds improved and as people began to accept administration intruding in their lives) the harmony became even more precarious. Delays lengthened as the administration's empirical process gathered more and more facts into the offices and onto desks.[71] Papers continued to be lost behind cartons and desks, prefects continued to send the wrong information on the wrong form, and the *commis d'ordre* continued to scratch his head as he tried to make sense of the chaos before him. Desperately, bureau chiefs reorganised desks and routines, established roll calls and surprise inspections. Nothing worked. The science of administration held within it the seeds of its own demise.

However, contemporaries did not explain the breakdown of administration by its logic or its mode of fact gathering and analysis. A division chief, waiting two weeks for a report he expected in two days, could not see the piles of paper engulfing the poor *rédacteur*. The public could not imagine the difficulties in bringing together facts from eighty odd *départements* and producing from them a clear, precise exposé. Though administrators were no longer purged in the name of creating a *tabula rasa*, they were 'reorganised' for failing to 'live up to their responsibilities', for bringing disorder to the administrative process. Offices were made and remade as they were deemed to have failed or to be superfluous. A climate of fear and distrust overshadowed the bureaux. The eve of each reorganisation saw a new batch of memoirs arrive in the Minister's office. Each held a history of an individual administrator's career, deposited to prove their rights to advancement. In the same way, however, that the administrative memory was paralysed by a glut of information, the abundance of protestations of loyalty and zeal devalued their message. Instead, administrators concentrated on proving their responsibility outside the office, as a good citizen, or through connections in the world of good society.

Though the science of administration could not achieve its aims, it continued to endeavour to do so. No one administrator stood outside the body to diagnose its sclerosis. Each was trapped within his own ambit, limited to his own relationships and responsibilities. The enlightened conviction that a common professionalism could structure a new France became mired in a morass of detail. The cold reality of the everyday chilled the ardour of the administrator who concerned himself more with avoiding the denunciation of his fellows than with recognising his common mission to regenerate the Nation. Harmony became less important than results; results became less important than survival. The French administration simply knew too much. Its organisation, modelled on a conception of natural order, collapsed under the weight of its task. The science of administration, based on empirical reasoning, depended on the flow of information from citizen to prefect to central bureau. Once this flow had been interrupted, Ministers looked for scapegoats, and found them by imagining a new kind of administrator, the 'bureaucrat', whose laziness threatened the administrative order.

NOTES

1 This narrative has been constructed primarily from a memorandum on the organisation of the Ministry of the Interior, dated 29 ventôse, year X, in Archives Nationales (AN), f/1a/634. I have also incorporated details from a number of other organisational memoirs in AN, f/1a/1. The Ministry of Police was modelled directly on the Ministry of the Interior [AN, f/7/3006]. The Ministry of Foreign Affairs also operated along similar lines, but was complicated by the special measures surrounding secret despatches ['Organisation des bureaux des Relations Extérieures, 22 frimaire an 4', Archives du Ministère des Affaires Étrangères (AAE), Organisation et Règlements du Ministère, vol. I (1547–1806), part 2]. Foreign Affairs was also much smaller. Personnel lists [AN, f/1bI/531] name 172 people employed in the Ministry of the Interior in year XI. Only 59 people worked in the Ministry of Foreign Affairs in nivôse, year X [AAE, Compatabilité (Volumes), vol. XVIII]. Because of this, bureau heads could deal directly with the minister.

2 The Ministry of Foreign Affairs kept three couriers of their own who could be depended on to handle diplomatic material. The Ministry of Interior used local couriers or those sent to them from the *départements*.

3 See AN, f/1a/634, on the delays involved in moving paper between offices.

4 Such a request was answered in 'Observations sur la nature des pasturages de l'Arrondissement de Pontarlier, département du Doubs', 21 July 1813, AN, f/10/252. The close relationship between the Parisian Agricultural Society and the Bureau of Agriculture is described in 'Société d'Agriculture', AN, f/10/211. Several correspondents' reports can also be found in AN, f/10/252.

5 'Ordre du travail du Ministre avec les Chefs de Division', AN, f/1a/1.

6 The punishing schedule of a commis d'ordre is described by A. Didot and Lefebvre in a letter to the Minister of Police, pluviôse year V, AN, f/7/3006. Both claimed to work from nine in the morning until six in the evening without a moment's rest, staying late on the evenings when military service had interrupted their ordinary day's work.

7 As attested in the note on Mardlez, Bourgogne and Gebert, AN, f/10/225. The difficulty of getting information from other bureaux through 'official' channels is described in AN, f/1a/634.

8 Prefects were increasingly provided with blank templates and forms so that their information could be easily absorbed into the communication channels in the ministry; see, for instance, 'Envoi au Manuel des Administrateurs', AN f/1a/57. For a criticism of prefects' correspondence, see AN, f/1a/634. Ambassadors were equally sloppy in their correspondence with the Ministry of Foreign Affairs, which also attempted to order and regulate their correspondence; see 'Pour servir de Règle à la correspondence des Employés, vendémiaire an IV', AAE, Organisation et Règlements du Ministère, vol. I (1547–1806), part 2. Rémy Fleurigeon, *Code Administratif, ou recueil par ordre alphabétique de matières de toutes les Lois nouvelles et anciennes, relatives aux fonctions administratives et de police, . . . jusqu'au premier avril 1809 . . .*, 6 vols (Paris, 1809), also provided sample forms and procedures for the local administrators to follow.

9 See the Ministry of Police order forbidding visitors both from other bureaux and outside the ministry, 20 thermidor year VIII, AN, f/7/3006.

10 W. G. Runciman (ed.), *Max Weber: Selections in Translation* (Cambridge, 1978), pp. 341–54; Max Weber, *The Theory of Social and Economic Organization*, trans. A.R. Henderson and Talcott Parsons (London, 1947), pp. 302–12; a useful

summary of Weber's ideal type is provided by Catherine Kawa, *Les Ronds-de-cuir en Révolution: les employés du ministère de l'Intérieur sous la Première République (1792–1800)* (Paris, 1996), p. 21.

11 Runciman, *Max Weber: Selections in Translation*, pp. 341–54

12 Works on French administration are legion and it is only possible to provide a sample. The *fermes générales* have long been seen as the most 'bureaucratic' of eighteenth-century administrations: see George T. Matthews *The Royal General Farms in Eighteenth-Century France* (New York, 1958), and Vida Azimi, *Un modèle administratif de l'ancien régime: les commis de la ferme générale et de la régie générale des aides* (Paris, 1987). Several other works deserve mention: R. M. Rampelberg, *Aux origines du ministère de l'intérieur: Le Ministre de la Maison du Roi 1783–1788, Baron de Brueteuil* (Paris, 1975); Jean-Pierre Samoyault, *Les Bureaux du Secrétariat d'État des Affaires Étrangères sous Louis XV* (Paris, 1971). If the eighteenth century has been mined so diversely, the history of nineteenth-century administration is dominated by one man, Guy Thuillier; see *La Vie Quotidienne dans les Ministères au XIXe siècle* (Paris, 1976); *Bureaucratie et bureaucrates en France au XIXe siècle* (Geneva, 1980). Thuillier's work is highly problematic owing to his dependence on literary, rather than archival material. More recently, William Reddy's intervention in the field, discussing the accumulation of honours in the Ministry of Interior, has been a breath of fresh air. Nevertheless, an unsteady chronology reveals his ambiguity about the development of office structures in the period: William Reddy, *The Invisible Code: Honor and Sentiment in Post-Revolutionary France, 1814–1848* (Berkeley and Los Angeles, 1997), pp. 114–83. *Longue-durée* studies include two other eclectic works by Guy Thuillier, *Témoins de l'Administration de Saint-Just à Marx* (Paris, 1967), and *La bureaucratie en France aux XIXe et XXe siècles* (Paris, 1987); see also P. Legendre *Histoire de l'administration de 1750 à nos jours* (Paris, 1968). Works on Revolutionary administration include Edith Bernadin, *Jean-Marie Roland et le Ministère de l'Interieur (1792–1793)* (Paris, 1964); J. F. Bosher, *French Finances 1770–1795: From Business to Bureaucracy* (Cambridge, 1970); Clive Church, *Revolution and Red Tape: the French Ministerial Bureaucracy, 1770–1850* (Oxford, 1981); Jacques Godechot, *Les Institutions de la France pendant la Révolution et l'Empire*, new edn (Paris, 1970); Kawa, *Les Ronds-de-cuir en Révolution*; Fréderic Masson, *Le Département des Affaires Etrangères pendant la Révolution, 1787–1804*, reprint of the 1877 Paris edn (Geneva, 1977). For a fine example of an in-depth study of the work done in the bureaux, though also accepting the Tocquevillean thesis: Harold T. Parker, 'Two administrative bureaus under the Directory and Napoleon', *French Historical Studies*, 4 (1965), 150–169.

13 Alexis de Tocqueville, *The Ancien Régime and the French Revolution*, trans. Stuart Gilbert, fifth impr. (Manchester, 1976), see especially pp. 49–51.

14 Kawa, *Les Ronds-de-cuir en Révolution*, pp. 509–10.

15 Colin Jones, 'Bourgeois revolution revivified: 1789 and social change', in Colin Lucas (ed.), *Rewriting the French Revolution* (Oxford, 1991), p. 96.

16 Louis Bergeron, *France under Napoleon*, trans. R. R. Palmer (Princeton, 1981), pp. 53–4.

17 Guy Thuillier, *La Vie Quotidienne dans les Ministères au XIXe siècle* (Paris, 1976), pp. 110–11.

18 For this reason, handwriting was taught in special schools: see Alfred-Louis-Auguste Franklin, *Dictionnaire historique des arts, métiers et professions exercés dans Paris depuis le treizième siècle* (Paris, Leipzig, 1906), p. 287.

19 Fleurigeon, *Code Administratif*, I, pp. 10–11.

20 Some biographical detail is available in 'Dictionnaire Biographique des Employés du Ministère de l'Intérieur', ftp://ftp.univ-orleans.fr/pub/kawa. This database is an annex to Catherine Kawa, 'Les employés du Ministère de l'Intérieur pendant la Première République, Approche prosopographique de la bureaucratie révolutionnaire, 1792–1800', Doctoral thesis, Université de Paris I, 1993.

21 'Administration' prior to 1750 was used only in description (*administration des finances* rather than *administration financière*). It was only after 1788 that the neologism, 'bureaucracy', grabbed the public imagination. See Guy Thuillier and Jean Tulard, *Histoire de l'Administration Française* (Paris, 1984), p. 5.

22 Note that the various positions in the ministry hierarchy – *rédacteur, expéditionnaire, commis d'ordre* – derived from their various functions in the movement of correspondence, and not their perceived position in a hierarchy of status.

23 Charles-Jean-Baptiste Bonnin, *Principes d'Administration Publique*, 3rd edn, 3 vols (Paris, 1812), I, pp. xiv–xv. Bonnin explicitly contrasts administrative science with the creation of a bureaucratic and arbitrary authority. The copy of this work in the British Library [1391.e.14] belonged originally to Joseph-Marie De Gérando, Secretary-General of the Ministry of the Interior (1804–10).

24 Bonnin, *Principes d'Administration Publique*, I, p. xiv.

25 *Ibid.*, pp. vii–viii.

26 *Ibid.*, p. xv.

27 *Ibid.*, p. xxvii. Another interesting depiction of this 'chain' is to be found in 'Cercle figuratif de l'administration de la République francaise', AAE, Mémoires et Documents, France, 1414.

28 Bonnin, *Principes d'Administration Publique*, II, pp. 210–11.

29 *Ibid.*, p. 211.

30 *Ibid.*, p. 217.

31 Several remained left over in the offices of the Bureau of Agriculture, and were inventoried during one of its moves, AN, f/10/225.

32 A Ministry of Police memorandum in year VI advised employees to use the imperative in regulating the action of subordinate authorities, AN, f/7/3007.

33 Bonnin, *Principes d'Administration Publique*, II, p. 220.

34 See especially Pierre-Jean-Georges Cabanis, *Rapports du physique et du moral de l'homme*, 2 vols (Paris, 1802). On the medical revolution, see Elizabeth A. Williams, 'The French Revolution, anthropological medicine and the creation of medical authority', in Bryant T. Ragan Jr and E. A. Williams (eds), *Recreating Authority in Revolutionary France* (New Jersey, 1992); Martin S. Staum, *Cabanis: Enlightenment and Medical Philosophy in the French Revolution* (Princeton, 1980). David M. Vess, *Medical Revolution in France, 1789–1796* (Gainesville, Florida, 1975) also deals with the movement of revolutionaries into politics and administration. It is important to note that the term 'medical revolution' was coined by the doctors themselves.

35 Pierre-Jean-Georges Cabanis, *Coup d'Oeil sur les Révolutions et sur la Réforme de la Médicine* (Paris, 1804), p. 5.

36 *Ibid.*, p. v; see also Staum, *Cabanis*, pp. 268–9; Elizabeth A. Williams, *The Physical and the Moral: Anthropology, Physiology, and Philosophical Medicine in France, 1750–1850* (Cambridge, 1994), pp. 78–81.

37 Nicole and Jean Dhombres, *Naissance d'un nouveau pouvoir: sciences et savants en France, 1793–1824* (Paris, 1989), p. 64.

38 *Ibid.*, pp. 42–5, 743–6.

39 Staum, *Cabanis*, p. 287

40 Sieyès, Roederer, and even Talleyrand have been named as 'Ideologues', believers in the application of natural principles to society and politics: see Keith Michael Baker, *Condorcet: From Natural Philosophy to Social Mathematics* (Chicago, 1975), pp. 272–85. Cabanis was to play an important political role again under Napoleon as a member of the Council of Five Hundred.

41 Cabanis, *Coup d'Oeil . . .* , pp. 176, 193; Williams, 'The French Revolution, anthropological medicine', pp. 82–5 (Condillac), pp. 92–3 (the Montpellier vitalists).

42 John Locke, *An Essay Concerning Human Understanding*, ed. Peter N. Nidditch (Oxford, 1975), p. 55: 'the yet empty Cabinet'.

43 *Ibid.*, pp. 119–20.

44 *Ibid.*, pp. 117–18.

45 Etienne Bonnot de Condillac, *An Essay on the Origin of Human Knowledge*, reprint of 1756 English edn (New York, 1971), pp. 49–54.

46 Condillac, *An Essay on the Origin of Human Knowledge*, pp. 56–8.

47 Masson, *Le Département des Affaires Etrangères pendant la Révolution*, pp. 143–81, lists a great number of those dispossessed. See also Church, *Revolution and Red Tape*, pp. 241–2.

48 For examples of such oaths see Masson, *Le Département des Affaires Etrangères*, pp. 87, 140–1.

49 *Ibid.*, pp. 146–7.

50 'Observation sur le travail du bureau d'analyse (prairial, an V)', AAE, Organisation et Règlements du Ministère, vol. I (1547–1806), part 2; 'Ordre du Travail des Bureaux du Ministère de l'Intérieur (VI)', AN, AD/I/78; Bonnin, *Principes d'Administration Publique*, II, pp. 222–5.

51 Condillac, *An Essay on the Origin of Human Knowledge*, pp. 171–257.

52 George Louis Le Clerc (Comte de Buffon), 'Des sens en général', in *Histoire Naturelle, générale et particulière*, new edn, 127 vols (Paris, year VII–1808), 20 (Histoire de l'homme, II), pp. 35–6

53 J. Balteau, M. Barroux, M. Prévost, *et al.*, *Dictionnaire de Biographie Française*, Paris, 1933– , vol. 15, pp. 1197–99; Hoefer, *Nouvelle Biographie Générale*, 46 vols (Paris, 1852–66), 19, pp. 142–6.

54 Joseph-Marie De Gérando (Baron), *De la Génération des Connoissances Humaines* (Berlin, 1802), p. 12

55 De Gérando, *De la Génération des Connoissances Humaines*, p. 14

56 What happens in both epistemology and administrative science can also be seen more generally in revolutionary attitudes to the national heritage. After an initial period of vandalism, and attempts to destroy all vestiges of the old regime, the French became avid collectors. The Abbé Grégoire's speech, delivered to the Convention on 31 August 1794, on the need to organise and classify museums chronologically, to open them up to instruct the public, is cited most often as the turning point. Its effect was to turn the Louvre into a palace of the arts, housing a collection of masterpieces from France and all over Europe. What had been a royal palace and the preserve of nobility became a national museum, assembling works from the King's collections, from those of emigrated aristocrats and from the properties of the Church. Its displays 'revealed' the principles that had driven past regimes. See Andrew McLellan, *Inventing the Louvre: Arts, Politics and the Origins of the Modern Museum in Eighteenth-century Paris* (Cambridge, 1994); Jean-Pierre Babelon, 'The Louvre: royal residence and temple of the arts', in Pierre Nora, *Realms of Memory: The Construction of the French Past*, trans. Arthur Goldhammer, 3 vols (New York, 1998), III (Symbols).

57 'Copie de l'Organisation des Bureaux de la Quatrième Division de l'Intérieur (Brumaire an V)', AN, f/1a/1.
58 See the papers pertaining to Vitry and Bardel, AN, f/1bI/11–14. Both were members of the 'Bureau Consulatif du Commerce' in year X (AN f/1bI/15). Vitry had served in the central administration since the Year IV. He had previously be a perpetual secretary of the Agricultural Society and sole administrator of the *dépôt de mendicité* in Lyon. Bardel, also a member of the 'Bureau Consulatif des Arts et Manufactures' retained his position as a Government Inspector. He had also helped bring several precious manufacturing processes to France.
59 Letter from the 'Bureau Consulatif de l'Agriculture', 28 messidor year 7, AN, f/10/225.
60 AN, f/1bI/15.
61 The Ministry of Foreign Affairs, exceptionally, had used its archives to teach students at an ill-fated school of administration between 1712 and 1719; Guy Thuillier, *La bureaucratie en France aux XIXe et XXe siècles* (Paris, 1987), pp. 20–37. They were nevertheless completely reorganised during the Revolution.
62 AN, f/1a/590–2. For a summary history of the Ministry of the Interior archives up to Year XIII, see the letter from Carré d'Haronville to the Minister, undated, AN f/1a/634.
63 Masson *Le Département des Affaires Etrangères*, p. 415.
64 AAE, Dossiers Individuels (Origine–1830), Volumes Réliés, vol. 63 (Sautereau).
65 AN f/10/255
66 This is one argument for the usefulness of the Archives presented by Scipion Mourgues, 'Rapport présenté au Minister de l'Intérieur', 17 thermidor an XI' AN, f/1a/590-2.
67 Jean Baillou, *Les Affaires Etrangères et Le Corps Diplomatique Français*, 2 vols (Paris, 1984), I, p. 379
68 Talleyrand to Bourjot, 19 May 1807, AAE, Personnel dossier, 1ere série, Bourjot baron de, vol. 44.
69 'Rapport – 5e Division (Archives)', AN, f/1a/590.
70 Jacques Ymbert, *L'art du ministre; par un Excellence* (Paris, 1821), part 1 (Le ministre qui s'en va), p. 42.
71 For example, in 1805, the Ministry of Interior received 64,000 letters: it responded to 35,000 and produced 921 initiatives for local administrators to promote in the *départements*, all with a staff of 200 odd clerks: Thuillier, *La Vie Quotidienne dans les Ministères*, p. 80.

7 The Life and Opinions of Leonard MacNally (1752–1820): Playwright, Barrister, United Irishman, and Informer

Thomas Bartlett

'It will be said I have imitated STERNE'[1]

Scholarly investigations into the 'secret' war conducted against Revolutionary France in the 1790s have revealed the efforts of the British Secret Service to gather intelligence on French war plans, to foment royalist uprisings in order to disrupt the French war effort, even to assassinate key members of the French Directory in 1798–99.[2] Such researches will in time force a reappraisal of the usual dismissive verdict on the contribution of the British Secret Service to the defeat of France in the wars of 1793–1815: more immediately, they make necessary a revision of the historical origins of what has been called the 'British Intelligence Community'.[3] Unfortunately, there has been no recent inquiry into how Dublin Castle conducted its undercover war against the United Irishmen and their French allies in the 1790s, and those interested in that separate but closely related topic have had, for the most part, no choice but to rely on the volumes published by the nineteenth-century historians, W. J. Fitzpatrick and R. R. Madden.[4] Despite differences in approach, both these authors had in fact a common agenda: both were concerned to emphasise the near-omniscience of Dublin Castle's intelligence gatherers in the 1790s; both were eager to point the moral that young Irishmen should always eschew secret conspiracies because of the ubiquity of informers; and both were dedicated to exposing those who had betrayed their comrades and to revealing how much they had received for their treachery. Taxed with having an obsession with the sordid underbelly of the Irish revolutionary movement, Fitzpatrick indignantly denied that he had 'sought to dishonour Ireland by showing it as always abounding in spies, betrayers etc'.[5] Madden, for his part, answered his critics in a similarly robust manner:

Of what avail is it to enter into these disgusting details? To that question I answer: the utility of the task entirely depends on the amount of insecurity to treachery which similar disclosures of secret perfidy are calculated to produce, and the obloquy their disclosure is sure to bring sooner or later on those who practice treachery.[6]

Such non-historical or moralistic objectives have in large measure prevented the emergence of a balanced assessment of the importance of Dublin Castle's network of agents. Two hundred years on, the ubiquity of spies and informers, the consequent omniscience of the Castle, and the contribution of both to the failure of the United Irishmen, remain axiomatic. A reassessment is overdue.

The following brief study of Leonard MacNally – author, playwright, duellist, barrister, United Irishman, *and* Dublin Castle's most important, long-term, paid informer (*c.*1795–*c.*1819) – may shed light on the effectiveness of informing as a means of intelligence gathering and contribute towards a reconsideration of the role and function of the Irish government's spy system in the Age of the Democratic Revolution. On a narrower level, it may also help answer the question: why did MacNally turn informer?[7]

I

Details are sketchy about MacNally's early life. He was born in Dublin in 1752 and came, we are told, 'from a very respectable Irish [Catholic] family who suffered much by forfeitures'.[8] His grandfather, according to Richard Lalor Sheil, lost out badly as a result of 'discoveries' into various land transactions made by him in Dublin city. William McNally, his father (*obit.* 1756), was a grocer. MacNally appears to have converted to the Established Church in the 1760s.[9] He was entirely self-educated, and in 1774, after a brief career as a specialist grocer and purveyor of 'wines of every denomination, the choicest in their qualities, on the lowest terms, and in the smallest quantities', he entered the Middle Temple in London to study law.[10] In 1776, he was called to the Irish Bar, where he practised for a time, but money, as ever, proved elusive, and he returned to London in the late 1770s where he earned his living by journalism and by writing for the stage.

Already in 1779, he had written *The Ruling Passion, a Comic Opera* which, though it was performed in Dublin, was not published, nor did it transfer to London. Undeterred, MacNally wrote *The Apotheosis of Punch: a Satirical Masque with a Monody on the death of the Late Master Punch* (1779) which was dedicated to Richard Brinsley Sheridan, and put on, we are told, 'at the Patagonian Theatre, Exeter 'Change [London], with universal applause'.[11] In May 1782, MacNally scored his first clear theatrical success. His *Retaliation; or the Citizen a Soldier*, a frivolous tale of intrigue, was performed in the Theatre Royal, Covent Garden, and was regularly listed over the following years. The farce had, one critic observed, 'considerable merit . . . and the dialogue is well seasoned with wit'.[12] Disappointment, however, quickly followed. In September 1782, MacNally's *Prelude for Covent Garden*, written to mark the official opening of the refurbished Theatre Royal, was a resounding flop. A contemporary noted:

The author with a partiality to his own countrymen which we know not how to censure had drawn the character of an Irishman as one possessed of qualities which he had rather imprudently denied to other persons in the drama, consisting of English, Scotch, Welsh and French. This circumstance gave offense and before the conclusion of the piece, the clamour became too great for anything to be heard. It was therefore left aside.[13]

In May 1783, MacNally had another failure with *Coalition*, a musical farce, also performed at Covent Garden. The audience were apparently disappointed 'at not finding it of a political nature' – MacNally had been a very public supporter of the Fox-North coalition[14] – and, though they generously 'gave it a favourable reception', it closed after the opening night. It was not published.[15]

However, MacNally was quickly able to put this setback behind him, for a month earlier, his *Tristram Shandy: a Sentimental, Shandean Bagatelle . . . by the author of Retaliation* had been produced at the Theatre Royal. The critics had been dismissive ('very indifferently executed' noted one), but the public liked it, and it went on to receive regular productions over the next few years.[16] MacNally followed up this success with his most popular theatrical work, *Robin Hood: or Sherwood Forest, a Comic Opera*, which was first performed at Covent Garden in April 1784. Once again, the critics were less than enthusiastic ('by no means agreeable . . . [Robin Hood] . . . is dwindled down to a mere sententious pedant'), but the opera (music by William Shield) attracted large audiences, on three occasions taking in more than £200 and, in the words of a modern authority, 'was therefore among the most successful productions of the time'. It was very frequently performed during the later 1780s and 1790s in both the Theatre Royal and Drury Lane.[17]

Robin Hood was the high point of MacNally's career as a playwright. Later works were greeted with much less acclaim. Admittedly, *Fashionable Levities, A Comedy*, first performed in April 1785 'met with good success' and was revived at regular intervals until about 1800;[18] but the farce, *April Fool: or the Folies of a Night*, which opened in April 1786 and was 'tolerably well received', was soon forgotten, as was MacNally's *Richard Coeur de Lion, an Historical Romance from the French of M. Sedaine*, first performed in October 1786, and 'very soon consigned to oblivion'.[19] Later plays also disappeared without trace: the reception of *Critic upon Critic*, which opened in Covent Garden in 1792 (two years after MacNally's return to Dublin) is not recorded; and a similar fate befell *Cottage Festival: an Opera*, which was mentioned in the *Monthly Mirror* for December 1796, and about which nothing more was heard.[20] *Cottage Opera* may in fact be the play referred to by MacNally, under his *nom d'espion*, 'JW', in one of his letters to Dublin Castle: 'My friend [i.e. MacNally himself] has written a play and sent it to Covent Garden theatre. The object is to show the necessity of a permanent connection between Great Britain and Ireland.'[21]

As well as writing plays during his time in London, MacNally had also supported himself by editing the *Public Ledger*, a morning newspaper, and he had published *Sentimental Excursions to Windsor and other Places* (London, 1781), a work which, like his play *Tristram Shandy*, revealed his admiration for the writings of Laurence Sterne.[22] In contrast to such frivolities, MacNally also read for the English bar in 1782–3 (admitted 1786); and he published *The Claims of Ireland and the Resolutions of the Volunteers Vindicated* (London, 1782), the 'Cause of the Irish Discontents', 'Vision', later reprinted as 'Negro Slavery', and possibly, 'Account of the Important Revolution in Ireland' (all in the *European Magazine*, April/June/August 1782).[23] All these works were strongly patriotic and drew comparisons between the Irish situation and that of unfortunate peoples elsewhere. The *Claims of Ireland* also brought MacNally to the attention of Charles James Fox for whom he acted in the Westminster election of 1782.[24]

On a more private note, MacNally married his first wife some time in the early 1780s: nothing is known about her except her death on 27 March 1786.[25] He then married Francis I'anson or Janson of Richmond, Yorkshire, and Bedford Row, London, for whom he composed the well-known ballad, 'The Lass of Richmond Hill' (music by James Hook).[26]

Having apparently forsaken his career as a playwright, MacNally returned to Dublin in or around 1790 where he began to practise once again at the Irish Bar. He also threw himself into radical politics, signalling his arrival on the scene by writing *An Address to the Whig Club* (Dublin 1790), in which he called for an end to corruption, denounced 'the purchased dependants of the British minister', and urged the newspaper press to 'drag [venal politicians] before the people'.[27] With sentiments such as these, it is not surprising that he found the mildly reformist stance of the Dublin Whig Club uncongenial and that he should gravitate immediately towards the more radical Society of United Irishmen when it was founded in Dublin in November 1791.

MacNally proved an extremely active member of the Society, being first noticed by Thomas Collins, a member of the United Irishmen and a Dublin Castle spy, in December 1791.[28] From then on, Collins recorded him as attending regularly, speaking frequently and often proposing new members.

In June 1792 he was appointed one of a committee (along with William Drennan and Theobald Wolfe Tone) charged with drawing up a congratulatory address to James Napper Tandy on his recent acquittal.[29] In April 1793, MacNally showed his commitment to the United Irishmen by fighting a duel with a fellow barrister, Jonah Barrington, who had spoken disparagingly of its members.[30] This satisfactory settlement of an 'affair of honour' was all the more relished by the United Irishmen because of Napper Tandy's recent (and galling) failure to 'blaze' when similarly denounced in public.[31] Again, MacNally was one of the select group who drew up the United Irish proposals for parliamentary reform, and he vigorously defended the omission of a provision for a secret ballot from their report. A secret ballot, he said in January 1794, 'would only corrupt the morals of the people by holding out a mode of deception'.[32] He was also present at the final meeting of the Society of United Irishmen on 23 May 1794. On that date, Dublin Castle, as a result of information received concerning negotiations between a French agent, the Revd William Jackson and members of the United Irishmen, issued an order banning the society.

With the outbreak of war between Britain (and Ireland) and revolutionary France in February 1793, Ireland had once again become an object of French attention. Early in 1794, Jackson had come to Dublin on behalf of the French revolutionary government to investigate the likely reaction in Ireland to the arrival of a French force. Unfortunately for him, from an early date he had been placed under British government surveillance. In particular, he had been accompanied to Ireland by John Cockayne, a London solicitor who was employed as an informer by William Pitt, the Prime Minister.[33] It appears that both Cockayne and Jackson had known MacNally in London, and they made him their first port of call in Dublin. MacNally, 'merely no doubt from that hospitality in which Irishmen are never deficient' (as the Attorney-General archly put it at Jackson's subsequent trial), offered them dinner, and facilitated contacts with known radicals including Archibald Hamilton Rowan (then in Newgate Prison) and Theobald Wolfe Tone.[34] When the British government and Dublin Castle had intercepted sufficient incriminating material concerning Jackson, he was seized and put on trial charged with high treason. Those who had been in contact with him were closely questioned. Rowan acknowledged his guilt by escaping from gaol and fleeing the country. Tone, too, conceded the strength of the case against him by undertaking to go into permanent exile in order to avoid prosecution. MacNally was almost certainly interrogated but, curiously, there was, it seems, no immediate threat of legal action against him. Indeed, a casual observer at Jackson's trial might not have associated the MacNally who acted as go-between for the United Irishmen and the French agent, with the MacNally who then acted as junior defence counsel for the defendant. It was, it seems, some time after the arrest of Jackson in late April 1794 that MacNally embarked on his career as a government informer.

II

The timing of MacNally's decision to turn informer appears to point to at least one of his motives: self-preservation. As Camden put it: 'There is so much evidence against this person [MacNally] that he is, I am informed, completely in the hands of government.'[35] MacNally had been gravely compromised by his association with Jackson and there was a chance that he would be taken into custody. Even if he were not charged and put on trial, for a rising barrister to be so closely identified with the 'revolutionary party' in Ireland would mean inevitably that, whatever the outcome, his professional career would be damaged, perhaps irreparably. It seems clear, for example, that this last consideration weighed with another struggling barrister, Theobald Wolfe Tone, when he made up his mind to leave Ireland.[36] Did MacNally turn informer in order to head off a crippling prosecution?

Before addressing this question, we should consider the possibility that MacNally had been an informer long before the arrival of Jackson in Dublin. Certainly, both Madden and Fitzpatrick strongly impute treachery to him in 1792, even as early as 1790. Madden, in particular, suggested that Napper Tandy's defence strategy at his trial in 1792 had been disclosed to the prosecution by MacNally, Tandy's counsel.[37] Contemporaries, too, certainly had their doubts about him. In March 1792, Collins, the Castle informer at meetings of the Dublin United Irishmen, intriguingly described MacNally in February 1793 as 'one of us';[38] and a year later, Martha McTier, William Drennan's sister, and a close observer of the United Irishmen, posed the question, 'Are you or your society safe with a member such as MacNally?'[39] However, on examination, such suggestions of earlier treachery are unconvincing. There is no evidence of collusion between MacNally and the prosecution at Tandy's trial; Collins's remark surely meant that MacNally was a United Irishman, not that he was a fellow spy (We may note that Collins later denounced MacNally to his handler, John Giffard, as an 'agitator');[40] and the context of Martha McTier's comment strongly suggests she feared MacNally's recklessness or levity, not his capacity for betrayal. For his part, W. E. H. Lecky, while he acknowledged the 'cloud of suspicion and discredit' that hung over MacNally's reputation, found no evidence to support the accusation of treachery prior to the Jackson mission;[41] nor have I discovered any letters to substantiate it.

In the aftermath of Jackson's arrest, however, doubts about MacNally multiplied. Some time after the banning of the United Irishmen, Collins wrote that MacNally 'was suspected [by them] of being a spy';[42] and Drennan recorded that in August 1794 both Richard McCormick and Thomas Addis Emmet had sworn they would never attend the reconstituted secret Society of United Irishmen if MacNally were a member. Drennan, however, had spoken out in his favour: 'In reality, I believe he has not been treacherous and I don't think levity a good ground for objection'; and MacNally was admitted. Drennan would soon repent of his kindness: 'I really do wish now that he had been rejected, though', he added, by way of another explanation for supporting his candidacy, 'I thought it was wrong to make such a man a declared enemy'.[43] However, it was by that point too late. Beginning in late 1794, or possibly early 1795 – certainly by March of that year – MacNally's letters, invariably signed 'JW', started to find their way into the hands of the top officials in Dublin and London.[44] His letters do not seem to have ceased until a few years before his death in 1820.

It seems probable, then, that MacNally, confronted by evidence of his complicity with Jackson, was induced to turn informer; and it seems likely that it was John Pollock, clerk of the crown on the Leinster circuit (and attorney to the Marquess of Downshire) who 'turned' him. Pollock was a determined and intelligent supporter of the Protestant Ascendancy, and throughout the 1790s both he and his patron and friend, Downshire, were active in the secret war against the United Irishmen.[45] Pollock was from the beginning in regular receipt of JW's informations and he distributed them as he saw fit – to his master, Downshire, and to Edward Cooke, Under-Secretary in Dublin Castle. Through Cooke, MacNally's letters found their way into the hands of the Prime Minister, William Pitt, or of the Home Secretary, the Duke of Portland or of the Chief Secretary to the Lord Lieutenant, Thomas Pelham.[46] Pollock's legal work would necessarily have brought him into contact with MacNally and the two would have been able to communicate by letter, or indeed through personal contact, without arousing undue suspicion. It was also Pollock who, in the early years, arranged payment for MacNally.

In any discussion of the motivation of an informer, it is inevitable that the question of financial reward will be raised. Certainly, Madden and Fitzpatrick devoted much time and effort to tracking down the payments made to various renegades, MacNally included. And there is no doubt that MacNally and the others were persistent (some might say insatiable) in their demands for money. In September 1795, MacNally tactfully reminded his handler of 'a private subject respecting myself' and requested action. By July 1796, he had abandoned delicacy, and was even prepared to allow money to be sent directly to his home in Dominick Street; 'It will be safely received there', he wrote, adding, 'it is my sole dependence'. However, a few months later, he complained that he was 'totally exhausted in cash' and petulantly declared 'this is not the way others are treated'.[47] Still aggrieved in May 1797, he then issued an ultimatum: 'I cannot proceed unless what I wrote about is complied with'. By January 1798, he had grown both desperate and piteous in his demands: 'I am in deep distress for want of money . . . neglect to me is cruelty'.[48] In the event, it was not until June 1801 that MacNally was awarded a secret pension of £300 p.a.;[49] until then he had to be content with amounts of between £50 and £300 doled out periodically through Pollock's agency.[50]

Such sums can scarcely be regarded as extravagant, and financial inducement can scarcely have been the sole motive for MacNally's betrayals for, if money had been his God then he ought to have abandoned radical politics, because his association with the United Irishmen was gravely damaging his legal career. Such a withdrawal was feasible: William Drennan, one of the founders of the United Irishmen backed away from the society after 1795 and, after a lean period, pursued a successful career as an *accoucheur* or lying-in doctor; Peter Burrowes, a lawyer and friend of Tone, forsook his flirtation with radical politics and made a successful legal career;[51] and John Keogh, the Catholic activist, also distanced himself from his former friends after 1795.[52] Perhaps MacNally could not in fact escape: once bought, he had no option but to stay bought. Yet there is no indication in any of the 160 or so extant letters from MacNally over the period 1795 to 1815 that he regretted his clandestine activities or that he sought a way out: on the contrary, as the years passed, he evidently warmed to his role as informer.

In addition, as, ostensibly, an open and avowed supporter of the United Irishmen, MacNally ran no small risk from the depredations of crown forces in the period of the rebellion. His house was raided and items seized in June 1798: at around the same time, he confessed that it was 'extremely hazardous [for him] to appear in the streets . . . that his family, all females, live in terror' and that he fully expected 'to be taken into custody and treated with severity'.[53] Lecky's conclusion on this matter may therefore be accepted: 'MacNally lost much more by his politics than he ever gained from the government . . . ; had his politics from the beginning been of a different type his professional talents would probably have raised him to the bench'. MacNally's persistent demands for payment from the Castle have to be viewed in this light. He was a talented – if overly dramatic – barrister, and he was a legal scholar with, by the early 1800s, several notable publications to his name. He could legitimately have expected to make his career and his fortune at the Irish bar: instead he ended up, as Drennan sniffed, 'a sort of Newgate solicitor much looked down upon by the Bar . . . a notorious United I[rishman]'.[54] MacNally gave up career expectations ('everything *professional*', he wrote, 'is lost on account of my *politics*')[55] and he forfeited much peace of mind in return for an annual stipend so meagre that when it ceased on his death, its absence plunged his family and dependants (eight in all) into penury. What *was* his motivation?

It is possible that principle played some part in MacNally's desertion of the United Irishmen. There is no sign that he ever harboured revolutionary or separatist notions; and an informer noted his uneasiness in 1793 at the increasingly subversive tone of discussions among the United Irishmen; for MacNally, the Jackson mission may have proved the last straw.[56] In February 1798, when he remarked that separatism had been 'the object of the United Irishmen of Dublin from its origin *though many who supported the measures of that society were ignorant of its principles*' – was he including himself among their number?[57]

Moreover, MacNally's confidential position with the Castle gave him the opportunity to voice, with impunity, trenchant criticisms of the government's security policy and of the army's activities. 'I write to you', he assured his contact, 'with the free and uninfluenced mind of a friend who wishes to represent everything that occurs to his observation with undisguised truth, considering that is the only means by which you can with justice and propriety guide your judgement'.[58] There was no dissembling in MacNally's letters, and to that extent he retained his earlier radicalism. He pointed out the folly of treating suspects in a cruel manner: whether officially authorised or not, he wrote, activities such as half-hanging, house-burning or flogging inevitably 'attach to government . . . and become causes in the mouths of subtle men to initiate and provoke resentment in the vulgar mind'.[59] He condemned the ghoulish practice of displaying rebel heads on spikes: 'I venture to say', he wrote, 'that if the heads of the rebels on the balcony of Carlow gaol were taken down, it would be felt as an act of grace – they are objects of disgust, not of terror'.[60] And he was wholly opposed to the judiciary's policy of exemplary justice, such as that visited on thirteen prisoners at the Spring assizes at Maryborough:

In my opinion, many of the convictions were not so much owing to conclusive evidence as promptitude in juries determined on making examples, for the defences set up by the prisoners were treated too often with inattention, laughter and contempt, everything against them received as truth. In some cases the judge's authority could scarcely preserve the decorum necessary to a court of justice and this conduct was severely felt and bitterly complained of by the local people to those in whom they could confide. I apprehend it has instilled more resentment than terror and that they consider the sufferers under sentence [of death] objects of vengeance rather than of justice.[61]

Moreover, after the rebellion, MacNally was independent enough to argue against the official wisdom that 'the rebellion was carried on merely at the instigation of papists and for the special purposes of their religion'. In his opinion, such a notion 'looses [*sic*] ground hourly. . . . with [Protestant Dissenters] it never had much credit and at present it has little or none'.[62]

Lecky was sufficiently impressed by such forthright comments to argue that 'if the advice of MacNally had been more frequently listened to some of the worst consequences of the rebellion might have been avoided'.[63] Secure in the belief that he had the ear of the Chief Secretary and Lord Lieutenant, MacNally no doubt flattered himself that his strictures on the forces of law and order were being duly noted and even acted upon. In his own lights, he was acting as a patriot: perhaps he justified to himself his betrayals in this way?[64]

In addition, MacNally did not confine himself only to protesting against military excesses: on several occasions he described at length and in very unflattering terms, the state of Ireland and the condition of its peoples. Presumably he derived some satisfaction from the fact that his analyses of the country were going directly to the top officials in Dublin and London (though it remains anybody's guess what use, if any, they made of them). He was happy to confirm Theobald Wolfe Tone's bleak account of Irish society – for which (in a sense) Tone had been exiled – but possibly he reckoned that, coming from him, such remarks would carry greater weight, and that remedies might even be forthcoming.[65] Perhaps he believed that if he could help prevent an insurrection, then he would have done no small service to his country. But there was, inevitably, a dark side to MacNally's treachery, one which cannot be overlooked in any discussion of principle.

In his brilliant study of the sixteenth-century secret agent Giordano Bruno, John Bossy remarks that informing, 'contrary to an impression which has been put around, . . . always involves betraying your friends or people you have caused to believe your friends'.[66] MacNally's basest betrayals involved those of his clients who knew him and trusted him and who were at their most vulnerable: men charged with high treason, on trial for their lives. He betrayed the secrets and defence strategies of William Jackson, Henry and John Sheares, Robert Emmet – who all paid with their lives – and many others now forgotten. He handed over to the Castle Jackson's last letters to his wife, and he held back Emmet's to his brother. He alerted the prosecution at the Maidstone treason trials in early 1798 to the thrust of the Irish defence witnesses' testimony.[67] A few months later, he urged the Sheares brothers to stand their trial together, even though the guilt of one would surely seal the fate of the other. And when the veracity of the principal prosecution witness against the brothers, Captain J.W. Armstrong, was called into question by his former commanding officer – 'I would not pay much attention to what he did say nor give much credit even to his oath' – MacNally withheld this embarrassing letter from the defence counsel, i.e. himself.[68] Even in relatively minor cases, he appears routinely to have disclosed the defence strategy to the prosecution.[69] It is difficult to square such perfidy with any recognised definition of principle.

Could it be that it was the element of risk in informing that attracted MacNally to informing, and led him to persist in it? He was, after all, a notorious duellist who had lost a thumb in one encounter and who walked with a pronounced limp after another. No stranger to danger, he may have relished the perilous situations in which he inevitably found himself. 'I have risqued everything, even my life' he wrote:[70] perhaps that was part of the attraction? As noted above, in 1798 MacNally's life and property were threatened by those who knew him only as a prominent United Irishman.

At the same time, there was always the possibility of discovery by the other side – his hitherto unsuspecting United Irish friends. MacNally well knew that the offices of Dublin Castle were famously insecure; he claimed that the United Irishmen had penetrated the Irish Post Office; and he understood therefore that the chance of being unmasked as an informer was always high.[71] Was this part of the thrill?

This is not to suggest that MacNally was reckless in his behaviour, deliberating courting danger. On the contrary, he took every precaution to shield his identity and protect his activities. He burned all communications from the Castle;[72] he rarely used a courier: 'I well know servants ought not at present to have the slightest confidence reposed in them.'[73] He commended to his correspondent 'the prudence of making extracts from my letters and burning the originals'.[74] He adopted the initials 'JW' as his signature, almost never employed any kind of salutation, sometimes disguised his handwriting,[75] and always referred to himself as 'my friend', 'our friend', or simply as MacNally. It would have been difficult to deduce that MacNally was himself the author of those letters which were delivered to Dublin Castle from 1795 on.

For his part, MacNally always weighed carefully the impression he might create in seeking information at the Castle's request, for an impertinent question or an unexpected appearance could easily arouse suspicion. 'It would have been impossible for me to have gone to the place you mentioned' he explained patiently in one of his letters, 'without giving very reasonable cause for particular and perhaps jealous inquiry into my motives that probably might lead to suspicions extremely injurious [to me]'.[76] On another occasion, he warned:

The strictest and most deliberate caution will be necessary on your part in conducting yourself on the business I communicated yesterday. The existence of *our friend* [i.e. MacNally] may depend on your prudence. The slightest suspicion would stop all communication to him [and] might destroy him and his family.[77]

And, of course, the very fact that he operated entirely undetected for nearly twenty-five years shows that whatever secret excitement he derived from his dangerous work must have been restrained by cold calculation and tempered by the need for self-preservation.[78]

Finally, in the light of what we know of MacNally's later career as a paid informer, does a scrutiny of his creative writing during the 1780s offer any hint of what was to come, or hold out any clue as to his motivation for his subsequent betrayal of his associates and clients? In his brief discussion of MacNally, Lecky concluded that he was 'a strangely composite character' in whom were combined 'singularity and melancholy'.[79] The literary or theatrical tone to Lecky's description is apt, for MacNally can be read as a character in a novel or as an actor in a play as well as a figure on the historical stage. On several occasions, he referred to 'the character I assume' and 'the part I have taken', and it was vital for him to play his public role as agitator to perfection.[80] He would have been delighted at the way he was frequently denounced to Dublin Castle, for it offered proof that he was staying in character. For example, Francis Higgins, the editor of the *Freeman's Journal* and a dedicated Castle informant, described MacNally as 'a thorough-paced firebrand [who] justly merits the punishment due to traitors'; he regularly reported that he was illegally schooling defence witnesses in their testimony, even dressing up 'common vagrants' to take the stand, and he alleged that MacNally was active in helping to regroup the United Irishmen after the debacle of 1798.[81] Army officers, too, had no love for him and they were exasperated by his legal tricks. Major General Fawcett complained to the Castle that MacNally had served a writ of *habeas corpus* on him in respect of two prisoners.[82] The shock and disbelief that greeted disclosure of his long-standing private deception can only be understood by reference to the complete success of MacNally's long-running public performance.

It is, however, MacNally's secret role over the years that concerns us: was this pre-figured in his theatrical or prose writings? Given that so many of MacNally's popular works for the theatre – *Robin Hood, Retaliation* and *Fashionable Levities* – all involve some measure of deception, deceit and disguise, it is tempting to see in them ominous signposts to his future career in subterfuge. A recurrent theme in his plays is that no-one-is-who-or-what-they-seem-to-be. Thus one of Robin Hood's men, Edwin, had fought in Palestine 'under a borrowed name' and he marries Angelina who, for her own reasons, first appears in the opera dressed as a man. Robin Hood himself is, of course, not at all an unknown and penniless forest outlaw, but is in fact 'the brave earl of Huntingdon' who through ill-fate has been forced to conceal his true identity. As he tells his beloved, Clorinda (who also appears in disguise):

You know the wrongs I have suffered – my services overlooked – banished on a false accusation; stigmatised with the imputation of a rebellious spirit.[83]

Similarly, *Fashionable Levities*, with its stock minor characters – Mr Ordeal, Widow Volatile, Cheaterly and so on – also turns on duplicity. Patrick Welford, an Irishman, is Constance's true love but, cheated out of his money, he was forced to flee. He has now returned clad in livery ('A livery? Yes, it is a disguise I own'): it transpires eventually that Patrick is not Irish but 'a gentleman'. Later in the comedy, Douglas the Scotsman (who is not in fact Scottish) denounces the villainous Cheaterly in terms that might later have given MacNally pause for thought:

Men like you, habituated in deceit, become callous to humanity – destitute of principle, they are not deterred by the compunctions of conscience but will insure the profits of their cunning even at the price of blood.[84]

And yet, the temptation to read MacNally's plays (with one exception) as indicators of his future duplicitous role ought to be resisted: so very many plays at that time (and since) have hinged on disguise or deception that no conclusions can be drawn. The exception is MacNally's *Tristram Shandy: a Sentimental, Shandean Bagatelle*, a work which, with his prose work, *Sentimental Excursions to Windsor and Other Places*, is possibly worth further consideration.

   Laurence Sterne's *Tristram Shandy* was published in instalments in London between 1759 and 1767 and, despite rather tepid notices from the leading literary critics of the day, proved very popular. It would now be regarded as one of the two great Irish novels (or anti-novels) in English. The novel is impossible to summarise since it deliberately avoids narrative, plot, or conclusion. It 'proceeds' in a biographical sense *towards* the narrator's conception – he is truly misbegotten – and it is punctuated by numerous digressions and studded with all sorts of typographical tricks, pages of asterisks, rows of squiggles, and with blank and black pages. It is very funny. Leonard MacNally was much taken with it, and by Sterne's other prose writings. 'Imbibing his [Sterne's] opinions' wrote MacNally, 'has sweetened whatever portion of acidity, Nature, misfortune and disappointment have mixed in my composition', and, as we have seen, he adapted *Tristram Shandy* for the London stage, and he published a parody on Sterne's *Sentimental Journey* (1768). MacNally may even have chosen the initials 'JW' in homage to Sterne's drinking companion and would-be biographer, the famous radical, John Wilkes.[85] Just as Sterne was consciously subversive of all literary conventions, perhaps MacNally relished flouting other codes of conduct by informing on his companions and clients? To do so by *writing* would surely have added to the enjoyment. After one interminable digression in *Tristram*, the narrator confesses: 'But this is neither here nor there – why do I mention it? – Ask my pen – it governs me – I govern not it'.[86] MacNally, ever prolix, might have agreed.

III

In his note recommending MacNally for a pension of £300 p.a., Edward Cooke commented that he was 'not much trusted but I believe [he] has been useful'.[87] Too much should not be made of Cooke's apparent faint praise for MacNally's services: 'useful' carried a much higher approval rating in the eighteenth century than it does today; and the money involved appears to have been the usual sum awarded to those informers whose services were especially valued. Samuel Turner, a key informer at the very heart of the United Irishmen's continental projects, was awarded a like amount, and the quality of his information has never been questioned. Similarly, Francis Higgins, who had been instrumental in the betrayal of Lord Edward Fitzgerald, was given £300 p. a. for his pains. It is true that some others received pensions running into thousands of pounds – e.g. Thomas Reynolds whose information led to the arrest of the Leinster Directory of United Irishmen in March 1798 – but such large amounts were always conditional on testifying in open court: neither MacNally, nor Higgins nor Turner ever acted as witnesses for the prosecution.[88]

MacNally's clandestine services to government lay in a variety of areas. We have already noted his practice of divulging the defences of his clients to the prosecution, and his propensity for lengthy depictions of the public mood in the late 1790s has also been cited: little more needs to be said on these points. However, it may be questioned whether MacNally's betrayal of his clients – given, in general, the overwhelming nature of the evidence against them – was all that significant in securing convictions. Again, his lengthy discussions of the state of Irish opinion (though very entertaining, and extremely useful to later historians!) may well have been entirely disregarded by the Castle. In this respect at least, MacNally may have been viewed, not as someone who had his finger on the pulse of Irish insurgency nationwide, but merely as an opinionated (and importunate) know-all.

MacNally's solid services lay in other areas. He had excellent contacts with some of the leading Catholic activists and through them he could keep the Castle informed on their thinking and plans. MacNally's earliest letters date from February–March 1795, a time when Catholic hopes of full emancipation had been dashed by the abrupt recall of the Lord Lieutenant, Earl Fitzwilliam. Dublin Castle and London were most anxious to learn how Irish Catholics would react to this crushing setback, and MacNally duly obliged. He reported how the members of the Catholic Committee had put together a delegation to plead their case before

George III in London; how this delegation had returned from England 'discontented, disappointed and disgusted'; and how Henry Grattan had assured the Catholics that, notwithstanding this reversal, he would bring forward a Catholic Bill when the Irish Parliament reconvened.[89] This last piece of information confirmed the view taken by Lord Downshire, to whom it was passed on, presumably by MacNally's handler, John Pollock, that the whole Catholic agitation had in fact been orchestrated from the beginning by Grattan 'as a party matter and not at all thought of or intended by the Papists themselves'.[90] This 'insight' may have stiffened London's determination to face down the Catholic demand for emancipation. Certainly, MacNally's letters on this topic ended up, after several copyings, in William Pitt's post-bag, an indication, surely, of the value attached to them. Again, some years later, MacNally described in detail the reaction of Catholic lay leaders to the proposed Union with Great Britain. Initially, he wrote that they had been hostile but that then their attitude had softened so that by February 1799 he noted that 'they [lay Catholic leaders] persevere in neutrality on the Union question: that is, they will do nothing that can render them responsible in the aggregate'.[91] After the Union, too, MacNally supplied the Castle with intelligence on the Catholic question: at least two Chief Secretaries, Sir Arthur Wellesley in 1807 and William Wellesley Pole in 1811, received communications from JW on this perennial issue.[92]

It was, however, MacNally's constant information on the plans and activities of the United Irishmen which most impressed Dublin Castle (and which today elicits a whistle of appreciation from historians). On the face of it, JW was ideally placed to supply vital intelligence. As a senior member of the United Irishmen – though never one involved in military activity – he was in constant contact with leading figures within the revolutionary movement and he was privy to some of their secrets. Moving easily within their social circle, MacNally was in a position to report on the absences (or arrivals) of key players, on journeys which they had undertaken, on the gossip which inevitably was circulating among them, and on their personal rivalries. It was from such 'hints and circumstances' that MacNally predicted that a second French invasion was to be attempted in the latter half of 1797 or early 1798.[93] He cited a 'combination of circumstances arising from a variety of conversations and facts which, taken separately would not appear serious' as confirming him in this opinion.[94] Especially, MacNally declared that 'the affectation of ignorance, the ironical denial of fact accompanied by the most pleasant smiles from inward satisfaction are proofs beyond doubt [of an invasion]'.[95] Dublin Castle presumably found such 'low-grade' information valuable in attempting to build up a picture of the nature and extent of the threat that confronted it.

Crucially, MacNally was on intimate terms with James Tandy, son of James Napper Tandy. Tandy was no revolutionary, but his father, a long-time radical, was very active in the conspiracy, having fled from Ireland to the United States at the time of Jackson's arrest, moved thence to France, then on to Ireland with a small French force in 1798 and eventually to Hamburg. Throughout this period, and for some years after the rebellion, Napper Tandy kept in touch with his son who, for his part, saw no harm in showing his father's letters to another long-time radical, and James's own confidential friend, Leonard MacNally. Using these letters, MacNally revealed to Dublin Castle that 'a kind of seditious convention is now forming in America . . . [through which] . . . a correspondence was [being] carried on between the leaders of the United [*sic*] here and persons in France, through the medium of fugitive friends,' and he correctly identified these latter to be Dr James Reynolds, Archibald Hamilton Rowan, Theobald Wolfe Tone and Napper Tandy himself.[96] From Tandy's letters to his son, MacNally was also able to inform Dublin Castle in 1796 that, while in Philadelphia, Napper Tandy had been on a 'most intimate footing' and had enjoyed 'unlimited confidence' with the French minister there, and that he had acted as a 'kind of vouchee for Irish commissioners [to the French]'.[97] In mid-1797 he revealed that Napper Tandy was in Hamburg, that Edward Lewins and Tone were in Paris, that both had been given French military rank, and that an expedition by the French was in urgent preparation.[98] In addition, MacNally, through his friendship with James Tandy, picked up stray bits of information about the likes of Lord Edward Fitzgerald (whom MacNally did not consider to be central to the conspiracy) and Arthur O'Connor, a prime object of suspicion in British government circles. Sensationally, MacNally reported in December 1797 that there was a plan, devised by Fitzgerald and O'Connor, to raise sectarian riots in Dublin and elsewhere on Christmas eve by breaking the windows of Catholic chapels and yelling 'the Orangemen!' Fortunately, MacNally wrote, the Catholic bishops had got wind of the plot, cancelled some masses and the threatened disturbances had been avoided.[99] This information was described by Camden as 'very important intelligence' and he lost no time in summoning a 'cabinet' to Dublin Castle to consider it – or in transmitting it to London.[100]

On the face of it, then, it would appear that MacNally played a major role in the Castle's 'secret war' particularly in the years before the rebellion. Camden and Cooke in Dublin, and Pelham and Portland in London, all accepted him as an 'authority' on the United Irish conspirators, and their letters have numerous references to information provided by MacNally, a.k.a. 'JW' or 'my friend' or 'our friend'.[101] And yet, can we accept without question their estimation of his worth? MacNally's prime source – the letters of Napper Tandy – are undoubtedly interesting, but their author was emphatically not the leading conspirator that the Castle believed him to be. Napper Tandy had long been a thorn in the side of Dublin Castle, but in the mid-1790s, after his flight from Ireland, his star had waned considerably. At the same time, however, his vanity and self-esteem had waxed substantially. In Paris, he hugged the limelight, refused to adopt an alias, and boasted about his military expertise. Acutely jealous of Tone and Lewins, who were already well established in the French capital, he contrived a plan to arraign them before a tribunal of Irish refugees on charges of acting without authority. Poorly informed on French intentions, and lacking any detailed knowledge of affairs in Ireland, Tandy succeeded only in sowing confusion and spreading disinformation among the United Irishmen – and in misleading Dublin Castle. Late in 1797 and early 1798, for example, he sent confident reports (which, as we have seen, MacNally duly passed on) that the French were planning another expedition to Ireland: in fact, the opposite was the case. Napper Tandy was, in short, impossible. Eventually, after the rebellion, even Dublin Castle came to see that he was not the threat they had once imagined. Cornwallis resisted (unsuccessfully) his extradition back to Ireland from Hamburg and he was duly tried for treason at Lifford Assizes in 1801; but the death sentence passed on him was respited and, after a short interval, to the Castle's relief, he was allowed to go into exile in France.[102]

Furthermore, it should be noted that while Tandy's highly suspect information (transmitted via MacNally) was eagerly accepted by Dublin Castle, significant intelligence also provided by MacNally was sometimes ignored. For example, from a very early date, MacNally was aware of the abilities and determination of Theobald Wolfe Tone. In September 1795, he had written:

Tone is a keen sensible man, argues with plausibility and cunning and writes with perspicuity and elegance. . . . No man in Ireland knows so well their [the Catholics'] resources or the real situation of the country; of course no man [is] as capable to further the scheme of an invasion and I shall not be surprised to hear of his being shortly at Paris.[103]

Again, it was MacNally who broke the news to the Castle that Tone had been in Paris for some time and that he had played a key role in organising the French invasion of Ireland, and he claimed that Tone's early memoranda on Ireland constituted 'the ground work of all subsequent negotiations' between the French and the United Irishmen.[104] MacNally also revealed that Tone had been 'actually on board one of the ships on that expedition [to Bantry Bay]'.[105] Some months later, he followed this up with the information that 'Tone is in the French army and in consequence of his great

attention and adroitness is a colonel of Brigade or Brigade Adjutant'.[106]
Notwithstanding such reports, no particular attention was paid to Tone:
Dublin Castle remained firm in its belief that Napper Tandy was central to
the conspiracy, and that Tone was not. As a result, the Castle seriously
underestimated Tone's role in the revolutionary decade.

Throughout the 1790s, Dublin Castle had its own preconceived ideas as
to what was important information, and what was not – a near-fatal
weakness in any intelligence-gathering organisation. In addition, until the
early months of 1798, it lacked anything approaching a proper information
processing structure, whereby information could be properly assessed,
collated, dispersed or discarded: hence Dublin Castle could not transform
the very large amount of information that came into its possession into
real intelligence. For this reason, key information from its many informers –
MacNally among them – stood a good chance of not being properly
assessed.[107]

Lastly, in measuring MacNally's real contribution to the intelligence
wars of the 1790s, we should note that, contrary to received wisdom, the
Directory of the United Irishmen did in fact manage to keep its plans quite
confidential. MacNally was not a member of that inner circle of United
Irishmen charged with organising a military structure and preparing for a
French expedition, and his attempts to penetrate this group, by and large,
came to nothing. In June 1797, MacNally confessed that 'intelligence
flattering to their [United Irish] views has undoubtedly been received . . .
within a few days, but by whom brought or through what medium or from
whom sent is a secret known only to those who have received it and who
communicate only by hints and in general terms that "France will support
the Irish people"'.[108] He frequently admitted that he came up against a
'secrecy almost inpenetrable' in his quest for information. 'On the grand
object [invasion]', he lamented, 'I am indefatigable but cannot come to
the desired point so profound is the secret kept'.[109] A more modest assessment of MacNally's contribution to 'secret' war of the 1790s would therefore
appear to be in order.

IV

MacNally's later career may be quickly sketched in. After the rebellion, he
continued to act for the United Irishmen as their defence counsel, and he
was able to convey useful information to the Castle at the time of Robert
Emmet's *émeute* in 1803.[110] However, Napper Tandy's death in that year
in France meant that his prime source of secret information was gone, and
JW's letters to Dublin Castle in consequence became fewer.[111] It is evident,
too, that his finances were in an increasingly parlous state, especially as his

'family' was growing. In 1797, he had noted that 'I have four unprotected females to maintain and cloth [*sic*] – two daughters and two neices – and I have a son'.[112] In 1815, he claimed that he had eight children 'all depending on me'.[113] In 1817, he stated that 'I have a wife, four sons, three daughters, a sister and a neice to maintain by my sole industry'.[114] Before then, he had published his work, *Justices of the Peace*, which went through two editions, each of 1,000 copies,[115] and while this had eased his financial situation somewhat, income from his legal work, some journalism (and his secret pension) could not support his family and he was eager for legal office. In November 1815 he applied for the position of magistrate of Dublin, and a month later, he solicited the post of Chairman of County Carlow on the death of Morgan O'Dwyer.[116] In October 1817, he put his name forward for the post of second counsel to the police establishment, an employment which, he wrote, because of 'my long standing at the bar and continual practice in the crown courts', he felt well qualified for.[117] He was unsuccessful in these applications.

MacNally died on 13 February 1820. As the informer JW, he had once unblushingly declared that it was 'very probable' that the Catholic archbishop of Dublin, John Thomas Troy was 'up' – i.e. a sworn and secret United Irishman; he had claimed several times that Catholic priests were the principal agents for disseminating sedition and disaffection; he had revealed the plans of Catholic activists for more than twenty years; and he had been a professed Protestant all his life: but on his deathbed, MacNally sent for a Catholic priest.[118]

NOTES

My thanks to C. J. Woods and Richard Aylmer for their comments on successive drafts of this paper. The usual disclaimer applies.

1   Leonard MacNally, *Sentimental Excursions to Windsor and other Places* (London, 1781), p. 59; cf. Laurence Sterne, *A Sentimental Journey through France and Italy* (London, 1767).

2   On the secret war against France, see especially, Elizabeth Sparrow, 'The alien office, 1792–1806', *Historical Journal* 33 (1990), 361–84; Elizabeth Sparrow, 'The Swiss and Swabian agencies, 1795–1801', *Historical Journal* 35 (1992), 861–84; Elizabeth Sparrow, 'Secret service under Pitt's administration, 1792–1806', *History* 83 (1998), 280–95; Elizabeth Sparrow, *Secret Service: British Agents in France, 1792–1815* (London, 1999); Michael Durey, 'The British Government and the plot to assassinate the French Directory', *History* (forthcoming). I am indebted to Professor Durey for letting me read his article in typescript. Olivier Blanc, *Les Espions de la Révolution et de l'Empire* (Paris, 1995) is interesting but rather sensational.

3 The best history of the British Secret Service is that by Christopher Andrew, *Secret Service: The Making of the British Intelligence Community* (London, 1985) but he dates the origins of the Secret Service to the Victorian period, and writes that previously 'over Europe as a whole the gains from eighteenth-century espionage and covert action were probably smaller than the time and energy spent on them' (quotation at p. 24, 1986 pb. edn).

4 W. J. Fitzpatrick, *Secret Service under Pitt* (London, 1892); W. J. Fitzpatrick, *The Sham Squire and the Informers of 1798* (Dublin, 1872); R. R. Madden, *The United Irishmen, their Lives and Times*, revised edn, 4 vols (Dublin, 1857–60). I have made a brief statement on this topic in 'Informers, informants and information, the intelligence war of the 1790s', in T. Bartlett, D. Dickson, D. Keogh and K. Whelan (eds), *The 1798 Rebellion* (Dublin, forthcoming); and I have attempted an assessment of Francis Higgins in Cathal Póirtéir (ed.), *The Great Irish Rebellion of 1798* (Cork, 1998), pp. 125–37. For the approach of a literary critic to informing, see Julia M. Wright, 'Handling informers in the 1790s', *Éire-Ireland*, 32–3 (1997–8), 144–69.

5 Fitzpatrick, *Sham Squire*, p. xvii.

6 Madden, *United Irishmen*, 2nd series, p. 576.

7 MacNally continues to fascinate: see the poem about him by Seamus Heaney, 'The old icons', which concludes 'the very rhythm of his name/ a register of dear-bought treacheries/grown transparent now, and inestimable': in Seamus Deane *et al.* (eds), *The Field Day Anthology of Irish Writing* (Derry, 1991), III, pp. 1373–4.

8 [Henry MacDougall], *Sketches of Irish Political Characters* (Dublin, 1799), pp. 256–7.

9 As a Catholic, MacNally's grandfather was barred from undertaking transactions in property and liable to heavy penalties if discovered. Fitzpatrick, *Secret Service*, p. 210. Fitzpatrick is also the source for MacNally's conversion but there is no record of this in the published lists: Eileen Byrne (ed.), *The Convert Rolls* (Dublin, 1981).

10 Madden, *United Irishmen*, 2nd series, 2nd edn (Dublin, 1858), p. 569.

11 Title page of published play (London, 1779).

12 Published London, 1782: D. E. Baker, Isaac Reed and Stephen Jones (eds), *Biographica Dramatica or, a Companion to the Theatre*, 3 vols (London 1812; reprint edn New York, 1966), III, p. 202.

13 *Ibid.*, pp. 176–7.

14 'In 1783, we find him [MacNally] again in London, distinguishing himself by speeches in the Shakespeare tavern in favour of the memorable coalition': Baker *et al.*, *Biographica Dramatica*, I, p. 477

15 *Ibid.*, II, p. 110

16 *Ibid.*, III, pp. 351–2; for details of productions, see Ben Ross Schneider Jr *et al.*, *Index to the London Stage, 1660–1800* (Carbondale, Ill., 1979), p. 534.

17 Baker *et. al.*, *Biographica Dramatica*, III, p. 215; Stephen Knight, *Robin Hood: A Complete Study of the English Outlaw* (Oxford, 1994), p. 150; R. B. Dobson and J. Taylor, *Rymes of Robyn Hood: An Introduction to the English Outlaw* (Stroud, revised edn, 1997), p. 45; Schneider, *et al.*, *Index*, p. 534.

18 Baker *et. al.*, *Biographica Dramatica*, II, p. 223; Schneider, *et al.*, *Index*, p. 534.

19 Baker *et. al.*, *Biographica Dramatica*, III, p. 206; Scheider, *et al.*, *Index*, p. 534.

20 Baker *et. al.*, *Biographica Dramatica*, II, pp. 131, 143.

21 JW to _____, n.d. [1796?], National Archives, Rebellion Papers, 620/10/121/161: MacNally went on to write: 'He hopes the manager [of the theatre] will have taste enough to lay it before the Lord Chamberlain and the Lord Chamberlain sufficient judgment to licence it'. I have found no copy of this play.

22 Intriguingly, a certain 'JW' penned a series of travel accounts in the province of Munster in 1794–5: this may have been MacNally: *Hibernian Magazine*, Oct., Nov., Dec. 1794, Jan., Feb. 1795.

23 E. W. Pitcher, 'Leonard MacNally: A few facts on a minor Irish author of the eighteenth century', *Notes and Queries* 28 (1981), 306–8.

24 Fitzpatrick, *Secret Service*, p. 183.

25 The *Dictionary of National Biography* (Oxford, 1938), XIII, p. 588, records Miss Janson as being MacNally's first wife: but Pitcher, citing various entries in the *European Magazine*, IX, XI, XXIV (1786–95), writes of an earlier marriage: Pitcher, 'Leonard McNally', p. 306. Frances Janson died in 1795 and in May 1799, MacNally married Louisa, daughter of the Revd Robert Edgeworth.

26 'One of the classics of Anglo-Irish song': Robert Welch (ed.), *The Oxford Companion to Irish Literature* (Oxford, 1996), p. 344.

27 Leonard MacNally, *An Address to the Whig Club* (Dublin, 1790), pp. 7, 11.

28 R. B. McDowell (ed.), *Proceedings of the Dublin Society of United Irishmen* (Dublin, 1998), p. 7.

29 *Ibid.*, pp. 11, 12, 24–5.

30 James Kelly, *'That Damn'd Thing called Honour': Duelling in Ireland 1570–1860* (Cork, 1995), p. 203. Needless to say, Barrington's account of his duel with MacNally is almost entirely unreliable: Barrington, *Recollections of Jonah Barrington* (Dublin, n.d.), p. 307.

31 James Kelly, 'Napper Tandy, nationalist and republican', in J. Kelly and U. MacGearailt (eds), *Dublin and Dubliners* (Dublin, 1990), pp. 12–13.

32 McDowell (ed.), *Proceedings*, p. 105.

33 See, Marianne Elliott, *Partners in Revolution: The United Irishmen and France, 1793–1815* (New Haven, 1982), pp. 62–8.

34 'Proceedings in the Court of King's Bench . . . against the Reverend William Jackson', in Thomas McNevin (ed.), *Lives and Trials . . .* (Dublin, 1846), p. 209.

35 Camden to Portland, 20 May 1795, quoted in Lecky, *Ireland*, III, p. 377.

36 Marianne Elliott, *Theobald Wolfe Tone: Prophet of Irish Independence* (New Haven, 1989), pp. 221–4.

37 Madden, *United Irishmen*, III, p. 575; Fitzpatrick, *Secret Service*, p. 150

38 McDowell (ed.), *Proceedings*, p. 19.

39 Mrs Martha McTier to William Drennan, 8 Feb. 1793 in Jean Agnew (ed.), *The Drennan-McTier Letters*, 3 vols (Dublin, 1998), I, p. 135.

40 McDowell (ed.), *Proceedings*, p. 46.

41 W. E. H. Lecky, *A History of Ireland in the Eighteenth Century*, 5 vols (London, 1913), III, pp. 375–6.

42 McDowell (ed.), *Proceedings*, p. 140.

43 Drennan to McTier, 20 Aug. 1794 in Agnew (ed.), *Drennan-McTier Letters*, pp. 213–14.

44 The earliest letters from JW that I have found are in the Pitt Papers, Public Record Office, London (PRO 30/8/327), and in the Downshire Papers, Public Record Office of Northern Ireland (D 607/c/56). Neither is dated but internal evidence suggests early 1795, possibly February.

45 There is a short notice of Pollock's role in Fitzpatrick, *Secret Service*, pp. 365–7. A useful cache of Pollock's papers has been calendared in PRONI, Mic 634: I am indebted to Dr A. P. W. Malcomson for drawing these papers to my attention.

46 Pelham was absent from Dublin continuously from 1796–8.

47 JW to Pollock, 24 Sept. 1796: National Archives [hereafter NA], Rebellion Papers 620/25/108.

48 NA, Rebellion Papers, 620/10/121/29, 32, 35, 42: JW to —- [Pollock? Cooke?],
    17 Sept. 1795, 26 July 1796, 30 May 1797, 2 Jan. 1798.
49 In a memorandum written in late 1800, Edward Cooke recommended MacNally for
    a pension of £300: Charles Ross (ed.), *Cornwallis Correspondence* (London, 1859), III,
    p. 320. See also, 'Pensions to Loyalists [*c.* 1800], by [Edward Cooke?] PRO, Colonial
    Office Papers 904/7/9–11. MacNally pronounced this sum to be a 'handsome
    remuneration . . . [though] . . . I am ignorant when it commenced and when
    and where I am to apply': JW to ——, n.d. [1801?], NA, Rebellion Papers,
    620/10/118/23. For MacNally's applications for further funding see below.
50 See 'Account of Secret Service Money, 1797–1804', in J. T. Gilbert (ed.), *Documents
    Relating to Ireland, 1795–1804* (Dublin, 1893), pp. 26, 40 for payments by Pollock
    to JW. I would suggest that earlier payments by Pollock of £50 (15 Nov. 1797),
    £100 (10 Nov. 1797) and £300 (11 Dec. 1797) to an unidentified person went
    almost certainly to MacNally (pp. 6, 7).
51 Burrowes wrote to the earl of Clare, the Irish Lord Chancellor, distancing himself
    from radical politics (and Wolfe Tone): Burrowes to Clare, 1795, in T.W. Moody,
    R.B. McDowell and C. J. Woods (eds), *The Writings of Theobald Wolfe Tone* (Oxford,
    1998), I, pp. 519–21. (My thanks to C.J. Woods for calling this letter to my
    attention.).
52 John Larkin (ed.), *The Trial of William Drennan* (Dublin, 1991); Maureen Wall, 'John
    Keogh and the Catholic Committee', in Gerard O'Brien (ed.), *Catholic Ireland in the
    Eighteenth Century* (Dublin, 1989), pp. 163–70. But see also the memorial of
    barrister Edward Purdue to the Lord Lieutenant, Lord Whitworth in which he claimed
    that because he was a strong government supporter in 1798 his 'Roman Catholic'
    clients left him and he lost business subsequently: NA, Official Papers 432/14, *c.* 1815.
53 The soldiers seized a musket, four swords and a sword cane; one of the swords was a
    family heirloom having been taken by a 'near relation' at the battle of Fontenoy
    (1745); a silver cup was also stolen. A 'protection' from Lord Castlereagh was torn up
    in MacNally's face: MacNally to —— , 24 May, 2 June, and n.d. [early June] 1798:
    NA, Rebellion Papers 620/10/121/104, 107, 117.
54 Drennan to McTier, 17 May 1806 in D. A. Chart (ed.), *The Drennan Letters*
    (Belfast, 1931), p. 361.
55 JW to ——, 2 Jan, 1797 [*recte* 1798]: NA, Rebellion Papers, 620/10/121/42.
56 Lecky, *Ireland*, III, p. 376.
57 JW to ——, 4 Feb. 1797 [*recte* 1798]: NA, Rebellion Papers 620/10/121/49: my
    emphasis.
58 JW to ——, n.d. [*c.* Apr. 1798?]: NA, Rebellion Papers, 620/10/121/97.
59 JW to ——, 1 Jan. 1797 [*recte* 1798]: NA, Rebellion Papers, 620/10/121/41.
60 JW to ——, 27 Apr. [1802?]: NA, Rebellion Papers, 620/10/121/10.
61 JW to ——, n.d. [*c.* Apr. 1798]: NA, Rebellion Papers, 620/10/121/97.
62 JW to ——, 12 June 1798: NA, Rebellion Papers, 620/10/121/113.
63 Lecky, *Ireland*, III, p. 380.
64 Nancy Curtin, *The United Irishmen* (Oxford, 1992), p. 112.
65 Tone's account, wrote MacNally,was 'justly conceived and accurately written': JW
    to ——, 12 Sept. 1795: NA, Rebellion Papers, 620/10/121/27.
66 John Bossy, *Giordano Bruno and the Embassy Affair* (Yale, 1991), p. 143.
67 JW to ——, n.d. [early 1798]: NA, Rebellion Papers, 620/10/121/152.
68 JW to ——, 14 July 1798: NA, Rebellion Papers, 620/12/121/120.
69 Madden, *United Irishmen*, 2nd series, pp. 576–8. That the prosecution saw nothing
    amiss in being briefed on the intentions of the defence in the key treason trials of the

period bears witness to the corruption and abuses inseparable from a counter-insurgency policy which had at its core a disregard for the legal norms.

70 JW to ——, 4 Feb. 1797 [*recte* 1798]: NA, Rebellion Papers, 620/10/121/49.

71 'The Castle is surrounded by emissaries; every person who goes in or comes out is reported and it is probable there are enemies in its offices, for the party certainly have very minute intelligence': JW to ——, 14 May 1797: NA, Rebellion Papers, 620/10/121/56. See also the report of the informer B[oyle], 1 Feb. 1797: 'Some of the Castle servants have been sworn and also the greater part, if not the whole of the workmen employed in the Ordnance yard.': NA, Rebellion Papers, 620/18/3.

72 JW to ——, 30 Dec. 1802: NA, Rebellion Papers, 620/10/121/24.

73 JW to ——, 29 [May 1797?]: NA, Rebellion Papers, 620/10/121/62.

74 *Ibid.*

75 See for example the handwriting in JW to ——, 20 May 1797: NA Rebellion Papers, 620/10/121/57. It is possible MacNally was drunk on this occasion.

76 JW to [Mr C?], n.d. [1795?]: NA, Rebellion Papers, 620/10/121/26.

77 JW to ——, 6 [Jan.?] 1798: NA, Rebellion Papers, 620/10/121/43.

78 Perhaps not everyone was taken in by MacNally? A live snake was reportedly sent to MacNally from the convict colonies in Australia in 1804: Kevin Whelan, *Fellowship of Freedom: the United Irishmen and 1798* (Cork, 1998), p. 49.

79 Lecky, *Ireland*, III, pp. 379–80.

80 JW to ——, [Sept. 1796?], 7 July 1797: NA, Rebellion Papers, 620/10/121/34, 69.

81 Higgins to [Cooke], 27 Sept. 1796, 17 Dec. 1797, 18 May 1801: NA, Rebellion Papers, 620/18/14. In November 1797. Higgins reported that MacNally had told him that government had offered him a sinecure appointment but that he had rejected it. Clearly infuriated, Higgins had bet him 100 guineas that the story was a fabrication 'which completely put him [MacNally] down'; Higgins to Cooke, 26 Nov. 1797: NA, Rebellion Papers, 620/18/14.

82 Maj-Gen. Fawcett to Thomas Pelham, 15, 25 Feb. 1798: NA, Fraser MS, I, no. 26.

83 L. MacNally, *Robin Hood or Sherwood Forest: a Comic Opera*, new edn (London, 1787), pp. 5, 10, 34–5, 57.

84 L. MacNally, *Fashionable Levities*, 2nd edn (London, 1783), pp. 57, 66, 88. Note how dismissive MacNally was of the suggestion that to show their loyalty, barristers should always appear in military uniform during the rebellion: 'What does it [wearing a uniform] do but furnish a disguise?': JW to ——, 12 June 1798: NA, Rebellion Papers, 620/10/121/113.

85 A. H. Cash, *Laurence Sterne, the Later Years* (London, 1986), pp. 180–4, 348

86 Laurence Sterne, *The Life and Opinions of Tristram Shandy, Gentleman* (London, Penguin edn, 1978), p. 345.

87 'Pensions to Loyalists' n.d. [*c.* Dec. 1800], PRO, Colonial Office Papers, CO 904/7/9–11: a similar document published in *Cornwallis Corr.*, III, p. 320 has 'faithful' in place of 'useful'.

88 *Ibid.*; Fitzpatrick, *Secret Service*, pp. 305–7; Bartlett, 'Prime Informant', p. 136.

89 See the letters in the Pitt Papers, Mar.–Apr. 1795: PRO, 30/8/327/307–10.

90 Marq. of Downshire to [Pitt?], Apr. 1795: PRO, 30/8/327/317.

91 JW to ——, 14, 23 Feb. 1799: PRONI, Downshire Papers, 607/G/ 66, 76.

92 Fitzpatrick, *Secret Service*, pp. 197–200: See also MacNally's discussion of anti-Union sentiment among Irish Catholics in 1810: JW to ——, 6 June, 18 Sept. 1810 (PRO, HO 100/158/168; HO 100/159/160). MacNally's post-Union activities would repay further investigation.

93 JW to ——, 19 Sept. 1797: NA, Rebellion Papers, 620/10/121/76.

94 JW to ——, 4 Feb 1797 [*recte* 1798]: NA, Rebellion Papers, 620/10/121/49.

95 JW to ——, 19 Sept. 1797: NA, Rebellion Papers, 620/10/121/76.

96 JW to ——, 12 Sept. 1795: NA, Rebellion Papers, 620/10/121/29; JW to ——, 20 Feb. 1798: NA, Rebellion Papers, 620/10/121/92.

97 JW to ——, 26 July, 17 Aug. 1796, 3 July 1797: NA, Rebellion Papers, 620/10/121/32, 69; 620/24/165.

98 JW to ——, 30 May [1797], 3 Jan. 1798: NA, Rebellion Papers, 620/10/121/145, 88.

99 JW to ——, 26 Dec. 1797: NA, Rebellion Papers, 620/10/121/86. Another Castle informant, Francis Higgins, reported about this time that there were plans for a 'general rising' during the 'holydays' but that these had been laid aside: Higgins to Cooke, 22 Dec. 1797: NA, Rebellion Papers, 620/18/14. This and MacNally's reports seem to have been based on unfounded rumours.

100 Camden to Pelham, 26 Dec. 1797: BL Add. MS 33105/299.

101 Camden to Portland, 26 Feb. 1798: PRO, HO 100/75/128–9; Portland to Camden, 2 March 1798: PRO, HO 100/75/142; Cooke to Pelham, 26 Dec. 1797: BL Add. MS 33105/307.

102 Kelly, 'Napper Tandy', pp. 16–18: Tandy's trial was at Lifford, County Donegal, because it was the nearest town to Rutland Island, where he had made landfall in September 1798.

103 JW to ——, 17 Sept. 1795: NA, Rebellion Papers, 620/10/121/29.

104 JW to ——, 22 Sept. 1797: NA, Rebellion Papers, 620/10/121/77.

105 JW to ——, 3 July 1797: NA, Rebellion Papers, 620/10/121/69.

106 JW to ——, 3 Jan. 1798: NA, Rebellion Papers, 620/10/121/88.

107 This point is further developed in my 'Informers, informants and information'.

108 JW to ——, 21 June 1797: NA, Rebellion Papers, 620/10/121/68.

109 JW to ——, 12 Oct. 1797: NA, Rebellion Papers, 620/10/121/80.

110 JW to Marsden, 25 Sept. 1803 in Michael MacDonagh, *The Viceroy's Post-Bag* (London, 1904), pp. 401–3.

111 His letters in 1805 and 1806 lacked the detail of earlier letters and tended to confirm the absence of any threat to British rule: NA, Rebellion Papers, 620/14/188/ 37, 50 and 620/14/200/3. In September 1805, he told the Castle that the family of Thomas Addis Emmet had arrived in New York: NA, Rebellion Papers 620/14/1, 2, 3.

112 JW to ——, 3 July 1797: NA, Rebellion Papers, 620/10/121/69.

113 MacNally to ——, 3 Nov. 1815: NA, Official Papers, 433/12.

114 MacNally to [Sir Robert Peel?], 18 Sept. 1817: BL Peel Papers, Add MS 40270/139. My thanks to Ms Gillian O'Brien for this reference.

115 MacNally to ——, 3 Nov. 1815: NA, Official Papers, 433/12.

116 *Ibid.*; MacNally to ——, Dec. 1815: NA, Official Papers 432/12.

117 MacNally to [Sir Robert Peel?], 18 Sept. 1817: BL Peel Papers, Add MS 40270/139.

118 JW to ——, 22 May 1797: NA, Rebellion Papers, 620/10/121/58; Daire Keogh, *The French Disease: The Catholic Church and Radicalism in Ireland, 1790–1800* (Dublin, 1992), pp. 127–8: Fitzpatrick, *Secret Service*, p. 209. For a sharply written profile of MacNally see Desmond Ryan, 'Leonard MacNally, patriot and rogue', *Irish Press*, 8 Sept. 1953: cutting in NLI, F. S. Bourke Papers, MS 10, 724/5.

8 The Improvement of Communication in International Freight Markets, *c.* 1830–1870

Yrjö Kaukiainen

Introduction

In November 1843, Captain Sylvander, master of the Finnish ship *Veloce* was unloading tar and deals in Liverpool. At the same time, he tried to find a new freight and in the course of which (as he wrote to his shipowner) he not only contacted 'most local shipbrokers but even corresponded . . . with the major trading ports around the North Sea'. In fact, he managed to agree on a shipload of salt to Trieste and was even promised a freight of grain from Odessa to Marseilles.[1]

This case, while in no way unique, illustrates quite well the state of European freight markets just before the abolition of the British Navigation Acts. Above all, it demonstrates certain features which can be regarded as omens of integration between the earlier discontinuous local markets. Thus, the good captain contacted several shipbrokers around the North Sea (probably in London, Amsterdam and Hamburg). This meant that it was possible to negotiate for a freight without actually being present at the prospective loading port; an agreement also could be made in advance, at least a few months before the respective voyage was due to start. Such features were a substantial improvement from older times when freight markets were small and limited (many ships actually carrying goods owned by the owners of the ships), in essence, spot markets.

In an earlier article[2] I have suggested that the development of international freight markets was quite rapid in the 1830s and 1840s. This was still, geographically, a limited process which was mainly confined to the big West-European ports like London, Hamburg, Amsterdam and Marseille. There also was some degree of integration between these centres. I have also suggested that one of their main advantages consisted of the fact that they were important centres of information and in command of better-than-average communications.

It is not difficult to understand that modern freight markets depend heavily on communication: basically, what they are all about is exchanging information between those who needed cargo space and those who could supply it. The faster such information can be found the faster the ships are able to secure new employment; and, vice versa, it can be claimed that limitations and imperfections in information transmission meant that the commercial actors incurred substantial opportunity costs. But this approach also opens up much wider perspectives. Information and communication have always been important agents in historical development; therefore, improvements in the speed and reliability of information transmission can be regarded a positive impulse in many kinds of economic activity, and in cultural development as well.

A common belief, however, seems to be that not much happened in this respect before the introduction of electric telegraph. On the other hand, it is clear that international mail connections gradually became quicker as well as more frequent and reliable,[3] but – so far – fairly little data can be found to indicate how much this affected the speed of information, for example. In order to find more substantial, and systematic, empirical evidence I collected data from the well-known maritime journal, *Lloyd's List*. In many respects, it is an ideal source; having a wide network of agents all over the maritime world it was able to publish shipping news and 'intelligence' (lists of ships arriving and departing) from all the important ports in Europe as well as overseas. Moreover, it enjoyed a favoured treatment by the Royal Mail[4] which meant that very few private information systems were able to produce equally quick, or quicker, communication. Thus, we can expect that, in terms of both speed and reliability, *Lloyd's List* commanded the best available flows of information thorough the period in question.

The data

In general, newspapers are very practical sources for the study of information transmission; since they endeavour to publish news as soon as possible, the time differences between the news datelines and their publishing dates represent quite well the actual transmission times.[5] Yet, a few caveats must be observed. First, it is not certain that all news were printed at the first opportunity; in addition to lacking competition between papers, the prosaic factor of the lack of printing space may have accounted for additional time lag between receiving and publishing dates. Moreover, this was also caused by the simple fact that early newspapers normally were printed only twice a week. As such time lag obviously diminished when papers were printed more frequently, a fall in the age of news may not have depended wholly on the development of communication.

These caveats do not loom large as far as *Lloyd's List* is concerned. Time was such a concern for the paper that, at least from the 1830s onwards, it endeavoured to publish all lists and reports received before the actual printing. Moreover, during most of the period which is actual in this study, it regularly published notices indicating which foreign papers and shipping lists had been received ('Foreign Papers and Shipping Lists received this day'); since they also record the original datelines, the computing of time lags becomes a very simple exercise. Only for the early 1830s do we lack such notices and they even disappear gradually during the year 1870. This means that, for the beginning and the end of the period, time differences must be computed in a traditional way from datelines and publishing dates. This of course involves some risk of introducing time lags from other sources than communication, and the risk is particularly acute for the 1830s. At that time, *Lloyd's List* was only published twice a week, on Tuesdays and Fridays (whereas, from 1837 onwards, it was published six times a week), and it is obvious that some information regularly missed the printing days. This is also indicated by the fact that, even concerning lists from Western Europe, substantial variances in times were observed.[6] However, much of this time lag can be corrected simply by subtracting one day from the average dispatch times.[7]

As the study concerns brief and extremely standard news or notices, the annual number of potential observations is very high. Therefore, to make the task more manageable, the data was collected as a series of decadal samples (years 1830, 1840, 1850, 1860 and 1870). In order to allow for seasonal variations each annual sample was divided in two, covering, more or less, the months of February and August. The aim was to collect about 250 observations (non-British ports) for each sampling month (or 500 a year).[8] In one sample, that of 1830, the periods were, however, increased to two months (February–March and August–September), which produced a total of almost 1000 observations. This was regarded as necessary because the variances (partly for reasons of data explained before) were larger than they became later on.

There are, of course, different ways to present the data. Perhaps the most natural one would be to compute average transmission times between each port and London. On the other hand, it may be claimed that the shortest times present a better gauge of what was technically possible. In this case, it was decided to compute median values; since they are much less affected by exceptionally slow cases of transmission, they can be regarded as a kind of compromise between the two alternatives presented above. In addition, the total variance between shortest and longest times was recorded; in fact, this is very substantial data in determining how regular and reliable the communications with different ports were.

The data for 29 selected ports are presented in Table 1. They only comprise a fraction of the total data computed, but they suffice quite well to demonstrate the main trends. Above all, it can clearly be seen that there was a global improvement in the speed of communication, and in most cases the change was quite impressive. What perhaps is most interesting is the fact that this transition was already in full motion a decade or two before the diffusion of electrical telegraph.

A more detailed account of the development in different parts of the world follows.

At the verge of change: communications around 1830

The first sample year, 1830, still represents 'pre-industrial' times; at least the most dramatic phase of the 'transport revolution' was just beginning. It is true that steam packets had already been sailing between England and Ireland for ten years and almost equally long between Dover and Calais, but the total amount of operational railways was still less than 200 kilometres (and, excluding one short French line, all of these were to be found in England).[9] There also were networks of optical telegraph (semaphore) in Western Europe but their commercial use was extremely limited – *Lloyd's List*, at least, seems not to have relied on such connections at all. Accordingly, information mainly travelled with conventional mail which meant that its speed was not much faster than it had been in the middle of the eighteenth century: the old rule of thumb claiming that overland transport was only seldom able to cover more than about 100 kilometres in 24 hours[10] still applied in most European countries. In practice, it was only in England and France that substantially faster stagecoach lines were to be found. The best English lines reached speeds of ten miles an hour (that is, over 350 km in 24 hours) in the early 1830s.[11] Almost equally quick connections were to be found on the best French *routes nationales* such as from Paris to Bordeaux and Calais.[12] Against this background, and the fact that steam packets already crossed from Calais to Dover in less than five hours, it is surprising that Paris news was at least four days old when published in *Lloyd's List* (see Table 1) – obviously crossing a national border involved some bureaucracy and loss of time (but it is also possible that Paris news was not regarded as urgent as that from great ocean ports).

Outside these core areas the speeds of communication dropped significantly. The data from *Lloyd's List* indicate that between Paris and Marseilles, for example, 160 kilometres a day was the common maximum, and similar rates must have been reached on the route between Trieste and the Channel coast; on the other hand, corresponding rates were below 100 between Paris and Naples or Venice. Best connections with Constantinople accounted

Table 1. Median intervals in days between dispatch and receipt/publication in *Lloyd's List*, London, of shipping lists and foreign newspapers.

Figures in brackets indicate differences between quickest and slowest dispatch (as for 1830, this figure has been reduced by one). Cases with only one observation are given in square brackets [ ]. In 1870, cases with at least some messages obviously being relayed by telegraph have been indicated with an asterisk (*).

Port	1830	1840	1850	1860	1870	D 1830/ 1860
Gothenburg	8 (5)	9 (6)	7 (12)	5 (2)	5 (4)	3
St Petersburg	17 (6)	10 (2)	10 (4)	7 (1)	3 (5)*	10
Copenhagen	10 (7)	7 (5)	6 (10)	3 (1)	3 (5)*	7
Hamburg	5 (5)	4 (5)	4 (10)	2 (0)	2 (0)	3
Antwerp	3 (3)	2 (0)	1 (1)	1 (0)	1 (1)	2
Paris	4 (4)	2 (0)	1 (1)	0 (1)	0 (0)	4
Bordeaux	7 (5)	4 (1)	3 (0)	2 (0)	1 (0)*	5
Lisbon	13 (6)	7 (0)	6 (2)	6 (3)	5 (4)	7
Cadiz	22 (11)	11 (1)	9 (1)	9 (0)	5 (2)	13
Gibraltar	18 (13)	11 (2)	8 (5)	8 (8)	6 (3)	10
Marseilles	9 (6)	8 (3)	4 (0)	2 (0)	2 (1)	7
Naples	23 (9)	12 (4)	10 (3)	5 (4)	5 (3)	18
Trieste	13 (6)	10 (0)	7 (1)	4 (3)	4 (5)	9
Constantinople	30 (11)	25 (4)	17 (9)	10 (6)	10 (12)*	20
Odessa	25 (8)	17 (1)	11 (2)	10 (3)	10 (16)*	15
Alexandria	53 (22)	18 (8)	[12]	9 (4)	[2]*	44
Madeira	31 (24)	17 (13)	—	14 (4)	15 (7)	17
Capetown	69 (19)	66 (32)	67 (20)	[39]	[35]	[30]
Bombay	129 (70)	47 (36)	[30]	27 (3)	23 (8)	102
Singapore	176 (47)	115 (25)	—	[52]	36 (41)	[124]
Batavia	131 (60)	[122]	—	[60]	19 (27)	71]
Sydney	142 (24)	137 (5)	109 (46)	54 (7)	54 (8)	88
Valparaiso	122 (56)	111 (62)	66 (3)	[47]	46 (5)	[75]
Buenos Aires	76 (25)	—	72 (19)	[40]	33 (7)	[36]
Rio de Janeiro	58 (29)	64 (34)	53 (6)	28 (1)	28 (3)	30
Havana	37 (10)	39 (8)	25 (11)	19 (3)	[18]	8
New Orleans	47 (11)	35 (30)	23 (8)	19 (9)	18 (14)*	28
New York	26 (10)	21 (13)	12 (2)	13 (4)	9 (13)*	13
Quebeck	35 (8)	32 (15)	14 (5)	12 (3)	13 (3)	23

Source: Lloyd's List, 1830–70 (microfilms in Merseyside Maritime Museum).

some 100 kilometres in 24 hours while those with Odessa (supposing a route via Kraków and Dresden) were marginally quicker.

The picture is quite similar as far as Northern Europe is concerned. While Hamburg enjoyed fairly quick connections with London (at least when steamships could be used),[13] those of Copenhagen or Stockholm were much slower (100–120 km in 24 hours), obviously because mails in both cases had to cross stretches of water in traditional post boats (which also counted for big delays in bad weather). Surprisingly, the most efficient mail connections in that part of Europe were those of St Petersburg (about 150 km per 24 hours between the city and the Channel coast).

Looking at overseas connections, it is clear that they relied exclusively on sailing vessels with correspondingly long and unpredictable transmission times. Yet there was a clear trend to speedier passages. Thus, for example, 120–140 days from Batavia to London compared quite favourably with the typical passages of some 200 days by the eighteenth-century East India men.[14] Relatively speaking, even greater improvement took place on the North Atlantic where fast-sailing American packet-ships had, in the course of the 1820s, totally outrun Royal Mail's New York packets. Being able to sail to Liverpool in three weeks or less and back to New York in five, they cut down the typical passage times of the late eighteenth century by about a half.[15]

Another 'early-modern' feature was the large overall variances between fast and slow despatch times. On short distances, the latter often exceeded the former by more than one hundred per cent; even on long ocean routes variances of over fifty per cent were recorded (see for example Bombay and Calcutta). Seasonal variations were also an integral element in North European and certain overseas connections. Thus, for example, mails from Hamburg or Copenhagen reached London in much shorter times, on average, in summer than in winter (and in winter, of course, hardly any shipping lists arrived from the Baltic);[16] monsoons also affected greatly the sailing times to India as winter storms in respect to North American connections.

Measured by the speed of communication, the World was still quite big in the early 1830s. The remotest ports of Europe were some four weeks away from London as also were the nearest coasts of North America. The distances to Buenos Aires and Cape Town amounted to more than two months, and Sydney was no less than four-and-half months from the centre of the British Empire.

The development of communication between 1830 and 1860

Although a number of national telegraph networks and even a cable crossing the Channel were already in existence in the early 1850s, this new mode of communication gained an international breakthrough only during the following decade.[17] In practice, international communication relied in traditional mail still around 1860. This was also the case of *Lloyd's List*: the notices of 'Foreign Papers and Shipping Lists received this day' hardly contain any examples of data transmitted through cable (for 'papers' this would, of course, have been impossible). This material thus gives a good picture of the development of communication thorough the last three decades of 'pre-telegraph' era.

The data tell an interesting and convincing story. There was a global and substantial reduction of despatch times. Of the twenty-nine examples with data for both 1830 and 1860 presented in Table 1, only four record a reduction below 50 per cent (of which just one, Havana, amounted to less than a third) and in no less than eleven cases was the reduction at least two thirds. The latter include a few ports in the Baltic (Copenhagen), the Western and Central Mediterranean (Marseilles, Naples, Trieste) and in the Far East (Bombay, Singapore). Equally important as the shortening of 'normally quick' dispatches is the fact that variances between fast and slow cases, as well as seasonal variances, also experienced a universal decline. Finally, it must be pointed out that this was, with few exceptions, a fairly even, or evolutionary, development.

It is obvious that if arithmetical averages instead of medians had been computed the reductions would have been slightly larger. (This 'safety factor' should even compensate for the fact that the data of 1830 may include cases of delayed publishing.) Thus, it seems reasonable to claim that European, as well as global, communications experienced dramatic improvement in the span of the three decades which preceded the 'telegraph revolution'.

What factor, or factors, accounted for this remarkable increase in the efficiency of communication? Above all, it should be asked whether this was a result of 'exogenous' technological development or did it rather depend on demand, that is, the demand for quicker transmission of information which was induced by the growth of international trade and transport. Unfortunately, historical problems can seldom be answered in terms of such dichotomy – however, a closer look on the actual improvements may still increase our understanding on the nature of the process.

As far as Western and Central Europe is concerned, railways are normally regarded as a dominant element in the 'transport revolution'. Already by the late 1830s, trains were able to travel twice as fast as the best stagecoaches and, in Britain, they quite rapidly replaced the latter as carriers of mail.[18] However, in spite of this great potential, the impact of railways was fairly marginal in the Continent until the late 1840s. The first obvious example is the building of the Paris–Calais and Paris–Marseille trunk lines; this was reflected in a dramatic shortening of dispatch times from Marseille between 1840 and 1850. In the following decade, similar cases can be found for Trieste (which was connected with Vienna in 1859) and St Petersburg (line between Warsaw and the Russian capital being finished before 1860). However, many important railway lines, such as Paris–Madrid, Bologna–Ancona or the Mont Cenis line between France and Italy, were only finished in the 1860s or 1870s, that is, in a period when telegraph already was offering much faster means for international communication.[19]

With regard to the limited role of railways before 1850, it is obvious that improvements on many overland routes depended mainly on advances in traditional transport technology. In the construction of roads (tarmac and asphalt surfaces), carriages and the organisation of coach lines, the first half of the nineteenth century witnessed a development which some scholars have regarded 'revolutionary'.[20] This mainly applies, however, to Western and Central Europe, and is reflected in the shortening of transmission times from, for example, Paris and Marseilles in the 1830s, or Danzig or Trieste between 1830 and 1850. Yet, it is possible that road connections also improved in the periphery since a similar development can be observed for Odessa and Constantinople.

However, since Europe is, in effect, a peninsula with long coastlines, steamships continued to improve communications, in particular before 1850. By the 1820s, there was, for example, steamer connection between Kiel and Copenhagen (although Lloyd's mails seem not to have been using it that early),[21] and regular lines from Hull to Gothenburg as well as between Stockholm, Helsinki and St Petersburg were established in the following decade; all this was reflected in quicker mail connections from both the Swedish and Russian capital.[22] In Southern Europe, at least Cadiz, Genoa and Naples obviously gained quicker communication in the 1830s for similar reasons; in the first case the credit obviously belongs to the new P & O Gibraltar-line, while in the two others this seems to have depended on Italian steamers.[23]

Steamships also entered ocean routes in the 1830s and 1840s. In the North Atlantic seaway this took place during the last years of the 1830s; a turning point was the summer 1838 with the crossings of the *Sirius* and the *Great Western* which were soon followed by other prospective steamer lines. The first North Atlantic mail contract (which started the famous Cunard-line) led to the beginning of a regular service in July 1840. Even these first steamers were able to shrink the eastward crossing time from about nineteen days (which was the clipper-packet average in 1836 from New York to Liverpool – and still happened to be the second fastest dispatch time between New York and London in the sample of 1840) to twelve, and westward times even more.[24]

Steam packets were already carrying mail in the Caribbean and the Gulf of Mexico by about the middle of the 1830s and a regular steamship traffic between England and the West Indies was started in 1842, after a mail contract had been concluded with a new company, the Royal Mail Steam Packet Company. The traffic network also extended to Chagres on the Isthmus of Panama which was connected with the Pacific coast (Panama) by a 50-mile mule track and, in 1841, another British company, the Pacific Steam Navigation Company, started service on the west coast of South America between Panama and Valparaiso (although it received mail subsidy only in 1846). In the 1840s, Americans also started a line between New York and Chagres (as well as between Panama and California).[25] The effects of these new lines can be seen in the 1840s and 1850s as a moderate reduction of dispatch times from the West Indies and a quite substantial one from Valparaiso. On the other hand, direct steamship service down the east coast of South America (via Madeira and Tenerife) was only started in the beginning of the 1850s. This seems to have reduced dispatch times from Buenos Aires and Rio by almost a half (see Table 1).[26]

Communication between Europe and the Far East did not only benefit from steam technology but from a geographic reorientation as well. Increasing European presence in Egypt made it possible to create a shortcut route to India via Alexandria and Suez. Already by the early 1830s, the East India Company had started irregular steamship traffic between Bombay and Suez, and this came onto a more regular basis in 1835 when the Admiralty extended the Malta line to Alexandria (in 1840, this line passed to the P & O). Although the overland travel remained a bottleneck until 1858 when a railway between Alexandria and Suez was opened, the new shortcut made a dramatic reduction in mailing times between London and Bombay. The times were already halved by the 1830s and another twenty days were saved during the next two decades. (The opening of the Suez Canal did not, in fact, reduce the passage times at all because the ships had to travel slowly and to stop for the night – it was only in 1888 that all British mails started to be carried through the canal.)

The East India Company carried the Bombay mail until 1854 but, ten years before, the P & O extended its services east of Suez, to Ceylon, Calcutta (before then, messages from Calcutta to Bombay had been carried by native runners who travelled this distance in eleven to fourteen days), Singapore and Hong Kong.[27]

In the late 1840s (at least in 1847), there was also a steamer line serving Batavia, the capital of the Dutch East Indies.[28] Mail services to Australia proved more difficult to arrange: the first trials in the beginning of the 1850s did not last long and it was only after 1859 (when P & O took it over) that a regular and reliable steamer service between Ceylon and

Australia was established. Roughly at the same time (1857), a mail contract with the Union Steam Ship Company started regular services to South Africa.[29] Accordingly, connections to these parts of the world remained at the 'pre-steam' level equally long as those of Brazil and Argentine.

In terms of time, European as well as global distances shrank by more than half between 1830 and 1860. It is now time to return to the question of the respective roles of supply (new technology) and demand (for information) in the process. While a well-founded answer would require much better data a few general remarks seem possible. First, it is clear that European overland communication relied on old technology until the 1840s and, in vast parts of the continent, the 1850s. Accordingly, what improvement there was before those times did not depend on new inventions making an increase in travelling speeds so cheap that it would have taken place even without heavy demand. Quite on the contrary, it seems probable that there was a continuous striving for improvements because of the demand for quicker communication.

On the other hand, the role of steamships was so visible right from the 1830s that the importance of the new technology cannot be denied. But even in this case, it was a fairly costly progress. In the beginning, steamships were economically successful only on fairly short distances with a good flow of travellers; for longer journeys they were uneconomical because their carrying capacity was low and the consumption of fuel very high. Many overseas post lines would, indeed, have been economically disastrous unless they had received public aid. In concluding the first mail contracts, the British post office actually yielded to pressure and lobbying which the merchants of the city, in particular, were actively engaged in. The initiatives of the East India Company (and other groups with interests in Far East trade) in developing the Mediterranean route also indicate that there was a steady demand for quicker communication.

The impact of telegraph

As was mentioned earlier, the electric telegraph had been slowly gaining ground since the late 1840s. But around 1860, it was still hardly relied upon for transmitting 'shipping intelligence' to *Lloyd's List* – probably the unit value of such data was not high enough to justify as expensive a medium as the telegraph then was. It must also be remembered that the part of Europe which, at that time, was covered by telegraph network already enjoyed good, and continuously improving, 'surface' communication. As late as in 1870, most of the European data published in the *List* were sent by mail to London; obviously, the connections were regarded quick enough for such general purposes. It was only when communicating with Archangel,

St Petersburg or the Black Sea area (obviously also Marseilles) that telegraph was relied on. This was also the case with New York, San Francisco, Aden or Calcutta.

In overseas communication the telegraph certainly made a dramatic difference. If dispatch time from London to Calcutta and San Francisco could be shortened by a month, or to New York and Archangel by a week it seems like a revolution. However, if we compare these gains with what was achieved during the preceding three decades, the revolution does not seem as impressive. Table 2 presents a comparison of selected overseas dispatch times in 1830, 1860 and those attained by telegraph. It can be seen that in most cases the reduction before 1860 amounted to more days than the difference between 1860 and subsequent telegraph times. There are only three examples – Cape Town, Buenos Aires and Barbados – in which this was not the case but there were also others, such as Alexandria, Calcutta or Bombay with the 'pre-telegraph' advances clearly outpacing the latter. As a graphic indication – whatever it is worth – it can be pointed out that the sum of the earlier differences ('a–b' in the table) exceeds the latter ('b–c') by some fifty per cent; indeed, even if the 'pre-telegraph' advances had been measured only from 1840 onwards they would have slightly exceeded the 'b–c' figures. Thus it can be claimed that, at least in overseas communication, telegraph resulted in a roughly similar improvement in speed as that achieved by the development of surface mail in two decades.

The role of telegraph was less dramatic in Europe, where the quality of conventional communication was already very high. This can also be demonstrated by the data in Table 1. As far as the thirteen European ports are concerned, the overall reduction in dispatch times to London amounted to no less than 65 per cent during the three decades after 1830. Thus it was physically impossible for the telegraph to reduce the actual times by an equal amount.

This conclusion is not, however, intended to belittle the importance of the telegraph. It is clear that the development of surface mail was approaching its limits, at least in Europe, in the 1870s and 1880s (in fact, a performance comparable to the present) and better speeds were only possible with a totally new technology. But at the same time, it is useful to remember that the telegraph did not transform all communication: in many cases, it was too expensive to be used for other than the most urgent messages. It thus vastly increased the division between 'express' and 'bulk' information. Since the latter was concerned with the common everyday needs, the development of faster and more reliable surface mail connections continued to be an important matter even after the 'telegraph revolution'.

Table 2. The development of the speed of overseas communication before and after the introduction of the telegraph (days between despatch and receipt/publication of overseas news etc. in London).

To London from	a: 1830	b: 1860	c: 1870–	a–b	b–c
Alexandria	53	9	2	44	7
Madeira	31	14	2	17	12
Cape Town	69	39	4	30	35
Bombay	129	26	3	103	23
Calcutta	137	39	2	98	37
Hong Kong (1840)	141	54	3	87	51
Sydney	142	53	4	89	49
Valparaiso	122	47	4	75	43
Buenos Aires	76	41	3	35	38
Rio de Janeiro	58	28	3	30	25
Barbados	37	21	4	16	17
Havana	37	19	4	18	15
New Orleans	47	19	3	28	16
New York	26	13	2	13	11

Source: Columns a and b, see Table 1; column c, Jorma Ahvenainen, 'Telegraphs, trade and policy', in W. Fischer, R. M. McInnis and J. Schneider, *The Emergence of a World Economy*, II: 1850–1914 (*Beiträge zur Wirtschafts- und Sozialgeschichte*, Band 33, Wiesbaden, 1986), p. 507 (table 1).

Conclusion

The material drawn from the *Lloyd's List* indicates that a major overall improvement took place between 1830 and 1860; in terms of actual dispatch times, it well matched those which came into effect after the introduction of the telegraph, in the 1860s and 1870s. The pace of development was quite different in different parts of the world but, roughly speaking, this was a process of diffusion with its centre in Western Europe.

It was an evolutionary development, which continued into the 1860s and 1870s because the transition to electric telegraph did not affect all transmission of information and was, moreover, a gradual process. And while steam shipping was in a key role in the development of global connections until about 1860, it is worth emphasising that even traditional road traffic made substantial advances between 1830 and 1850. It was also suggested above that this was a demand-derived process.

However, with regard to the validity of the empirical material, a few reservations must be made. The horizon of *Lloyd's List* does not necessarily produce an all-encompassing and balanced view of the world; it may be a fair representation of the 'information horizon' of London, but this differed somewhat from those of, say, Paris, Hamburg or St Petersburg. Thus, for example, the mails received by *Lloyd's List* hardly ever travelled over Central Europe's north–south overland arteries which were of central importance to North German or Scandinavian merchants; neither does the material illustrate the nature of wintertime communication in the Baltic world. It is also clear that the material emphasises the role of Royal Mail and British steamship companies but it is good to remember that French postal systems were important in the Mediterranean (as was also the steamship company Messangeries Imperiales) and the old Habsburgian Thurn und Taxis mail system was in a key position in Central Europe until the 1860s.

However, since the emphasis in this study is in maritime trade and freight markets, the London-centred material must be regarded as quite satisfactory. Already by 1830, London was one of the biggest ports in the world and it also later developed into the undisputed centre of international shipping business. Thus, we may say that, even if *Lloyd's List* cannot present us a true overall mirror image of global information networks, it at least represents quite well one sector of them, the maritime one. And, concerning the wider picture, this sector was important enough and subject to the same universal constraints as the rest of the global information system; therefore, its development could not be markedly different, rather it reflects at least the broad outlines in the overall development in communication.

The aim of this study was not to analyse in any detail the impact of information in the development of either freight or commodity markets. Yet its main result makes an interesting parallel to what we know of the latter. As demonstrated by Simon Kuznets in the 1960s, international trade started to grow at an unprecedented pace after the Napoleonic wars and the speed of growth actually peaked in the period 1840–73. According to Douglass C. North, a similar development can also be seen in the development of ocean shipping productivity. Information is so important for both of these markets that the improvement of communication must have been a major background factor in the growth process. Of course, it was not the only one, nor necessarily the most important – the development of industrial production (and technology), growth of populations (and demand) and institutional changes (economic policies) all played an important role. Yet, it is difficult to believe that rapid growth of trade and overseas transportation could have been possible without a simultaneous improvement of information transmission.

NOTES

1 Finnish National Archives, Archives of the Malm Trading House, Letters Received: capt. Sylvander to P. Malm, Liverpool, 5 Nov. 1843.

2 Yrjö Kaukiainen, 'International freight markets in the 1830s and 1840s: the experience of a major Finnish shipowner', in Gelina Harlaftis and David J. Starkey (eds), *Global Markets: the Internationalization of the Sea Transport Industries since 1850*, Research in Maritime History, no. 14 (St John's, Newfoundland, 1998).

3 See, in particular, Howard Robinson, *Carrying British Mails Overseas* (London, 1964), pp. 105–83.

4 John J. McCusker, *Essays in the Economic History of the Atlantic World* (London and New York, 1997), pp. 162–6.

5 As for the exploitation of newspapers, see e.g. Ian K. Steele, *The English Atlantic 1675–1740* (New York and Oxford, 1986), pp. 158–9.

6 On the other hand, neither of the publishing days seems to have been better in terms of short dispatch times. A test was made by comparing the age of news in Tuesday's and Friday's papers and, at least as far as mail from Western Europe was concerned, no substantial systematic difference was found. It seems that Lloyd's agents often were able to estimate optimum mailing days so that their reports arrived in London just before printing deadlines.

7 Supposing a random flow of correspondence, it may be supposed that a third of news was printed without delay while another third missed was delayed by one day and one more third by two days; thus the average 'time lag' was one day.

8 This may sound a satisfactory sample but, since the number of individual ports often exceeded one hundred, not all of them were adequately covered. On the other hand, data from ports along certain communication routes, such as the Baltic or the Mediterranean, can be analysed as logical series and, in such a context, data for various ports can supplement each other.

9 Robinson, *Carrying British Mails*, pp. 118–20; Simon P. Ville, *Transport and the Development of the European Economy, 1750–1918* (Houndsmill and London), p. 115.

10 Fernand Braudel, *The Structures of Everyday Life* (Frome and London, 1988), p. 424. As Braudel expressed it, higher speeds were 'very infrequent and a great luxury'.

11 Howard Robinson, *The British Post Office: a History* (Princeton, 1948), pp. 234–5.

12 Quite often mails from Bordeaux reached *Lloyd's List* in only two days' longer time than those from Paris. Supposing that they were carried via Paris this suggests speeds of almost 300 km in 24 hours.

13 The first mail contract for Holland and Germany was given to the General Steam Navigation Company in 1831, but its ships had been sailing on the route from the mid-1820s and also carried private ship letters. Robinson, *Carrying British Mails*, p. 123.

14 See e.g. Erik Göbel, 'Danish companies' shipping to Asia', in J. R. Bruijn and F. S. Gaastra (eds), *Ships, Sailors, Spices, East India Companies and their Shipping in the 16th, 17th and 18th Centuries* (Amsterdam, 1993), p. 105.

15 Robinson, *Carrying British Mails*, pp. 114–15. According to Steele, *The English Atlantic 1675–1740*, pp. 158–9, London-datelined news, published in New York and Boston papers, was on average more than 80 days old still around 1740. These figures, of course, refer to the slower, westward, passage. It seems that, in the second decade of the nineteenth century, British sailing packets were able to do the passage in 45–80 days.

16 This, in fact, is a substantial limitation in the material. Other news and mail certainly moved in the North and, not infrequently, travelling by sleigh could be faster even than by wheeled carts in summertime.

17 As is commonly known, the first successful laying of an Atlantic cable took place in 1866. In Scandinavia, this was also an important year since the Danish telegraph company Det store nordiske telegrafselskab was established then; subsequently it built lines to Norway, Sweden, Finland and Russia. In 1865, London was already linked with Karachi by using overland European and Turkish lines.

18 Robinson, *The British Post Office*, pp. 241–2.

19 See, in particular, Simon P. Ville, *Transport and the Development of the European Economy* (Hong Kong, 1990), pp. 114–30.

20 See, in particular, Francois Caron, 'L'évolution des transports terrestres en Europe (vers 1800–vers 1940)', in H. van der Wee and E. Aerts (eds), *Debates and Controversies in Economic History* (A-sessions, Proceedings, Tenth International Economic History Congress, Leuven, August 1990), pp. 86–7; Ville, *Transport and Development of European Economy*, pp. 15–16.

21 *Diary of a Tour in Sweden, Norway and Russia in 1827 with Letters by the Marchioness of Westminster* (London, 1879) tells of a tour with a ship from London to Hamburg, overland to Kiel and on a steamer to Copenhagen. Total travelling time from London to Copenhagen amounted to five and a half days.

22 See e,g, Yrjö Kaukiainen, *A History of Finnish Shipping* (London and New York, 1993), p. 86. As a result, Stockholm enjoyed for some time faster communication with London than St Petersburg .

23 Robinson, *Carrying British Mails*, p. 164. The Admiralty also had steamers on the Malta-line at least since 1835, replaced by the Peninsular Company (later P & O) in 1837, but even the voyage from England to Gibraltar took nine days (Robinson, *Carrying British Mails*, pp. 124, 164).

24 Robinson, *Carrying British Mails*, p. 124–36; see also Freda Harcourt, 'British oceanic mail contracts in the age of steam, 1838–1914', *Journal of Transport History*, 3rd series, 9 (1988), 2–3.

25 As the first Pacific railway was opened in 1869 this was the quickest connection between the east and west coasts of the US for two decades.

26 Robinson, *Carrying British Mails*, pp. 124, 148–55. Americans even built a railway across the Isthmus, between Panama and Colon (Aspinwall), which was completed in 1855.

27 *Ibid.*, pp. 158–71; Harcourt, 'British oceanic mail contracts', pp. 3–4.

28 See Yrjö Kaukiainen, 'International freight markets in the 1830s and 1840s', p. 20.

29 Robinson, *Carrying British Mails*, pp. 175, 185–97; Frank Broeze, 'Distance tamed: steam navigation to Australia and New Zealand from its beginning to the outbreak of the Great War', *Journal of Transport History*, 3rd series, 10 (1989), 3–7. New Zealand was for a long time serviced by a feeder line to Sydney.

9 Print, Politics and Protestantism in an Imperial Context: New Zealand *c.* 1769–1870

Tony Ballantyne

The evangelical revival, which energised the social activism and reoriented the theology of the Protestant tradition from the 1730s, was a truly global phenomenon. From its origin a transatlantic movement, growing out of revivals amongst European settlers in North American as well as in Great Britain and in many of the German lands, evangelicalism was nourished by the networks of information exchange and the new religious institutions integral to European expansion and community-building.[1] Initially these networks and institutions were primarily concerned with reforming the spiritual and social lives of Europeans and European colonists, but, as the eighteenth century progressed, increased attention was directed towards indigenous communities. The pioneering work of David Brainerd, a leading New England evangelical, amongst the Delaware Indians in the 1740s marked an important shift in the practice of mission, but it was not until the 1790s that a powerful and widely accepted argument for missions aimed at non-Europeans was elaborated.[2] William Carey's *An Enquiry into the Obligation of Christians to Use Means for the Conversion of the Heathen* (1792) articulated a new obligation for British Protestants to spread the gospel and constructed this task as a global campaign. Inspired by reading Cook's accounts of the Pacific and drawing upon North American examples, Carey argued that the gospel had to be carried to all corners of the Earth.[3]

The technology of print and (the agglomeration of skills that we denote as) literacy were fundamental to this globalising mission. While the evangelical revival was fed by a trans-Atlantic republic of letters,[4] the printing press was embraced by evangelicals as a powerful instrument of social change as it facilitated the production of cheap Bibles and extensive bodies of instructional literature and socio-political commentary. Not surprisingly, evangelicals placed heavy emphasis on the dissemination of Scripture and the cultivation of Bible-reading amongst domestic European populations, but print and literacy took on added importance in the 'contact zones' of empires. Within these spaces, which, as Mary Louise Pratt argues, were characterised by the 'interactive' and 'improvisional' exchanges of cultural encounter, Christian literature was believed to be a stabilising influence. Scripture and instructional texts inculcated appropriate models of piety and ethics into turbulent, predominantly male, settler populations, while they were an even greater instrument of change when aimed at non-Christian indigenous communities.[5]

This chapter explores the role of the printed word in New Zealand, at the distant and unstable fringe of Britain's empire, where Britons encountered the various tribal groups collectively known as Maori, a non-literate Polynesian community unified by a shared linguistic and cultural heritage and almost a millennium of settlement in New Zealand. The central aim here is to sketch the cultural impact of literacy, the print medium and the Christian message upon Maori, within the broader context of a long-term intensification of contact with Europeans and New Zealand's eventual transition to colonial status in 1840. Thus this essay is concerned with the interface between social communication, religion and colonialism, and seeks to explore the ways in which Maori adapted to the complex social changes which characterised this new order. My central contention is that Maori engaged with, and appropriated, print and Christianity as they reassessed and recast pre-colonial mentalities and political idioms.[6] This transformation should not be understood as a revolution from above, imposed by all-powerful Europeans, that destroyed pre-existing 'oral' traditions. Even within the context of the increasing disparities of power which characterised colonial society, Maori interest groups directed and shaped these transformations and found ingenious ways of marrying the old with the new, creating a society where orality and literacy were frequently interdependent rather than mutually exclusive. Most importantly, print and the Bible provided successive generations of Maori leaders with new skills and knowledge that could be turned against Pakeha.[7] The radical potential of the Bible, particularly when wrenched free of missionary control, was clear, as one Maori bluntly stated in 1843, 'this is my weapon, the white man's book'.[8]

Historiographical models

It is necessary, however, to begin by locating this paper within the existing historiography of social change within the colonial Pacific. Until the 1970s the dominant model for the interpretation of social change within the Pacific was the 'fatal impact' model, an interpretation elaborated forcefully in Alan Moorehead's popular history of the same name.[9] European intrusion into the Pacific was seen as calamitous, unleashing a radical and rapid social revolution that led to massive depopulation, undermined chiefly authority and undercut traditional social systems and cultural values. In an influential 1967 article, Gordon Parsonson suggested that Polynesians embraced literacy, believing it to be the ultimate source of European power, and argued that the resulting 'literate revolution' was central in the dismantling of traditional belief systems.[10] Such models of destabilising social revolutions have been revised in light of new interpretations that emphasise indigenous agency and the constructive power of cross-cultural contact,[11] but even the most theoretically informed of historians can still write of the 'fatal impact of the Euro-Americans'.[12]

Essentially, there have been two different interpretations of the relationship between oral tradition and literacy in the Maori context. The first, the New Zealand version of 'the fatal impact' school, identifies literacy as a corrosive force that undermined the vitality of Maori oral tradition, and, as a result, played a central role in the construction of Pakeha hegemony. This model has exhibited considerable longevity, as some educationalists and historians continue to identify literacy and printing as forms of cultural imperialism, even equating literacy with becoming English.[13] The second position, which we might term the 'cultural continuity' argument, suggests that literacy and Christianity actually had limited impact on indigenous mentalities and that Maori culture in 1900, or even 2000, continues to be shaped by the power of the spoken word and exhibits a fundamental cultural continuity with pre-European traditions.[14] This interpretation was developed most fully in the late D. F. McKenzie's seminal *Oral Culture, Literacy and Print in Early New Zealand: The Treaty of Waitangi*, which argued that the notion of a 'literacy revolution' amongst Maori in the 1830s and 1840s was a product of evangelical missionaries, who were extreme proponents of a European 'literacy myth'. In McKenzie's view, print and Christianity had little effect on Maori in the nineteenth century and even in the twentieth: indeed he suggests that Maori retain an emphasis on the primacy of the spoken word as 'the written and printed word is not the mode they [modern Maori] habitually use'.[15]

This chapter counters both these interpretations, by stressing the ways in which Maori leaders quickly adapted to literacy and Christianity, and their ability to use both the ideas and the printing press to fashion new cultural spaces and political idioms within the colonial order. Just as a miller in early modern Europe might read creatively, constructing an idiosyncratic and 'extravagant cosmology', literate Maori fashioned new worlds from the vernacular Bible, building histories and identities inconceivable a century before.[16] By the 1860s indigenous leaders were articulating a diverse array of new identities and political agendas. Some identified primarily on sectarian lines as Anglican, Methodist or Roman Catholic, others aligned themselves with new pan-tribal political movements which attempted to restrict the flow of land and power to the settlers, while others still identified themselves as 'Tiu' or 'Hurai', literally Jews, as God's chosen people who were destined to cast off their Pakeha oppressors. These new identities were hybridised as they blended pre-colonial traditions and values with new ideas derived from the Old or New Testament. In this context oral tradition and printing were frequently intedependent: political leaders required both the *mana* (prestige, charisma) and oral skills of an old chief, but they also drew upon an encyclopaedic knowledge of the Bible in their letters, petitions and newspapers. As preachers, prophets, pamphleteers and warriors the Maori leaders of the mid-nineteenth century moved between worlds, switching roles and shifting idioms as they negotiated the often treacherous waters of colonial politics.

Contact

The transformation of Maori from a wholly oral society to a literate, or at least a partly literate society, was one of the most important results of contact with Europeans. Although a Dutch expedition led Abel Janszoon Tasman, an experienced seaman in the service of the Vereenigde Oostindische Compagnie, initiated contact between Europeans and Maori in 1642, it was the 'rediscovery' of New Zealand by Captain James Cook in 1769 that established sustained contact with Maori. Where Tasman's crew spent less than a week in the far north of the South Island, fleeing in the wake of the death of four sailors at the hands of the Ngati Tumatakokiri tribe, Cook's *Endeavour* spent six months circumnavigating and charting the coastline. The rich documentation produced by this venture was not only the product of an Enlightenment concern with natural and human diversity, but also reflected a reorientation of British imperial ambitions towards Asia and the Pacific. Cook, summing up his impressions of New Zealand's landscape and its indigenous population, concluded: 'was this Country settled by an Industrus people they would soon be supply'd not only with the necessarys but many of the luxuries of life'.[17]

The printed word was fundamental in disseminating this understanding and transforming it into reality. The accounts of Banks and Cook, synthesised in John Hawkesworth's popular compilation, stimulated a "Pacific" craze in Europe.[18] The Pacific loomed large in Enlightenment debates over the development of 'civilisation' and the qualities of 'natural man'. Economic exploitation followed intellectual assimilation at pace, as European and American sealers, whalers and traders attempted to tap the Pacific's rich natural resources from the 1790s. Euroamerican sojourner communities developed close to major natural resources, in the case of

New Zealand clustered near the fine timber of the far north and the seal colonies of the southern coastline. As carriers of Eurasian diseases and metal tools, and as transmitters of the pull of distant markets in Sydney, Canton, Boston and London, these commercial agents initiated profoundly important transformations in the demographic profile and material culture of the communities they lived amongst. Nevertheless, as they inhabited the hybrid world of the beach and the port, and were subject to indigenous control, these sealers and traders rarely aspired to, yet alone exercised, the authority to transform indigenous mentalities.

But the desire to effect religious and social change was at the heart of the Protestant missionary enterprise. From the foundation of the first Church Missionary Society mission in late 1814 and the establishment of Wesleyan Missionary Society mission in 1823, Maori were incorporated into a social world fundamentally reshaped by evangelicalism. In order to understand the transformations in Maori mentalities that resulted from this encounter, it is important to sketch the values held and inculcated by missionaries, particularly with regard to literacy and the Bible. This is an important omission within the existing historiography: most importantly, D. F. McKenzie uses the evangelical 'myth of literacy' to discount the extent of Maori literacy. While McKenzie meticulously anthropologises Maori attitudes to print, missionary attitudes do not receive the same close treatment. Greg Dening warns us against such approaches, 'an anthropology of natives and a history of strangers', arguing that an 'anthrohistory' of both native and newcomer is the appropriate model for writing the history of culture-contact.[19]

Evangelicalism and the power of print

At one important level, the evangelical revival was a rediscovery of the centrality of scripture to faith: indeed Richard Altick has described evangelicalism as 'bibliolatry'.[20] The vernacular Bible was fundamental to the evangelical world-view, for not only was it the product of divine inspiration, but it was also a valuable moral guide, a store of historical fact, a guide to the natural world (God's other great 'book') and the key text for domestic devotion. Bible-reading structured and permeated evangelical life as it was seen as a window to God, best accessed by the individual reader but also effective if read to illiterate members of the community or shared with family members over meals, during idle moments and on the Sabbath.[21] Evangelical enthusiasm ensured that the Bible reached more and more Britons: the British and Foreign Bible Society undertook a vast campaign, disseminating their cheap Bibles to as many households as possible.[22] This drive was extremely successful, with the Bible dominating the reading material of many nineteenth-century families: around 1840, even in poor urban neighbourhoods, over seventy-five per cent of British families owned a Bible.[23]

Although evangelicals envisaged the Bible as the primary text for the reading Christian, other forms of literature were also seen to forward the cause of spiritual and social reform. John Wesley declared himself to be a '*homo unius libri*' (man of one book – i.e. the Bible), but he nevertheless placed heavy emphasis on the value of Christian literature for the reformation of the soul, believing that '[r]eading Christians' were 'knowing Christians'.[24] Wesley, a man of almost incomparable energy, played a central role in the creation of a literature-hungry evangelical readership: his fifty-volume *The Christian Library* communicated a body of spiritual literature, frequently in a condensed and pithy format, while his monthly *Arminian Magazine* reached a large and loyal readership.[25] These texts, which directed the reading Christian to correct models of religious devotion, social responsibility and work discipline, were designed to counter the lure of popular literature and entertainments. A host of voluntary organisations and missionary societies from across the evangelical spectrum extended these campaigns in the nineteenth century, expanding upon the body of 'improving' literature created by early tract societies from the late seventeenth century. The Religious Tract Society, founded in 1799, disseminated over twenty-three million publications in Britain and Ireland in the decade following 1840, while in the same period the Society for the Propagation of Christian Knowledge published around four million items per annum.[26] These projects were undertaken with the hope of inculcating new models of piety and sobriety and disseminating 'useful knowledge' to a Christian readership. Such campaigns took on extra meaning in the 'Celtic fringes' of the Highlands and Ireland, where evangelical organisations launched extensive proselytisation and educational campaigns in the hope of liberating the peasantry from illiteracy and Catholic 'superstition'.[27]

Instructional literature was only one product of evangelical presses. Print, for evangelical Protestants intent on remaking the world, had many functions. The press was an effective fund-raising tool, as missionary reports of souls saved and the heathen awaiting the gospel in Africa, Asia and the Pacific were written not only to keep Christians at home informed, but also to solicit the donations that were essential to the continued function of missionary societies. In the early nineteenth century, a host of new evangelical periodicals flourished and provided a metropolitan audience with lively accounts of the trials of the mission field and detailed discussions of the various communities, from the Highlands of Scotland to Tahiti, from England's industrial cities to rural Bengal, amongst whom the missionaries worked. Journals such as *The Methodist Magazine* and *The*

Evangelical Magazine were hugely popular, with circulations in the vicinity of 20,000, circulation figures which placed them amongst the most influential journals of the day, clearly eclipsing, for example, the sales figures of *The Edinburgh Review.*[28] As this evangelical book market grew, new specialised journals developed, tailoring their material and language to meet the sensibilities of specifically youth and female readerships.[29]

Offering a mix of illustrations, pictorial and textual exoticism, religious commentary and political discussion, missionary periodicals created a global picture of British missionary activity, at a moment when evangelical propagandists could link missionary expansion with the national interest. During the Napoleonic wars a Church Missionary Society publication argued that:

> At this hour, religion, Protestant Religion, is the bulwark, shield, sword and glory of Britain; and if Providence had placed under her domain the provinces of the distant East, it is hard to say for what purpose, worthy of the Judge of Earth, it is done, unless it be, that we may impart to them the blessed religion of Jesus.[30]

Of course Anglo-French conflict contained, and to some degree was animated by, religious tensions, and missionaries proved themselves adept at manipulating these. Claudius Buchanan, Chaplain to the East India Company and a leading theorist of mission, argued in his *Colonial Ecclesiastical Establishment* that British imperial strength could be used to extend the 'National church' and elsewhere he argued that Protestant missions in Asia, 'defenceless and unprotected', required government support to 'counteract the influence of the ecclesiastical power of ROME'.[31] Anglicanism, Buchanan maintained, could provide a stabilising influence which would weld an increasingly disparate and diverse empire together.[32]

Similar arguments were articulated in the North American context after the American Revolution. In 1786 William Knox, a member of the Society for the Propagation of the Gospel and the former Under-Secretary of State for the Colonies, wrote that the 'Prevalence of the Church of England' in Britain's remaining North American colonies was that best means of ensuring the colonists' continued 'Fidelity and attachment' to British interests.[33] Although, as the nineteenth century progressed, evangelicals would frequently express deep-seated suspicions of the state and of colonial companies (expressed forcefully in debates over the charter of the East India Company, the New Zealand Company's plans for colonisation and the provision of resources for Indian Christians), faith, morality and imperial patriotism were increasingly entwined between 1783 and 1815 as British imperial holdings were consolidated in Ireland, the Mediterranean and beyond.[34]

Mission and the project of translation

A missionary presence was established in New Zealand at the very end of this period: in fact Samuel Marsden preached the first sermon of the Church Missionary Society mission at Oihi in the Bay of Islands, on Christmas Day 1814. Marsden soon returned to New South Wales, leaving the fledgling mission at Rangihoua (close to Oihi) in the hands of the first three missionaries: William Hall, a carpenter, John King, a shoe and rope maker, and Thomas Kendall, a farmer and teacher. It was these three missionaries, but especially Kendall, who would have to struggle with a problem that Marsden had left them with: translation. Although Marsden had enjoyed regular contact with Maori visiting the New South Wales colony and had established a close relationship with Ruatara, the Ngapuhi *ariki* (chief) who acted as a patron of the mission, it was immediately clear that communicating Christian doctrine to Maori was going to be a difficult task. After Marsden's initial sermon:

The Natives told Duaterra [Ruatara] that they could not understand what I meant. He replied, that they were not to mind that now, for they would understand by and bye; and that he would explain my meaning as far as he could. When I had done preaching, he informed them what I had been talking about.[35]

Confident of Maori intellectual abilities and full of zeal Marsden felt 'much gratified' with his reception, believing that mission labour in New Zealand would be 'crowned and blessed with success'.[36]

The linguistic and cultural translations challenging the early missionaries living amongst Maori were nothing new, at least within the broad sweep of Christian history. Of course translation was deeply embedded in Christian tradition, occupying both a prominent position in the Bible and the historical experience of the early church. At a theological level, many Christian commentators had understood the Incarnation itself was an act of translation, remembering that Jesus himself was described in this way: 'And the Word was made flesh, and dwelt among us' (John I:14). Lamin Sanneh has traced the development of the mission impulse from the time of Paul, arguing that out of the encounters between Jew and Gentile and then between Christianity and Greek culture, a distinctive tradition of Christian mission developed. The chief characteristic of this missionary impulse, in Sanneh's view, was the fundamental importance attached to translation and cross-cultural communication in the preaching of the gospel. Even when the hierarchy of the medieval church upheld Latin as the sacred language of liturgy, vernacular languages were crucial media for religious exposition and individual devotion.[37] Unlike Islam, which would place such a heavy emphasis on the revealed nature of Arabic and the resulting perfection of the *Qu'ran*, ensuring a profound cultural continuity within the Islamic world, Christianity quickly became a vernacular faith, as distinctive localised traditions developed amongst the Celts, Slavs, Copts and Ethiopians.[38]

Sanneh suggests that a tension between this long-standing tradition of 'vernacularisation' and the assimilationist aims of empires, whether medieval, early modern or modern, has been at the heart of the globalisation of Christianity. One of Sanneh's objectives is to draw attention to the importance of translation within the Catholic tradition of mission, particularly as it developed within the Spanish imperial world from the sixteenth century. Sanneh notes that while Protestants emphasised the translation of Scripture itself because it was their 'crucial standard of authority', Roman Catholic missionaries undertook the translation of the catechism, their 'teaching authority', into a multiplicity of languages in the Americas, the Philippines, Japan and India.[39]

In the South Asian context Jesuit missionaries gained few converts but some, most notably Robert de Nobili, made significant progress in the 'vernacularisation' of Christianity. But until the 1760s European knowledge of Indian languages, apart from the Persian of north Indian courtly tradition, was disorganised and unreliable. Under the patronage of Warren Hastings, the Governor of Bengal, skill in Indian languages was a foundation of the Company's administration and a huge effort was devoted to the study of Indian languages.[40] Company servants, most notably men like Nathaniel Brassey Halhed and John Gilchrist devoted themselves to the study of vernacular languages like Hindustani and Bengali, producing grammars, dictionaries and translations.[41] From the 1792 the East India Company found an unlikely ally in this linguistic project in the form of the British Protestant missionaries whose preaching the Company were attempting to restrain. Where the Company was attempting to gain a command of Indian languages in order to cement their authority, Protestant missionaries sought such linguistic knowledge as the first step in the Christianisation of India.

The Baptist William Carey, whose *An Enquiry into the Obligation of Christians to Use Means for the Conversion of the Heathen* was pivotal in offering a theological justification (through the doctrine of 'means') for overseas missionary activity and turned the gaze of British Protestants to their vast empire, embodied the centrality of language to Protestant mission enterprise. Although a humble shoemaker, Carey, the moving force behind the foundation of the Baptist Missionary Society and the establishment of the Baptist Serampore mission, exhibited considerable linguistic ability and even greater drive as he devoted himself to the study of Indian languages. Under Carey's influence, the Baptist Missionary Society saw that the translation of scripture into the vernacular languages of mission fields was fundamental to the success or failure of evangelisation. Carey led the way, working in close consultation with indigenous language experts on grammars of South Asian languages and translations of scripture. Carey was responsible for six complete translations of the Bible (Assamese, Bengali, Hindi, Marathi, Oriya and Sanskrit) and contributed to some 29 other translations, while he also authored (or, more correctly, co-authored) grammars and dictionaries of Bengali, Marathi and Sanskrit.[42] This Indian experience was crucial as a model for missionaries elsewhere; it confirmed the tradition of the cultural vernacularisation of Christianity and placed even greater emphasis on language in missionary policy: it was an example followed throughout the Pacific.

Orthography, translation and print

Within the New Zealand context, however, translation proved a serious barrier to the fulfilment of Marsden's high expectations. As Marsden began preparations for the foundation of the New Zealand mission he stressed that the missionaries required books to guide them: the Bible was to offer spiritual solace and moral direction in a strange land, while 'useful' manuals would guide the missionaries in their trades and provide a body of knowledge that might be eventually communicated to Maori. Marsden insisted that the Church Missionary Society supply William Hall, the carpenter, with the 'necessary Books and draughts'.[43] Marsden attempted to provide the missionaries with the best possible linguistic training, as he prepared to sail with two of the first missionaries to New South Wales (where they would spend some four years). He was delighted to find a Maori, 'a very fine young man', aboard. Marsden hoped that this fortunate coincidence would allow William Hall and John King to gain 'some Knowledge of the New Zealand language' preparing 'their minds for more easily understanding the natives when they arrive'. Such instruction would be supplemented by an attempt to systemise the knowledge gained as Marsden planned to 'draw up a short Vocabulary' in co-operation with the Hall, King and the 'New Zealander'.[44]

But here, as in his reflections on his first sermon in 1814, Marsden's hopes were too high. With the exception of Kendall (and James Shepherd, a gardener and lay missionary, who arrived in 1820) the early missionaries sent by the Church Missionary Society to New Zealand had limited linguistic ability. Hampered by poor education, meagre resources and constant fears about the security of the mission, the initial progress of the mission was uneven. Kendall was responsible for the mission school where Maori learnt to read and write and were introduced to the basic elements of the Protestant tradition.

Kendall quickly collated *A Korao no New Zealand; or, the New Zealander's First Book*, a work published in 1815 that identified basic elements of the grammar and provided a vocabulary of everyday terms and some very basic cultural concepts. The orthographic scheme in this work was muddled and inconsistent, as Kendall represented single phonemes with a variety of letters (/r/ with 'dd', 'rr' and 'r') and failed to develop a consistent scheme for the depiction of vowel sounds (confusing a and u, i and e) and length. In addition to a simple word list, Kendall's text also contained parallel English and Maori sentences such as 'Behold! Jesus Christ is the great and good Atua [god], the great and good friend to white and black men; to all men.'[45] Many of these phrases embody Kendall's uncertainty over the linguistic and cultural translations he was undertaking. 'God', a term fundamental to missionary project, was especially problematic. There was a disjunction between the English word 'god' and '*atua*', the Maori term that missionaries identified as the nearest possible equivalent. In the Polynesian world, where the boundary between the material world and supernatural was thin and porous, '*atua*' could designate culture heroes, malevolent spirits, departed ancestors, chiefs of high standing as well as the supernatural beings resembling the 'gods' missionaries looked for.[46] Initially at least Maori found the concept of the Christian God as elusive as the missionaries found Maori *atua*: did God have a body? Where did he live? Was he English? Why did this God seem both loving and angry?

This disjunction between cosmologies led many missionaries and travellers to doubt that Maori had any equivalent of religion. Kendall himself, for example, argued that the Maori 'does not, so far as I can learn, bow down to a stock [*sic*] or a stone; but he magnifies himself in a god.' The only elements he could discern in the Maori world-view were 'pride and ignorance, cruelty and licentiousness'.[47] While on occasion Kendall translated 'God' as 'Atua Nue' [*atua nui*] – 'the great God' (a rendering that implicitly recognised the multiplicity of Maori *atua*), he also produced Maori sentences which simply incorporated 'Jehovah' and 'Lord' as the name of the 'Atua Nue'. In a similar vein the English words 'Paradise', 'Satan' and 'the Devil' featured in the Maori sentences.[48] While linguistic and cultural uncertainties imposed some limits on the vernacularisation of Christian terms in *A Korao no New Zealand*, the sample sentences affirmed the value that the early missionaries were placing on vernacular literacy: 'It is good to read the language of New Zealand'.[49]

This early linguistic work was extended and refined in 1820, when Kendall returned to England. Accompanied by the influential *ariki* (senior chief) Hongi Hika and the younger Hohaia Parata Waikato, Kendall travelled to Cambridge with the hope of fixing a basic framework for the acquisition and study of Maori. In Cambridge Kendall and the *ariki* worked with Samuel Lee, professor of Oriental languages, a prominent translator and grammarian who undertook a range of linguistic work for the Church Missionary Society. Lee was at the forefront of Scriptural translation and linguistic scholarship and it was hoped that his assistance would help resolve the orthographic problems that the missionaries were struggling with. Lee's grammar, in reality a heavily collaborative work, was a marked improvement upon Kendall's earlier work. While Lee's orthographic scheme still contained some redundant consonants and the rendering of certain phonemes remained uncertain (with /r/ represented as both 'r' and 'd' and /p/ as 'b' and 'p'), the identification of key vowel sounds and length was both more accurate and consistent than in Kendall's earlier work.[50] This work, in the tradition of *A Korao no New Zealand* and grammars in other colonial contexts, contained extensive sample dialogues: the missionary and 'his pupil' discuss the name of God, the Bible, the significance of the Sabbath, the Ten Commandments, the Fall, the Incarnation of Jesus and the Crucifixion.[51] As a grammatical text and teaching-aid this 1820 grammar provided missionaries with a basic framework for the preparation of sermons in Maori and was an essential starting-point for the long and difficult process of Scriptural translation.

As we have seen from the discussion of Kendall's work, early efforts at translation were *ad hoc* efforts lacking co-ordination and authority. Falling back on what they knew best, the early 'mechanic' missionaries were more at ease communicating new agricultural skills and the proper use of European technology than immersing themselves in the profoundly important linguistic and hermeneutical questions raised by biblical translation. In the wake of Kendall's grammatical work, it was a lay missionary James Shepherd and an assistant industrial agent to the Christian Missionary Society mission, William G. Puckey, who began translating significant sections of the Gospel. As the mission passed from Marsden's control, greater emphasis was placed on the education of missionaries and co-ordinating the translation programme. From 1826 a committee of missionaries and their associates (including gifted 'natural' linguists like Puckey) worked together on a collection of key texts, including Genesis, John I, the Ten Commandments, the Lord's Prayer and an small assortment of hymns. Although this work was painstaking and intellectually challenging, significant progress was made, when the resulting pamphlet was printed in Sydney, with the assistance of the New South Wales chapter of the British and Foreign Bible Society. Between 1827 and 1834, as translation work continued in New Zealand, the mission was reliant on printing presses in Sydney to produce various compilations of Scripture, catechisms, prayers and hymns. While this arrangement allowed Maori to be introduced to printed scripture, there was much dissatisfaction amongst the missionaries who were unhappy about the quality of the Sydney-produced material and the delays engendered by their reliance on distant presses.[52]

Finally, in 1834, the New Zealand mission received a trained printer, the missionary William Colenso, and a functioning printing press. A gifted and resourceful man, Colenso learnt to make the most of his meagre materials and quickly adapted to working in Maori. In fact, the pressure on Colenso quickly mounted, as the mission press failed to keep up with a strong Maori demand that had grown steadily since 1830, and evidence suggests that, in some locations at least, literacy outstripped the supply of Bibles.[53] As Colenso's press produced substantial runs of vernacular material, large numbers of Maori converted to Christianity and many more incorporated aspects of the new belief into their world-view, even if they did not formally convert. In response to this increased demand, the Christian Missionary Society press produced three and a half million pages of Maori language texts between January 1835 and the beginning of 1840, and produced a further two million pages in 1840.[54] In 1841, 1843 and 1845 the Maori New Testament was reprinted in runs of 20,000. By this stage, the missionaries had saturated the market: my conservative calculations suggest that there were two New Testaments in circulation for every three Maori in 1845.

Vernacularisation and New Zealand's colonial status

Missionary translations and the printing boom were crucial cultural contexts for the debates in the late 1830s which would determine the future relationship between the British Crown and Maori. From the missionary perspective, the success of the printing press and a new found Maori interest in Scripture were signs of a great age of conversion: by 1840 one missionary was, perhaps over optimistically, able to suggest that 'full three-fourths' of local Maori had 'embraced the gospel'.[55] The battle was not entirely won, however. Throughout the 1830s the missionaries feared that while great progress had been made, the spiritual status of Maori was fragile. As the white trading community grew in the far north of the North Island and New England whaling ships visited the Bay of Islands with increasing frequency, the missionaries feared that Maori were being 'contaminated' by this contact. Whites were exploiting Maori women, introducing muskets, tobacco and alcohol into coastal communities and the immorality of white sailors and traders was undercutting the positive effects of Christianity. The missionaries attempted to construct a social boundary around Paihia, the new mission headquarters, to limit the 'degrading' effects of Kororareka, the nearby port-town, which the missionaries dubbed the 'Hell'.[56]

The missionaries' attacks on settler morality were extended and elaborated by James Busby, the British resident who arrived in the Bay of Islands in 1833. Hamstrung by meagre resources and lacking military support, Busby was unable to exercise authority over the Bay's white population, but his depictions of social change were extremely influential. In his reports Busby, like the missionaries, attacked the impact of the traders and whalers, stressing that they were primarily responsible for 'permanent anarchy' of the Bay. European-introduced disease and muskets were leading to rapid depopulation, a 'decrease' that local Maori 'were perfectly sensible of'.[57] Many Church Missionary Society missionaries argued that any further white settlement should be prevented and that the aspirations of the New Zealand Company, which was planning the foundation of colonies, should be blocked.[58] Underpinned by humanitarian concern and a desire to control European incursions in New Zealand, such arguments actually facilitated colonisation, as they created an image of Maori enfeeblement which not only 'necessitated' annexation but also fashioned an image of a weak and diminishing 'native' population easily displaced, an attractive image for speculators and settlers.

By 1839 the tide of opinion had shifted. Some leading missionaries, including Henry Williams, supported formal British intervention, especially after the New Zealand Company dispatched its first colonists in September 1839. Once organised white settlement was inevitable, the Colonial Office, also under evangelical sway, decided (with 'extreme reluctance') that annexation was the only solution. A treaty would provide the best means of extinguishing Maori independence, which had been officially recognised by the Colonial Office in 1835, while, in return, Maori would receive law and the rights of British subjects. Ultimately on 6 February 1840 at Waitangi, after heated discussion, 43 chiefs from the far north (they would be followed by almost 500 more) signed a Treaty that guaranteed chiefly authority and resource rights, but transferred sovereignty over New Zealand to the Queen.

The treaty they signed was in Maori, a text which fundamentally transformed the future of New Zealand, but whose ambiguity and imprecision encapsulated the problems of linguistic and cultural translation that had troubled the missionaries over the previous twenty-five years. Hastily translated from an English draft by Henry Williams and his son Edward, the Maori text failed to convey accurately several key concepts, particularly the shades of meaning and significance attached to 'sovereignty' in British legal tradition. As one historian has observed, the language the Williams used was 'Protestant missionary Maori', an idiom heavily moulded by earlier scriptural translation.[59] The two key terms in the Treaty '*te tino rangatiratanga*' and '*kawanatanga*' were both used in Maori scripture.

Rangatiratanga, an old term denoting 'chieftainship', had been used by the missionaries to describe God's kingdom, while 'kawana' (a transliteration of Governor) was used in the scripture to describe the authority of rulers: Pontius Pilate, for example, was described as a kawana. In the context of the Treaty, however, 'rangatiratanga' was supposed to convey the 'possession of lands', while 'kawanatanga' was supposed to designate 'all the rights and powers of Sovereignty'.[60]

The imprecision of these translations and the cultural disjunctions which framed the Treaty continue to exercise political activists, lawyers and historians. In particular, the role of the missionaries continues to be debated: were they simply the pawns of empire that played a central role in the colonisation of New Zealand and the destruction of Maori culture?[61] Where modern historians have tended to depict missionaries as purveyors of print and the Protestant work ethic, as either agents of modernisation or, more typically in the New Zealand case, as 'cultural imperialists' intent on destroying native culture as the first step in evangelisation, a very different picture is conveyed by contemporary British and settler sources. The missionaries' critics, the advocates of colonisation, particularly in the 'systematic' forms pursued by the New Zealand Company, attacked evangelical missionaries as obstacles to cultural assimilation and social modernisation. Even after the Treaty made organised white settlement a possibility, *Fisher's Colonial Magazine and Colonial Maritime Journal* attacked the cultural and linguistic policies of the missionaries. The printed form of the Maori language was, it suggested, 'formed by Mr. Lee from the sounds of two natives, brought from New Zealand by Mr. Kendal [*sic*]'.[62] The sole object of this 'creation' was 'to keep the native aloof from the English settler'. As self-appointed and 'nominal' protectors of Maori interests, missionaries were a serious barrier to the development of colonial society: the way ahead was clear: 'Cultivate the English language by every possible means, and lead the native to forget his own'.[63]

Edward Gibbon Wakefield, the leading theorist of systematic colonisation and moving force behind the New Zealand Company, launched a polemical attack against missionary language policy in the same journal in 1845. His argument began:

A NEWSPAPER in the Maori, or native New Zealand language, has been published at Auckland, in New Zealand. It is a great mistake to laud this paper; it is in truth a link added to that chain, which has been gradually forged for the purpose of surrounding the natives as a distinct race, and to prevent their amalgamation with the settler, and consequent civilization and attainment of real Christianity.[64]

Wakefield and many other critics overlooked the significant transformations in faith and morality the missionaries hoped to effect through the vernacularised gospel as they argued that the central thrust of missionary policy was the maintenance of indigenous culture and language. Here Wakefield clearly rejects the notion of an indigenous Maori Christianity (or Christianities), equating 'real Christianity' with British culture and 'amalgamation' as the assimilation of Maori into British norms. The 'true, the only way, to really and not nominally Christianise the aborigines, is to first teach them our language; by degrees they will adopt our habits, they will amalgamate, civilisation will follow, and Christianity'.[65] Edward Gibbon Wakefield's son, Edward Jerningham, argued that Anglicisation was a necessity because of the cultural and linguistic poverty of Maori: 'The Maori language is essentially a poor one, and it possesses in particular but few words which express abstract ideas'.[66] For the Wakefields, a civilised colonial world of trade and politics necessitated the destruction of the Maori language.

Patterns of literacy

But the Maori language exhibited a strength and vitality that was not easily crushed. The missionaries insistence on the vernacularisation of Christianity and the productivity of the mission presses created a body of printed material that would serve as a touchstone for decades to come. Even when some missionaries began to favour teaching Maori English in the mid-1840s and Maori grew increasingly sceptical of missionary intentions as the settler population grew, the Bible remained fundamentally important to Maori communities.[67] This was made clear when missionaries began to revisit the earliest translations, refining them and striving for greater consistency: such revisions were contested by Maori who believed that, as the Word of God, the Maori Bible was perfect and should not be altered.[68]

By 1860 the vernacular Bible had saturated Maori society, with one Maori New Testament per capita in circulation, a remarkable figure given that these communities were non-literate less than fifty years before. Of course, the diffusion of printed texts is not necessarily an indicator of literacy. This was particularly the case in Maori society where the accumulation of goods was integral to the construction of personal status and was an important vehicle for inter-tribal competition.[69] McKenzie has also demonstrated that in many instances Maori used books as charms and talismans or even used the paper in the construction of cartridges for their firearms.[70] He suggests that Maori literacy and Maori conversion was a mirage, born out of missionary propaganda and their overwhelming stress on the power of print and the gospel.[71] For McKenzie the most telling evidence of Maori literacy, or continued non-literacy, is the 'ability or inability to write a signature'.[72] He notes that of the 520 or so chiefs who

signed the Treaty of Waitangi only 72 were able to sign their name, leading
to the conclusion that perhaps thirteen or fourteen per cent of the population were literate.

This test, however, is problematic. While a signature might be taken as
an easily quantifiable measure of literacy, it can be misleading. We know
that in many societies, including Maori, individuals could often read
without having the ability to write. Moreover, religious literacy of the
type common among Maori (as until at least 1850 Scripture dominated
vernacular printing), was focused on reading, and within such a context
less premium might be placed on the ability to write.[73] McKenzie's sample,
moreover, is not representative, as the senior chiefs who signed the Treaty
typically belonged to an older social order. Although some of the chiefs
acted as patrons and protectors of missionaries and merchants, they were
the section of indigenous society least acquainted with Christianity and
literacy. Missionary schools, which were central in the dissemination of
literacy, accepted Maori of both genders and of all classes: but the pupils
were more frequently from the bottom half of the society. For the Maori
elite their *mana* (power, status) was derived from their ancestry, their ability
to wage war, and from the accumulation of *taonga* (precious goods,
including food, weapons, and even missionaries). The older chiefs had
limited use for literacy and some resisted consorting with the lowly types
who attended missionary schools.[74] Conversely Christianity and literacy had
a greater appeal to those at the bottom of the social order, particularly former
slaves, who were conspicuous as 'native teachers', spreading Christianity
and literacy well beyond the frontiers of missionary influence.[75] For these
'little-people', literacy allowed them to function as intermediaries between
the Pakeha and older, more traditional Maori. Most importantly, however,
it allowed them to access Christianity, which proclaimed an egalitarian
vision and promised eternal suffering for sinners, doctrines that had
obvious appeal for ex-slaves.[76]

Contrary to McKenzie's insistence that vernacular literacy was a
'chimera', recent scholarship has recovered substantial evidence of a large
number of nineteenth-century Maori with both the ability to read and
with confident hand-writing, an important point in light of the weight
McKenzie attaches to the signature as an indicator of literacy.[77] Our
best estimates of the extent of vernacular Maori literacy come from
A. S. Thomson's exhaustively researched *The Story of New Zealand* (1859),
which suggested that approximately one half of the adult Maori population
could read Maori and that around one third could both read and write.[78]
But such figures do not convey important variations within the population,
particularly patterns shaped by region and age. Certain Maori tribal groups,
Ngati Whatua for example, were renowned for their literacy; generally

coastal tribes which were engaged in frequent contact with Pakeha enjoyed higher rates of literacy than those in the inaccessible interior.[79] Equally importantly, literacy was embraced more readily by a younger generation, which grew up with a closer knowledge of Pakeha than their elders. In 1841 the perceptive traveller R. G. Jameson noted that literacy was extremely widespread among those Maori between ages ten and thirty. While older Maori were less interested in this skill, young Maori placed high value on it and even taunted illiterate Pakeha.[80]

This generation gap became clear as some younger Maori expressed an interest in using the print medium to preserve oral traditions. Leading government officials and amateur ethnographers offered indigenous informants free lodgings, money or other gifts in return for recording various tribal traditions. Younger Maori, who were literate, familiar with Christianity, and accustomed to the market economy, seized these opportunities. However, their elders were not pleased, as they believed that such knowledge was *tapu* (sacred) and sharing it with Pakeha would not only undermine its *tapu* status and also might also lead to illness and death. But these elders were unable to stem the tide. Younger Maori eagerly embraced literacy, becoming avid letter-writers and used their new skills to request detailed biblical exegesis from missionaries, to preserve genealogies and to record patterns of land holding. Effectively these innovations 'disembodied' knowledge: old traditions were no longer the sole preserve of wise elders and *tohunga* (religious specialists), as Pakeha and Maori of all ranks could read and reflect on these new 'fixed' versions of tradition at their leisure.[81]

Maori faith and politics: the imbrication of literacy and orality

The profound political impact of Christianity and literacy is most clear from the late 1850s. Although there is much evidence to indicate waning Maori interest in missionary-Christianity in this period, the Bible, Christian theology and literacy shaped political activism and notions of community. Here we can note three important strands in Maori thought which reveal the interdependence between older oral traditions and literacy, and the imbrication of pre-colonial beliefs and new ideas derived from the Bible: the King Movement, loyalist or neutral Maori Christianity, and Maori prophetic traditions.

Christianity played a crucial (but often neglected) role in the elucidation of the ideology and aims of the King Movement, which was founded in 1857 by Waikato Maori in the hope that the alienation of Maori land could be controlled. While the movement's aim was to limit Pakeha influence in the 'King Country', its ideology and political language was profoundly Christian. Iwikau Te Heuheu, who presided over the investiture of Te Wherowhero Potatau as the first king, asserted the primacy of Christianity in Kingitanga (the culture of the King Movement):

Potatau, this day I create you King of the Maori People. You and Queen Victoria shall be bound together to be one (pai-here-tia kia kotahi). The religion of Christ shall be the mantle of your protection; the law shall be the whariki mat for your feet, for ever and ever onward.[82]

This investiture ceremony reflected the remarkably swift integration of Christianity into the construction and projection of political authority. Not only did Iwikau Te Heuheu insist on the cohesive and protective role of Christianity, but the Maori Bible was also the central ritual object in the coronation.[83] Ultimately, the power of God sanctified and legitimised the power of the new King. The Maori king was responsible for the main-tenance of law and order within Kingitanga's *aukati* (boundary), known by Pakeha as 'the King Country', while the Queen's sovereignty was recognised by all New Zealanders, Maori and Pakeha, outside the *aukati*: 'The King on his piece; the Queen on her piece, God over both; and Love binding them to each other'.[84]

Other Maori Christians, however, felt uneasy with the agenda of the King Movement. They placed their religious identity as Christians first, pledging allegiance to the Crown as long as it acted in a Christian manner. William Williams, the Church Missionary Society missionary based at Tuuranga (Gisborne), reported in 1863 that the local Rongowhakaata leader Anaru had rejected the overtures of King movement. Anaru asserted that Christianity, not the King Movement, was the basis of his own community's future: 'there was no unity except under the Gospel and no sure foundation but Christ'.[85] These arguments were frequently restated at meetings and in innumerable letters by those Maori who rejected the legitimacy of the Maori king. Ngati Kahungunu leaders from Gisborne, for example, wrote to the Governor to reassure him that they were loyal and that 'cultivation' and 'the buying of clothes, and vessels' were their interests, not war. 'The heart which has enmity towards God or man is an evil thing. Love to God and man is peace with God, the Queen, and her subjects.'[86]

But these 'loyal' Maori did not see themselves simply as 'Maori Christians', rather they were 'Mihinare Maori' (missionary/Anglican Maori), 'Weteriana Maori' (Methodist Maori) or 'Katorika Maori' (Catholic Maori). From the late 1820s distinctive sectarian identities emerged as Wesleyan and Catholic missionaries joined the Anglicans in the New Zealand mission field. Maori religious affiliation was often determined by old agendas as denominational identity became a new vehicle for kin-group rivalries and, in turn, Christian identities became a means of re-inscribing boundaries between rival kin-groups. Both Catholicism and Methodism also became 'denominations of dissent', allowing kin-groups to emphasise their autonomy from both the control of Pakeha and powerful Maori Anglican groups.[87]

The intensely sectarian programmes of the missionaries undoubtedly deepened these tensions. Both Wesleyan and Anglican missionaries drew on pre-existing Maori resentment of the French to launch sustained anti-Catholic campaigns and print was their most important vehicle.[88] In response to the establishment of the Catholic mission the Church Missionary Society produced a raft of anti-Catholic pamphlets drawing on the stock images of evangelical Anti-Catholicism.[89] As a result, Maori routinely called Jean-Baptist Pompallier, the Catholic Bishop, the 'Anti-Christ'.[90] The strength of these sectarian identities became clear in the 1850s when missionaries of various denominations were embroiled in heated doctrinal debates that drew intense Maori interest.[91]

These more orthodox identities have been generally overlooked by historians who have seized on the more radical and sensational responses to Christianity and the host of Maori prophets, millennial movements and healing cults have provided rich material for historians.[92] The characteristic feature of these prophetic movements was their active engagement with the Old Testament. Whereas the first two strands of Maori Christianity focused on the New Testament and the figure of Christ, the prophetic movements drew heavily on the narratives and parables of the Old Testament, which was printed in its entirety in Maori in 1858. In 1864 one leading colonial reported that Maori were 'exceedingly fond of reading the books of the Old Testament, in which they find described a state of civilization not unlike their own'.[93] The angry and vengeful God of the Hebrews was far closer to Maori *atua* than the God of the New Testament. The Christian God was, as one Maori observed, 'too quiet, too lazy, and so no good for the Maori'.[94]

The Old Testament's narratives of enslavement and its promise of salvation for God's chosen people held great appeal for Maori who had experienced the hardships of disease, depopulation, land sales and war. Pai Marire (or Hau Hau),[95] the most important prophetic movement of the 1860s, consciously emphasised the Maori-Israelite link and its founder, Te Ua, signed himself as 'Te Ua Jew' or 'Te Ua a peacable Jew'.[96] He described his homeland, the Taranaki, as 'waahi o Keenana' (the land of Canaan) and 'Iharaaira' (Israel) while the land-hungry Pakeha were 'nga Paarihi' (the Pharisees).[97] The Old Testament was integral to the teachings of the other great prophet of the 1860s, Te Kooti Arikirangi. Te Kooti saw himself as a Maori Moses, a leader who would free a persecuted group from bondage and functioned as a conduit for God's instructions to his Chosen People. In services, parables, and prophecies Te Kooti consistently identified Maori as the Israelites and Pakeha as the Egyptian oppressors.[98] Over the next two decades, Te Kooti delivered a series of parables promising that he would drive the 'wicked' out of the Promised Land.[99] These parables were the product of a powerful concordance between Old Testament notions of prophethood and *matakite*, the gift of foresight.[100] Te Kooti assured his followers that divine favour insured success:

Fear not because thy cry hath reached unto God, and God hath heard thy crying, hearken I will strengthen thee and will cause thee to know the things whereof I had spoken unto your forefathers, to Abraham to Isaac to Jacob and all their children down to David.[101]

As this quotation shows, the Maori identification with the Israelites had gone beyond a simple analogy between the Maori and Israelite experience of oppression. Te Kooti insisted that Abraham, Isaac, Jacob and David were the forefathers of Maori. Te Ua also insisted that Maori actually were Jews. 'Ua Rongopai' ends with the injunction: 'kei hoki ki te Whare o Taapeta, engari e hoki ki te Whare o Heema' –'Do not return to the House of Japheth, but return to the House of Shem'.[102] Te Ua accepted the threefold division of humanity into the descendants of Japheth (Taapeta), Shem (Heema) and Ham (Hama) conveyed in missionary translations and texts.[103] It is important to note that just as there was a powerful similarity between the gifts of prophethood and *matakite*, the Old Testament's strong emphasis on genealogy was in keeping with Maori tradition where, as we have seen, *whakapapa* was fundamental to individual or group identity. In fact Christianity and pre-colonial tradition became increasingly imbricated and as Christianity spread, many Maori *whakapapa* (genealogies) began to assimilate the genealogies of the Old Testament. Noa (Noah) and Heema (Shem) began to appear as ancestral names in Maori genealogies which defined the history and identity of the kin-group.[104] But in the new world of the 1860s these genealogies were increasingly recorded in a written form: Maori and Judeo-Christian elements were woven together in new printed narratives and genealogies, which enjoyed the authority that Pakeha, and increasingly Maori, conferred upon the printed word.

Conclusion

These new hybridised visions of tradition are a telling emblem of the profound impact of both print and the Bible on Maori mentalities. If we examine the King Movement, the range of Maori sectarian identities or Maori prophetic traditions, we can see a weaving together of the old and the new. The dominant models in New Zealand historiography – 'the fatal impact' or 'cultural continuity' arguments – fail to illuminate the con-structive and creative response of Maori to the rapid and painful changes wrought by colonialism. Certainly old values and traditions were challenged and re-evaluated: the old men who signed the Treaty of Waitangi struggled with the new world of the 1860s. By this time indigenous society and culture were increasingly hybridised, as Maori embraced many Judaeo-Christian ideas as well as drawing upon those elements of tradition which remained powerful. In the new and mixed world of a colonial society some degree of accommodation was inevitable. The dynamism of these cross-cultural exchanges, where Christianity and tradition were interwoven and literacy and oral tradition were frequently interdependent, is a powerful reminder of the ability of 'traditional' societies to adapt quickly and effectively to new technologies, ideas and political orders: an insight of some importance in this age of globalisation where technology and social communication are changing so rapidly.

NOTES

1 R. Cawardine, *Trans-Atlantic Revivalism: Popular Evangelicalism in Britain and America, 1790–1865* (Westport, CT, 1978); R. E. Davies, *Jonathan Edwards and his Influence on the Development of the Missionary Movement from Britain* (Position paper 6, North Atlantic Missiology Project, Cambridge, 1996); John B. Frantz, 'The awakening of religion among the German settlers in the middle colonies', *William and Mary Quarterly* 3rd series 33 (1976), 266–88; J. Mason, *Moravian Connections with English Calvinists during the Missionary Awakening in England, 1770 to 1790* (Position paper 3, North Atlantic Missiology Project, Cambridge, 1996) and *The Influence of Moravian Missionary Thought on the British Missionary Movement* (Position paper 18, North Atlantic Missiology Project, Cambridge, 1996); M. A. Noll, D. W. Bebbington and G.A. Rawlyk (eds), *Evangelicalism: Comparative Studies of Popular Protestantism in North America, the British Isles and Beyond, 1700–1900* (Oxford, 1994). A National University of Ireland, Galway Millennium Fund Grant assisted the research for this chapter. The author would like to thank Chris Bayly, Elizabeth Eisenstein, William O'Reilly and, especially, Niall Ó Ciosáin for their responses to earlier versions of this paper.

2 Jonathan Edwards, *An Account of the Life of the late Reverend Mr David Brainerd: Minister of the Gospel* (Edinburgh, 1765).

3 Andrew Porter, 'North American experience and British missionary encounters in Africa and the Pacific, *c.* 1800–50', in Martin Daunton and Rick Halpern (eds), *Empire and Others: British Encounters with Indigenous Peoples 1600–1850* (London, 1999), p. 348; D. W. Bebbington, *Evangelicalism in Modern Britain: A History from the 1730s through to the 1980s* (London, 1989), p. 42.

4 Susan O'Brien, 'A transatlantic community of Saints: the great awakening and the first evangelical network, 1735–1755', *American Historical Review* 91 (1986), 813.

5 Mary Louise Pratt, *Imperial Eyes: Travel Writing and Transculturation* (London, 1992), p. 7.

6 On 'appropriation' see Roger Chartier, 'Culture as appropriation: popular cultural uses in early modern France', in Steven L. Kaplan (ed.), *Understanding Popular Culture: Europe from the Middle Ages to the Nineteenth Century* (Berlin, 1984), pp. 229–53.

7 'Pakeha' is the Maori word commonly used by all New Zealanders to designate the non-Maori population.

8 Cited in Peter Lineham, 'This is my weapon: Maori response to the Bible', in Robert Glen (ed.), *Mission and Moko: Aspects of the Work of the Church Missionary Society in New Zealand, 1814–1882* (Christchurch, 1992), p. 178.

9 Alan Moorehead, *The Fatal Impact: An Account of the Invasion of the South Pacific 1767–1840* (London, 1966). A similar argument of cultural crisis was elaborated in Harrison M. Wright, *New Zealand 1769–1840: Early Years of Western Contact* (Cambridge, Mass., 1967).

10 Gordon Parsonson, 'The literate revolution in Polynesian'?, *Journal of Pacific History* 2 (1967), 39–58.

11 Most notably: I. C. Campbell, 'Culture contact and Polynesian identity in the European age', *Journal of World History* 8 (1997), 29–55.

12 Greg Dening, 'Writing, rewriting the beach: An essay', *Rethinking History* 2 (1998), 43–72 (p. 60).

13 E.g. Kuni E. H. Jenkins, 'Te ihi, te mana, te wehi o te ao tuhi: Maori print literacy from 1814–1855: literacy, power and colonisation' (Master's thesis, University of Auckland, 1991) and *Becoming Literate, Becoming English* (Auckland, 1993).

14 For a critical evaluation of both the 'fatal impact' and 'cultural continuity' arguments see Kwen Fee Lian, 'Interpreting Maori history: A case for historical sociology', *Journal of the Polynesian Society* 96 (1987), 445–72.

15 D. F. McKenzie, *Oral Culture, Literacy and Print in Early New Zealand: The Treaty of Waitangi* (Wellington, 1985), p. 15, n. 19.

16 Carlo Ginzburg, *The Cheese and the Worms: The Cosmos of a Sixteenth-century Miller*, ed. John and Ann Tedeschi (Baltimore, 1992), pp. 27–54 (p. 32).

17 J. C. Beaglehole (ed.), *The Journals of Captain James Cook on his Voyages of Discovery:* I *The Voyage of the Endeavour 1768–1771* (Cambridge, 1968), p. 276

18 John Hawkesworth, *An Account of the Voyages Undertaken by the Order of His Present Majesty for Making Discoveries in the Southern Hemisphere*, 3 vols (London, 1773); P. J. Marshall and Glyndwr Williams, *The Great Map of Mankind: British Perceptions of the World in the Age of Enlightenment* (London, 1992), p. 258.

19 Dening, 'Rewriting the beach', p. 170.

20 R. D. Altick, *Victorian People and Ideas* (London, 1974), p. 191. More recently David Bebbington has identified 'biblicism' as one of the four fundamental traits of evangelical faith (along with activism, conversionism and crucicentrism). Bebbington, *Evangelicalism*, pp. 5–17, especially 12–14.

21 Elisabeth Jay, *The Religion of the Heart: Anglican Evangelicalism and the Nineteenth-Century Novel* (Oxford, 1979), p. 148; Altick, *Victorian People and Ideas*, p. 192.

22 Leslie Howsam, *Cheap Bibles: Nineteenth-century Publishing and the British and Foreign Bible Society* (Cambridge, 1991).

23 David Vincent, *Literacy and Popular Culture: England 1750–1914* (Cambridge, 1989), p. 174.

24 R. P. Heitzenrater, *The Elusive Mr Wesley:* I, *John Wesley – His Own Biographer* (Nashville, 1984), 149; Bebbington, *Evangelicalism*, p. 68

25 *Ibid.*

26 Vincent, *Literacy and Popular Culture*, p. 175.

27 See, for example, the discussion of religious tracts and popular culture in Niall
    Ó Ciosáin, *Print and Popular Culture in Ireland, 1750–1850* (Basingstoke, 1997),
    pp. 132–53.
28 R .D. Altick, *The English Common Reader: A Social History of the Mass Reading
    Public, 1800–1900* (Chicago, 1957), p. 392. In 1810 *The Edinburgh Review* printed
    12,000 copies of each edition: John Clive, *Scottish Reviewers: The Edinburgh Review,
    1802–1815* (London, 1956), p. 134.
29 Periodicals aimed at the juvenile market proliferated in the 1840s: examples
    include *Juvenile Missionary Magazine* (London Missionary Society, 1844–94),
    Children's Missionary Monthly Newsletter (Inter-denominational, 1843–61) and the
    Church Missionary Juvenile Instructor (Church Missionary Society, 1844–90).
    Journals targeted specifically at women enjoyed greater popularity in the second half
    of the nineteenth century, reflecting the rising involvement of women in the mission
    field: titles such as *The Indian Female Evangelist* (Inter-denominational, 1872–93);
    India's Women (Church of England Zenana Missionary Society, 1881–95) and
    Quarterly News of Woman's Work (London Missionary Society, 1887–95: circulation
    c. 10,000) were largely aimed at a female readership.
30 *Church Missionary Society Proceedings* (1811), p. 201.
31 Claudius Buchanan, *Colonial Ecclesiastical Establishment* (London, 1813); Claudius
    Buchanan, 'The Three Eras of light' in *Eight Sermons* (London, 1812), p. 275.
32 Buchanan, *Colonial Ecclesiastical Establishment*, p. 112.
33 Cited in Andrew Porter, 'Religion, missionary enthusiasm and empire', in Andrew
    Porter (ed.), *The Oxford History of the British Empire:* III *The Nineteenth Century*
    (Oxford, 1999), p. 223.
34 W. Stafford, 'Religion and the doctrine of nationalism in England at the time of
    French Revolution and the Napoleonic Wars', in S. Mews (ed.), *Religion and
    National Identity* (Oxford, 1982), p. 385.
35 *Missionary Register*, Nov. 1816, pp. 470–1.
36 *Ibid.*
37 Lamin Sanneh, *Translating the Message: The Missionary Impact on Culture* (New York,
    1989).
38 *Ibid.*, pp. 50–87. The *Qur'an* itself denotes Arabic (and the very text) as *i'jaz*
    'inimitable eloquence'. See, for example, *Qur'an* 10: 38–9; 11: 1–2; 28: 49.
39 Sanneh, *Translating the Message*, 3, pp. 88–101.
40 Rosane Rocher, 'British Orientalism in the eighteenth century: the dialectics of
    knowledge and government', in Carol Breckenridge and Peter van der Veer (eds),
    Orientalism and the Postcolonial Predicament: Perspectives on South Asia (Philadelphia,
    1993), pp. 215–45.
41 Rosane Rocher, *Orientalism, Poetry, and the Millennium: The Checkered Life of
    Nathaniel Brassey Halhed, 1751–1830* (Delhi, 1983); Richard Steadman-Jones,
    'Colonialism and linguistic knowledge: John Gilchrist and the representation of
    Urdu in the late eighteenth and early nineteenth centuries' (PhD thesis, University of
    Cambridge, 1998).
42 S. P. Carey, *William Carey, DD, Fellow of Linnaean Society* (London, 1926); William
    Carey, *A Grammar of the Bengalee Language* (Serampore, 1801); *A Grammar of the
    Mahratta Language* (Serampore, 1805); *A Grammar of the Sungskrit Language, Composed
    from the Works of the Most Esteemed Hindoo Grammarians* (Serampore, 1804).
43 Samuel Marsden to Josiah Pratt, 28 June 1808, *Marsden and the New Zealand
    Mission: Sixteen Letters*, ed. P. Havard-Williams (Dunedin, 1961), p. 19.
44 Marsden to Pratt, 28 August 1809, *ibid.*, pp. 22–3.

45 Thomas Kendall, *A Korao no New Zealand; or, the New Zealander's First Book; being An Attempt to compose some Lessons for the Instruction of the Natives* (Sydney, 1815), pp. 22–3.

46 John Owens, 'Religious disputation at Whangaroa 1823–7', *Journal of the Polynesian Society* 79 (1970), 289–90; Herb Kawainui Kane, 'Comment', *Current Anthropology* 38 (1997), 265.

47 *Missionary Register* (1819), p. 466; A. J. Ballantyne, 'Imperial networks, ethnography and identity in colonial India and New Zealand' (PhD thesis, University of Cambridge, 1999), pp. 125–33.

48 Kendall, *A Korao no New Zealand*, pp. 32–3, 34–5.

49 *Ibid.*, pp. 30–1.

50 Compare the nineteen consonants (including 'ng') of Kendall and Lee's Grammar with the nine consonants of the later grammars. Eventually ten consonants were settled upon, with the aspirated form 'wh' differentiated from 'w'. See Colenso's comments on this process: William Colenso, *Fifty Years Ago in New Zealand: a Commemoration: a Jubilee Paper: a Retrospect: a plain and true story read before the Hawke's Bay Philosophical Institute, October 17th, 1887* (Napier, 1888), pp. 24–7, 47–9.

51 Church Missionary Society [Thomas Kendall and Samuel Lee], *A Grammar and Vocabulary of the Language of New Zealand* (London, 1820), pp. 114–24.

52 Peter J. Lineham, *The Bible Society in New Zealand* (Wellington, 1996), pp. 7–13.

53 Nathaniel Turner to Wesleyan Missionary Society, 27 May 1836, reprinted in *Missionary Notices*, 256 (Apr. 1857), pp. 453–4.

54 *Missionary Register* (1840), 512 and (1841), 510; Wright, *New Zealand, 1769–1840*, p. 53. D. F. McKenzie has questioned the value of these statistics, noting that measurement in sheets is the standard form used by printers and bibliographers. Using this measurement he calculates the output of the mission press at 145,775 completed sheets. He further notes that these sheets represented only sixteen distinct works. But McKenzie's figures need to be contextualised against the size of Maori society: a total population of about 70,000 in 1840 and the 25,000 or so Maori in the missionary's sphere of influence. In the 1835–40 period the Paihia Press produced approximately 5,400 copies of the New Testament (122,500 of the 145,775 completed sheets) which is a significant output in relation to this small population.

55 Robert Maunsell to CMS (Christian Missionary Society), 8 June 1840, C.N. 064, Hocken Library, Dunedin.

56 Tom Griffiths, 'Boundaries of the sacred: the Williams family in New Zealand, 1823–30', *Journal of Religious History* 13 (1984), 40.

57 James Busby to Lt Gov. Arthur, 16 August 1833, qMS–0352, Alexander Turnbull Library, Wellington.

58 *Proceedings of the Church Missionary Society*, 1838–9, pp. 144–6.

59 R. M. Ross, 'Te Tiriti o Waitangi: texts and translations', *New Zealand Journal of History* 6 (1972), 136.

60 *Ibid.*, 135–57; Claudia Orange, *The Treaty of Waitangi* (Wellington, 1987), pp. 40–3.

61 E.g. Ranginui Walker, *Ka whawhai tonu matou: Struggle Without End* (Auckland, 1990), pp. 81–2, 85–7, 90–7.

62 Anon., 'New Zealand – The Aborigines and Their Language', *Fisher's Colonial Magazine and Colonial Maritime Journal* 2 (Jan.–Apr. 1843), 455.

63 *Ibid.*, 456–7.

64 E. Wakefield, 'The New Zealand language', *Fisher's Colonial Magazine and Colonial Maritime Journal* 2 n.s. (1845), 281.

65 *Ibid.*, 284.
66 E. J. Wakefield, *Adventure in New Zealand* (Christchurch, 1908 [1837]), p. 194.
67 C.J. Parr, 'Maori literacy 1843–1867', *Journal of the Polynesian Society* 72 (1963), 211–34.
68 Lineham, *Bible Society*, pp. 21–3.
69 The centrality of accumulation in kin group rivalries see Ann Parsonson, 'The expansion of a competitive society', *New Zealand Journal of History* 14 (1980), 45–60
70 McKenzie, *Oral Culture, Lieracy and Print in Early New Zealand*, p. 30.
71 *Ibid.*
72 This literacy test is borrowed from David Cressy, *Literacy and the Social Order: Writing and Reading in Tudor England* (Cambridge, 1980), p. 53.
73 Keith Thomas, 'The meaning of literacy in early modern England', 102–3. On this disjunction in Maori society see n. 78 below.
74 Some chiefs, however, did send their children to missionary schools. See Patricia Bawden, 'The mechanic missionaries: how effective were they?' in Robert Glen (ed.), *Mission and Moko: Aspects of the Work of the Church Missionary Society in New Zealand, 1814–1882* (Christchurch, 1992), p. 41.
75 Ballantyne, 'Imperial networks, ethnography and identity', pp. 177–8, 244.
76 For a discussion of the role of slavery in pre-colonial Maori society see F. Allan Hanson and Louise Hanson, *Counterpoint in Maori Culture* (London, 1983), pp. 178–85.
77 Brownyn Elsmore, *Like Them That Dream: The Maori and the Old Testament* (Tauranga, 1985), p. 25; Lyndsay Head and Buddy Mikaere, 'Was 19th century Maori society literate?', *Archifacts* 2 (1988), 17–20; Shef Rogers, 'Crusoe among the Maori: translation and colonial acculturation in Victorian New Zealand', *Book History* 1 (1998), 182–95.
78 A. S. Thomson, *The Story of New Zealand*, 2 vols (London, 1859), II, p. 297.
79 Waitangi Tribunal, *Report of the Waitangi Tribunal on the Orakei Claim* (Wellington, 1987), section 4.1.
80 R. G. Jameson, *New Zealand, South Australia and New South Wales* (London, 1841), pp. 260–2.
81 On a discussion of print and the disembodiment of knowledge among South Asian Muslims, see Francis Robinson, 'Islam and the impact of print in South Asia' in Nigel Crook (ed.), *The Transmission of Knowledge in South Asia: Essays on Education, Religion, History and Politics* (Delhi, 1996), pp. 62–97.
82 James Cowan, *The New Zealand Wars: A History of the Maori Campaigns and the Pioneering Period*, 2 vols (Wellington, 1922), I, p. 446.
83 Lindsay Cox notes that a Maori Bible was prominent in the ritual of coronation and this same Bible has been used in the coronation of the five subsequent monarchs. Lindsay Cox, *Kotahitanga: The Maori Search for Political Unity* (Auckland, 1993), p. 52.
84 *The New Zealander*, 3 July 1858.
85 Frances Porter (ed.), *The Turanga Journals* (Wellington, 1974), p. 592.
86 Tamati Hapimana, Te Rangituawaru, Tamihana Ratapu and Te Waka Perohuka, 'Reply from Ngati Kahungunu, No. 1', 14 July 1860, *Great Britain Parliamentary Papers*, 1861 (2789), 101.
87 James Belich, *Making Peoples: A History of the New Zealanders from Polynesian Settlement to the End of the Nineteenth Century* (Auckland, 1996), p. 219.
88 Maori in the north of North Island were suspicious of the French, who they called 'wi-wis' or 'oui-ouis', in the wake of reprisals following the death of the explorer

Marion du Fresne. Hugh Carleton, *The Life of Henry Williams* (Wellington, 1948), pp. 254–5. British missionaries also feared that the French might pre-empt the annexation of New Zealand, and in the wake of annexation French influence was suspected to lie behind Maori resistance to the Treaty of Waitangi and the northern war of 1845–6. William Colenso, *The Authentic and Genuine History of the signing of the Treaty of Waitangi* (Wellington, 1890), p. 34; James Stack to CMS, 4 April 1840, Hocken Library and Archives, Dunedin, CN/O78.

89 William Colenso, *He Pukapuka Waki; he wakakite atu i nga henga o te Hahi o Roma* [A Book of Errors, revealing the errors of the Church of Rome] (Paihia, 1840); *Ko te tuarua o nga Pukapuka Waki* [The Second Book of Errors] (Paihia, 1840).

90 Jean Baptiste Francois Pompallier, *Early History of the Catholic Church in Oceania* (Auckland, 1888), p. 44.

91 Jane Thomson, 'The Roman Catholic mission in New Zealand, 1838–1870' (MA thesis, Victoria University of Wellington, 1966).

92 Especially Bronwyn Elsmore, *Mana from Heaven: A Century of Maori Prophets in New Zealand* (Tauranga, 1989) and *Like Them That Dream: The Maori and the Old Testament* (Tauranga, 1985).

93 John Gorst, *The Maori King* (Auckland, 1959 [1864]), p. 103.

94 Cited in Elsmore, *Like Them That Dream*, pp. 72–3.

95 Pai Marire means 'good and peaceful'. The followers of Te Ua would repeatedly chant 'hau' as a charm as they went into battle, hence the name 'Hauhau'.

96 Paul Clark, *'Hauhau': The Pai Marire search for Maori identity* (Auckland, 1975), p. 17.

97 Lyndsay Head, 'The Gospel of Te Ua Haumene', *Journal of the Polynesian Society* 101 (1992), 14–15, 16–17, 28–9.

98 Greenwood, *The Upraised Hand* (Wellington, 1942), p. 25; W. Hugh Ross, *Te Kooti Rikirangi: General and Prophet* (Auckland, 1966), p. 52.

99 Judith Binney, 'Myth and explanation in the Ringatu tradition', *Journal of the Polynesian Society* 93 (1984), 368–70.

100 *Ibid.*, 348.

101 Ross, *Te Kooti*, 31

102 Head, 'The Gospel of Te Ua Haumene', pp. 28–9.

103 For example one 1847 CMS text described Europeans as the descendants of 'Hapeta' (Japheth): CMS, *He Whakapapa, ara Nga Mahi menga aha noa a te Atua raua ko tana Hahi* (Auckland, 1847).

104 L. G. Kelly, 'Some problems in the study of Maori genealogies', *Journal of the Polynesian Society* 49 (1940), 241.

10 Informing Empire and Nation: Publicity, Propaganda and the Press 1880–1920

C. A. Bayly

This chapter suggests that the British Empire of the later nineteenth century can be rewardingly studied as an extended political arena which saw an unprecedented globalisation of information alongside novel attempts by governments and elites to control its diffusion. Anthropologists and sociologists have recently become interested in the formation of global society and international public culture, but a strong historical perspective is absent from most of their work.[1] To some extent, of course, human society has always been 'globalised', if only by the long-distance migration of human communities and by the spread of the world's great religions. Historians, however, are in strong position to discuss ruptures – points at which new and dynamic forces of globalisation became apparent – and in doing so examine the claims made for the revolutionary character of contemporary developments.

The expansion of the European empires can been seen as one violent aspect of the early stages of the building of international society. European conquest and settlement linked previously loosely connected world civilisations through networks of military coercion and communications. Scholars have recently filled out the older narrative of imperial annexations with studies of the multi-lateral exchange of geographical, botanical, linguistic and scientific knowledge which accompanied it. This process is now no longer seen as a purely Eurocentric one. Much more is now known about the parallel global growth of non-European diasporas – slave and free – which accompanied the expansion of Europe.[2] Historians and literary historians have meanwhile debated the representations and knowledge forms by which these new experiences of discovery, conquest and exploitation were domesticated into existing systems of knowledge: physiocracy, Scottish enlightenment developmental stage theory and, latterly, scientific racism. More and more sophisticated studies have also appeared analysing non-European responses and reactions to these territorial and cultural incursions.

Two broad but complementary approaches could be taken to characterise the historical writing on empire as the globalisation of knowledge. The first approach comprises what we might call the horizontal interpretation in that it stresses intercontinental exchange. Typical works of this sort include Ian K. Steele's studies of communication during the first British Atlantic Empire and Thomas Richards, *The Imperial Archive*.[3] Peter Marshall and Glyndwyr Williams, *The Great Map of Mankind*,[4] again, showed metropolitan thinkers assimilating and comparing observations and prejudices gleaned from a wide range of travels and new international contacts. In all these interpretations, the technical expansion of communications plays a critical role in the argument, though change is understood to derive from ideological as well as technical innovation.

The second approach – the lateral interpretation – is more anthropological in feel. Benedict Anderson's *Imagined Communities* is its best-known representative.[5] This approach examines the ways in which groups in different societies received and transformed messages and representations from within themselves and from across cultural borders. It is concerned with how such messages relate to structures of power and prevailing ideologies. It consists in analysing the properties of what is called here the 'information orders' of different human communities as they have evolved over time.[6] Information orders were influenced by, but cannot simply be reduced to the social, ideological or political structures of different societies. They can display markedly different characteristics at similar levels of economic and political change. So, for instance, the use of block-printing, associated with Buddhist and Confucian orthopraxy, was much more general in coastal China and Japan than it was in the middle east and south Asia which demonstrated roughly similar levels of pre-colonial economic development. In turn, these long-standing information orders influenced the way in which new messages derived from the globalisation of communication were received in east Asia.[7]

This chapter will employ both of these broad approaches in analysing the evolution of the British Empire and colonial nationalisms as systems of information between 1860 and the First World War. The process was a dialectical one. The international spread of communications and the discourses associated with western expansion were assimilated, moulded or rejected by publicists in different societies. They were transformed and diffused along lines created by the internal networks of specific information orders. Later, they were propelled back into metropolitan debate by colonial writers or early nationalists. More tenuous links of communication also developed between different extra-European societies, between the Islamic modernists of Cairo and Bombay, for instance.

If we think of the horizontal expansion of communication during the expansion of Europe as a form of globalisation we might consider three phases. First, in the fifteenth to early eighteenth century, European trading diasporas, often armed and predatory, expanded in competition with non-European commercial and cultural migrations. These reflected, but also stimulated, the growth of world trade and consumption. The contingent non-European diasporas included Muslim trading and cultural networks throughout Asia and north Africa and the Chinese commercial diaspora in the Indian Ocean and South China Seas.[8] During the early modern period, the formation of western knowledge of the world was powered by commercial fact-finding and the birth of colonies of settlement, but new observations were fitted into broad renaissance typologies of barbarism and civilisation.

The next main phase, from 1750 to 1850, witnessed the establishment of European-style armies in parts of Asia and Africa and dense settler populations in the Americas, Africa and Australasia. The bearers of information between metropolis and colony now needed to take a much closer interest in the medical topography, revenue and crop-bearing capacity of the new dependencies and of the military resources of remaining indigenous states. Knowledge and representations of knowledge were still largely cast in the form of Scottish enlightenment and French models for universal civilisation and this still enshrined a cultural and evolutionist rather than a biological and conflict-driven understanding of human progress. Captain Cook's 'Voyages' and the Napoleonic *Description de l'Egypte* were classic artefacts of this phase.

The third and fourth phases of modern globalisation were also driven by new international forms of communication and the massive expansion of capitalism. The impact of the global stockmarket, computer, television and Internet marks our current phase. In the late nineteenth century, however, the key changes registered the advent of the electric telegraph, the international posting of stock market listings, the steamship, mass publishing and the spread of press syndicates. These changes were cumulative, interconnected and registered themselves in the realm of culture, but technical changes certainly underpinned them. Key dates here include the laying of the Government of India's Persian Gulf Telegraph Line in 1863 and the opening of two Atlantic cables in 1866.[9] In 1876 Australia and New Zealand were linked to Europe. African submarine telegraphs had been laid by 1889. No less important, however, were the attempts to control and channel information as Reuters and other news agencies spread through Asia in the 1860s.[10] Mass newspaper publication, which took off in Britain, Europe and America in the 1880s,[11] imposed new formats on news, but also allowed powerful political figures to influence its diffusion.

States – domestic and colonial – responded to the gathering velocity of communication with new weapons of censorship and surveillance.

While the revolution in communication empowered various groups of activists, it also provided novel means of control by which states and elites could influence what people thought. As we know, the rise of colonial nationalism in the late nineteenth century was marked by the emergence of communities of readers of printed information within colonial societies. But nationalists also attempted to bypass local colonial governments and exploit these new informational skills in London, Paris and Lausanne. In the process, they learned from each other. Thus Indian, Egyptian and Irish nationalists borrowed and concerted with each other from the 1870s onwards.[12] Nationalism, like the purposive imperialism of the late nineteenth century was globalised, and by much the same series of events. To imagine the Nation and the Empire, people had also to imagine an international ordering and hierarchy.

The expansion of information skills was received unequally in different colonial societies. This is where the second, more anthropological approach may help us. The form of imperial rule and of nationalist mobilisation was moulded by the information orders of the various colonised societies. These information orders, in turn, reflected the *longue durée* of knowledge-use and information projection within indigenous societies and also the specific interests of different colonial powers.

In India, as I tried to show in my book *Empire and Information*, colonial knowledge was more than an epiphenomenon of the process of dominion. But it was, indeed, driven centrally by the imperative of land-revenue collection and military control. Up to the 1840s, the British were dependent on the expertise of native writers, informants, runners and intelligencers who had been central to the pre-colonial systems of revenue extraction and arbitration. India was already a literacy-aware, if not a highly literate society. Huge volumes of information moved around the subcontinent outside the purview of the colonial power. This explains the paradox of the existence of the massive, detailed archival effort of the East India Company and Crown alongside sudden collapses of British knowledge and power. These collapses were accompanied by information panics when the colonial authorities lashed out desperately at the chimeras they saw haunting them: stranglers in the 1830s, Muslim fanatics in 1857, Indian 'Fenians' – the phrase was often used – in the 1880s, and Bengali anarchists in the 1900s.

Let us consider two other contemporary colonial societies, Malaya and Egypt, where different styles of information order moulded the confrontation between British power and indigenous leaderships. In the Malay world the early burst of enlightenment knowledge-collection, pioneered by Stamford Raffles and John Crawfurd in the 1810s, was not maintained.[13] Commercial interests were not afforced with a drive for revenue and an engagement with the peasantry, as in India. Officials in the 1880s mourned the complete stagnation of British knowledge about either Malay or Chinese. Only Christian missionary institutions continued to accumulate random material about local peoples.

It was not until the 1890s that the British government and indigenous elites in the Malay and overseas Chinese worlds began again to collect, codify and publish material relating to Malayan society on a large scale. Whereas fairly full gazetteer and census material was published from the 1850s in India, there was a fifty-year gap in southeast Asia. When, after 1890, this changed, the impetus came partly from the expansion of trading interests in rubber and tin. It also resulted from a colonial information panic about the rise of Pan-Islamic consciousness in the Muslim east and the Confucian revival in the South China Sea.[14] This conjunction is not surprising. The growth of commercial information was almost always accompanied by, or lodged within a deepening range of cultural and political contacts. Thus, rising exports of East Asian produce resulted in the growth of Muslim pilgrimage to Mecca and Medina and a countervailing flow of Pan-Islamic ideas back to southeast Asia. The very concentrated expansion of bureaucratic knowledge and social communication which took place after 1890 was, however, segmented into Chinese and Malay subsets to a much greater extent than it had been even between the con-structed categories of 'Hindu' and 'Muslim' in India. To adapt the dictum of the twentieth-century century scholar-administrator, J. S. Furnivall, Malaya was a bifurcated informational order, just as it was a plural society. This profoundly affected the nature of Malaya's nationalisms and Malayan people's understanding of modernity in the twentieth century.

Egypt, occupied by Britain after 1882, displays yet another pattern. Here the British rested on the detailed system of surveillance and control which had been built up by the khedives, the Egyptian viceroys, on a French model, since 1802.[15] The pattern of local control by gentry literati, which could also be seen in post-Mughal north India, was deeper and more pervasive in Egypt. Social communication was dense because of the intellectual connections of the village landholder with the Cairo teaching mosques and the close articulation of Egypt's produce markets in cotton and grain. The khedives had instituted censuses, poll taxes and revenue information; labour was tightly accounted. This system of surveillance the British used to some effect after the occupation of 1882.[16]

As with India, again, this was a literacy-aware society, but not a highly literate one. A small elite of sophisticated professional people and landlords, armed with a rapidly developing press, dominated a poor, but by no means ill-informed population. The British never, however, established any degree of cultural hegemony even to the extent they did in India. The Islamic and Arabic teaching system stretching from the al-Azhar mosque in Cairo to the countryside and on to the wider Muslim world was powerful and flexible.[17] European influences were anyway predominantly French, not English; nationalist newspapers were able to dodge British press restrictions by claiming French protection.[18] Those French connections stretched to Paris, Lausanne and Brussels, without benefit of the British media. Egypt was therefore informationally ungovernable long before it rose in outright rebellion in the aftermath of the First World War. In Egypt, the British had acquired little cultural legitimacy. Their legal and conceptual categories had only minimal influence on indigenous Egyptian perceptions of themselves.

The chapter now investigates several of these themes in greater detail. In particular it assesses the changes in information diffusion and the concomitant rise of new globalising ideologies within the British Empire between 1860 and 1914. It also shows how early nationalists and reformers were able to begin to turn these changes to their advantage. First, however, the chapter will try to show how what, for risk of jargon, might be called an 'information' approach to social and political history can illuminate one major event in the contest between empire and popular unrest. This was the foundation in 1885 of the Indian National Congress.

The early Congress, along with the Egyptian movement of 1882, was the most powerful challenge to imperial control within the non-white British Empire. Conventionally, the emergence of organised nationalism has been seen as a product of social strains in India after the Rebellion of 1857. The argument goes that the growing professional and merchant class was alienated from government by its lack of access to wealth and preferment.[19] More recently, historians have turned from various forms of materialist social analysis to the analysis of discourse. Partha Chatterjee and Sudipta Kaviraj, among others, have discussed the appropriation by nationalist ideologues, especially in Bengal, of the statist and racialist assumptions of contemporary European thought.[20]

Yet the early Congress was much more than a reflection of ideological appropriation and social strains. It was specifically designed as a movement of publicity, communication and sociability. Its leaders sought to communicate the fears of the people to the rulers and to stir debate amongst the people about the poverty of the subcontinent. It was consciously designed to exploit the informational order of colonial India and the subcontinent's links to Britain. An explosion of English-language and vernacular newspapers fed with information by the new cable service promoted knowledge of Irish and radical agitations within and outside the British parliament.[21] Information about radical liberalism and early socialism in Britain and about pan-Islamic movements in the Ottoman Empire made Indians aware of the wider background to their demands for political representation. To imagine a national community, Indian nationalists had also to imagine, and to begin to create political connections for a global struggle for self-determination.

The British and Irish leaders of the early Congress movement are no longer fashionable figures. But they were critically important both in terms of the legitimacy they conferred on indigenous debate and because of the publicity in Britain which they were able to summon up. They were experts in communication above all. The founder of the Congress, Allan Octavian Hume, was, we need to remember, son of the Scots radical politician, Joseph Hume, a long-time critic of the East India Company.[22] Even as an officer in the Indian Civil Service, Hume believed that a vigorous free press would make government more open and accountable and hence more popular. According to him, official deafness to popular discontent voiced in the vernacular press allowed the Rebellion of 1857–9 to gain momentum. In 1863, Hume, then a district magistrate, founded *The People's Friend* at which he hoped would be popular journal of loyal opposition.[23]

The idea of pre-empting further rebellion by communicating the people's woes to government lay behind Hume's urgent search for an all-India political organisation in the 1870s and 1880s. His biographer, William Wedderburn, another early Congress leader, recalled that Hume's fears came to a head in the early 1880s when he learned from what were said to be Indian informants of the depth of hostility to the government around the country. He was most impressed by the warnings of the itinerant Hindu monks who were 'an important factor in the Indian problem'. Some of these, Wedderburn reported, were imposters but most were 'of the highest quality, like the ancient Hebrew Prophets' who gave moral instruction to the populace.[24] According to Wedderburn, some of these men had lent Hume the ledgers in which they kept the regular letters of their disciples. This correspondence revealed an acute level of distress and deep grievances against the government.

Here Hume and his supporters seem almost to be throwing into reverse the reasoning behind the traditional information panics of the Anglo-Indian bureaucracy. We must fear the night-time murmurings and secret messages of the natives, he implies. But we must bring discontent out into the open and use a National Congress to pre-empt a new Indian Mutiny. Conversely, it is revealing that the government agencies enlisted to spy on the early Congress leadership were lineal descendants of the venerable Thuggee and Dacoity Department founded in the 1830s to unearth the dastardly plots of the stranglers.[25] The Viceroy, Lord Dufferin, proprietor of the Clandeboye estate near Belfast, brought to bear another version of colonial information panic on the issue. He decided to discourage Hume and the Congress on the grounds that it was a similar organisation to the Irish Land League and was distributing seditious literature in the countryside.[26]

William Wedderburn's treatment of this aspect of the early Congress movement is, however, rather ambivalent. For Hume and a substantial section of the early Congress leadership were heavily influenced by the ideas of the Theosophical Society about occult communication. The Indian holy men Wedderburn mentions were apparently not merely Indian monks and renouncers, but included spiritualist adepts. Theosophy had been spreading rapidly in India after 1879 when its major proponents, Col. Olcott and Madame Blavatsky, had reached India, ostensibly to sit at the feet of Swami Dayananda Saraswati, founder of the Arya Samaj or Aryan society which was an important movement of religious reform within Hindu society.[27]

Blavatsky and Olcott, however, went their own way, establishing theosophical lodges throughout the subcontinent, especially among lawyers, journalists and other high caste intelligentsia in southern and western India. The aim of the movement was to tap into the ancient wisdom of India through the medium of occult knowledge. This knowledge was to be derived from a group of Mahatmas or Great Souls who resided in the Himalayas. According to Olcott and Blavatsky, the occult brotherhood had worked through all history in the interests of creating a New Mankind. They had headed off revolutionary violence in France in 1848 and had helped the British power[28] during the Mutiny of 1857. Now in the early 1880s, it warned Hume through its chief adept, Koot Homi, that a new Mutiny was at hand.[29]

Indian Nationalism, of course, was much more than a 'derivative discourse' of western statism or occult romanticism. It rooted itself in and was imbricated by living Indian traditions of Indo-Islamic political ethics and right government.[30] India during this period exhibited a bifurcated information order. The widest audience could be reached by blending together the ideas of traditional patriotism with theosophy and Anglo-Celtic agrarian radicalism. The organisation's early leaders realised this. They distibuted 50,000 copies of a pamphlet, *A Conversation between Moulvee Furreedoodeen and one Rambuksh of Kumbakhtpur* throughout the Indian Empire.[31] This little book, widely called the 'Congress catechism', adopted the traditional dialogue, now used increasingly in government school books, to interrogate the weaknesses of government policy.

Congress leaders believed that Indian representation and publicity in the metropolis was also crucial. It was intended to form a powerful lobby in London. Though this effort failed in the short term, Indian editors and politicians of the nascent associations tried to influence the new British public which had been created by the Third Reform Bill.[32] Campaigns were mounted to get Indian representatives into Parliament in 1885 and Indian press offices and associations were set up in London.

The issue of spiritualism, Empire and nationalism provides a good example of how new ideologies as well as new media were set to work in the later nineteenth-century world. It reminds us that information revolutions which purport to diffuse useful and rational knowledge to mankind have often proved to be niches for adepts of occult, secret knowledges and forms of communication. The sixteenth-century revolution in printing and its networks of humanist correspondents had allowed secret neo-platonic and magical lore to circulate, for instance. Even in the present era, the computer and Internet revolution was initially powered by counter-culturists and new-lifers, as much as by the military and capitalism. In its maturity the technology has also fostered conspiracy theorists, obsessive genealogists, astrologers and esoteric religious sects.

The changes of the nineteenth century allowed theosophy to propagate itself, moving backwards and forwards between east and west. A. P. Sinnett, editor of the Anglo-Indian newspaper, *The Pioneer*, who had been present at Hume's and Blavatsky's seances at Simla in 1881, later went on to reorganise theosophy in London. He remained in contact with the men who tried to put the Indian problem in front of the expanded British electorate in the general election of 1885.[33] His book, *The Occult World*, neatly captured the conceptual link between international spiritualism and the expanding information networks of empire. Sinnett's works, for instance, became a formative influence on the romantic Irish nationalism of the young W. B. Yeats.[34] Theosophy, Sinnett wrote, was not arcane religious lore. It was instead hard, modern, scientific fact. It was 'as true as the London Post-Office Directory; as the Parliamentary reports people read in the morning are true'.[35] In this vision, the tap-tap-tap of the spirits in the seance was no different from the tap-tap-tap of the Morse codes in the telegraph room. Both brought the spirit of peoples together by ethereal messages.

That vaunted link between scientific information gathering and spiritualism was also clear in the contemporary writer, W. Scott Elliot's *The Story of Atlantis*, for which Sinnett wrote a preface. Scott Elliot's treatment of Atlantis, supposedly the last of the ancient Toltec civilisations which held sway before the emergence of the Fifth or Aryan race which 'inhabited India and colonised Egypt',[36] reads as an anthropological and racialist fiction. Or rather, it represents an even more imaginative version of the contemporary racialist and historical science. In this narrative of human history, races rose and fell, but each peak guided by the supernatural wisdom of the Ancient Seers was higher than the last. The humbler intellectual tools of imperial information-gathering were displayed here in evidence, too. Linguistic analysis was said to link the Toltecs to the ancient Mayan civilisation. Oceanographic surveys carried out by British and American gunboats 'Challenger' and 'Dolphin' provided the geological evidence for the ancient Atlantic civilisation.[37]

This discussion of what may seem a bizarre aspect of the world of early colonial nationalisms returns us to the major themes of this chapter. The global projection of imperialist and nationalist ideas between 1860 and the First World War took place in a widening space of ideology, publicity information-collection and government surveillance. Spokesmen of colonial liberation movements used the new media, but they also needed to frame their messages within a sufficiently generalised set of ideologies to influence the emerging international public. Two features broadly distinguished these ideologies from the global systems of the earlier enlightenment thinkers. First, as has often been observed, conflict, whether between races, nations, castes or classes, was particularly heavily emphasised in the age of Spencer, Marx and Gobineau. Secondly, secret and arcane knowledges, usually represented as forms of science, came increasingly to the fore. The rise of these new global doctrines was indirectly responsive to the new forms of communication. The colonial war correspondent sending his despatches along the telegraph brought constant news of distant nations and races locked in mortal conflict with each other and spread premonitions of the 'death of the native'. Equally, the mass dissemination of scientific information, from phrenology to biology, legitimated the idea that whole new realms of liberating knowledge lay just beneath the surface of human history, waiting to be made plain by masterful men, races or nations. Theosophy and racialist theory provided two doctrines particularly well adapted to the age of the telegraph, war correspondent and mass publishing, but there were others.

The collection of information by the agents of empire had never been wholly constrained within the bounds of testable scientific rationalism. The scares about the thugs, Chinese secret societies or African bush-drumming had driven forward, but also subverted, the colonial state's desire for knowledge about its subjects. By the same token, much of the information built up by scholar officials and men on the spot in disciplines such as astronomy and medicine was created in the search for secret knowledges and ancient wisdoms. The archaeological effort in Egypt which formed the cultural dimension of the British and French presence in the country began with attempts to tap the supernatural power of the Pyramids.[38] Even in the 1880s and 1890s a kind of racial and religious messianism saturated the works of figures such as the archaeologist, Flinders Petrie. The British, it was argued, through their irrigation and engineering work were inaugurating the new age of the Pharaohs when Egyptians would once again resume their upward march as a civilisation.

Equally, though, the self-knowledge generated by the early nationalist project in much of the colonial world derived from a mystical and millenarian notion of nation, race and culture. Flinders Petrie's understanding of the rise and fall of races in the near east paralleled the debate in Egyptian nationalist circles about the Pharaonic heritage of its people. Early nationalists, such as Duse Mahomed Ali and Salama Musa, asserted that the Egyptian servitude to Turk and European was drawing to its close. At the same time, Coptic Christian separatists and their supporters took up the same theme to argue that it was the Copts alone who were the true descendants of the Pharaohs.[39] Muslim Egyptians were merely the offspring of Arab predators. We should note that the use of the themes of race by nationalists did not always or necessarily imply an aggressive racism similar to that espoused by extremist European settlers. The terms were flexible ones and sometimes meant something akin to our contemporary use of 'culture' and 'civilisation'.

Another powerful and globalising ideology which served a similarly ambiguous purpose derived from the Biblical doctrine of Atonement. The idea that the British were a chosen people and that this could justify their overseas expansion had, of course, been abroad since the time of Cromwell. It flowered again during the French revolutionary and Napoleonic wars, as Linda Colley showed.[40] It was also used to naturalise British conquest in the extra-European world. Apologists for Empire asserted that Britain had been saved by Providence from destruction during the revolutionary and Napoleonic Wars in order to advance its civilising project.[41]

Atonement for the sin of slave trading through purposive imperial expansion was also a reigning theme in British expansion on the west coast of Africa. By the later nineteenth century, the supposed decay of Islam had imparted a new messianic urgency to the activities of the established Church and dissenting groups. The salvation of slaves was cited as a justification for the British occupation of Egypt in 1882 and later acquisitions in east Africa. Empire would save the African from the slaver.

By the same token, however, the sin of slavery and the networks of abolitionism played an important part in the early formulation of pan-African ideologies of liberation in west Africa, as J. Ayo Langley has shown.[42] The first generation of black writers from Liberia or Sierre Leone, all of whom had British or American abolitionist connections, argued for the expansion of European trade and capital as had the Bengali patriots of a generation before. But English-educated Africans, such as Alexander Crummell, also insisted that Africans should be ceded a proper place among the nations. Crummell wrote *The Negro Race not under a Curse*, along with his Smithian and evangelical *The Duty of a Rising Christian State* of 1853, which examined Liberia and Sierre Leone. During the next generation, the slow expansion of west African education and suspicion of the motives of the European powers encouraged a protective, patriotic tone among African publicists.[43] By the turn of the century, Pan-African world congresses were arguing that Europeans should atone for the evils of slavery by liberating Africans from colonial rule.

The globalising ideologies of the late nineteenth century fall, then, into several overlapping categories: Christian messianism, spiritualism, scientific racism and radical political economy. The ideologies themselves were all universalising ones. They could be used both to legitimate conquest and to plead for the liberation of a newly envisaged homeland.

Equally important were the strategies of the new media which projected and formed these discourses. The expansion of information networks through cable, railway, telegraph and steamship – the hardware, as it were – has already been mentioned. It was, however, the tactics and policies of editors and other publicists which registered the greatest change between the 1870s and the outbreak of the First World War. These were changes in 'software', in a sense. Imperial publicists such as Cromer, Curzon, Colvin and Milner were taking the argument for Empire onto the streets of Britain through the mass press and into its drawing rooms through fast-selling books. But, again, fledgling nationalist movements, revolutionary conspir-acies and occult cells, as much as publicity-hungry proconsuls, appropriated the changes in communications. Greater range and density of commu-nications, unless tightly policed by the state, could allow marginal or heterodox voices to make themselves heard or to organise clandestinely. This was why the expansion of communications brought in its wake more vigorous attempts by the colonial and domestic state to control the press and access to the telegraph and mails.

W. T. Stead, one of the pioneering journalists of the late nineteenth century, exemplified the links between the new journalism, globalising ideologies and the informing of emergent nationalisms. Stead was brought up in the Gladstonian tradition as editor of the *Pall Mall Gazette*.[44] Predictably, he was hostile to Islam and to the Ottoman Empire in particular. Publicising the Armenian atrocities and the plaints of Ottoman Christians against Muslim oppression, much of what he wrote in the early part of his career implicitly or explicitly justified British imperial advance in the Middle East and North Africa. He played an important part in 'Sending Gordon' to Khartoum.[45] In this, he stood apart from Wilfrid Scawen Blunt and his European and Egyptian allies who rather improbably accused this son of the Congregational manse of capitulating to capitalists.

On the other hand, Stead's Gladstonian concern for the oppressed and links to the Aboriginal Protection Society made him sensitive to other forms of imperialism and to the struggle against slavery. He took a particular interest in the Congo. In 1891, E. D. Morel, who worked for a Liverpool firm with links to the Belgian Congo, became what we would now call a whistle-blower.[46] Morel informed Stead of a form of slavery in the Congo in which the Belgian authorities had created a forced labour corps of upwards of 13,000 people. Stead's article 'Cannibal Christendom in South Africa', published in the *Review of Reviews* in 1893, stirred a furious debate, which both looked back to earlier polemics about slavery and anticipated later arguments about African liberation.[47]

Indian nationalist writers were soon in contact with Stead. William Digby, later author of the ironically titled *Prosperous British India* and an intimate of the Congress leadership, wrote to Stead in 1891. He alerted him to Indian official statistics which revealed four million excess deaths from fever in eight years.[48] Digby asserted that this was merely statistical massaging of famine mortality. Stead, who had hitherto believed British rule in India to be benign, gradually changed his position. In 1901 he wrote an article 'What is my duty to the people of India?' Here he argued that the British should relinquish power as soon as possible and refrain from race pride. Soliciting views, Stead initiated another violent debate which followed in the wake of Lord Curzon's passage at arms with Dadhabhai Naoroji, the father of economic nationalism. Old India hands savaged Stead for lack of patriotism. Dadhabhai Naoroji and William Wedderburn came to his defence, arguing that British rule had impoverished the subcontinent. Later, Stead attracted further notoriety by publicly attacking Kipling's poetry as an incitement to imperial expansion.

The high point of public controversy came with Stead's albeit guarded criticism of the government and the 'pitiful tragedy of Jingo fever' during the South African War. His real importance, though, lay more in the organisation of the media than in the message. Stead was devoted to the idea of cheap mass publishing for the education of the common man. The 1884 Reform Act and the expansion of mid-Victorian education had given him and his brother editors an audience and a market. Better printing technology and syndicated international news over the telegraph had given them the copy. Stead's personal innovation was a cheap journal that published digests of news and critical notices of publications in an easy style. His aim, as he put it, was to 'democratise the best thought of the world'. *The Review of Reviews* was able to take information to readerships which did not have the means to purchase a sufficient range of daily, weekly and monthly publications to fully brief themselves. It was, therefore, colonial subjects as much as the British lower middle class and educated working class who made use of the new service.

Bipan Chandra Pal, journalist and Bengali radical, denounced by the Indian authorities as an extremist, wrote to Stead as follows:

We [the Indian editors] are too poor to subscribe to newspapers and magazines. To us, therefore, your *Review of Reviews* placing us in direct touch with the moving thought of the modern world came as a godsend. The number of your subscribers [in India] may not be large but I can assure you that the influence of your paper is very considerable among my English educated countrymen, who have always appreciated your generous sympathy with Indian aspirations.[49]

Indian editors copied, lent and otherwise distributed material from *The Review* to each other. They were released from dependence on the Anglo-Indian journals of Bombay and Calcutta. More direct access to material on Egyptian nationalist struggles, the rise of Japan and Gandhi's campaigns in South Africa globalised Indian nationalism with very significant consequences. Vernacular newspapers borrowed and cribbed international news from their English contemporaries. But they also provided a forum for religious, moral and local debates and news items which were sometimes picked up and broadcast by the English-language media in their turn.

Alongside *The Review*, other ventures of Stead were his Masterpiece Library, which was designed to spread the use of great books, and 'penny dreadfuls' such as the *Daily Paper* founded in 1904. These not only spread information widely but also increased the size of the reading public and alerted it to the travails of the overseas world. In his last years, before perishing on the *Titanic*, Stead argued for a European peace conference, heralded a United States of Europe and publicised the issue of the female suffrage. On Ireland, he argued for immediate Dominion status, holding that otherwise the Irish 'instead of the cement in the fabric of our race' would remain 'an element of division and weakness'.[50] Physically, in the metropolis of London, and virtually, through the international community of print created by mass publishing, aspirant nationalisms were learning from each other.

A second revealing incident regarding the role of the Press in the globalisation of colonial nationalism in this period concerns the abduction of the Chinese nationalist, Sun Yatsen, in London in 1896.[51] Sun was born in China in 1866; he was educated in medicine in Hawaii and Hong Kong where he became a Christian. In 1895 he plotted to overthrow the provincial government in Canton as a prelude to ending the Manchu dynasty, which he regarded as itself foreign and over-dependent on the will of imperialist governments, especially the British. Sun fled to London, where in 1896, he was allegedly kidnapped by members of the Chinese Legation who included its chief linguist, Sir Halliday Macartney. Sun was later released as the result of intervention by the British government. He was hailed in some English newspapers as a Christian hero, imprisoned by barbarous Tartars. His fame spread to China, Japan and America. A book, *Kidnapped in London*, supposedly written by Sun, confirmed this heroic status and sold thousands of copies.

The facts of the case have recently been thoroughly re-examined by John Wong. What interests us here is the light it throws on two themes: the use of the imperial press by emerging nationalist ideologues and the role of the metropolis itself as a conduit for and mould of ideas about national liberation. While Sun Yatsen was a willing accomplice in his rise to celebrity status, he did, as Wong has demonstrated, have many allies. His former mentor in Hong Kong the Scottish medical doctor, Dr James Cantlie, was the real author of *Kidnapped in London*. A Scots proponent of national liberation movements and fierce enemy of Manchu 'barbarity', Cantlie also introduced Sun to a circle of minor nationalist publicists from Ireland, India and the dominions and to radical thinkers among British Israelites.[52] This lumpen intelligentsia, now gathered in London, played an important part in the spread of nationalist ideas. The British press, eager for hot news that would interest the new mass readership helped his cause greatly. Dastardly orientals in London undermining British liberties made good copy. Thus the *Globe*: 'Strange Story! Conspirator kidnapped in London. Imprisoned at the Chinese Embassy!'[53] Later the *Daily Telegragh*, which had already printed 250,000 copies, praised Sun for conspiring against the 'stupid barbarity' of his own country.[54]

While this adventure in London helped to project Sun's image across the world, it also provided him with contacts and ideas which shaped his later views and may well have helped formulate his famous 'Three Principles of the People', the founding text of Nationalist Chinese Government. In London, Sun encountered Japanese Pan-Asianists, Irish radicals and socialist activists. Impressed by what he read of indigenous resistance to British advances in southern Africa, Sun seems to have remembered particularly King Lobengula's resistance to Cecil Rhodes, which he heard about while in London.[55]

Proponents of sub-nationalism and ethnic or religious separatism also quickly appropriated the new media possibilities. Indian Muslims seeking special status and their British supporters lobbied brilliantly in London, using connections in the Lords, the Bar, London club-land and the press. Egypt's Coptic separatists were less successful, but as canny in their use of media. Kyriakos Mikhail, the Coptic press's representative in Britain during the controversy over Coptic special electoral representation in 1910–11 caught the tone of pre-First World War racial discourse perfectly and projected it back into the metropolitan arena. His early career had been as a special correspondent for *Al-Watan*, a Coptic community newspaper. Later as proprietor and manager of 'The Egyptian News and Information Bureau', Alexandria, he was responsible for the collection and diffusion of information on Egypt in Europe and *vice versa*.[56] His publication in *The Freedom of the Press in Egypt* (3 editions 1911–14) carried advertisements for Thomas Cook and other firms pioneering learned tourism to Egypt. 'The genuine Egyptians', Mikhail proclaimed, 'are the Christian Copts. They alone trace an unadulterated descent from the race to whom the civilisation and culture of the ancients were so largely due.'[57] Because of their practice of Christian endogamy 'they have kept their blood pure from admixture with semi-barbarous Arabs and savage Kurds, or other foreign elements whom the licentiousness of Mohammedan family life has introduced into the country'.

The years after 1880 also marked the coming of age of statistics. This is the third dimension of change addressed by this chapter. Here, again, early colonial liberationists quickly adapted the new science to their own interests. Domestic European governments counted and categorised their citizens with greater and greater precision. They were impelled by the need to tax them, pension them, call them up for military service and, increasingly, to monitor their health. Before the First World War, international standards of data evaluation and comparison were being put into place. These efforts extended to European dependencies, though, as we have seen, they were subject to considerable regional variation. Nevertheless, censuses and reports on trade and production abounded by 1900, created in the interest of Parliamentary committees and of colonial governments increasingly called to justify themselves in the public arena. Clandestine surveillance of seditionists through the Criminal Intelligence Department or Reporters on native newspapers paralleled these public efforts, especially after Indian, Egyptian, Irish and socialist cells turned to armed action after 1900. Statistics became both a discourse of power and an aid to policy-making and debate.

As many historians have shown, the colonial state's categories of caste, tribe, religion, gender or class set, became to one degree or another the discursive context for indigenous publicists.[58] Hindus in India and Copts in Egypt, for instance, began to argue that they were declining in numbers or under-represented in subordinate government service. Nationalists moved remarkably quickly to turn the colonial state's methods of data collection and publication against it in international debate. William Wedderburn, whom we have earlier seen as a bemused onlooker of theosophy, started his career in the Bombay Civil Service. He monitored the famines in western India in the 1870s, the riots against incoming moneylenders and the workings of the Deccan Agriculturalists Relief Act of 1875. He used his statistical knowledge of rural society to fight the nationalist cause in India and later in London where he became an MP. His expert analyses of government blue books and famine reports paralleled the work that his nationalist contemporaries Dadhabhai Naoroji and R. C. Dutt did on trade statistics from Parliament and the Manchester Chamber of Commerce. Spheres of nationalist information gathering overlapped. As Liberal MP for Banffshire between 1887 and 1894, Wedderburn also travelled to the so-called congested agricultural districts of Ireland as rural conflict intensified.[59] He later projected the findings back into India by means of speeches to the Indian Famine Union and *Manchester Guardian*.[60] The Famine Union and associated relief work in western India were among the first political activities undertaken by the young G. D. Gokhale, later founder of the Servants of India Society and mentor of Gandhi.

Similar conceptual links, in this case also drawing in Occupied Egypt were made by Wilfrid Scawen Blunt and Keir Hardie, the Labour leader. Blunt spent time in Anglo-Irish jails for his vigorous investigative methods and penchant for publicity which were regarded ill by Dublin Castle and the landlords.[61] The activities of these men shadowed the imperial expertise and knowledge deployed by administrators such as the Earl of Dufferin, an Irish landlord who reported on Egypt and ruled India, or Lord Cromer who brought his knowledge of Indian finance to Egypt.

The early collection of statistical knowledge by the British in India derived as much from military as from revenue concerns. Before population statistics came the medical topography of cantonements and military stations. The death of British soldiers from disease was something that could not be tolerated either by military opinion or by the Treasury. Here also early nationalists found useful ammunition. Florence Nightingale, as is well known, spread her activities as medical and temperance watchdog in the Crimea to the garrisons of post-Mutiny India and other parts of the eastern Empire. In her last years, however, she became convinced that poverty and famine among the indigenous population were the root cause of death among the European garrisons. To save the lives of British sailors and soldiers, the Empire would have to be better governed. By 1885 she had joined the Indians and renegade Indian officials in London in trying to force Indian issues onto the electoral agenda. She proposed to Wedderburn the establishment of an independent service of press cablegrams from Indian editors to London.[62] This would correct the biases of the weekly Indian telegram to *The Times* from its Calcutta correspondent. Recently enlisted to stir up racial hatred in Britain against the Ilbert Bill, its appearance on Monday morning systematically misled the British reader on Indian matters, Florence Nightingale believed.

Finally, this chapter attempts to draw together the different arguments through an analysis of the Imperial Press Conference of 1911. All the themes which have been discussed are seen here in action: the expansion of communications and new modes of press activity; competing ideologies of race and national efficiency; the use of publicity by indigenous spokesmen to globalise issues of national self-determination. Above all, the Conference showed the British government and imperial administrations paying careful attention to the politicised lobby of press and communications media which had now formed at an international level.

The Press Conference marked one of W. H. Stead's last important appearances before his fateful rendevouz with *SS Titanic*. It was convened by Harry Brittain, Unionist MP for Acton and himself a director of several newspapers.[63] Brittain's purpose was very much part of Tory Imperialism and of the wider movement to cement links between English-speaking peoples. Newspaper editors and proprietors from all over the British Isles, Dominions and India gathered in London. It was a measure of the importance attached to it by British politicians, though, that practically every Liberal Minister and senior member of the Tory opposition was present. The reason was clear. Press messages sent over the cables had more than trebled between 1900 and 1909,[64] and they were set to increase further. This then was a serious attempt to influence public opinion around the world at a time when the arms race that led to the First World War was reaching its crescendo.

In speeches to the Conference much was made of communications 'cementing the Empire' and of the 'gathering of the tribes to the ancient shrine' of England. To this end, the combined weight of editorial and political influence was brought to bear on the major telegraph companies which were forced to reduce their rates on newspaper stories by 25 per cent. The change in rates led to a further surge in the volume of press messages over the cables before the guns opened fire in August 1914. This aspect of the Conference fits well into the pattern of imperial propaganda which John MacKenzie has traced in media as varied as the press, learned societies, the music hall and school books.[65]

Yet this festival of imperial publicity was lit by subterranean nationalist conflagrations. Dominions delegates constantly harped on their new equality with Britain.[66] Their home despatches contrasted the poverty and eugenic weakness of the British working class with the prosperity which arose from generous social welfare in the Dominions. Statistics were employed to prove these discrepancies. The issue of language and identity also surfaced. An Afrikaner delegate from Bloomfontein, who had fought against the British in the Anglo-Boer war, rejected the hegemonic project of promoting the English language, lauded at the conference by Winston Churchill.[67] The editor of the *Toronto Globe*, J. A. Macdonald, likewise rejected Sir Edward Grey's lazy emphasis on Anglo-Saxon racial unity, disavowing a drop of what he called 'Sassenach blood' and arguing that all races, including the French 'must be encircled by our Canadian nationalism, otherwise we can have no genuine imperialism'.[68]

It was at this meeting that the Bengali editor-politician, Surendranath Banerjea, confronted the aged but vigorous imperial propagandist, Lord

Cromer. Banerjea was the only non-white editor officially accredited to the conference; the other so-called Indian delegates were expatriate Britons. Cromer accused the Egyptian and Indian journalists of sedition. Banerjea bit back. In Banerjea's own account, the Dominions' editors applauded him for 'wiping the floor with Lord Cromer'.[69] Banerjea had earlier affirmed that he wanted cheap cablegrams from India to counteract the 'false, misleading telegrams regarding Indian opinion' with which the British public was fed, presumably by *The Times*. Now he denounced revolutionary terrorism as a vile perversion brought from the west, alien to India's traditions of non-violence.[70]

The expansion of communication within the Empire clearly gave nationalists as much as imperialists a wider sense of each other and of the vices of imperial policy. It allowed them to bypass conservative or reactionary colonial governments and to bring to bear pressure directly on British politicians. These politicians themselves included increasing numbers of former journalists or polemicists who had written on the overseas world. Nationalists quickly exploited this second information revolution to 'write back', as Edward Said puts it, against the colonial powers.

It is a truism that by some kind of osmosis historians project their own present onto the historical past. The imperatives of global development as well as the interests of expanding capitalism ensured that the immediate post war generation of historians wrote global history in terms of economic conjunctures and the struggles of emerging capitalism. Analyses of colonial and nationalist ideologies of the last twenty years represent a response to the discursive steamroller of the Free World during the Vietnam era and the Cold War – an attempt by the fly to escape the fly-bottle. Our growing contemporary concern with information, the history of printing, statistics and the diffusion of news can perhaps be seen as an attempt to draw both of these concerns into a common framework. In the 1960s, Marshall McLuhan announced 'the medium is the message': a phrase which later became hackneyed by overuse. I have tried to suggest that a fruitful approach to the emergence of imperialism and nationalism would combine analysis of the ideologies and discourses of empire and nation with an understanding of how the media themselves were developing within a global information order. In this way we can see exactly how and when networks of modernisers and anti-colonialists were able to take the offensive against imperial discourse and power at an international level.

The extent to which these changes in media and ideology empowered people beneath the level of the small nationalist elites is, of course, another question. Heavy costs, both cultural and monetary, were extracted from colonised people trying to gain access to the new media and techniques. The cost of paper, telegrams and printing technology was high. So too was the cost of the education required to know how to use them. All the same, networks of popular communication and contacts between the populace and intelligentsia, especially in India and Egypt, were probably denser than we have been accustomed to believe. The explosions of 1919–23 across the Empire were legitimation crises born of the repeatedly transmitted news that imperial government was in disarray, as much as they were reflections of simple economic strains. The rise of the Wafd agitation in Egypt was measured by the volume of press reports and cables directed to Egypt from the European peace conference and occupied Istanbul. Equally, the Khilafat movement in India rose and fell in intensity in close relationship to reports of the activities of British troops in the environs of the Islamic holy places and the seat of the Khalifa. Once received in India, news of Allied duplicity was broadcast by proscribed pamphlet, speeches at the mosque, through networks of sufi brotherhoods and by means of Hindu holy-men. The oldest, as well as the most modern, components of the information order were brought into play with the result that the political messages of anti-government resistance were heavily coloured by religious rhetoric and imagery, with problematic consequences for the future of a unified Indian nationalism. Both government and Congress emerged from the war with a keener sense of the vital importance of propaganda and communication.[71]

An approach to political change through the issue of communications and the programming of messages may help, therefore, to restore a sense of historical context and historical change to a discipline which has appeared to lurch from materialist reductionism to discursive reductionism. But whatever future research uncovers in this respect, information history seems to have come of age, along with the Internet.

NOTES

I wish to acknowledge the help of Deep Kanta Lahiri-Choudhury, who is working on the history of the Indian telegraph, in reformulating the ideas in this paper.

1   See, for instance, the journal *Public Culture* (Chicago), though an exception to this general rule is Arjun Appadurai, *Modernity at Large: Cultural Dimensions of Globalization* (Minneapolis, 1996).

2   Philip D. Curtin, *Cross-cultural Trade in World History* (Cambridge, 1984) provides an introduction to some aspects of this vast topic.

3   Ian K. Steele, *The English Atlantic 1675–1740: A Study in Communications and Community* (New York, 1986); Thomas Richards, *The Imperial Archive: Knowledge and the Fantasy of Empire* (London, 1993).

4 P. J. Marshall and G. Williams, *The Great Map of Mankind: British Perceptions of the World in the Age of Enlightenment* (London, 1982).

5 Benedict Anderson, *Imagined Communities* (London, 1983).

6 See C. A. Bayly, *Empire and Information: Intelligence Gathering and Social Communication in India, 1780–1880* (Cambridge, 1996), pp. 3–9. I have adapted this concept from Manuel Castells, *Information Technology, Economic Restructuring and the Urban-regional Process* (Oxford, 1989).

7 Joseph Needham, *Science and Civilisation in China*, 5, *Chemistry and Chemical Technology. Part I. Paper and Printing*, by Tsien Tsieu-Hsuin, (Cambridge, 1985), pp. 377–83, passim.

8 For the overseas Chinese, Leonard Blussé, *Strange Company: Chinese Settlers, Mestizo Women and the Dutch in VOC Batavia* (Dordrecht, 1986); for Iranians and others, see e.g., Sanjay Subrahmanyam (ed.), *Merchant Networks in the Early Modern World* (Aldershot, 1996). V. Purcell, *The Chinese in Southeast Asia* (Kuala Lumpur, 1980).

9 For an overview see Andrew Porter, *An Atlas of British Overseas Expansion* (London, 1992), pp. 148–52; Charles Bright, *Submarine Telegraphs: Their History, Construction and Working* (London, 1898).

10 Donald Read, *The Power of News: The History of Reuters 1849–1989* (Oxford, 1992).

11 See, e.g., Joel Wiener (ed.), *Papers for the Millions: The New Journalism in Britain 1850 to 1914* (New York, 1988); Mitchell Stephens, *A History of News* (London, 1988).

12 See e.g., Briton Martin, *New India 1885* (Berkeley, 1969), p. 209; these connections are documented in Anne Taylor, *Annie Besant: A Biography* (Oxford, 1992).

13 The following paragraph is based on T. N. Harper, 'Globalism and the pursuit of authenticity: the making of the diasporic public sphere', *Sojourn: Journal of Social Issues in South-east Asia*, 12 (1997), 261–93; cf. R. J. Wilkinson, *Papers on Malay Subjects* (London, 1900).

14 This merged easily into fears engendered by the rise of Japan, the Boxer Rebellion, the threat of Pan-Islamism, Indian terrorism, etc. See, e.g., the many works of Valentine Chirol, *The Times* senior editor on oriental matters.

15 A. al-Sayyid Marsot, *Egypt in the Reign of Muhammad Ali* (Cambridge, 1983).

16 Robert L. Tignor, 'The "Indianization" of the Egyptian administration under British rule', *American Historical Review* 68 (1963), 636–61; Roger Owen, 'The influence of Lord Cromer's Indian experience on British policy in Egypt, 1883–1907', *St Antony's Papers*, 17 (1965).

17 J. R. I. Cole, *Colonialism and Revolution in the Middle East: Social and Cultural Origins of Egypt's 'Urabi movement* (Princeton, 1993).

18 Martin Hartmann, *The Arabic Press of Egypt* (London, 1899); cf. e.g., E. Gorst to E. Grey 8 Jan., 7 Mar., 11 Mar., 1910, Foreign Office Confidential Print, lxxii, Further Correspondence respecting the affairs of Egypt and the Soudan, 9909.

19 Anil Seal, *The Emergence of Indian Nationalism: Competition and Collaboration in the Later Nineteenth Century* (Cambridge, 1968); J. R. McLane, *Indian Nationalism and the Early Congress* (Princeton, 1977).

20 Partha Chatterjee, *Nationalist Thought and the Colonial World: A Derivative Discourse?* (London, 1986); Sudipta Kaviraj, *The Unhappy Consciousness: Bankimchandra Chattopadyay and the Formation of Nationalist Discourse in India* (Delhi, 1995).

21 Uma Dasgupta, *Rise of an Indian Public: Impact of Official Policy, 1870–1880* (Calcutta, 1977), pp. 1–51, for the cost and management of the Indian press in the 1860s and 1870s.

22 William Wedderburn, *Allan Octavian Hume, CBE* (London, 1913; reprint Delhi 1974), pp. 1–5.

23 A. O. Hume, Magistrate, Etawah to Secretary to Government, North Western Provinces, 10 Jan. 1861, North Western Provinces General Proceedings, 26 Jan. 1861, 55 and 56, 216/4, Oriental and India Office Collections, British Library, London.

24 Wedderburn, *Hume*, p. 83.

25 Richard J. Poplewell, *Intelligence and Imperial Defence: British Intelligence and the Defence of the Indian Empire 1904–24* (London, 1995).

26 Sir Auckland Colvin, Lieutenant Governor of the North-Western Provinces and Oudh, to Lord Dufferin, 25 April 1888, Dufferin Papers, Oriental and India Office Collections, British Library.

27 The best account of this remains, Briton Martin, *New India 1885* (California, 1969), pp. 45–78.

28 *Ibid.*, pp. 63–4.

29 *The Mahatma Letters to A. P. Sinnett from the Mahatmas M and K.H.* (London, 1923).

30 See C.A. Bayly, *Roots of Nationality in South Asia: Patriotism and ethical Government in the Making of Modern India* (Delhi, 1998).

31 Wedderburn, *Hume*, p. 63.

32 *Ibid.*, pp. 55–6.

33 Martin, *New India*, pp. 261–2

34 R. F. Foster, *Paddy and Mr Punch* (London, 1993), p. 221.

35 A. P. Sinnett, *The Occult World* (1881; 9th edn London, 1969), p. 181.

36 W. Scott-Elliot, *The Story of Atlantis and the Last Lemuria* (1996; rev. edn, 1962), p. 1.

37 *Ibid.*, p. 3.

38 Margaret S. Drower, *Flinders Petrie: A Life in Archaeology* (London, 1985), pp. 29–30, 40; John Ward, FSA, *Pyramids and Progress* (London, 1890), p. vii.

39 Kyriakos Mikhail, *Copts and Muslims under British Control* (London, 1911), p. viii; C. A. Bayly, 'Representing Copts and Indian Muslims', in L. Fawaz (ed.), *European Modernity and Cultural Difference from Mediterranean Sea to the Indian Ocean, 1890s–1920s* (New York, forthcoming).

40 Linda Colley, *Britons: Forging the Nation, 1707–1837* (London, 1990); C. A. Bayly, *Imperial Meridian. The British Empire and the World 1780–1830* (London, 1989), pp. 136–47.

41 See, e.g., Claudius Buchanan, *Colonial Ecclesiastical Establishments* (London, 1813), p. 11.

42 J. Ayo Langley, *Ideologies of Liberation in Black Africa, 1856–1970: Documents on Modern African Political Thought from Colonial Times to the Present* (London, 1979).

43 *Ibid.*, intro. pp. 38–45.

44 Ray Boston 'W. T. Stead and democracy by journalism', in Joel Wiener (ed.), *Papers for the Millions: The New Journalism in Britain 1815–1914* (New York, 1988), 91–106.

45 Frederic Whyte, *Life of W. T. Stead* (London, 1925), I, p. 117.

46 E. D. Morel, *King Leopold's Rule in the Congo* (London, 1904) and William Roger Louis and Jean Stengers (eds), *E. D. Morel's History of the Congo Reform Movement* (Oxford, 1968).

47 Whyte, *Stead*, II, p. 215.

48 *Ibid.*, pp. 220–1.

49 *Ibid.*, p. 226.

50 *Ibid.*, p. 323

51 J. Y. Wong, *The Origins of an Heroic Image: Sun Yatsen in London, 1896–7* (London, 1986).

52 *Ibid.*, pp. 228ff.

53 *Ibid.*, p. 46.

54 *Ibid.*, p. 175.

55 *Ibid.*, pp. 218ff.

56 Kyriakos Mikhail, *The Freedom of the Press in Egypt: An Appeal to the Friends of Liberty by Kyriakos Mikhail* (3rd edn, London, 1914).

57 Kyriakos Mikhail, *Copts and Muslims under British Control* (London, 1911), p. viii.

58 Notably, Bernard S. Cohn, *An Anthropologist among Historians and Other Essays* (Delhi, 1987).

59 S. K. Ratcliffe, *Sir William Wedderburn and the Indian Reform Movement* (London, 1923), pp. 68–73.

60 *Ibid.*, p. 114; anon (ed.), *Speeches and Writings of Sir William Wedderburn* (Madras, 1918), pp. 149–53, 181–7, 323–8.

61 W. S. Blunt, *The Land War in Ireland: Being a Personal Narrative, in Continuation of 'A Secret History of the English Occupation of Egypt'* (London, 1912).

62 Ratcliffe, *Wedderburn*, pp. 123–4.

63 Thomas H. Hardman (ed.), *The Parliament of the Press: The First Imperial Press Conference. 1909; illustrated with a preface by the Earl of Rosebery KG* (London, 1909).

64 *Ibid.*, p. 137.

65 John MacKenzie, *Propaganda and Empire: The Manipulation of British Public Opinion 1880–1960* (Manchester, 1985).

66 Cawthra Woodhead, 'The Imperial press conference', *The African Monthly*, 7 (Dec. 1909), 151–2.

67 *Ibid.*, p. 197; cf. 4.

68 *Ibid.*, p. 184.

69 S. N. Banerjea, *A Nation in Making* (1925, repr. Bombay, 1963), p. 243.

70 *Parliament of the Press*, pp. 49, 164 ff; Woodhead 'Imperial press conference', p. 276, noted Banerjea's 'exceptional lung power and knowledge of English'.

71 Milton Israel, *Communications and Power: Propaganda and the Press in the Indian Nationalist Struggle* (Cambridge, 1994).

11 Media and Power: Charles Stewart Parnell's 1880 Mission to North America

Alan O'Day

> Oratory is the usual avenue to leadership in a democratic movement, and Mr Parnell is one of the few who have arrived at power neither by that road nor by military success. . . . So far from glittering with the florid rhetoric supposed to characterise Irish eloquence, his speeches were singularly plain, bare, and dry. Neither had they any humour.[1]

Introduction

Colin Matthew has drawn attention to the function of rhetoric in later Victorian Britain and its subsequent decline.[2] In the late nineteenth century, he observed, only two avenues of communication were then available – speeches and the printed word. Speeches, he pointed out, were 'not simply or even mainly declaimed to those present'.[3] Gaining attention in the press could quickly elevate a politician to public stature.[4] Joseph Chamberlain and Lord Randolph Churchill are two such instances. A 'nationally integrated reporting system offered the means for a nationally integrated political rhetoric', Matthew maintained.[5] His perceptive analysis of communication affords an appropriate framework for consideration of Charles Stewart Parnell's exceptional and innovative use of the media in order to project himself. Like William Gladstone, John Morley and Herbert Asquith, Parnell was catapulted into public esteem despite the fact that none of them controlled a machine, spent vast sums of money on politics, had a base in the localities or exercised vast patronage.[6] Parnell even carried the process a step further. His mission to Northern America at the beginning of 1880 afforded him an international platform for influencing opinion at home.

Dissections of Charles Stewart Parnell's mystique – the magnetism he exerted on Irish Catholics – are two-a-penny.[7] Conor Cruise O'Brien, for one, points to Parnell's attributes for leadership while also observing that he happened also to be endowed in a most exceptional degree with the less tangible qualities of leadership: prudence and daring, firmness and flexibility, far-sightedness and tactical sense. That he should have been also – as he was – gifted with imposing stature and great physical beauty makes it easier to understand the almost superstitious veneration with which many of his followers – especially his remoter followers – regarded him. Few leaders in modern times have looked so very like a leader.[8]

F. S. L. Lyons notes that Parnell 'impressed all who met him – Irish farmers and parliamentarians, Fenians at home and overseas, English politicians of whatever shade – with his extraordinary ability to control men and events and bend them to his steely will'.[9] That Parnell possessed exceptional gifts and that he had immense significance to the unfolding of Irish nationalism are beyond question. But it is less often recognised that he was Ireland's first modern media politician, in that he advanced himself and the national project principally through indirect means, that is at a physical distance, through the press and often by what now would be called 'sound bites'. Such means allowed Parnell to register his impress upon millions of Irish people at home and abroad who never heard or saw him in the flesh. Cruise O'Brien and Lyons assume physical chemistry in Parnell's influence, and, though there is an element of truth in this, it was not instrumental for most who followed him. His mission to North America when he was still a sectional figure and not leader of a party or even a faction is rightly seen as a decisive increment in Parnell's ascendancy. It is less frequently noted that this tour and the publicity engendered took place far from the heartland of Ireland's politics and the House of Commons, nor is there much analysis about why this distant enterprise served to make him in T. M. Healy's enduring synonym, the 'uncrowned king of Ireland'.[10]

Before Parnell, Daniel O'Connell created and mobilised a mass following. But O'Connell was proto-modern: he relied on visual effects, showmanship and potent demagoguery directed at huge crowds who physically flocked to his meetings,[11] although there was also an unseen audience. The foundations of his power were rooted in mobilising the physical crowd. He was feared by the government officials and the respect-able orders, who had a deep suspicion of public demonstrations, indeed of almost any species of mass gathering. Yet governments possessed means to mute this kind of offensive. In his case it did so by banning the monster meeting at Clontarf and O'Connell's appeal slipped into decline. The crowd to be sure did not disappear in Parnell's formulation but assumed a different and modern guise. Significantly, it was not a physical crowd which could be dispersed but an aggregation of people who never necessarily met. Creation of public opinion, electoral management and manipulation of information are hallmarks of this 'virtual' crowd. O'Connell was master of the outdoor platform, a visual image manager, Parnell, an aloof man uncomfortable in public gatherings which he always disliked,[12] commanded the sound bite. According to a journalist close to him, Parnell 'always referred to his American tour in 1880 with a shiver, and regarded it as a nightmare'.[13] He grasped how information presented in a fresh way could be controlled, disseminated and then forged together for the exercise of power. His methods actuated spells of 'information panic' among rivals, especially State officials who largely lacked the legal tools to respond efficiently. He created a 'crowd' that was all but immune to administrative and legal restraint. Parnell's achievement sustained mobilisation of most Catholics in Ireland behind the national agenda in spite of disappointments, delays and setbacks. Immense advances in the dissemination of information have tended to obscure Parnell's originality in Irish and for that matter British political annals.

Parnell appreciated that physical separation could enhance psychological proximity, a point made in a different sense by both R. Barry O'Brien and Lyons, who see aloofness as an essential part of his mystique. Converting limitations into assets, Parnell, an indifferent speaker, was little given to expressing ideas on paper, another earlier avenue of communication. His credentials as an ideologue and moral entrepreneur of Irish aspirations scarcely differed from many contemporaries; it was his use of the media that made Parnell a remarkable figure with his close associates acting as the 'spin-doctors' of a their day. During the divorce crisis of 1890–91, Parnell lost control of the information monopoly when many of his former acolytes opposed him; the forces he employed to such effect were then turned on their heads and instead directed at him. As a consequence he reverted to older channels of presentation which predictably were no match for his opponents' modern methods.

Parnell went to North America to solicit funds, arriving on 1 January 1880 and sailing home on 11 March. This brief spell is rightly recognised as pivotal to his political rise. During the tour an editorial in *The Times* grudgingly recognised that he had made a huge impact, but prophesied wrongly, 'when Mr Parnell returns he will find that his American triumph such as it is, has done very little towards strengthening his position in the English Parliament'.[14] When he came home, the *Freeman's Journal*, then suspicious of him, conceded, 'we have no hesitation in rendering to Mr Parnell the praise that is due to him, and which the country accords him'.[15] O'Brien portrays this episode as an increment in Parnell's great quest. First, he seized attention through parliamentary obstruction, then won the confidence of the Fenians, followed this by securing a foothold on power through the Irish in Britain, captured the support of Irish-America and the nation at home, building gradually towards an ascendancy over

British politics and finally converting Gladstone to home rule.[16] The mission has been the subject of specialist investigations, the most recent enthusing that it enlisted the moral and financial assistance of the American Irish, bolstering 'the home rule movement incalculably, forcing the British government to deal with an "Irish nation" whose boundaries extended beyond the shores of Ireland itself'.[17] M. V. Hazel also observed that 'in the course of his tour the period of his ascendancy over the Irish nationalist movement may most accurately be said to have begun'.[18] Michael Davitt anticipated recent academic literature, stressing the political rather than the financial outcome:

The political value of the mission to the league movement was enormous. Active sympathy for its objects was awakened throughout America, and all the bitter memories of landlord oppression and insolence were revived in the hearts of our exiled people, to help us to enlist the active co-operation of hundreds of thousands of Irish-American Land-Leagues in the combat against the landlord and Castle enemy of the old country.[19]

Robert Kee was the first to give due attention to the western phase of the mission, noting the varied public and American press responses to Parnell's speeches.[20] General acclaim for the humanitarian purposes, he wrote, was tempered by reservations about Parnell's attack upon the three other funds designed to aid the Irish peasantry, his wish to destroy Irish landlordism, and the intention that the crisis be turned towards securing Ireland's nationhood. Progression is a common theme – Parnell's advance from sectional to national spokesman. While these accounts are valuable, they are less illuminating about how he was able to use distant and obscure venues as a medium to communicate with an audience at home and the broader implications of this format for dispensing political information. Communication over vast physical space was not invented by the tour but was extended and amplified. This two-way street of communication received emphasis in 1886 when T. M. Healy observed of the House of Commons debates on home rule: 'This is not a closed secret Assembly. Every word which is spoken here is telegraphed wheresoever the English language is spoke.'[21] Mobilisation receives extensive airing in the theoretical literature on nationalism. Diaspora participation is treated as subsidiary and is usually discussed in the context of support for the home movement through provision of finance, morale, or safe havens rather than in terms of the globalisation of information. A communications revolution under-pinned sustained mobilisation. Certain constructs developed by theorists of communications assist interpretation of Parnell's mission. Paul Lazerfeld pointed out the essential ingredients – communicator, message, medium, receiver and effects – and the present discussion is conducted within these parameters.[22] He also saw the audience as a tissue of interrelated people rather than isolated individuals whom the communicator activates. For him, 'opinion leaders' fulfilled the role of 'intervening variables' between the media and audience. In George Gerbner's estimation the media had the function of forming the 'mass' by creating shared ways of selecting and viewing events by delivering to them technologically produced and mediated message systems, common ways of seeing and understanding the world which he calls the cultivation of dominant image patterns. Michael Gurevitch stressed the mutual dependence between the political communicator and the media. Politicians, he observed, command scarce resources and for the purveyors of the media there is pressure to give chief figures the lion's share of attention. Additionally, John B. Thompson noted the distinctive nature of the mass communication process, emphasising that messages are produced for an audience not physically present at the place of production, the necessity of an information storage mechanism which persists, the reproducible nature of information, and availability of the message.

Whereas Parnell's mission essentially conforms to these paradigms, O'Connell, in contrast, was hampered because vital preconditions were absent or insufficiently developed. By 1880 there were vast changes, making globalised Irish politics a reality. Three quarters of the population in Ireland were literate in English and the remainder had access to political information by word-of-mouth, enjoying 'virtual literacy'. After mid-century there was rapid growth of periodicals, catering for the enlarged audience. Between 1849 and 1879, railway track expanded from 428 to 2285 miles in Ireland with only remote hamlets remaining relatively inaccessible. This network allowed politicians to range widely and for a patriotic press in Dublin or other main centres to penetrate into all corners of the island. Furthermore, the rail system was vital to the growth of an efficient postal system. Letters per head rose from 2.9 annually in the mid-1840s to 17.3 in the early 1880s. By then letters posted in London normally reached Cork within 24 hours. The telegraph transmitted material quickly. By 1880 more than 1.5 million telegrams were dispatched in Ireland. North America underwent a similar transition. The Atlantic had been transformed into an information highway. People in the rural American middle-west were able to follow the events in the British Parliament through their local press if not quite instantly then within a mere day or two and this at a time when it still took five to seven days to traverse the Atlantic, itself a shortening of the passage from O'Connell's era. The main obstacle to politicians was not the speed of transmission but securing access to the means of communication.

Background to the mission

Parnell was born in 1846 into an Irish Church of Ireland gentry family possessing 'patriotic' credentials. His mother was of prominent American lineage. Parnell visited North America three times in his life, though a brother, John Howard Parnell, his mother, and three sisters, Anna, Fanny and Theodosia, lived there at the time of the mission in 1880. His initial visit (1870–71) was apolitical. So far as is known, Parnell made no contacts with Irish activists although he later claimed that the Fenian revolt in 1867 had ignited an interest in Ireland's politics. In testimony to the Special Commission on Parnellism and Crime, Parnell claimed to have supported the Liberal candidate for Wicklow at the general election of 1868 but his first known entry into politics came in early 1874 and shortly thereafter, when he stood in the parliamentary by-election for County Dublin on 18 March 1874, losing by 2183 votes to 1235; he was returned for Meath on 17 April 1875 by 1771 to 1050 for his two opponents combined. Parnell did not make much of an impression as a speaker on either occasion; his election speeches were only synopsised, even by sympathetic newspapers. Still a relatively obscure MP, he and John O'Connor Power travelled to the centenary of American Independence in autumn 1876. On his return Parnell outlined what would become his theme, the need to educate opinion, an opinion that extended outside Ireland and to people who were not automatically receptive to the national project. In Liverpool he stated:

They had another duty to perform, which was to educate public opinion in England upon Irish questions, which he looked upon as a difficult and almost impossible task – so difficult that he had often been tempted to think it was no use trying to educate English public opinion. The English press encouraged prejudice against Ireland. Englishmen themselves were in many respects fair minded and reasonable, but it was almost impossible to get at them – it required intelligence almost superhuman to remove the clouds of prejudice under which they had lived during their lives.[23]

The challenge then was to find ways of circumventing information blockage, resulting from the monopoly exercised by a hostile press, though at this stage he did not, in fact, suggest anything innovatory. His subsequent steps to locate a formula stuttered and the North American mission proved significant for breaking the logjam.

Between 1877 and 1879 Parnell experimented with techniques of communication, using with telling effect the forum of the House of Commons and to a lesser degree public appearances. Parnell saw that rapidly rising rates of literacy joined to the new technology, that is cheap rates for the transmission of material for newspapers under the Telegraph Act of 1868, and the swift circulation of ephemeral periodicals allowed him to reach the Irish people despite his lack of the traditionally valued gifts of oratory. His limitations proved a virtue, pressing upon him the need to use space in a fresh way. Parnell targeted the reading rather than a listening audience, grasping that short speech and memorable phrase were more effective than the florid public declamations favoured by contemporary Irish politicians. Furthermore, he understood that in order to reach Irish people at home and abroad he required the mediation of journalists. Unlike many of his contemporaries, he grasped that political communication rests on mutual dependence, a point made by Gurevitch, and so Parnell courted the humble reporter, a group which was to repay this consideration.

He had to undergo a learning curve. Between 1874 and the beginning of 1877 Parnell addressed audiences in Ireland fewer than twenty times and many of these occasions received slight notice in the press. Starting in 1877 he gained notoriety by making a nuisance of himself in the House of Commons, exploiting the opportunity for recognition in the country by manipulation of a media that published columns of parliamentary proceedings and, more importantly, commentary on these debates. Until the advent of the 'new journalism' late in the century, politics and the speeches of major figures were staples of the press. However, by the mid-1870s, the press was already reproducing parliamentary debates less fully and turning its focus to public speeches by major politicians. This conforms to Lazerfeld's notion of opinion leaders as 'intervening variables' between the media and audience and Gurevitch's that politicians command scarce resources, leading to pressure to follow the top people. To meet this buoyant demand the recently founded Press Association, Central News Agency and Exchange Telegraph engaged shorthand writers to cover the extra-parliamentary speeches of key figures and then sold the reports to newspapers in three forms – brief synopses, medium and verbatim accounts.[24] This was done for profit and the more copies sold the higher the return, thus reinforcing the tendency to focus on leading politicians. Initially, Parnell discovered that he could secure wide attention at home by participation at late hours in the distant Palace of Westminster. Moreover, although he was only one of a small set of so-called Irish 'obstructives', the press and in its wake people in Ireland identified the tactic and 'resistance' to British domination with him. By sometimes crude use of 'obstruction' and the forum of Westminster, he was able to sidestep the clergy and respectable elements in Ireland, obviating the need for an organisation or a public relations apparatus.

In late August 1877 Parnell reaped the first reward for his newly found status by being elected President of the Home Rule Confederation of Great Britain. In September he made a tour of northern English and west of Scotland towns to publicise the policy of parliamentary activism, a theme he promoted at several speaking engagements in Ireland as well. Parnell spoke in nine different places in Great Britain, usually to enthusiastic assemblages of receptive Irishmen who knew him by the reputation amassed essentially through an largely unsympathetic press. His speeches were reproduced verbatim in the local press and by traditional norms the tour was successful but Parnell's reach to an outside audience was constrained. The national press in London tended to allocate only brief references to his appearances and even Irish newspapers gave the tour measured acknowledgement. As a consequence historians, too, have tended to give these outings only limited attention: O'Brien refers to three of the speeches, devoting a paragraph to the campaign.[25] Public speeches, like parliamentary participation, could only transcend the narrow confines of an immediate audience when these were published in prominent newspapers. Parnell's efforts did not suggest that he was on the threshold of an innovatory form of political communication. During the next year he scarcely spoke in Ireland or elsewhere and 'obstruction' was blunted by an agile government that withheld a major Irish measure until late in the session, ensuring that the 'activists', should they delay government business, would bear responsibility for its loss. At the beginning of 1879 Parnell began a second tour of northern towns but this proved a dismal flop and was abandoned after merely three meetings. Both O'Brien and Lyons omit mention of this brief campaign.

By 1879 Parnell had achieved notoriety mainly by espousing a sectional point of view and concentrating energy disproportionately on topics of marginal concern to people at home. He gained notice but lacked a galvanising issue and obstruction had already been exposed as a limited piece of weaponry. Following Isaac Butt's death in May, William Shaw was elected party chairman. Parnell's future assumption of leadership was by no means inevitable, or perhaps even very likely. Early in the year Parnell spoke on the land question and then did so again at Westport on 8 June. His sound bite there quickly found its way into popular parlance: tenants should 'show landlords that you intend to hold a firm grip on your homesteads and land'.[26] As the agricultural crisis deepened, he took a more active role in the land agitation, accepting the Presidency of the Irish National Land League when it was founded on 21 October. As the League lacked funds, Parnell agreed to visit America to solicit for money to maintain its operations. John Dillon was selected to accompany him. An interesting backdrop to the tour is the vastly lower degree of interest roused by Dillon's appearances. This pattern confirms the hypothesis that the media bows to pressure to follow top people. Parnell was a media creation and once he became a 'major' figure, the press concentrated on his activities, not to the exclusion of other Irish agitators but they received less attention. It was a self-sustaining syndrome; Parnell was elevated to symbolic status and having attained this stature retained his centrality in the interactive media-political relationship. This may be seen as a form of take-off into self-sustaining media personality growth.

The tour, 2 January–11 March 1879

Parnell and Dillon left Queenstown on 27 December 1879, disembarking at New York on 2 January. Parnell kept a rough ledger of his visit and saved cuttings from local newspapers of his speeches. Both he and Davitt (who did not accompany Parnell) used the ledger in preparation of their testimony to the Special Commission on Parnellism and Crime. Volume XX [Parnell's evidence] describes portions of the tour. The ledger subsequently disappeared. However, Davitt made notes from it and his account in *The Fall of Feudalism in Ireland*, along with Parnell's testimony, form the fullest contemporary records.[27] O'Brien knew of the ledger but did not see it. Parnell claimed to have visited 62 cities and addressed forty to fifty meetings, although he made other impromptu speeches along the way.[28] Texts for most of the speeches have been located. Two compilations of Parnell's speeches, the first for the Special Commission and a small volume, *Words of the Dead Chief* (1892), omit addresses delivered in North America.[29]

Arrangements for the tour were, in part at least, in the hands of the Clan na Gael, a revolutionary organisation though Parnell denied its involvement. He stated, 'I am absolutely convinced that the arrangements for my tours were in nobody's hands. We had to complain most strongly of the want of any organisation to receive us or to arrange for our tours'.[30] No itinerary was established on arrival and the route followed was haphazard, geographically bounded in the United States by Massachusetts in the north-east to Richmond, Virginia in the upper south, extending as far west as Iowa but also including stops in Toronto and Montreal in Canada. During his testimony Parnell traced his route with the aid of a map. It took place in the depth of a harsh winter season. Dillon usually spoke at the meetings and made several speeches elsewhere. A third member of the troop, John Murdock, a Scottish radical land reformer, who American audiences found unintelligible was usually present as well. Parnell insisted:

we usually got invitations from the mayors of the cities either by telegraph or by letter, and Mr Dillon and I were left entirely to our own instincts as to which city we should visit first. On account of this, we made our tour in the most absurd fashion owing to the want of organisation. We went here, there, and everywhere, passing many important cities we had to return to, travelling over long distances of country. In one case we went from the eastern seaboard to Indianapolis down in the central west of America, a journey considerably over 1,000 miles and returned the next day. We travelled thousands of miles needlessly which we should have avoided had there been the slightest organisation.[31]

This misleading version has been restated in standard works. He spoke at Toledo and other cities in Ohio immediately after his stop in Indianapolis.

Parnell's speeches, though much less often those of his companions, were normally published verbatim in the local newspapers. Only the ethnic press, particularly *The Irish World* and the *Irish-American*, followed the mission across the country and routinely printed the texts. Parnell denied ever meeting Patrick Ford, proprietor of *The Irish World*. The texts found in the ethnic press were derived from local newspapers; Parnell maintained that no reporter of *The Irish World* was present at any of his meetings. Irish-American newspapers, of course, form a channel of communication within the diaspora. Nearly every city in the north and middle-west had an Irish-Catholic newspaper; perhaps half a million families subscribed to one of these. At the close of the century *The Irish World* had a circulation of 125,000 and the *Boston Pilot* some 75,000 and others reached figures of 20–50,000. But dissemination of information within the American Irish fold did not constitute true globalisation and Parnell himself testified to the Special Commission that his intention was to reach a general American audience. He addressed five state legislatures [New York, Virginia, Kentucky, Wisconsin and Iowa] and the House of Representatives in Washington, D. C. At each meeting the platform was occupied by pro-minent and usually respectable Irishmen, priests, Protestant ministers along with local and state officials, most of whom were not Irish. In Boston, for instance, Wendell Phillips was one of the speakers. There was no national newspaper and while the *New York Herald* gave the mission regular, if critical, coverage and its reporter accompanied the tour party,[32] the *New York Times* did not and Americans, while interested in the visit, usually experienced only its local manifestation. Nevertheless, local newspapers published one or more articles, usually with a photograph, about the impending visit just prior to Parnell's arrival and usually an editorial commented on the meeting and his speech. The published texts which were compiled by local staff are not as reliable as their contemporary counterparts in Great Britain and Ireland; Parnell rightly complained, 'the reporting in America was not very good outside of the great eastern cities'.[33] The news agencies did not send a team of experienced shorthand recorders; the reports they produced were based on local sources and truncated. This deficiency may account for the notorious 'last link' phrase at Cincinnati on 20 February when Parnell was reported as stating, 'and let us not forget that that is the ultimate goal at which all we Irish aim. None of us – whether we are in America or in Ireland; or wherever we may

be – will be satisfied until we have destroyed the last link which keeps
Ireland bound to England'.

An engrossing historiography centres on the Cincinnati speech; Lyons
suggested that Parnell, a passionate man, might have been swept along by
the enthusiasm he encountered in America.[34] Parnell's denial of the phrase
before the Special Commission was rather tentative but earlier he repudiated
it unequivocally in the House of Commons. The 'last link' section had
been circulating for some time beginning with Philip H. Bagenal's
pamphlet (1880) and repeated in a second tome (1882).[35] Edward Gibson
cited it in the House of Commons and then on 21 January 1886 it was
reproduced inaccurately and attributed to an obviously incorrect date by
a Conservative MP, when it was immediately repudiated by Parnell.[36]
G. O. Trevelyan correctly quoted the speech on 25 May, attributing the
report to *The Irish World*. Parnell responded, 'I have by me a verbatim
report of both of the speeches I made at Cincinnati on the day in question
five years ago, and no such words quoted . . . appear in those speeches' or
in any American speeches.[37] He offered to deliver the original text as it
appeared in the *Cincinnati Daily Gazette* to Trevelyan. Bagenal on 27 May
published the 'last link' phrase again in a letter to *The Times*.[38] Once more
the source was *The Irish World*. At the Special Commission a report in
another Cincinnati newspaper did contain the phrase and it is this account
of the speech which was duplicated by *The Irish World*. Parnell probably
had no knowledge of the alternative version though he would have realised
that opponents had been ransacking his North American speeches in
search of incriminating material.

The absence of systematic pre-planning, an unclear purpose, and controversy surrounding the three other funds threatened the mission. Funds
to relieve distress had been started by the wife of the Lord Lieutenant, the
Duchess of Marlborough (18 December 1879; £135,000), a second under
the chairmanship of Edmund Dwyer Gray, a parliamentary colleague and
proprietor of the *Freeman's Journal* (2 January 1880, The Mansion House
Committee; £180,000), and then while he was in America, James Gordon
Bennett, owner of the *New York Herald*, began a third fund. Parnell
attempted to discourage contributions to the rival funds; his stance became
a source of controversy as the mission progressed. Healy joined the tour at
the end of February at Davenport, Iowa in an effort to improve the
organisation but his participation lasted only about two weeks.

The mission suffered from an ill-defined and shifting rationale. Initially
the idea was to secure contributions for the operations of the Land League
and only incidentally to solicit funds for relief. Solicitation of funds for
relief quickly became pre-eminent [*c.* £60,000; *c.* £12,000 for the Land
League]. He told the Special Commission that 'our chief efforts were

directed to collecting money for the relief of distress. The proceeds of all my meetings were given for the relief of distress without exception'.[39] Prior to disembarking, Parnell granted an interview to the *New York Herald* during which he stated that though the original purpose had been political he now meant to give primacy to the relief of distress.[40] In his first public meeting held in Madison Square Garden, New York, on 4 January Parnell plugged the humanitarian theme:

Our object in visiting this country and I may say the intention we originally formed have been considerably modified by the pressure of circumstances. Originally we proposed only to address you on behalf of our political organisation, but the course of events in Ireland has culminated so rapidly – a terrible, far and wider spread of famine is so imminent – that we felt constrained to abandon our original intention, and to leave ourselves open to receive from the people of America money for the purposes of our political organisation and also money for the relief of the pressing distress in Ireland.[41]

On 14 January in Fall River, Massachusetts he pleaded,

the immensity of the famine, and the certainty that unless something is done very speedily, in six or seven of the large counties in the West of Ireland, thousands will perish of the most horrible of all deaths, famine; so we have changed in obedience to the dictates of humanity and ask you to assist us in endeavouring to remove the distress in Ireland.[42]

Relief remained a theme which he carried into Canada, stating at Toronto on 7 March:

This welcome sufficiently dispels the calumny which was heaped by the pro-British press upon the people of Canada – that they did not sympathise with the suffering people of Ireland. Your actions before we came here had indeed sufficiently dispelled that calumny, but I am glad that you have also reserved some of your sympathy for our mission, and while you have showed before our arrival that your hearts were opened and that your money was ready to alleviate the distress of Ireland, so also your wish to help us in preventing the recurrence of that distress.[43]

Parnell contrasted the humanitarian assistance freely rendered from overseas with the stingy response of the British government and people. The shift to a humanitarian appeal was not to everyone's satisfaction. Dr William Carroll reflected the considerable dismay inside the Clan na Gael, 'charity should have been kept separate from politics and such is the general feeling in Phila[dephia], especially among our friends the Newspapers'.[44]

The tour had other themes – discussion of the land question, the demand for self-government, and an explanation of the 'active' policy in Parliament, though this last soon drifted into the shadows as it became apparent that Americans failed to grasp it. Parnell argued at every meeting that the rural distress was artificial and a consequence of the 'feudal' land system. At

Baltimore on 13 February he said, 'we charge that the famines and chronic poverty of Ireland are due to the absurd and cruel system of land tenure. We have there a feudal land tenure'.[45] He urged that the problems of Ireland could never be remedied unless the system was abolished. In Detroit on 22 February Parnell intoned, 'there must be some cause why these artificial famines should be so frequent and so terrible, and we charge the cause of these famines upon the artificial system of land tenure which prevails in that country. [applause] That land system . . . is the feudal land tenure'.[46] On 27 February at Dubuque, Iowa he repeated,

The Irish famine is a famine of the means with which to buy food. The rack-rents which the landlords have been exacting have left the people without any means to buy food; and thus all the Irish tenantry who have endeavoured to pay these impossible rents now find themselves without the wherewithal to save their wives and little ones from starvation. What is this Irish system of land tenure? It is one which has been tried and found wanting, and abandoned in every other civilised country. All the nations which originally started with it, including America, have given it up, except Great Britain and Ireland. And we in Ireland intend to give it up now.[47]

The ultimate goal of self-government, or as he put it the right of nation-hood, too, was articulated at most meetings. At Brooklyn on 9 January he associated the land struggle with the national question, saying 'when we shall have struck the first blow, the first vital blow, at the land system as it now exists in Ireland, and then we shall have taken the first step to obtain for Ireland the right to nationhood for which she has struggled so long as so well'.[48] To his audience in a part of the country with a small Irish population, Dubuque, he stated on 27 February:

and when we have killed the Irish land system we shall have plucked out and ground to powder the corner stone of British misrule in Ireland, for one of the principal props of that misrule has been the system of land tenure there. Emigrate the Irish landlords and the British government will soon have to follow them. And you who have helped us today, when you have assisted our people to take their proper place amongst the nations of the world, you will have the proud satisfaction of knowing that you also did what you could, freely and spontaneously to gain the rights of Ireland.[49]

However, there was a little noticed object of the mission – to construct a dialogue with the British Government on Irish land in which American opinion was a lynchpin. At Madison Square Garden Parnell explained:

We want to relieve the people, but we also want to sweep away the bad system which has led to the distress. America has always come forward with unexampled liberality to relieve distress in Ireland, but all the charity of America cannot perma-nently relieve us. We must shame the British Government into doing us justice. We don't want to come to you in the guise of mendicants every year. The

American people must not forget that our great point is to reach the British Government by means of an open discussion of the Irish land question before the nations of the earth.[50]

As has been observed, Parnell stressed the virtue of educating British opinion as early as 1876. Yet he asserted at Leeds on 12 November 1879 that there continued to be the difficulty of reaching this opinion:

It was almost impossible to get through the cloud of prejudice which seemed to envelop the English mind regarding every Irish question. At the present moment the land agitation in Ireland, which was necessary in order to save the people from starvation and from being driven from the country, was subject to all kinds of misrepresentation The agitation – which was in every sense of the word perfectly constitutional, and carried on in the ordinary and legitimate method of public meetings – had been denounced by the English newspapers as communistic, revolutionary, and even murderous in character. (Laughter.) If they could get English public opinion enlightened upon Irish questions, and induce the House of Commons to enter into a full and fair inquiry into their position, he believed it would be evident that their cause was a perfectly just one, and people would wonder why they had ever opposed it.[51]

This intent, only feasible with modernised communications, sought a globalisation of opinion, transcending the diaspora, and through the transmission of information and exertion of pressure via the media. The British Government was to be educated by an American opinion, an opinion that would itself be shaped by the informing purpose of Parnell's mission. In this regard he anticipated the globalisation of localised crises that has emerged, especially since the mid-1980s. If this tour was dogged by inconsistencies and fluctuating aims, Parnell never lost sight of the intent to 'inform' and thereby create an American attitude that would influence the calculations of British leaders. His most deliberately prepared address during the visit, before the House of Representatives in Washington, D.C., underlined this conception. To an audience that had reservations about the nationalist intent behind the tour, he pointed out:

I feel it to be equally my duty to point out to you the cause which keeps Ireland in a condition of chronic poverty and brings on from time to time such horrible famines as that which is at present raging there. When the task is thrown upon America of feeding a people who have been driven into starvation by ruinous and unjust laws, surely you acquire a right to express your opinion very freely on the character of those laws and on the policy of maintaining them. And I have every confidence that the public sentiment of America will be a great assistance to our people in their present effort to obtain a just and suitable settlement of the Irish land question. . . . I do not seek to embroil your Government with the government of England; but we claim that the public opinion and sentiment of a free country like America is entitled to find expression wherever it is seen that the laws of freedom are not observed.[52]

He then said:

It will be a proud boast for America if, after having obtained, secured, and ratified her own freedom by sacrifices unexampled in the history of any nation, she were now, by the force of her public opinion alone, by the respect with which all countries look upon any sentiment prevailing here, if she were now to obtain for Ireland, without the shedding of one drop of blood, without drawing the sword, without one threatening message, the solution of this great question. For my part, I, as one who boasts of American blood, feel proud of the importance which has been universally attached on all sides to American opinion with regard to this matter, and I am happy in seeing and believing that the time is very near at hand when you will be able to say you have in the way I have mentioned, and in no other way, been a most important factor in bringing about a settlement of the Irish land question.[53]

This message was repeated constantly. In a State and to a body relatively uninfluenced by the pressure of the diaspora, the Wisconsin legislature, Parnell stated on 25 February, 'the public opinion of the people of this country will be of the utmost importance to the people of Ireland in settling the great land question'.[54] Throughout the engagements Parnell mixed the three themes of relief of distress, the need to mobilise world opinion behind ending the system of landlordism which he claimed was the cause of periodic famines in Ireland, and the aspiration of Ireland taking its place among the nations of the world.

Communication of the tour

While the humanitarian appeal received widespread support from an American public extending far beyond the Irish-America circuit, Parnell's critique of the land system was less generally accepted and the self-government demand with a concomitant hostility to Great Britain provoked dissent and frequently opposition in local newspapers. Moreover, Parnell alienated influential opinion by criticising the three other relief funds. Few American commentators were sympathetic to his attacks and indeed most were reluctant to draw distinctions between the different organisations seeking to provide emergency assistance to Ireland's rural destitute. And, finally, even though Parnell's early halting speaking style had improved, he remained infinitely more suited to the House of Commons than to populist demonstrations. At Philadelphia the local newspaper praised his 'manifest sincerity' rather than his qualities as a speaker; in Boston it was noted, 'he has some hesitancy in his speech, often corrects a word or phrase which he has uttered, and during the latter part of his address he was visibly affected'.[55] Alexander Sullivan claimed that Parnell achieved oratorical maturity in the course of the mission, noting 'when he first spoke in my hearing in public [at Indianapolis] his voice was unsteady, his address without evidence of previous mental plan, his ideas, each sharp and substantive, without cohesiveness, his feeling towards his audience timid and ineffectual'.[56] But, according to Sullivan, by the time Parnell reached Chicago he was an effective speaker. This opinion, though, is confuted by subsequent reports. From St Paul, Minnesota, it was observed, 'his manner is quiet, and his gestures few and it is evidently his subject more than his style that appeals to the audience. He makes no oratorical displays, and attempts no rhetorical flourishes, but states his views and facts so calmly that he seldom rouses the enthusiasm for which his countrymen are so noted' while the local newspaper at Peoria, Illinois, remarked 'his manner is not calculated to produce very much enthusiasm'.[57]

Parnell stuck essentially to the same formula in each appearance but in spite of the practice many of the speeches lacked finessse. His limitations were often accentuated by overlong preliminaries preceding his addresses. Still, the mission which lasted beyond Parnell's own stay was an outstanding triumph. His intention to bring American opinion to bear on British politicians may have been an illusory expectation, but during the North American tour Parnell certainly projected the demand for land reform to the forefront of the political agenda, focused attention on the Land League, and, in part, as a consequence scored successes in the general election held in April 1880, becoming party chairman the following month. Some of these things could have been possible without the tour but the trip hastened the process and quite possibly is the single foremost factor in enabling him to wrest the chairmanship of the parliamentary party.

Parnell's primary object was to influence opinion and in this context he sought to pull the levers of power in American life. His audiences at most venues were mainly Irish but he also visited several state capitals, spoke to many state governors, mayors, religious leaders and other prominent people, the majority being neither Irish nor beholden to Irish-American electors. For most of this audience the humanitarian motive of the mission greatly outweighed the political content. Parnell's wider function, then, was to have an impact on opinion for the longer term. It was this part of the tour that had the greatest implications, lifting him from being a mere agitator to a figure identified with compassion.

Overall, this mission achieved three things. It enlisted North American opinion behind the Irish farmers in their time of need, it placed the Irish problem in a context that was comprehensible and acceptable to middle-class Irish people overseas, though again underlining that this was mainly because of the humanitarian appeal, and it made Parnell into the foremost Irishman of his age. Only a comparatively small number of Irish-Americans saw or heard Parnell but most knew about him thereafter. And even though he never crossed the Atlantic again, his image loomed large.

However useful Parnell's trip was, its main significance lay not in specific accomplishments but in the way it was publicised in America, Great Britain, and most importantly in Ireland. This is a reminder that communication is both selective in terms of audience and uneven in its spread. The absence of a national newspaper in the United States meant that the mission was unevenly covered. The *New York Herald* followed his progress along the east coast during January but paid less attention to the western portion of the circuit. And, while Parnell emphasised the role of American opinion, he actually found that his trip had more impact at home. The nationalist weeklies, *The Nation* and *Ulster Examiner*, reported it extensively. More importantly, the *Freeman's Journal*, which had the largest circulation in Ireland and whose owner headed the rival Mansion House Committee, followed the tour in detail until early February and less completely thereafter, printing full or synopsised texts derived mainly from American newspapers. *The Irish Times*, which had little time for Parnell's politics, also followed the tour carefully, again printing a number of texts. It noted the Cincinnati meeting but used only the brief report supplied by Reuters. Like the *Freeman's Journal*, coverage of the eastern leg was more comprehensive than of the west. No Irish periodical sent its own reporting staff but they relied on cable services and local accounts of each meeting. Thus Parnell succeeded in reaching a wide audience in Ireland while speaking thousands of miles away. Interestingly, *The Times* also gave the mission substantial attention though the reports received from the Anglo-American Cables generally were brief. It took a critical, not to say hostile, view of the tour, sometimes reprinting unfavourable notices from American newspapers. Portions of a number of speeches based on local reports were printed and the trip was the subject of several editorials. The Cincinnati meeting was not noticed, though Parnell's declaration at Buffalo that Ireland had a 'right to separate nationality' was given adverse attention. Once more the eastern section received more attention than the later meetings. In this instance even a hostile newspaper ensured that Parnell's image was widely disseminated and that he reached a large 'unpresent' audience. And, in some ways, the brief notices served Parnell's purpose equally as well as printing full texts and reports for it kept the London political elite aware of the mission and, of course, enforced the sense that if Parnell was not yet the leader of the national movement he was assuredly its foremost figure.

Conclusion

Parnell was a pioneering figure. In tracing the evolution of political communication, Parnell assumes a pivotal place and the American mission of 1880 shows clearly that in the process of globalisation, physical proximity, if still valuable, was less decisive than access to the media. He elevated Irish political dialogue to a new plateau, creating a huge audience for himself. His mission is a foretaste of the now familiar trips by political leaders abroad designed to capture attention at home and in that respect was an advance on the methods employed by British politicians sketched in Colin Matthew's study. Parnell learned that he could communicate from almost anywhere and in doing so he made the Irish national platform mobile and less easily stifled than had proved true for his predecessors.

This brief incident fits certain key paradigms and also adds a dimension to the theoretical discussion. Lazerfeld's contention that the audience is a tissue of interrelated rather than isolated individuals whom the communicator activates and that 'opinion leaders' had the vital role of 'intervening variables' between the media and audience are illustrated in this case study, as is Gerbner's emphasis on the media's function of forming the 'mass' and creating common ways [among the Irish] of understanding the world. At the same time Gurevitch's stress on the mutual dependence between the political communicator and the media along with the pressure to give chief figures the lion's share of attention is validated. Dillon, whose part in the mission was ultimately larger than Parnell's, received vastly less attention then and subsequently, while Murdock has gone nearly unnoticed. But most of all, it confirms Thompson's observation that messages are produced for an audience not physically present at the place of production, the necessity of information storage mechanisms which persist, the reproducible nature of information and availability of the message. Although Parnell's message was important, ultimately his means of creating audiences and transmitting signals is the lasting legacy.

NOTES

I wish to thank Carla King for reading and commenting on this article and Patrick Maume for useful points. Also, I wish to thank my aunt, Helen E. O'Day, for her encouragement and support once again.

1 James Bryce, *Studies in Contemporary Biography* (London, 1903), pp. 241–2.
2 H. C. G. Matthew, 'Rhetoric and Politics in Britain, 1860–1950', in P. J. Waller (ed.), *Politics and Social Change in Modern Britain* (Sussex, 1987), pp. 34–58.
3 *Ibid.*, p. 43.
4 *Ibid.*, p. 46.
5 *Ibid.*, p. 48.
6 *Ibid.*, p. 52.
7 A discussion of some of this literature can be found in Alan O'Day, *Charles Stewart Parnell* (Dublin, 1998), pp. 65–76; D. George Boyce, '"The Portrait of the King is

the King": The Biographers of Charles Stewart Parnell', in D. George Boyce and Alan O'Day (eds), *Parnell in Perspective* (London, 1991), pp. 284–309.

8 Conor Cruise O'Brien, *Parnell and his Party 1880–90* (corrected impression; Oxford, 1964), p. 7.

9 F. S. L. Lyons, *Charles Stewart Parnell* (London, 1977), p. 612.

10 *Montreal Gazette*, 10 March 1880.

11 Gary Owens, 'Constructing the image of Daniel O'Connell', *History Ireland* 7 (Spring, 1999), pp. 32–6. This, of course, was not wholly absent in Parnell's case. See James Loughlin, 'Constructing the political spectacle: Parnell, the press and national leadership, 1879–86', in Boyce and O'Day (eds), *Parnell in Perspective*, pp. 221–41.

12 Katharine O'Shea, *Charles Stewart Parnell: His Love Story and Political Life* (London, 1914), I, pp. 235–36.

13 Edward Byrne, *Parnell: A Memoir*, ed. Frank Callanan (Dublin, 1991), p. 23.

14 *The Times*, 4 Feb. 1880.

15 *Freeman's Journal*, 22 March 1880.

16 R. Barry O'Brien, *The Life of Charles Stewart Parnell 1846–1891* (London, 1898), I, pp. 198–207, passim; see also F. S. L. Lyons, *Charles Stewart Parnell* (London, 1977), pp. 102–15.

17 M. V. Hazel, 'First link: Parnell's American tour, 1880', *Éire-Ireland* 15 (1980), 24; also, Wayne C. Minnick, 'Parnell in America', *Speech Monographs* 20 (1953), 39–48; Robert M. Post, 'A rhetorical criticism of the speeches delivered by Charles Stewart Parnell during his 1880 American Tour', PhD thesis, Ohio State University, 1961, and, 'Charles Stewart Parnell before Congress', *Quarterly Journal of Speech* 51 (1965), 419–25.

18 *Ibid.*

19 Michael Davitt, *The Fall of Feudalism in Ireland* (London and New York, 1904), pp. 193–210 (p. 210).

20 Robert Kee, *The Laurel and the Ivy: the Story of Charles Stewart Parnell and Irish Nationalism* (London, 1993), pp. 217–34.

21 *Parliamentary Debates* (*PD*), 306, c. 119, 25 May 1886).

22 For Lazerfeld and the other authorities discussed in this paragraph, see Oliver Boyd-Barrett and Chris Newbold (eds), *Approaches to Media: A Reader* (London, 1995).

23 *The United Irishman*, 18 Nov. 1876.

24 Matthew, 'Rhetoric and politics', pp. 43–4.

25 O'Brien, *Parnell*, I, pp. 149–50.

26 *Freeman's Journal*, 9 June 1879.

27 Davitt, *Fall of Feudalism*, pp. 193–206,

28 *Special Commission*, p. 25.

29 *Mr Parnell's Speeches, Letters and Public Address (Out of Parliament) in the United Kingdom 1879–88* (Dublin, 1889); Jennie Wyse-Power (comp.), *Words of the Dead Chief: Being Extracts from the Public Speeches and Other Pronouncements of Charles Stewart Parnell, from the Beginning to the Close of his Memorable Life* (Dublin, 1892).

30 *Special Commission*, p. 24.

31 *Ibid.*

32 T. M. Healy, *Letters and Leaders of My Day* (London, 1927), I, p. 82.

33 *Special Commission*, XX, p. 33.

34 Lyons, *Parnell*, pp. 112–13.

35 Philip H. Bagenal, *Parnellism Unveiled or, The Land-and-Labour Agitation of 1879–80* (Dublin, 1880), pp. 25–6; *The American Irish and their Influence on Irish Politics* (London, 1882), p. 201.

36   *PD*, 3rd Series, 302 (21 Jan. 1886), cc. 140, 151–2.

37   *Ibid.*, 304 (25 May 1886), cc. 99–100.

38   *The Times*, 27 May 1886.

39   *Special Commission*, XX, p. 36.

40   *New York Herald*, 3 Jan. 1880.

41   *New York Times*, 5 Jan. 1880.

42   *Fall River Herald*, 15 Jan. 1880.

43   *Toronto Globe*, 8 March 1880.

44   William O'Brien and Desmond Ryan (eds), *Devoy's Post Bag 1871–1928* (Dublin, 1948), I, p. 484.

45   *The Baltimore Sun*, 14 Feb. 1880.

46   *Detroit Free Press*, 23 Feb. 1880.

47   *Dubuque Herald*, 28 Feb. 1880.

48   *Brooklyn Daily Eagle*, 10 Jan. 1880.

49   *Dubuque Herald*, 28 Feb. 1880.

50   *New York Times*, 5 Jan. 1880.

51   *Leeds Mercury*, 13 Nov. 1879.

52   *Congressional Record*, X, pt 1 (2 Feb. 1880), pp. 664–5.

53   *Ibid.*

54   *Wisconsin State Journal*, 26 Feb. 1880.

55   *Philadelphia Enquirer*, 12 Jan. 1880; *Boston Evening Transcript*, 13 Jan. 1880.

56   Quoted in Callanan, *Healy*, p. 32.

57   *St Paul Daily Pioneer*, 28 Feb. 1880; *Peoria National Democrat*, 3 March 1880.

12 Orality Lost: The Archives of the Irish Folklore Collection and Folk Historiography of *Bliain na bhFrancach*

Guy Beiner

Orality found

This chapter sets out to rethink the relationship between oral tradition and history by way of offering a reappraisal of the Irish Folklore Collection. By demonstrating the value of the Folklore Collection as an oral history archive, I wish to call attention to a hitherto much neglected, but nevertheless extremely valuable, repository of sources for the study of Irish history. Preliminary theoretical and methodological background is followed by examples from a case study in an attempt to identify some of the unique possibilities and fresh insights folklore material offers the historian of modern history while, at the same time, teasing out some of the key problems entailed. In line with recent historiographical studies, the subject matter under examination is the concept of 'the past'.[1] However, the emphasis is on vernacular and popular historical discourses, conducted primarily through the media of 'orality',[2] and the dynamics of power at play during the course of shifts from orality into written form.

In reference to orality in an Irish historical context, there can be no clear-cut dichotomy between oral and literate cultures, such as that often employed by Africanists.[3] The advent of writing undermined the possibility of a state of 'pristine orality' and, despite widespread illiteracy throughout prolonged periods into the history of modern Ireland, oral tradition constantly interacted with influences of writing. A telling example in the context of Irish folklore collecting was the detection of the penetration of stories from the *Decameron* into the rich Gaelic storytelling repertoire of the Blasket Islands.[4] Another eye-opening case relates to eighteenth-century folk poetry, which was collected primarily from oral sources, yet Louis Cullen has shown that the documentation process in the late-nineteenth and early-twentieth century was permeated with influences of written sources.[5] Orality is a dynamic state, in constant transition as it negotiates and reconstructs itself through contacts with spheres of literacy. As a form of communication, orality is best considered within the larger parameters of popular culture, reshaped by multiple agencies and various media.

The Irish Folklore Collection[6]

At the heart of the Irish Folklore Collection lies the work of the Irish Folklore Commission (*Coimisiun Béaloideasa Éireann*), which functioned from 1935 to 1970 and was a direct continuation of the Irish Folklore Institute (*Institiúid Bhéaloideas Éireann,* 1930–5). Since 1970, the Collection has been incorporated into the Department of Irish Folklore of University College Dublin.[7] Under the supervision of the Commission's Honorary Director Séamus Ó Duilearga (James Hamilton Delargy), the recording and documentation of folklore were undertaken by a team of field workers, known as 'collectors'. The collectors were either full-time, part-time or specially assigned for a specific project. They were equipped with notebooks and, when possible, with recording devices to enable verbatim transcriptions (at first ediphones and later tape recorders).[8] The collectors were charged with collecting narratives and conducting ethnographic investigations of 'folk life material'. They operated mainly in their native area, making the best of their familiarity with the locality and their personal contacts in order to gain access to storytellers of local repute.

At first the collectors were guided by personal direction and periodic issues of instructions and questionnaires. Later, more comprehensive training was provided through instruction books written by the archivist of the Irish Folklore Commission – Seán Ó Súilleabháin, who had studied the classification of folklore in Sweden under the direction of well-known folklorists.[9] Ó Súilleabháin's *A Handbook of Irish Folklore* (1942), which became the collectors' indispensable *vade-mecum*, was instrumental in standardising folklore collecting in Ireland. This book included a chapter specifically dedicated to 'Historical Tradition' (chapter XI). The *Handbook* set rigorous standards for the written documentation of folklore, including several essential guidelines for the precise recording of oral history, namely:

2. Even very small or seemingly trivial items or information should be recorded

7. Record the information in the exact words of the speaker, if possible.

11. The collector should state clearly (either on a slip affixed at the head of each item or else as a note at the end) the name, age, and full address of the person from whom he recorded the information. It is most important that the source of information be given correctly.[10]

The collectors' fieldwork spanned over all thirty-two counties of Ireland, but focused primarily on Irish speaking areas, resulting in Irish language material consisting of roughly seventy per cent of the Main Manuscript Collection in 1970. There was also a distinct preference towards rural areas in the initial work of the Irish Folklore Commission,[11] whereas urban folklore collection has been more rigorously addressed in recent years (particularly through the Urban Folklore Project run in Dublin City in 1980–1).[12] As a result of the dedicated fieldwork of the collectors, the folklore archives host a rich assortment of different types of material: manuscripts in two major collections – the Main Manuscript Collection and the Schools' Collection, pictorial (including some 40,000 photographs and also drawings, paintings, plans and maps) and sound-record (including music, songs and folk narratives). The Main Manuscript Collection currently holds over 2,200 volumes.[13] The volumes include narratives collected through oral interviews with informants. Narratives were typologically divided into *scealaíocht* and *seanchas*. Generally speaking, *seanchas* relates to shorter more realistic forms while *scéalaí* are distinctly longer and more structurally complex tales. As a rule, folk history accounts fall under the category of *seanchas*, which alongside stories also includes other genres such as place names, songs, folk-poetry and sayings.[14] The Main Manuscript Collection also hosts questionnaires, which focused on specific topics,[15] and collectors' diaries, which offer illuminating commentary regarding the context in which the fieldwork was undertaken.[16]

The Schools' Manuscripts Collection [*Bailiúchán na Scol*] dates back to the Schools' Scheme project run in national primary schools around 1937–8.[17] Séan Ó Súilleabháin, the Irish Folklore Commission archivist, provided a concise guidebook in English and Irish, issued by the Department of Education, for the principals and teachers of National Schools[18] and sent out blank copybooks to participating schools. As a result 4,337 notebooks were collected, subsequently bound in 1,126 paginated volumes, arranged in sequence of province and county. The contribution varies from school to school and the quality of the material depends on the individual pupil along with the counselling and editing of the teacher.[19] Unlike the Main Manuscript Collection, the Schools' Scheme was conducted only in the twenty-six counties of the Free State.

The Irish Folklore Collection as an oral history archive

Oral historical sources are often divided into two categories:

(*a*) *Oral history*: recollections of contemporary events.

(*b*) *Oral tradition*: a body of knowledge which was transmitted orally over several generations and is the collective property of a community.[20]

The Irish Folklore Collection contains information on a wealth of community-shared traditions, collected through oral interviews, and is therefore an oral tradition archive *par excellence*. Folk-history, or folklore material of explicit historical nature (*seanchas*), appears in the archive both directly (in narrative form, namely stories about historical episodes) and indirectly (through references in place names, songs, ballads, folk-poetry, proverbs etc.).

Like all transcriptions of oral sources, the archival material in the Irish Folklore Collection is mediated through the working assumptions of its collectors. Amongst the main limitations of the archive from a historian's point of view is an underlying, somewhat romantic notion of folklore, which is often a-historical, tending to present oral tradition as an a-temporal and solid set of antique texts faithfully passed on with reverence from one generation to another. By focusing on the narrative, classification and primary analysis of the material in the archive often neglect crucial issues regarding historical context. Furthermore, the focus on Irish-speaking rural areas does not always accommodate major sociolinguistic and demographic trends in modern Irish history, namely emigration, migration (specifically to Dublin) and language shift. A characteristic nationalist prejudice in the founding period of the archive directed the working definition of folklore towards what was regarded as the culture of the 'native' population, often neglecting Ascendancy, Protestant and loyalist traditions. Moreover, elementary gender critique reveals the dominantly masculine nature of folklore collecting, as both collectors and informants were, quantitatively speaking, predominantly male.

Cathal Póirtéir observed that the major obstacle preventing the utilisation of folklore material by historians has been principally methodological:

As yet, in Ireland, no acceptable methodology has been arrived at between folklorists and historians to evaluate folk material as an historical source, although both the wealth of that tradition and its systematic collection in Ireland is very highly regarded by folklorists and ethnologists world-wide.[21]

Since most of the historical material in the folklore archive is not contemporary with the historical events and was recorded following multiple transmissions and performances, historians' suspicions often arise regarding the authenticity and value of the source material. An inspiring example of first steps towards addressing this lacuna can be found in the innovative work of Cormac Ó Gráda, who, in the context of Famine Studies, has moved beyond presenting anthologies of folklore sources and has delved into issues pertaining to analysis.[22] Niall Ó Ciosáin has recently advanced this direction by presenting a preliminary historical typology of famine narratives in the folklore archives.[23]

The challenges of oral history: towards a conceptualisation of vernacular historiography

Generally speaking, there are two basic schools of oral history research: positivist and interpretative. The positivist approach clings to an empiricist doctrine and is characterised by the historian's attempt to identify 'hard facts' in oral sources. The trustworthiness of oral sources is called into question as problems of unreliability and validity arise, mainly because oral accounts are mostly recorded at a later date and are therefore obviously not contemporaneous to the historical event.[24] Questions of unreliability can be overcome by checking the consistency with which an individual tells the story on different occasions and by collecting, if possible, several testimonies on one event. Careful selection of informants[25] together with reference to sociological research often contribute to overcoming problems of representativeness by allowing an evaluation of how typical and how central specific oral testimonies are to a society.[26]

The American folklorist and historian Richard M. Dorson laid out helpful criteria for assessing the validity of oral traditions, namely: corroborating testimony (the degree of conformity with other primary source material); support from mnemonic devices; presence of professional chroniclers and saga-men; continuities in locus of transmission (socio-demographic stability versus migration of peoples and their histories); and discounting individualistic and folkloristic elements in the narrative.[27] Historians' opposition to the positivist school's usage of oral sources can be overcome by integrating oral evidence into a comprehensive historical investigation, where archival printed material and oral sources correlate with one another in order to reveal their specificity and difference. In this regard, oral testimonies can be regarded as another contribution to the reservoir of primary sources, to be categorised perhaps as 'memory claims', highly susceptible to bias and therefore to be treated with particular caution.

The interpretative school of oral history calls attention to many of the unique characteristics of oral material and its ability to focus on mentalities.[28] As John Tosh has commented in a review of oral history:

oral research is less important as *histoire vérité* or as an expression of community politics than as precious evidence of how popular historical consciousness is constructed . . . The very subjectivity of the speaker may be the most important thing about his or her testimony.[29]

In a pertinent critique of the positivist approach to oral tradition, the anthropologist Elizabeth Tonkin argued persuasively that 'bias' 'is an essential part of any communication, and is not a flaw to which oral tellers are particularly prone'.[30] By offering a window into how individuals in a community remember their shared past, interpretative analysis is invaluable towards attempting an examination of social memory (a term which is more appropriate than the more familiar 'collective memory', for it calls attention to the fluid social dynamics constantly at play in the construction of communal discourses of the past).

An interrogation of social memory is at the heart of the new French historiographical school *Les Lieux de Mémoire* (translated recently as 'Realms of Memory'), spearheaded by Pierre Nora and involving the cream of France's contemporary historians. Yet Nora's project is built on the basic assumption of a binary opposition, according to which history today is irrevocably divorced from memory.[31] Whereas in Ireland, it appears that memory and history were not necessarily separated and they consistently interact in the world folklore. An open challenge facing Irish historical studies is the examination of the memory of historical events in folk discourses.

Maurice Halbwachs, the pioneer of the study of social memory, commented: 'Our memory rests truly not on learned history but on lived history.'[32] The English radical historian Raphael Samuel advocated that history is essentially a social form of knowledge, envisioning a historiography that would not be based on examination of historians' work alone, but instead recommended inspecting an 'ensemble of activities and practices in which ideas of history are embedded or a dialectic of past-present relations is rehearsed'. Samuel's concept of history as an activity with many practitioners advocates a democratisation of academic history towards what may be described as a 'folk history'.[33] The term 'folk history' is not new to Irish scholarship and signifies a recognised field within folklore studies.[34] However, it is often presented as an a-temporal, constant construction. Awareness of issues relating to multiple transmissions and performances reveals the dynamic and constantly changing nature of oral tradition. Therefore, folk history necessarily entails a complex contextual-historical understanding of the variable nature of repeated history-tellings, which may be termed 'folk historiography'.

An analysis of folk history transcends the confines of academic history, looking at popular reception of historical events and subsequent interpretation and manipulation in social memory. Folk history is complex and diverse by nature, incorporating multiple narratives performed by numerous narrators in various versions. Therefore, this is more a case of manifold 'folk histories' or rather 'folk historiographies'. It is a particularly difficult task to attempt to trace the changes over time within the various components of oral historiographies and chart the developments in popular reconstructions of the past. Jan Vansina has demonstrated how recurrent events tend to merge in recall, so that often only the first and last occurrence of habitual or repetitive activities are distinctly remembered.[35] In their study of social memory, Fentress and Wickham observed that in oral tradition without written records to freeze a version at any stage of transmission, there is no basis for comparison. The version as told by the storyteller seems the same as the version learned by the storyteller many years ago. And this version, in its turn, seems identical to the version first told, many generations ago, when the supposed event was still fresh in everyone's mind. There is no perception of the process of change, for this process obliterates itself in passing.[36]

Unlike a standard investigation of historiography, research of folk historiographies can never strive to be definitive.

Orality lost

By referring to 'orality lost', I would like to call attention to three processes in the transition of oral-folk history into written forms. Firstly, as already indicated, oral traditions are constantly changing and therefore social memory is inevitably exposed to processes of 'forgetfulness' – as traditions from the past are no longer practised and gradually disappear. Folklorists are driven by the urgency to document traditions of a passing world. Even if the expression of these sentiments is sometimes criticised as a literary trope of nostalgic nature, it is an indisputable fact that undocumented material is exposed to erosion and, particularly in times of rapid social and economic change, is ultimately doomed to extinction. Folklore collection is inevitably a limited project and, regrettably, many oral traditions remain unrecorded, only to be lost to posterity.

Secondly, it is necessary to acknowledge the inherent irony of most oral history work, which implies the unconscious shift from performance to text. Orality is often lost in oral history research, which tends to be based on transcripts of oral material. Likewise, the final product of oral history research is almost invariably published as a textual-printed product.[37] Researchers with ethnographic awareness, such as Elizabeth Tonkin, have pointed out that oral genres inherently include aspects of performance and are dependent on the circumstances and conditions of recitors and audiences. Therefore, they are social products and text cannot be separated from context.[38] Folklore collecting, in terms of written documentation of oral tradition, is essentially the 'fossilisation' of the living-oral recital of folk history. The folklorist Lauri Honko presented an innovative model for the 'folklore process', which she divided into 'two lives of folklore'. The 'first life' of folklore in this model relates to traditions in a genuine living environment and follows their documentation through collection, con-servation in archives and their initial scientific analysis. The 'second life' of folklore follows the utilisation of the material in the archive through 'recycling mechanisms' alien to the original cultural context.[39] It is often in this 'second life' that oral history research distances itself from the supposedly characteristic orality of its sources.

Thirdly, historiographical consciousness reveals the neglect and rejection of oral-folk history material by contemporary academic historians. Historians of the ancient world since Herodotus and Thucydides used oral sources, as did medieval historians and chroniclers and writers of history into the early-modern age.[40] It was in the nineteenth century that the Rankean school of historicism[41] confined history exclusively to written documents found in archives, delegitimising oral evidence. Folk histories are by nature democratic endeavours by which communities narrate their pasts in their own words. In his renowned post-colonial critique, Edward Said accused Western academics of assuming an oppressive, colonial role. Said called attention to the subtle dynamics of power and authority by which the people of the East were not permitted to represent themselves in Orientalist Studies but, instead, were represented by the Orientalist.[42] In much the same way, historians of today 'colonise' history, not allowing the people of the past a voice of their own, but speaking for them.

The disciples of the 'new Irish history' followed this direction, introducing what Ronan Fanning has identified as 'a striking characteristic of modern Irish historiography: a continuous compulsion to confront myth and mythology'.[43] By adhering to a fundamental dichotomy between 'history' and 'popular mythology' (implying a parallel binary opposition between 'truth' and 'myth'), mainstream Irish historiography openly rejected folk history, refusing to integrate oral tradition into historical research. This deficient legacy continues today into a so-called 'post-revisionist' historiographical climate. In the next section I shall illustrate briefly how oral tradition was neglected in recent high profile historiographic debate, demonstrating the overtones of 'orality lost'. Several constructive suggestions are made by indicating the possibilities entailed in redressing these missed opportunities and in attempting to tap into folk historiographies.

Speaking '98: folk historiographies of *Bliain na bhFrancach*

Anyone with interest in the history of modern Ireland could not have remained indifferent to the mighty wave of preoccupation with the Rebellion of 1798 that engulfed its bicentenary year. Perhaps one of the more neglected theatres, in what Ian McBride has termed 'Ninety-Eight Studies',[44] is the insurrection in Connacht. After the suppression of the better-known rebellions in Leinster and Ulster, a small French expeditionary force under General Jean Joseph Amable Humbert arrived in Killala Bay, County Mayo on 22 August 1798. Subsequently, several thousand local Irish recruits rallied to the rebel cause. Sweeping through Killala, Ballina and taking over Castlebar in the famous 'Races of Castlebar', the Franco-Irish army went on to campaign through the counties of Mayo, Sligo,

Leitrim and Longford, only to be decisively defeated at Ballinamuck on 8 September. Following the defeat of the remaining insurgents' contingency at Killala (23 September), low-scale guerrilla resistance continued for several months in the hills of Erris, Tyrawley and Connemara. This '98 arena was not on the front stage of the highly politicised 'battleground of memory' described, for example, by Kevin Whelan in his seminal essay on ''98 after '98: the politics of memory'[45] and is often presented as a clear-cut case of a relatively minor military campaign.[46] In his grand narrative, *Modern Ireland*, Roy Foster brusquely noted that 'the strange episode of the Republic of Connacht is a footnote to Irish history'.[47]

Yet, for the people of Connacht, all along the rebel army trail, into the midlands and around the surrounding periphery and neighbouring counties (from which recruits enlisted and to which fugitives escaped), 'The Year of the French' or *Bliain na bhFrancach* as it was popularly remembered in Irish speaking areas, was no 'footnote' in their notion of history. In local social memory, the Rebellion was a watershed event. It became a landmark in folk calendar, remembered as the most notable historical episode in recent, pre-famine times and a massive body of vibrant oral traditions was sustained into the twentieth century to be documented by the folklore collection project. An extremely rich repository of sources for reconstructing the folk historiographies of this episode are the numerous sources, which have survived largely unnoticed by historians, in the Main and the Schools' Manuscript Collections of the Irish Folklore Commission.

Alongside the material in the Irish Folklore Collection archives, another major accumulation of relevant documented oral traditions can be found in the work of Richard Hayes, whose study of *The Last Invasion of Ireland* (1937) remains to date the most comprehensive historical narrative of this somewhat neglected episode of 1798. Hayes spent the summers of 1935 and 1936 travelling in the footsteps of the Franco-Irish army. He collected a vast amount of oral traditions from people he interviewed en route, many of them descendants of those who participated in the rising.[48] Hayes's fieldwork and sensitivity to the value of oral traditions, combined with his exhaustive study of historical archive sources, offers an inspiring model for contemporary historians. Furthermore, because his work was contemporaneous to the initial drive of the Irish Folklore Commission fieldwork and to the Schools' Scheme, Hayes provides an excellent test case for a comparative reassessment of the Irish Folklore Commission collection process.

By critically comparing the way similar traditions were collected by a dedicated historian, trained folklore collectors and National School pupils, guided by their teachers, we can sharpen our understanding of the 'fossilisation' of oral tradition. One of Hayes's particular fortes was his ability to identify and maintain a working relationship based on mutual respect with local folk historians. These spontaneous collectors of oral tradition, who were occasionally overlooked by the collectors of the Irish Folklore Commission, provided Hayes with a wealth of valuable material. On the other hand, benefiting from his historical training, Hayes tended to limit his collection of oral tradition to specific events directly relevant to his subject matter. Folklore collectors were less focused and had a broader agenda, gathering 'indirect' information which put the material into a larger context and also offered access to more generic-circumstantial historical evidence. The enthusiasm of teachers and pupils in documenting traditions of 'The Year of the French' for the Schools' Scheme [the English name rather than the Irish was generally preferred in submissions for this collection] indicates the pervasiveness of this historical episode in social memory and also facilitated systematic collection in localities which were not adequately covered by Hayes or the Commission collectors. Altogether, critical evaluation of folklore collection exposes how written documentation of folklore, which I have characterised as a form of 'orality lost', also entailed subtle, often subconscious, power dynamics. Collection implied selection of informants, editorial processing of the information received and even discreet mechanisms of censorship through which certain versions of historical narratives were endorsed with approval and documented while others were brushed aside or reshaped.

Together, the three major oral tradition collections (the Main Manuscript Collection, the Schools' Collection and the work of Richard Hayes) provide a rich inventory of several hundred sources. They are supplemented by an array of references to relevant local traditions found in a miscellany of sources such as popular print, travel books, local histories and lore relating to aspects of material culture. Mining these numerous sources provides crucial data for an attempt to trace the development of folk historiography from the late eighteenth century, over the course of the nineteenth and into the twentieth century. Owing to the inevitability of 'orality lost' in the first sense (loss of traditions), which is an inherent component of the nature of oral tradition, *seanchas* sources are essentially fragmentary. Only bits and pieces of a rich and vibrant corpus of tradition survive to be collected. Therefore, working with historical-folklore sources is essentially a task of reconstruction. 'Orality lost' in the second sense (documenting and analysing oral sources in written form) involves removing folk traditions from their natural environment.[49] This, in turn, demands from the researcher of folk history a concerted effort towards recontextualisation of the fragments, so as to try and reimagine how they may have appeared and functioned within the community in a historical context. Both these concerns are not foreign to historical research and are in fact part of the stock and trade of the historian, regardless of the type of sources. However, 'orality lost' in the third sense (historiographical neglect of oral sources) signifies the preference to write history void of vernacular historical discourses, history which is fundamentally elitist in its claim to be 'empirical'.

Democratic history

One of the striking characteristics of folk historiography is the democratisation of historical heroes. Whereas conventional histories tend to focus on a limited pantheon of national heroes, folklore narratives present 'people's histories'. In general, the image of those national heroes who are remembered in social memory is transformed in folk history accounts so as to reflect popular reception and is then continuously modified and reshaped through storytelling performances. The finest example in modern Irish history of the way folk traditions transformed the image of famous historical characters is Daniel O'Connell, who generated more material than any other historical hero in Irish folklore. In oral tradition, O'Connell became a folk hero *par excellence* – he was known as 'The Counsellor' or 'The Liberator' and his image was canonised as a 'king without a crown'.[50] The adaptation of major historical figures to completely different folklore characters can occur within a short period. An account of a visitor to Cork in 1685 reveals that less than forty years from the Cromwellian campaign in Ireland a local mummers' performance featured 'Belsibub' with 'the bold usurper, Cromwell, whom he tweaked by his guilded nose'.[51] However, it is important to acknowledge that the transformation of historical heroes into folk heroes is not necessarily devoid of political influences. For example, in the context of 1798 popular memory, Kevin Whelan has claimed that the traditional Wexford mummers' rhymes were rewritten by a Bree schoolmaster named Sinott so as to incorporate the pantheon of '98 Wexford heroes as they were represented in Patrick Kavanagh's influential *A Popular History of the Insurrection of 1798* (Dublin, 1870; followed by multiple editions). Kavanagh's book was the founding text of the politicised and highly influential 'Faith and Fatherland' Catholic-nationalist school of 1798 historiography. The revised mummer rhymes were printed and circulated through the services of a small manual printing press (owned by an Adamstown blacksmith named Evoy) and soon gained rapid popularity as the standard-popular version used by Wexford mummers.[52]

Similarly, in the context of the folk history of *Bliain na bhFrancach*, French *Général Humbert* [ʋmbɛr], was transformed into Humbert [hʌmbɛrt][53] – quite a different character, reflecting the way his persona was perceived by Irish locals and reconstructed through history-telling traditions. However, analysis of all available folklore sources of this historical episode reveals that Humbert was merely a marginal character in the regional folk historiography. Whereas Humbert is the focus of attention in all written historical narratives of the French campaign in Connacht, in folk historiography his name is synonymous with the French army, the rebellion leadership or the rebel camp in general, but his character is not developed. He mainly functions as a contextual 'peg' to which relevant folklore was attached in social memory. The corpus of oral tradition inverts the historical canon and highlights other names, which are either marginal or do not appear at all in standard historical accounts.

A noteworthy example from the indigenous folk singing repertoire is a fragmented stanza of a popular song in Irish collected in 1946 by the Irish Folklore Commission collector, Michael Corduff, from ninety-year-old Mrs Bridget Corduff ('Biddy Rooney') in north-west Erris, County Mayo:

> Tá na Franncaigh i gCill Ala
> Is fada a g'Caill ar Chlainae Gaeil
> Togaidh suas ar gcroidhe is ur misneach
> Agus suil amac le Captin Kane[54]

> [O the French are in Killala
> Long have they been missed by '*Clan na Gael*'
> Rise up your hearts of courage
> and step forth with Captain Kane]

Incidentally, the storyteller, 'Biddy Rooney', was thus described by Corduff:

She it was, who could tell the stories and she delighted in telling them. She was born shortly after the year of the French landing in Killala and it was most interesting to hear her tales as she heard them from people who were eyewitnesses of the invasion – the ships coming into Kilcummin Bay, the march of the French army into Killala and on to Ballina, men who went from Erris to join up with the French forces, and such incidents of that memorable year in Irish history.

It is interesting to note how a woman born around the middle of the nineteenth century was considered to have been born 'shortly after the year of the French'. This is just one of the numerous indications that illustrate the centrality of this episode in the regional-historical folk calendar.

Several other fragmented variants of this song were collected around North Mayo,[55] though provenance and authorship are uncertain. The words were sung to the tune and chorus of 'Vive La', which was an authentic United Irish ballad.[56] It appears to have been a popular song in Mayo at least as far back as the middle of the nineteenth century and perhaps had a wider distribution throughout Connacht.[57] The subject of the song, Father Henry O'Kane (Ó Catháin), was a native Mayo priest from the barony of Tyrawley, whose family lived in the vicinity of Ballina.

He emigrated to France and became the parish *curé* near Nantes in Brittany (1788). After the French Revolution, he joined the French army and gained rapid promotion. O'Kane was commissioned as staff officer and interpreter in the French expedition to Ireland in 1798 and distinguished himself with acts of bravery throughout the Connacht campaign. Following the final defeat of the Rebellion, O'Kane was captured and court-martialled in Castlebar on a charge of high treason. Although sentenced to death, he received a reprieve and was returned to France, where he resumed his distinguished military career throughout the Republican and Napoleonic Wars, receiving the Legion of Honour and retiring in 1815.

A vigorous recruitment campaign was undertaken by Captain Henry O'Kane immediately after the French landing, initially in the baronies of Lacken and Erris and later throughout Mayo. As Hayes already indicated, the surviving fragments of the song probably echo a rallying song, voiced throughout Mayo and beyond to recruit local Irishmen to the ranks of the Franco-Irish army.[58] Is it then surprising that the local Mayo man, who travelled the countryside and recruited locals and later exhibited great valour in the battlefield, left a strong imprint on social memory? Indeed it is O'Kane who features in this native popular song and not the familiar national heroes Theobald Wolfe Tone or Napper Tandy, both of whom were on French vessels on their way to Mayo at the time. Yet an examination of the entire corpus of folklore sources discloses that O'Kane was far from being the main hero of *Bliain na bhFrancach*. Knowledge of him was not universal in social memory. Folk historiography radically differs from conventional historiography for it does not restrict itself to a select panel of central figures but, in a more democratic fashion, each community remembered its own heroes.

Folk historiographies of *Bliain na bhFrancach* preserve hundreds of names. Some are widely recognised, such as Irish insurgent leader General George Blake of Garracloon (though there are distinct regional differences between his image in the social memory of his home community in South Mayo–North Galway and the martyrology that developed around him in the vicinity of Ballinamuck, following his execution and subsequent clandestine burial by sympathetic locals). Only a few names transcended local tradition and received external recognition, such as the Gunner James Magee of the Longford militia who joined the rebels at Castlebar and whose valour on the battlefield assumed legendary proportions in folklore.[59] For years, Magee was remembered in oral traditions around Ballinamuck. Later, in independent Ireland, the Artillery Corps head barracks of the Irish Army in County Kildare was named after him and in 1944 the 'Magee Field Artillery Gun Trophy' was introduced. '*An Gunnadóir Mac Aoidh*' [Gunner Magee] was the subject of a well-known recitation by the Galway poet Eoghan Ó Tuairisc.[60]

Other names of local heroes were initially preserved in family tradition and then, through performances of storytelling and balladry, they gradually entered community tradition and subsequently received recognition as part of local folk history through the process of folklore collecting. Such is the case of Robin Gill of Edenmore, County Longford. Numerous stories are recorded about Gill's bravery at Ballinamuck and his escape after the battle. Close examination of the material reveals that many of the traditions relating to Robin Gill originated from a single source: his grand-nephew 'Grey Pat' – Patrick Gill of Edenmore, who was renowned locally as a storyteller with particular knowledge of Ballinamuck lore.[61] The combined efforts of Richard Hayes, Irish Folklore Commission collectors and the local Schools' Scheme contributions, awarded the traditions of Robin Gill (as told by 'Grey Pat') a stamp of approval and promoted their assimilation into the communal body of local historical lore.

While mainstream historians have only recently turned to research the involvement of women in the Rebellion,[62] oral traditions include a rich volume of material regarding women participation (despite male predominance in the folklore collection project). Research of the ways women are mentioned in folklore sources proves to be an invaluable resource in qualifying the democratic nature of folk historiographies. The silence of conventional historical sources, which airbrushed women out of the Rebellion, contributed to the prolonged neglect of women in academic historiography. In contrast, folklore sources, by showing the roles women actually played in the Rebellion (as they were subsequently remembered), the roles they were assigned in oral narrative traditions and the fictitious roles women were associated with in popular imagination, offer a more complex gender balanced insight into the way communities narrated their pasts.

Folk histories deal with subject matter often neglected by the writers of 'official' history. These are not necessarily confined to issues of provincial and insular concern, but may often expose oversights and significant lacunae in our understanding of the past. Hayes noted a 'saying in the west' (without specifying its origin and distribution): 'Is cosmhail le Blácaigh na Gearra-Chluana iad, ceann aca i n-arm Shasana, ceann eile i n-arm na hEireann!' [They are like the Blakes of Garracloon, one in the English army and the other in the Irish army]. This saying, which was used to mark quarrels between brothers or relatives, originated from the fact that although George Blake was a prominent rebel leader, one of his younger brothers was an officer in the English army at the time of the Rebellion.[63] Much historiographical debate has centred on the question of the sectarian nature of 1798 and yet a largely neglected aspect of historical research is internal strife within communities. Numerous accounts in folk history relate to elements of civil war, as relatives and friends from the same community and social background were sometimes pitted against each other, each siding with opposite camps.

Another example of eye-opening material in folk history can be found in several stories from counties Mayo and Galway which make allusions to some sort of a sabbatical amnesty. According to these traditions, after 'seven years' outlaws on the run returned to the community and, following a policy of reconciliation, relations improved between landlord and tenant.[64] Seven is of course a typological number which relates to a familiar folkloristic-storytelling motif and so from a positivist perspective may be dismissed as a-historical. But in a deeper sense, incorporating an interpretative approach, these reconciliatory narratives offer valuable insight into mentalité. They show how oral traditions explained the gradual processes of normalisation as, after an interval, areas which had been strongly affected by the Rebellion and traumatised by the terror that accompanied its suppression eventually settled down.

Reconstructing oral historiography

More than anything else, folk histories reveal provincial-vernacular historical consciousness in the heyday of standardised folklore collecting, between the 1930s and 1950s. Positivist analysis of oral tradition strives to sieve the kernels of historical facts dating back to the original events in 1798. The challenge of tracing folk historiographies of *Bliain na bhFrancach* requires, to paraphrase Michel Foucault (and Walter Benjamin), 'an archaeology of social memory' in order to bridge the gap between these tentative *terminus post quem* and *terminus ante quem*. Identifying strata of popular memory as it developed over a hundred and fifty years demands close analysis of the oral narratives and cross-referencing to all available historical sources in order to uncover information that can help recontextualise the traditions. When attempting to reconstruct the chain of transmission, it is important to acknowledge that folkloristic analysis also reveals 'pre-historic' layers of communal memory, incidents where events in 1798 were narrated using familiar motifs that relate to earlier periods in Irish history. For example, a somewhat subversive tradition of local resistance to the French was retold as a version of a familiar story about the 'Fool of Barr Rúscaí'[65] – an Erris legend originally set on the background of struggles between Gaelic chieftains.[66] In this sense, the memory of *Bliain na bhFrancach* began long before 1798.

Tracing folk historiography requires us to look beyond the editorial work of the *seanchas* collector and the folklorist and expose marks of amnesia obscured in enigmatic fragments of oral tradition. For example, the children's song 'Mise agus Tusa', still sung today in Mayo and Donegal, includes explicit references to the French invasion:

An raibh tú igCill Ala nó i gCaisleán an Bharraigh,
Nó an bhfaca tú an campa a bhí ag na Francaigh?
Mise agus tusa agus ruball na muice,
agus bacaigh Shíol Aindí, bacaigh Shíol Aindí[67]

[Were you in Killala or in Castlebar
did you see the camp that the French had?
Me and you and the pig's tail,
and *bacaigh Shíol Aindí, bacaigh Shíol Aindí*]

The Opies, in their study of children's lore, demonstrated how rhyming formula can contribute to the unconscious preservation of historical tradition.[68] In much the same way, it appears that children in the periphery of the north-west coast unwittingly kept alive the memory of the French in Mayo. Trying to come to terms with the puzzling name *bacaigh Shíol Aindí*, folklorists have speculated that this is a colloquial-esoteric reference to Scottish troops – 'Bucky Heelanders' – who left a strong impression on people of the locality, an argument recently reiterated by Ríonach uí Ógáin.[69] This is indeed a plausible explanation and there are several examples of locals remembering the presence of Scottish soldiers in 1798. Yet surprisingly, Richard Hayes's primary informant, Patrick O'Donnell of Newport, a local folk historian in his own right who was extremely knowledgeable in the oral traditions of 1798 in Mayo, wrote to Hayes following the publication of *The Last Invasion of Ireland* inquiring: 'I wonder would there be any possibility of discovering who this Aindi was?'[70] Apparently, the original meaning of the name was forgotten in the local folk historiography of the 1930s and had to be rediscovered (or perhaps invented) later by external researchers.

Negotiations of memory

Vernacular history telling is fascinating in its own right, yet isolated research of folk historiography can be detached from the larger social context. Social memory is continuously constructed and reshaped through dialogic negotiations between periphery and centre. Commemoration has been accepted in contemporary historical studies as a legitimate topic and in the context of 1798 much discussion has been directed to the impact of the centenary celebrations.[71] The commemorative ceremonies and popular publications of 1898 had great influence on folk memory and are referred to directly and indirectly in several accounts. For example, the ballad writing of the Irish language revival enthusiast William Rooney was extremely popular during the centenary and by the 1930s these songs had filtered into the folklore repertoire and were recited to Commission collectors as bona fide *seanchas*. Similarly, the centennial monuments in Ballina and

Castlebar triggered patriotic fervour throughout the route of the French invasion of Connacht, as other communities sought recognition for their contribution and involvement. Subsequently, local '98 monuments were erected into the mid-twentieth century at Knock (1904), Burrishoole (1912), Ballinamuck (1928), Lahardane (1937) and Achill (1944).

However, the wide-ranging scope of folk historiography suggests a broader approach towards memory and commemoration, looking beyond the high profile, nationally sanctioned events. Oral traditions are generated in concentric spheres of commemoration: personal, family, community, region and nation. Each sphere is characterised by hegemonic struggles over the subject and form of social memory, as the key questions of 'who is remembered?' and 'how are they remembered?' rarely entail simple answers. 'Orality lost' in its first and second sense (in terms of what is remembered and how it is recorded) is never devoid of power dynamics. These levels of commemoration constantly interact with each other, presenting a complex and dynamic model of folk history engagement. Folk history is in constant dialogue with 'official' versions of history which are projected from the centre. These are sometimes accepted and integrated and sometimes rejected, but most often modified and reconstructed in folk historiography. Yet the dialogic process mostly flows in one way, as academic histories tend to ignore the multiple voices of vernacular historiographies (thus enforcing what I have defined as 'orality lost' in the third sense of the term).

Orality refound?

An overview of the seemingly endless amount of lectures, publications and conferences in the bicentenary year of the 1798 Rebellion reveals a shameful neglect of folk historiography. The official 'Bicentenary Conference', which took place in Belfast and Dublin over five days in May 1998, included thirty-six papers delivered by many of the leading authorities on the Rebellion. Remarkably, not even one paper focused on oral tradition. In a high profile television documentary, one of the leading experts on 1798 and the French connection confidently announced that 'the oral history of 1798 was almost nil'.[72] This statement, which typifies the current historiographical scene, is a basis for an indictment in its own right, for it illustrates the refusal to admit that throughout the nineteenth and well into the twentieth century oral historical discourses on the memory of 1798 were taking place through various genres of folk history-telling within local communities.

Whereas the loss of unrecorded oral traditions and the difficulties of reproducing oral performance are inherent limitations of oral history work, the neglect of folklore sources in mainstream Irish history writing is an issue that can be addressed. During the bicentennial year, local history and heritage projects reclaimed many oral tradition sources.[73] Often this work was partial and, as in the case of local heritage representations, reductionist in its tendency to substitute the multiple voices of folk histories with simplified narratives. This in turn can be amended through more comprehensive historical studies of folklore sources. Moreover, local bicentenary commemoration generated extensive historical discourse, which remains to be explored in its own right as a contemporary stratum in an 'archaeology of social memory'. The task of recognising oral tradition, coming to terms with folk historiographies and tapping into popular historical discourses in social memory is a challenge contemporary Irish historiography has yet to face. The Irish Folklore Collection (supplemented by miscellaneous auxiliary material) offers unique archival resources towards furthering this direction. By engaging in the study of Ireland's rich oral tradition, Irish scholarship may be able to offer a significant contribution to the exploration of the nature of vernacular history and popular culture at large. In turn, perhaps this will enable a rethinking of history towards a definition that acknowledges the role of orality.

NOTES

1 See for example: Robert Gildea, *The Past in French History* (New Haven and London, 1994).

2 In her study on the interrelations between orality and literacy, Ruth Finnegan has treated these two media as forms of communication technologies; Ruth Finnegan, *Literacy and Orality: Studies in the Technology of Communication* (Oxford, 1988).

3 See for example Jack Goody, 'Memory in oral tradition', in P. Fara and K. Paterson (eds), *Memory* (Cambridge, 1998), pp. 73–94.

4 See James Stewart, *Boccaccio in the Blaskets* (Galway, 1988); Bo Almquist, 'The mysterious Mícheal Ó Gaothin, Boccaccio and the Blasket tradition', *Béaloideas* 59 (1990), 75–90.

5 L. M. Cullen, 'Poetry, Culture and Politics', *Studia Celtica Japonica* 8 (1996), 1–26.

6 As of yet no comprehensive history has been written of the work of the Irish Folklore Commission (IFC) and its archives. For general overviews see: Bo Almquist, 'The Irish Folklore Commission achievement and legacy', *Béaloideas* 45–7(1977–9), 6–26; Séamas Ó Catháin, 'The Irish Folklore Archive', *History Workshop Journal* 31 (1991),145–8; Seán Ó Súilleabháin, 'Tuarascáil an Cóimisiín' (unpublished article, 1970, IFC offprint collection). For a recent critical assessment of the institutionalisation of folklore studies in Ireland see: Diarmuid Ó Giolláin, *Locating Irish Folklore: Tradition, Modernity and Identity* (Cork, 2000), pp. 128–41.

7 Initially, the archives of the Irish Folklore Commission were located in Earlsfort Terrace and in 1949 were transferred to 82 St Stephen's Green. Today, they are situated on the Belfield campus of UCD.

8 Regrettably, owing to lack of adequate funding the ediphone cylinders were transcribed and then reused and consequently the original oral recordings were lost. All tape recording from full time collectors were preserved.

9 Initially a brief booklet in the Irish language was published by the Folklore of Ireland Society [*An Cuman le Béaloideas Éireann*] – *Laimhleabhar Béaloideasa* (1937).

10 Seán Ó Súilleabháin, *A Handbook of Irish Folklore* (Dublin, 1942), pp. xxii–xxiii. The standards for oral collectors had already been laid down by James Delargy after the founding of the Folklore of Ireland Society. See *Béaloideas* 1(1928), 5.

11 Acknowledging the existence of urban folklore, the instructions to the collectors delicately express partiality towards collecting rural traditions: 'Even city and town-born individuals possess traditional information concerning the ways and doings of those about them, It is in country districts, however, that information is to be obtained in greatest abundance.' Ó Súilleabháin, *A Handbook of Irish Folklore*, p. xi.

12 For example see: Éilis Ní Dhuibhne, 'Dublin modern legends: an intermediate type list and examples', *Béaloideas* 51 (1983), 55–70.

13 When the Irish Folklore Commission disbanded in 1970, the collection had 1,746 volumes, including 102 volumes inherited from the Irish Folklore Institute, collected prior to 1935. In addition to the notes taken down by the Commission's collectors, the Main Manuscript Collection also includes several privately collected manuscript collections which were donated or purchased by the Commission.

14 See Clodagh Brennan Harvey, *Contemporary Irish Traditional Narrative: The English Language Tradition* (Berkeley, Los Angeles and Oxford, 1984), pp. 4–6. For a more detailed typology of standard narrative genres in Irish folklore see: Seán Ó Súilleabháin, *Storytelling in the Irish Tradition* (Cork, 1973).

15 The 166 questionnaires conducted until 1970 are divided into general questionnaires, sent to specially recruited voluntary correspondents all over Ireland, and local projects. Their subjects addressed in questionnaires are wide ranging and cover different folklore topics. A well-known example of a questionnaire utilised by an historian is Roger McHugh's study of the 1945 questionnaire on the Great Famine. See: Roger McHugh 'The famine in Irish oral tradition', in R. D. Edwards and T. D. Williams (eds), *The Great Famine* (Dublin, 1957), pp. 389–436.

16 An example of a pioneering investigation of the context and subtext relating to a folklore collector's field work is Ríonach uí Ógáin's analysis of the diaries of full-time Irish Folklore Commission collector Michael J. Murphy. Ríonach uí Ógáin, 'Some comments on context, text and subtext in Irish folklore', *FFSS99* (Preprint, Folklore Fellows' Summer School 1999).

17 For an overview of the Schools' Scheme see: Séamas Ó Catháin, 'Súil Siar ar *Scéim na Scol* 1937–1938', *Sinsear* 5 (1988), 19–30; Séamas Ó Catháin, 'Scéim na Scol: the schools' scheme of 1937–1938', in Margaret Farren and Mag Hoken (eds), *It's Us They're Talking About* (Clonmany, County Donegal, 1999) – proceedings of the McGlinchey Summer School (13 pages, unnumbered).

18 Seán Ó Súilleabháin, *Irish Folklore and Tradition* (An Roinn Oideachais, 1937).

19 The pupils documented the folklore accounts they collected as essays in copybooks. So as to avoid repetition, selected material from the copybooks was transcribed into an official notebook. In many cases all collected material (including copybooks and official notebooks) was submitted to the Department of Education and forwarded on to the Irish Folklore Commission. The original copybooks were stored, unbound and unpaginated, in 1,124 boxes. The preservation of the copybooks alongside the manu-script volumes often enables a critical evaluation of the selective compilation process, uncovering material that teachers decided to exclude from the official notebook and revealing circumstances when the original composition was edited by the teacher.

20 See for example the seminal work of the Belgian anthropologist Jan Vansina, who made a pioneering methodological contribution to the historical study of oral tradi-tions; Jan Vansina, *Oral Tradition as History* (London and Nairobi, 1985), pp. 27–9.

21 Cathal Póirtéir, 'Folk memory and the famine', in Cathal Póirtéir (ed.), *The Great Irish Famine* (Dublin, 1995), p. 231.

22 A chapter is devoted to 'Famine memory' in Cormac Ó Gráda, *Black '47 and Beyond: The Great Irish Famine in History, Economy and Memory* (Princeton, 1999), pp. 194–225.

23 Paper presented at the Economic and Social History Society of Ireland's conference on Oral History (Royal Irish Academy, Dublin, 20 Nov. 1999).

24 For a review of the modern debate on 'euhemerism' [named after Euhemerus the Sicilian mythographer, who claimed in the fourth century BC that the gods of ancient Greek myths were really deified historical heroes] from the late nineteenth century until the 1960s, with references to native North American tradition, Polynesia, Icelandic sagas, Africa and Victorian folklorists, see R. M. Dorson, 'The debate over the trustworthiness of oral traditional history', in Fritz Harkart, K. C. Peeters and R. C. Wildhaber (eds), *Volksüberlieferung, Festschrift für Kurt Ranke* (Göttingen, 1968), pp. 19–35.

25 For example, Paul Thompson's oral history of Edwardian England utilised the archival record of the period to develop a sampling procedure, which led to the selection of five individuals chosen to be representative of different socio-economic levels of society (from the very rich to the very poor) so as to portray five vignettes of remembered Edwardian childhoods. See Paul Thompson, *The Edwardians: The Remaking of British Society* (London, 1975).

26 Alice Hoffman, 'Reliability and validity in oral history', in D. K. Dunaway and W. K. Baum (eds), *Oral History: An Interdisciplinary Anthology* (Walnut Creek, London and New Delhi, 1996), pp. 92–103.

   Italian oral historian Alessandro Portelli characterises oral history with the expression 'life *and* times' (putting the stress on the 'and' – the combination of the two), claiming that it is a field ranging in between the personal uniqueness of biography and the representativeness of social history. See: Alessandro Portelli, 'Oral history as genre', in M. Chamberlain and P. Thompson (eds), *Narrative and Genre* (London and New York, 1998), p. 26.

27 R. M. Dorson, 'The debate over the trustworthiness of oral traditional history', pp. 19–35.

28 The French oral historian Daniel Bertaux distinguished between two different approaches to interpretative oral history:
   (*a*) The 'hermeneutic' approach focuses on text. It applies literary criticism and communications theory to an individual document and discovers the interpretative power of the text by revealing levels of discourse, hidden meanings and ability to transmit messages.
   (*b*) The 'ethnographic' approach focuses on context. It locates the testimony within a society, examines what it tells about people and relations between them, and analyses the world of production. Levels of discourse and use of language are related to social domains.
   Since this is only a general overview, I will not pursue the differences between these two schools in contemporary oral history. For further discussion see Louise A. Tilly and Ronald J. Grele in *Irish Journal of Oral History* (1985), 3–46, esp. 45–6.

29 John Tosh, *The Pursuit of History* (Essex and New York, 1984), p. 181.

30 Elizabeth Tonkin, *Narrating Our Past* (Cambridge, 1992), p. 7.

31 Nora observed a recent emergence of historiographical consciousness, which, to his mind, has brought to a conclusion a long process of separation between history and social memory. See: Pierre Nora, 'General introduction: between memory and

history', in Pierre Nora (ed.), *Realms of Memory* (New York, 1996), I pp. 1–20, in particular p. 4.

32 Maurice Halbwachs, *The Collective Memory* (New York, 1980), p. 57 [translation of *La Mémoire collective* (Paris, 1950)].

33 Raphael Samuel, *Theatres of Memory* I, *Past and Present in Contemporary Culture* (London and New York, 1994), pp. 3–50.

34 See for example: Dáithí Ó hÓgáin 'An Stair agus an Seanchas Béil', *Léachtaí Cholmcille* 14, *Ar Scéalaíocht* (1983), pp. 173–96; Dáithí Ó hÓgáin, *The Hero in Irish Folk History* (Dublin and New York, 1985).

35 Jan Vansina, 'Memory and oral tradition', in J. C. Miller (ed.), *The African Past Speaks* (Kent and Connecticut, 1980), p. 264.

36 James Fentress and Chris Wickham, *Social Memory* (Oxford and Cambridge MA, 1992), pp. 39–40.

37 For an oral historian's awareness of this issue see: Alessandro Portelli, 'Oral history as genre', in Mary Chamberlain and Paul Thompson, *Narrative and Genre* (London and New York, 1998), p. 25.

38 Elizabeth Tonkin, *Narrating Our Pasts* (Cambridge, 1992), pp. 2–4.

39 Lauri Honko 'The folklore process', in *Folklore Fellows Summer School*, 1991, pp. 25–47.

40 For a review of historians' reliance on oral sources from Ancient Greece to Early-Modern Europe see David Henige, *Oral Historiography* (London, New York and Lagos, 1982), pp. 7–13.

41 The historian of early modern popular culture, Peter Burke, has termed the formation of the prevailing modern school of historiography as the 'Rankean counter-revolution'. Yet when referring to this paradigm of historiography as 'Rankean' it is important to acknowledge the Leopold Von Ranke was less confined to this orthodoxy than his followers were. As Burke himself observed: 'Just as Marx was not a Marxist, Ranke was not a Rankean'. See: Peter Burke 'Overture: the new history, its past and its future', in Peter Burke (ed.), *New Perspectives on Historical Writing* (Cambridge, 1991), p. 3.

42 Edward Said, *Orientalism* (orig. 1978; London, New York, Victoria, Toronto and Auckland, 1991), p. 21.

43 Ronan Fanning, '"The great enchantment": uses and abuses of modern Irish history', in Ciaran Brady (ed), *Interpreting Irish History* (Dublin, 1994), p. 146.

44 Ian McBride, 'Reclaiming the rebellion: 1798 in 1998', *Irish Historical Studies* 31 (1999), 395–410.

45 Kevin Whelan, *The Tree of Liberty: Radicalism, Catholicism and the Construction of Irish Identity 1760–1830* (Cork, 1996), pp. 133–75.

46 A typical example of the contemporary historiographic stance can be found in Herman Murtagh's recent essays which sum up the Rising in the West as an inevitable military failure, a narrative consisting exclusively of General Humbert's campaign: 'General Humbert's campaign in the west', in Cathal Póirtéir (ed.), *The Great Irish Rebellion of 1798* (Dublin 1998), pp. 115–24; and '1798: events in the West', paper presented at the 1798 Bicentenary Conference, Dublin Castle, 22 May 1998, to be published in Thomas Bartlett, David Dickson, Dáire Keogh and Kevin Whelan (eds), *The 1798 Rebellion: A Bicentennial Perspective* (forthcoming).

47 R. F. Foster, *Modern Ireland 1600–1972* (London, 1988), p. 280.

48 Richard Hayes, *The Last Invasion of Ireland: When Connacht Rose* (Dublin, 1937). The traditions published in the book are complemented by the raw material in his notebooks: Dr Richard Hayes's Papers, NLI MS 13799–13801.

49 Sound recording does not solve this dilemma, as implied by the term 'schizophonia', coined by R. Murray Shaffer to define 'packaging and storing techniques for sound and the splitting of sounds from their original contexts'. See Barbara Kirshenblatt-Gimblett, 'Folklore's crisis', *Journal of American Folklore* 111 (1998), 312–13.

50 See: Ríonach Uí Ógáin, *Immortal Dan: Daniel O'Connell in Irish Folk Tradition* (Dublin, 1995).

51 Alan Gailey, *Irish Folk Drama* (Cork, 1969), p. 8.

52 See Whelan, *Tree of Liberty*, pp. 171–2; Kevin Whelan, *Fellowship of Freedom* (Dublin, 1998), p. 127.

53 Frank O'Connor describes a meeting with an old man from County Longford, who recited stories he had heard from his grandfather, an active participant in the Rising. The grandfather used to refer to Humbert as 'u'ber'. Frank O'Connor, *Leinster, Munster and Connaught* (London), p. 286. From the transcriptions of most of the sources collected by the Irish Folklore Commission and the Schools' Scheme it appears that the letters h, m and t were pronounced distinctly.

54 IFC 1244: 251 [unedited]. IFC and IFC S = The Main Manuscript Collection and the Schools' Manuscript Collection, the number of either side of the colon representing the volume number and the page number(s) respectively. I would like to thank the Head of the Department of Irish Folklore at University College Dublin for his permission to publish material drawn from the Irish Folklore Collection at the Department of Irish Folklore at UCD, NUI Dublin.

55 IFC 1534: 522–3; IFC 1710: 197; IFC Disk 721–3; Hayes, *The Last Invasion of Ireland*, p. 218, 243; Hayes Papers, NLI MS 13800 (5).

56 Hayes notes that the refrain 'Vive la' served as a chorus. 'Viva la, United heroes' is the chorus of the song 'Rouse, Hibernians', which was reproduced by Richard Musgrave as evidence of a subversive text found on the mother of a killed Wicklow rebel in autumn 1798. Sir Richard Musgrave, *Memoirs of the Different Rebellions in Ireland* (Indiana, 1995, 4th edn; original 3rd edn, London, 1802), p. 703. As Georges-Denis Zimmerman noted, the tune 'Viva la! the French are coming' was a 'Rebel march song' recorded by antiquarian George Petrie in the middle of the nineteenth century. Sir Charles Stanford (ed.), *The Complete Collection of Irish Music as noted by George Petrie* (London, 1902–5), I and II, p. 254, no. 996; Georges-Denis Zimmerman, *Irish Political Ballads and Rebel Songs 1780–1900* (Geneva, 1966), pp. 160–1.

57 For example, a fragmented and corrupted version labelled 'When the French came into Killala' was collected for the Schools' Scheme in County Galway. In this version the reference to Kane by name was omitted and the song was mixed with what appears to be Anglicised influences – referring to the Duke of York marching his men to Castlebar. IFC S16: 77–8.

58 Hayes, *The Last Invasion of Ireland*, p. 243.

59 Traditions on Gunner Magee are widespread in folklore sources. For example: IFC 1858: 11–12; 100–2; IFC S219: 248–9; IFC S221: 5a; IFC S222: 619–20; IFC S225: 149–50; IFC S758: 56–8, 462–3; IFC S760: 133, 476–8; *The Last Invasion of Ireland*, pp. 227–8, 229, 231–2, 235, 324; *Béaloideas* 4 (1934/5), pp. 393–4; James P. Farrell, *Historical Notes and Stories of the County Longford* (Dublin, 1886), p. 106; Michael Connell MS reproduced in Rev. Owen Devaney, *Killoe: History of a County Longford Parish* (Cavan, 1981), pp. 129–33.

60 Eoghan Ó Tuairisc, *Lux Aeterna* (Dublin, 1964). For an English translation by Lt Col. Denis Burke see: Padraig Rehill (ed.), *Ballinamuck Bi-Centenary* (Longford, 1998), p. 123. Ó Tuairisc is also the author of the *L'Attaque* (1962), a historical novel set on the background of *Bliain na bhFrancach*.

61 IFC S758: 48–50, 432–4, 446–7; IFC S760: 129–30; IFC 1858: 10–11, 100–1, 120; Pádraig Mac Gréine 'Traditions of 1798: the battle of Ballinamuck', *Béaloideas* 4 (1934/5), pp. 393–5; Hayes, *The Last Invasion of Ireland*, pp. 231–5.

62 Almost eighty years of silence passed after Helena Concannon published her pioneer work on this subject: Mrs Thomas Concannon, *Women of 'Ninety Eight* (Dublin, 1919). Among the publications of recent rekindled interest in the field are: Séamas Ó Saothraí, *Heroines of 1798* (Bray, 1998) [which is partially based on an earlier booklet written by the same author in Irish: Séamas Ó Saothraí, *Mná Calma '98* (Dublin, 1966)]; Mary Cullin, 'Partners in struggle: the women of 1798', in Póirtéir (ed.), *The Great Irish Rebellion*, pp. 146–59; and a notable collection of essays: Dáire Keogh and Nicholas Furlong (eds), *The Women of 1798* (Dublin, 1998), which includes a couple of articles that make use of folklore: Maureen Murphy, '"The noggin of milk": an Old Testament legend and the battle of Ballinamuck', pp. 177–87 and Anna Kinsella 'Nineteenth-century perspectives: the women of 1798 in folk memory and ballads', pp. 187–99.

63 Hayes, *The Last Invasion of Ireland*, p. 268.

64 For example: IFC 195: 312–15, 227: 398–400; 528: 6–10, 662: 263–6, 1512: 313–18; S141: 32–4, S763: 155–6.

65 Told by seventy-four-year-old Miceál Ó Rodaigh, a farmer from Bangor, Erris, County Mayo, to Irish Folklore Commission collector Liam Mac Coishdealbha in 1939. IFC 625: 197–8.

66 IFC 572: 55–64; IFC 625: 330–3; IFC 665: 520–1; IFC 743: 450–4; IFC 1242: 263–5. See also: John O'Donovan, *O.S. Letters*, Mayo I (1838), T.S. p. 5, MS p. 14.

67 See: Seán Ó Brádaigh (ed.), *Songs of 1798* (Dublin, 1887), p. 15. A version of this song was collected for the IFC in 1953 by Leo Corduff and Seán Ó hEochaidh from Róise Ní Ghrianna (Róise na nAmhrán) of Aranmore, County Donegal, IFC Tape 1188a. The contemporary popular music group Clannad recorded a version of the song, claiming to have learned it locally in Donegal from Síle Mhicí of Dobhar, Gaoth Dobhar.

68 Iona and Peter Opie, *The Lore and Language of Schoolchildren* (Oxford, 1959).

69 Ríonach Uí Ógáin, 'Béaloideas 1798 Thiar', in Gearóid Ó Tuathaigh (ed.), *Éirí Amach 1798 in Éirinn* (Indreabhán, Conamara, 1998), p. 150

70 Letter dated 11 April, 1938 in Hayes' Papers NLI MS 13799 (3).

71 See for example: Timothy O'Keefe, 'The 1898 efforts to celebrate the United Irishmen: the '98 Centennial', *Éire-Ireland* 23 (1988), 51–73; Timothy O'Keefe, '"Who fears to Speak of '98?": the rhetoric and rituals of the United Irishmen centennial, 1898', *Éire–Ireland*, 27 (1992), 67–91; Senia Paseta '1798 in 1898: the politics of commemoration', *Irish Review*, 22 (1998), 46–53; Peter Collins, 'The contest of memory: the continuing impact of 1798 commemoration', *Éire-Ireland* 34 (1999), 28–50; Anna Kinsella, 'Who feared to speak in 1898', *Journal of the Wexford Historical Society* 17 (1998–9), 221–34; Kevin Whelan's astute observations in his essay "98 after '98: the politics of memory', in Whelan, *Tree of Liberty*, pp. 171–3.

72 'Rebellion', RTÉ, 1998.

73 For example see: Padraig Rehill (ed.), *Ballinamuck Bi-Centenary 1798–1998* (Longford, 1998); in particular Fr Owen Devaney, 'Ballinamuck in Song and Story' in *ibid.*, pp. 57–92, which draws extensively from the work of Richard Hayes and selected material from the IFC archives.

13 The View from Merrion Square: The American Embassy in Ireland, 1956–66

Gary Murphy

This chapter examines the reportage of the American embassy's diplomatic community in Ireland, based in Merrion Square, in their covering of ongoing political developments in Ireland during the late 1950s and early 1960s. It considers the quality and accuracy of such diplomatic reporting and explores the American perspective on political events in Ireland in this period. The mid-1950s onwards saw successive Irish governments actively pursue the European option as witnessed by Ireland's negotiations to join the European Free Trade Area from 1957 and her application for membership of the European Economic Community (EEC) in 1961. This pursuit of the European agenda had a wider significance than simple economics in that membership of any European trading bloc would have political implications in terms of Irish neutrality. Moreover once the Irish application to the EEC lapsed, after Charles de Gaulle's veto of the British entry bid, the Fianna Fáil government of Seán Lemass quickly set about realigning relations with the various economic interest groups in order to reapply for membership.

On all these issues the American embassy reported back to Washington. Its reports examined political, economic and military affairs in Ireland and they shed important light on how the Americans viewed the Irish government's position on a number of international issues, most notably the political implications of EEC membership and the NATO question. They are also important in their analysis of the increasingly complex, and at times fractious, relationship between government and sectional interest groups during this period; a time when farmers' organisations, the trade unions and business interests came into the foreground of Irish politics. This chapter examines the reliability of these embassy reports and assesses their historical usefulness in the context of what we already know from Irish government records and other archives of the period.

The relationship between Dublin and Washington in the twentieth century has been analysed by Seán Cronin in his groundbreaking 1987

work, *Washington's Irish Policy 1916–1986*, and more recently in relation
to the immediate post Second World War era by Troy Davis in his *Dublin's
American Policy: Irish-American Diplomatic Relations, 1945–1952*.[1] Other
scholars have used the American files in parts, but there has been no
systematic attempt made either by Cronin, Davis or others to assess the
quality of reportage that the American embassy in Dublin sent back to the
State Department in Washington. This chapter analyses the files during a
crucial decade in modern Irish history, one which saw the retirement of
Eamon de Valera as leader of Fianna Fáil, the emergence of a new style of
economic policy, associated with Seán Lemass, which incorporated the
major interest groups into policy formation for the first time, and the Irish
government's historic decision to apply for membership of the EEC.

American diplomatic reporting from Ireland, as indeed from anywhere
else in the world at this time, involved the embassy simply reporting what
they were being told by sources they believed they could trust. The
structural dynamics of diplomatic reporting for the American foreign
service in a country such as Ireland, theoretically neutral, but seen by the
State Department as being essentially in the Western hemisphere, were
pretty basic. In the case of Ireland the American embassy would have
typically had between two to four officers: a chargé d'affaires, political
officer, economic officer and an agricultural attaché, who would arrive at
their posts with no particular knowledge of local issues and would support
the ambassador, a political appointment. The first year of the post would
be essentially devoted to acquiring basic local expertise which would mostly
mean meeting people such as politicians, government officials, journalists
and academics who 'seem to know what they are talking about'. Diplomatic
reporting for officers of the American foreign service thus consisted of
evaluating and reporting what these sources said.[2]

On the other end of the spectrum, in Washington, cables, as such
reports are known, would first be seen in the central communications
room of the Department of State. The Department of State is split up into
various regional sections and at this time Ireland was in the bureau of
British Commonwealth and Northern European Affairs. Each bureau has
an assigned desk officer for each country within its confines. Thus the desk
officer for Ireland would be the first person to evaluate such reportage from
the embassy and would have to make the primary decision on whether
any material emanating from there should be seen at higher levels within
the Department of State. Within the system the next step would be for
the desk officer to make weekly and monthly summations on Ireland to the
office of the Director of British Commonwealth and Northern European
Affairs. It would be then from this office that any material to be sent to the
Secretary of State's office, on the seventh floor, would be decided upon.

Within the Secretary of State's office itself, there would be another vetting procedure on summations before a final decision on what the Secretary should see would be made.[3] At the height of the Cold War Ireland was not an important player geopolitically for the Americans and as such cables from Merrion Square were rarely seen above the level of desk officer at the bureau of British Commonwealth and Northern European Affairs. Nevertheless, these reports for historians are an important source as they inform us of how American opinion of events in Ireland was shaped.

Reporting from informed sources is the lifeblood of all diplomatic activity and Ireland in this period was no exception. For the British, for example, use of such sources was a key way of assessing what was going on in Ireland: 'I report this with all reserve as no more than cocktail party gossip, but my source is a reliable businessman with political connexions and it seems to make sense',[4] wrote Gurth Kimber, chargé d'affaires of the British embassy in Dublin to G. W. Chadwick of the Commonwealth Relations Office in February 1959 on the questions of who would succeed de Valera as Taoiseach and who would be the Fianna Fáil candidate for the presidency in the same year.

The return to office of Fianna Fáil, with an overall majority after the March general election of 1957, saw the ageing and increasingly blind de Valera reinstated as Taoiseach. Within three months the American embassy were reporting back that de Valera was contemplating retirement and had decided that Dr James Ryan, newly appointed Minister for Finance, should succeed him. The reasoning for de Valera's choice, according to the reporting officer, John La Fréniere, makes for interesting historical analysis. The 1957 general election was called when the inter-party government of 1954–57 folded due to the defection of Clann na Poblachta. More importantly, however, it masked internal difficulties within Fine Gael, which was sharply divided over the economic policies of its Minister for Finance, Gerard Sweetman. Fine Gael had attempted to avert an election when it approached Fianna Fáil on 5 February with a view to forming an alliance. Rumours of Fine Gael's overtures caused de Valera to issue a statement on 10 February wherein he admitted to receiving two members of Fine Gael and 'listening' to a proposal which he found 'impossible'. According to de Valera, when he mentioned it to the Fianna Fáil committee 'as a matter of course', the committee dismissed the proposal and he so informed the Fine Gael representatives. La Fréniere reported to the State Department on 18 February that a merger was still a possibility:

The reporting officer has learned reliably that a rapprochement between Fianna Fáil and Fine Gael might occur should Fianna Fáil not obtain a working majority out of the election. It is reported that Seán MacEntee and Seán Lemass, lieutenants of de Valera, very much favour combining with Fine Gael to form a government, if this becomes necessary. It was learned that the two parties would be prepared to come to an agreement on basic economic principles and on national commitments; however it seems unlikely that de Valera and General Richard Mulcahy, the Fine Gael leader, would serve in the same cabinet because of long and deep seated animosities.[5]

The Fine Gael party papers, located in UCD, offer some light on the veracity of this report. Alex Bolster a Fine Gael member had submitted a policy document to Mulcahy, outlining various proposals on how a national government would be constituted. Mulcahy went public on 18 February calling for a spirit of co-operation in government between Ireland's political parties.[6] There is, however, no evidence in the MacEntee papers, also in UCD, to suggest that he was in any way willing, or made any attempt to align Fianna Fáil with Fine Gael, however putatively before the 1957 election. Moreover Lemass, in an interview with John F. McCarthy in 1969, maintained that although the possibility of a national government had been raised by Fine Gael, and that he had indeed met a member of Fine Gael in the Shelbourne hotel, he had informed this individual that the idea was 'completely impractical'. He was of the opinion that the whole scheme was designed to give people the idea that they could vote Fine Gael, and almost by proxy get a Fianna Fáil led government.[7] The idea of a national government was mooted at various times before the April election by a number of national newspapers, most particularly the *Cork Examiner* and the *Irish Independent* and was something that the British embassy picked up on. For them the issue revolved around the succession of de Valera with the British Ambassador, Alexander Clutterbuck, noting: 'there are rumours that some of the old guard such as Mr Aiken would not be prepared to serve under Mr Lemass, who is the heir apparent'.[8] Later the US embassy would see these personality problems as opening the way for James Ryan to succeed de Valera as a compromise choice.

By August, however, La Fréniere was informing the State Department that an informed source was now reporting that both Lemass and MacEntee had fallen out of favour with de Valera causing him to lean towards Ryan as his likely successor:

This change of attitude by de Valera toward his two able lieutenants is said to have come about in early February 1957 when the then inter-party government was trying to avert the general election that was threatening, and members of Fine Gael approached members of Fianna Fáil with a view to forming an alliance with Fianna Fáil or even a national government. . . . According to the source mentioned above, President Sean T. O'Kelly was secretly conducting the 'merger' negotiations between the Fine Gael leaders and Lemass and MacEntee. . . . It is reported that the above-mentioned negotiations had proceeded to an almost final stage when Lemass and MacEntee decided it was time to include de Valera in their plans.

Mr de Valera's reaction was one of extreme annoyance and displeasure with his two colleagues and he bluntly rejected the proposals. The chief had spoken and that was that. The source states that since then Mr de Valera has indicated that he considers Dr Ryan as the person in the party who should succeed him.[9]

Some months earlier when de Valera was forming his cabinet he had Ryan appointed to Finance at Lemass's insistence with MacEntee moving to Health.[10] De Valera, astute politician as he was, had undoubtedly realised that Fianna Fáil had gone to the country in 1948 and 1954 with conservative economic records and had been defeated in both. The economic crisis the Fianna Fáil government confronted in 1957 was so severe that there was every likelihood that a conservative approach would only exacerbate the problem and more importantly return the party to opposition at the next election. De Valera thus decided that change was necessary. It was a change brought about by electoral fortunes, not a deliberate break with traditional Fianna Fáil economic policies.

The belief, reported by the embassy, that Ryan was de Valera's chosen successor has some merit in that a number of commentators were of the view that Ryan could emerge as a compromise candidate between Lemass and Frank Aiken, who did not come into the equation at all for the American embassy. While it is unlikely that any American official had much regard for Aiken's political nous because of his stance on nuclear issues at the United Nations, his omission is nevertheless surprising. The British embassy, for instance, was convinced up to the end of 1958 that Ryan could emerge as a compromise candidate between Lemass and Aiken.[11]

MacEntee, as a result of his move to Health after the election of 1957 was never really a serious candidate to replace de Valera. By August, when La Fréniere was writing his memo, MacEntee had indeed been sidelined from the main focus of government economic policy, but Lemass most certainly was at the hub of government decision making. By this stage he was in the process of reorienting relations with the various interest groups and was fashioning a more active economic policy, which eventually would have interdependence with Europe at its core. No other evidence exists for any plotting by Lemass, MacEntee and O'Kelly. For their part the British, for instance, while conscious of the approach by Fine Gael, were not aware of any attempt by senior figures in Fianna Fáil to move towards the formation of a national government.

While the US embassy was much concerned with de Valera's imminent retirement in 1957, paradoxically when he eventually did retire their coverage was brief. What was more important for the Americans, however, was how Lemass would shape up as Taoiseach. Within two months of his becoming Taoiseach the embassy noted how, for Lemass, the European dimension to economic policy had quickly become paramount to government thinking:

Although Ireland has demonstrated in the UN that it has a wide interest in foreign affairs that do not directly affect the interests of Ireland, the country has failed to show a realistic interest in foreign affairs that do have a direct bearing on its progress. In this regard the opposition . . . have been most critical of the Taoiseach's failure to cope with Ireland's interest in European markets . . . it appears that the necessity of foreign cooperation is being brought home to Lemass and that he now realises that he must deviate from his government's policy of indifferent isolation and take an active role in establishing a place for Ireland in the European trade pattern.[12]

By the end of 1959, the embassy was of the opinion that Lemass's thoughts on European trading blocs were induced by his being 'now apparently concerned about his political future and is no doubt anxious to expand Ireland's trade prospects beyond the established practice of concentrating on trade with Great Britain'.[13] Although we now know that Lemass's thinking on economic and trade issues had considerably liberalised in the years immediately before he became Taoiseach, the embassy was accurately reporting the then conventional wisdom; a conventional wisdom that was in fact quite erroneous. Although he had been the apostle of protectionism in the 1930s and had seen government industrial policy underpinned for two decades by the protectionist regime, it is quite clear that by the time Fianna Fáil regained office in 1957, Lemass was of the opinion that a new approach to economic management was needed in Ireland. By the time he became Taoiseach his programme entailed active engagement with the major interest groups, and at the centre of this engagement would be some form of association with one of the emerging European trading blocs.[14]

While Lemass well realised that Irish economic policy formulation was inhibited by the close nature of the trading relationship with Britain, it is ludicrous in the extreme ever to think of him not being anxious to expand Ireland's trading horizons over and above the British market. Britain was the crucial market for Ireland, but Lemass knew that it could not be the only one. It was not a question of his political future, but more a question of the whole economic future of the Irish State that made him search for greater market exploitation than simply the British option.

Ireland's economic links with Britain again came to the American embassy's attention with the signing of the Anglo-Irish agreement of April 1960. Maintaining that the agreement had important political connotations and that its effects would be more psychological than material, the embassy astutely commented on the increasing role that the agricultural interest groups, particularly the National Farmers Association (NFA), were playing in Irish politics. It noted that James Dillon, leader of Fine Gael since October 1959, had advocated a strong agricultural economy and had linked his plans for increased agricultural production with closer association with Great Britain. Lemass, meanwhile, had managed to negotiate at least a foothold in the British market towards parity of prices and the embassy reported that this would 'no doubt tempt the leaders of both Irish political parties to strive for increasing advantages in the British market'.[15]

The point about the NFA's increasing importance as an effective lobby group was a valid one. From their inception in 1955, the NFA had built up an increasingly professional and vocal presence. It expressed profound disappointment at the Anglo-Irish trade agreement and was insistent in its demands to government that the EEC was the place to be. Once the trade agreement was signed the government adopted a wait and see approach in terms of membership of a European bloc as they were unwilling, quite naturally given Ireland's still quite high dependence on the British market, to make any move without the British. In May 1961 the NFA called on the government to open negotiations with the EEC to secure Irish membership whether the British applied or not. In adopting this position the NFA held that such membership was vital for the future of the Irish economy and that Irish agriculture was at the stage where it could compete confidently with its European counterparts. The embassy picked up on the significance of this declaring that:

this plea serves to dramatise a conviction which has been growing among agricultural interests in Ireland and is not nearly so widely shared by representatives of Irish industry many of whom frankly are scared of the prospect of the competition which they would face if Ireland joined the EEC. It is considered unlikely that the pressure from agricultural interests will be sufficient to induce any change in the policy of the government which long has pointed to the difficulties with Britain which would be engendered by an independent Irish move toward the EEC.[16]

While no Irish government was going to make any move on European matters without taking cognisance of British moves, the American analysis as regards the other Irish interest groups contained a certain grain of truth.

Lemass's attempts to align the various interest groups with government policy gathered pace after the government's historic decision to apply for membership of the EEC in July 1961. The Committee on Industrial Organisation was formed later the same year and was quickly followed by the Employer-Labour Conference (NELC) and the National Industrial and Economic Council (NIEC). These institutions paralleled the state's new-found commitment to some sort of planning and can be seen as part of a continuing corporatist-style initiative of Lemass to involve the unions and industry in the policy of economic development.[17] However, the American embassy was none too impressed with these developments maintaining that the

Government sets much store by this conference as a means of working out agreements between labour and management on long-term policies . . . However the embassy has not been especially impressed by the amount of enthusiasm with which the FUE or ICTU has been approaching the conference. Both parties have been diligently preparing for it, but neither side has indicated to the embassy that it has any great prospect of success.[18]

A year later with the establishment of the NIEC, the embassy noted that:

The establishment of such a council has been a major objective of the Lemass government in the course of the past year in order to associate all interests with governmental economic policies. . . . Since agriculture is the stagnant element in terms of overall economic growth the ICTU insisted that it be excluded from the frame of reference. Consequently there is no representation of agricultural organisations on the NIEC. This ignoring of agriculture at a time when farm organisations are showing more and more vociferousness may be self defeating.[19]

It is quite true that the government placed much store in both the NELC and the NIEC in terms of harmonising relations with the unions and the employers and no doubt the embassy was correct in its assessment of the attitudes of both groups to the NELC. In February 1963, after the government had published a White Paper entitled *Closing the Gap*, which called for wage restraint, the ICTU withdrew from the NELC, which substantiated the analysis deriving from Merrion Square.

On the question of the NIEC, however, the embassy's reading of the situation showed a fundamental flaw in its understanding of government interaction with the farming community. It was not a question of the government simply bowing to union interests and ignoring agriculture at the behest of the unions. By the early 1960s the NFA were deeply suspicious of Lemass's courtship of the unions. What the NFA was looking for was not to be a participant in some form of tripartite body with unions and employers, and hence they were not unduly bothered about the demands that were emanating from the trade union movement. What the NFA sought was a separate formalising of relations with government wherein farmers' incomes would keep pace with those of urban workers. The NFA wanted to sit at the top table with government; they most categorically did not want to have to share this table with employers and trade unionists. For the NFA, agriculture was the lifeblood of the Irish economy and as such they were of the opinion that state-farmer relations should be on a formal footing, alongside any such body that the government might set up with the other sectional interest groups. This formalisation of relations eventually did take place in February 1964 when in the Dáil Lemass gave official recognition to the NFA:

We recognise that the NFA has a special status among farmers organisations insofar as it is interested in all branches of agriculture and we made it clear to them that we welcome the prospect of regular comprehensive consultations and discussions with them in connection with the formulation of agricultural policies in the broad sense as well as their practical co-operation in respect of the different aspects of agriculture.[20]

Notwithstanding the formalisation of relations between the government and the NFA, relations continued to be fractious. The Minister for Agriculture, Paddy Smith, eventually resigned in October 1964 over what he saw as the sacrificing of rural to urban interests. The embassy originally reported that Smith's resignation had caught his colleagues and the public by surprise and was principled and courageous.[21] The following week's report told a different story, however, maintaining that

there are indications that Smith's action . . . may not have been as principled as was initially indicated. Various reports from generally reliable sources echo the theme that a cabinet reshuffle was contemplated and that Smith, along with one or two of his older colleagues, was to make way for the appointment of younger Ministers.[22]

This was something that the newspapers of the time were widely reporting, with 'Backbencher' in *The Irish Times* noting 'the young men were preparing to take over with the blessing of Mr Lemass. The berths were all but allocated', while a later editorial in the same paper maintained that 'it is widely believed that he [Smith] anticipated only by a short time the end of his Ministerial existence'.[23] Undoubtedly the embassy's second report was more accurate. John Horgan has commented on how Lemass was reported to have had up to 17 resignation statements from Smith in his drawer,[24] and it was only when Lemass learned that Smith was attempting to get the press to announce his resignation that Lemass himself acted in accepting the resignation and appointing Charles Haughey to succeed Smith.

The whole debate about the place of sectional interest groups in the policy process can be traced back to the decision by the Fianna Fáil government of Lemass to apply for membership of the EEC. This decision was described by William Tyler, Assistant Secretary of State for European Affairs, as the first move by the Irish government to participate in international affairs, and particularly in the economic affairs of Western Europe. Maintaining that Ireland was shedding its 'narrow provincialism', Tyler proclaimed:

the decision to apply for membership of the EEC is most significant. Though obviously motivated to a large extent by a feeling that Ireland would be excluded from the British market the decision is not merely a reaction to this prospect. There is evidence that Irish leaders weighed their decision carefully and concluded that Ireland must become a member of the Common Market. This is further borne out by the Prime Minister's declaration that Ireland is ready to assume all obligations, political as well as economic, of membership of the EEC.[25]

While some were doubtful about the European option, most notably parts of the industrial and trade union sectors,[26] Tyler's analysis is substantially correct. Lemass continually stressed the political obligations of EEC membership once Ireland applied. This came to the fore when the Minister of Lands, Micheál O Moráin delivered a speech in his native Castlebar in February 1962. He pointed out that it would be unrealistic to ignore the fact that all members of the EEC were in NATO and that neutrality in the context of East-West divisions was something that had not been envisaged by the Irish people. He went on to argue that between communism and the free world 'neutrality . . . is not a policy to which we would even wish to appear committed . . . it may be necessary for us to share any political decisions for the common good'.[27] While this speech caused quite a furore within both Fianna Fáil and the country at large, there can be little doubt that Lemass was aware of it in advance. In an organisation as tightly knitted together as the Fianna Fáil cabinet, it is inconceivable that Lemass would not have known of such a speech, hinting as it did of a fundamental change in Irish foreign policy.[28] At a parliamentary party meeting nine days later under questioning from Deputy M. J. Kennedy, Lemass 'gave a lengthy explanation to the party' of Moran's speech.[29] While the minutes of this meeting are no clearer than that, it does appear that Lemass was able to convince his colleagues that the economic benefits of membership were paramount and in any event there was no stipulation that entry to NATO was a prerequisite for joining the EEC. This was something the embassy picked up on:

It is much to be doubted that the Government wished to prepare the people of Ireland for admission into NATO . . . Rather it would seem that the Government felt that the time had come for the public at large to start thinking about what is inevitable if Ireland becomes a member of the EEC, namely a marked change in its present neutral status and complete independence of action . . . By raising the subject of NATO, the Government was sure of stirring the public into awareness that there were significant political implications in the application for membership in the EEC.[30]

The main problem that the NATO question posed was that the then Minister for External Affairs, Frank Aiken, and his department in general, showed a general caution towards European events in this period. Lemass's relationship with Aiken was problematic and Aiken played little role in formulating European policy. Aiken did outline his views on the EEC in April 1962 when he told the Dáil that 'the best contribution we can make to the world and world peace is to keep ourselves as free as we can to make suggestions that a member of a bloc could not make'.[31] Throughout this debate Aiken was heckled by the opposition as to whether joining a bloc compromised Irish independence in foreign affairs. To the US embassy this reflected the belief of a number of individuals both inside and outside political life that Aiken was 'less than enthusiastic over the prospect that membership of the EEC may entail some diminution of the independence of action which he has always championed as the proper role for Ireland in international affairs'.[32] There is some dispute amongst historians as to what extent Aiken was really interested in the EEC, with Joe Skelly in particular maintaining that Aiken and the Secretary of External Affairs, Con Cremin, played crucial roles in the Irish application.[33] The files of the Departments of the Taoiseach and Foreign Affairs would seem to suggest, however, that it was Lemass and the Secretary of Finance, T. K. Whitaker, who took the key decisions.[34]

For the State Department the Irish application was inevitably tied up with the British application and took a distinct second place to it. John R. Burke, officer in charge of Irish affairs at the bureau of British Commonwealth and Northern European Affairs, wrote to Edward Prince, First Secretary at the embassy in Dublin to this effect in April 1962 maintaining:

For the moment, Departmental attention is riveted, as you can appreciate, on the UK negotiations with the six at Brussels. Like a Cape Hatteras barometer the prognosis for the negotiation seems to shift daily from fair to stormy and though everyone continues to maintain that ultimate membership is the only possible result, there are those who consciously cross their fingers and touch wood as they say it. . . . The Department has not yet felt called upon to take a firm position on the Irish application. This is due to two factors: (1) the aforementioned preoccupation with the progress of the UK bid and (2) the many statements indicating that the Irish application was tied with that of the UK, and that it would probably be withdrawn should the UK negotiation fail.[35]

For their part, the British in essence also supported the Irish application. Christopher Audland, then a First Secretary in the British delegation, has stated that the British supported the Irish application on two levels:

from a trade point of view it made sense to us that Ireland be included, considering that we had such a large stake in the Irish market, and the government also felt that if both countries were in the community, it could help to move to a solution on Ulster. That was something that was not in the public eye at the time but it was most definitely important to us.[36]

However, the view of the State Department that the British application would eventually succeed was shown to be erroneous when, in January 1963, de Gaulle famously uttered 'non' to the British.

De Gaulle's veto of the British application led to the lapsing of Ireland's own application, and saw the embassy comment with just a touch of hyperbole that 'Irish official opinion realises that the economic future of Ireland is hanging in the balance in the present crisis over the future of the EEC'.[37] Lemass immediately began a process of developments, which would enable the Irish State to reapply for membership. He told the Dáil in February 1963 that the 'suspensions of the British negotiations should be viewed as a temporary setback and not as a final breach'.[38] The collapse of the negotiations provided the government with the motivation to move quickly to reduce tariffs and to prepare for a second application. An activist Taoiseach, Lemass had brought his party with him in the search for a more dynamic economic future, and in the process had fundamentally changed their economic philosophy. Assisted by dynamic elements within the civil service he had embarked on a route that assumed interdependence with other economies. To secure a consensus on this he engaged in meaningful and formal dialogue with economic interest groups. The American ambassador, Harold McCloskey, noted these changes in a politico-economic assessment of Ireland in May 1963:

The Irish continue to see an expanded EEC as the nucleus of a cohesive integrated Europe of which they want very much to be part. For these reasons they have made a complete political commitment to the ideals of the EEC and have shown no reservation about any of its doctrines, although they hope that accession to military pacts outside the EEC itself (e.g., NATO) will not have to be part of their political commitment. This commitment to the political aspects of EEC also influenced the economic aspects of membership when they foreswore seeking any particular economic concessions other than a minor modification of the transition period for the harmonisation of tariffs. In spite of the breakdown of the Brussels negotiations, the Irish are proceeding upon the premise of eventual EEC membership and determination to be ready for it colors most of their economic and political problems at the present moment.[39]

On such an assessment was American foreign policy towards Ireland predicated. Over the next three years the American embassy at Merrion Square followed events closely as the Fianna Fáil government, re-elected in 1965, sought to pursue the policy of entry to the EEC. By 1966 the embassy was arguing that the State Department should 'discreetly encourage greater Irish participation in Europe and European organisations and should likewise offer appropriate encouragement to Irish efforts to develop and broaden their economy'.[40] For the previous decade Merrion Square had been reporting back on these issues to a State Department that had been receiving valuable if not always entirely reliable information from its officers in Dublin.

NOTES

I would like to thank the research committee of Dublin City University for generously providing me with the opportunity to undertake research in Washington DC on which this chapter is based.

1 Seán Cronin, *Washington's Irish Policy 1916–1986: Independence, Partition, Neutrality* (Dublin, 1987); Troy Davis, *Dublin's American Policy: Irish-American Diplomatic Relations, 1945–1952* (Washington, 1998).

2 This section is based on the author's interview with George Dempsey, 14 Nov. 1999. Dempsey is a former American diplomat who served in a number of stations across the world, including Ireland where he was based between 1988 and 1992.

3 As above.

4 Public Records Office, London (hereafter, PRO) Dominions Office (hereafter DO), 35/7906. G. Kimber, Dublin embassy, to G. W. Chadwick, Commonwealth Relations Office, 10 Feb. 1959.

5 National Archives and Records Administration, Washington [hereafter NARA], Record Group [hereafter RG] 59, Box 3168, 740A/00/2–1857, Dublin Embassy to State Department, 18 Feb. 1957.

6 Alex Bolster to Richard Mulcahy, undated but by context early Feb. 1957. Fine Gael Archives, UCD, P39/GE 62.

7 Interview of John F. McCarthy with Seán Lemass, 14 August 1969, copy in possession of the author.

8 PRO, DO 35/5195, Clutterbuck to Lord Home, 23 March 1957.

9 NARA RG 59 Box 3168, 740A/00/8-857, Dublin Embassy to State Department, 8 Aug. 1957.

10 Brian Farrell, *Seán Lemass* (Dublin, 1971), p. 95.

11 PRO, DO, 35/790, G. Kimber, Dublin, to G. W. Chadwick, Commonwealth Relations Office, 3 Dec. 1958.

12 NARA RG 59 Box 3170, 740A/00 (W)/8–659, Dublin Embassy to State Department, 6 Aug. 1959.

13 NARA RG 59 Box 3170, 740/00 (W)/12–3059, Dublin Embassy to State Department, 30 Dec. 1959.

14 Gary Murphy, 'Government, interest groups and the Irish move to Europe, 1957–1963', *Irish Studies in International Affairs* 8 (1997), 57–68.

15 NARA RG 59 Box 1651, 740/00/4-1460, Dublin Embassy to State Department, 14 Apr. 1960.

16 NARA RG 59 Box 1652, 740/00(W)/5–460, Dublin Embassy to State Department, 4 May 1960.

17 Gary Murphy, 'Towards a corporate state? Seán Lemass and the realignment of interest groups in the policy process 1948–1964', *Administration* 47 (1999), 92–3.

18 NARA RG 59 Box 1652, 740/00(W)/5–2562, Dublin Embassy to State Department, 25 May 1962.

19 NARA RG 59 Box 3947, Pol 6–1 Ire, Pol 7 Ire, Dublin Embassy to State Department, 3 Oct. 1963.

20 Dáil Debates, vol. 206, col. 1794, 16 Feb. 1964.

21 NARA RG 59 Box 2343, Pol 2–1 Ire, Dublin Embassy to State Department, 9 Oct. 1964.

22 NARA RG 59 Box 2343, Pol 15–1 Ire, Dublin Embassy to State Department 16 Oct. 1964.

23 *The Irish Times*, 10 and 15 Oct. 1964.

24 John Horgan, *Seán Lemass: The Enigmatic Patriot* (Dublin, 1997), p. 356.

25 NARA RG 59, Office of British Commonwealth and Northern European Affairs, Alpha-Numeric files relating to Ireland, Box 1, Tyler to S/P – Mr McGhee, 11 Aug. 1961.

26 For the trade union movement's attitude to Europe, see Gary Murphy, 'Fostering a spurious progeny?: the trade union movement and Europe, 1957–1964', *Saothar* 21 (1996), 61–70.

27 The text of O'Moráin's speech can be found in National Archives, Department of the Taoiseach, S.17246A.

28 See Horgan, *Seán Lemass*, p. 223; Dermot Keogh, 'Irish neutrality and the first application for membership of the EEC', in Michael Kennedy and Joseph Morrison Skelly (eds), *Irish Foreign Policy 1916–1966: From Independence to Internationalism* (Dublin, 2000), p. 277.

29 Fianna Fáil Parliamentary Party Minutes, Fianna Fáil archives, 441/B, 14 Feb. 1962.

30 NARA RG 59 Box 1651, 740a.00/2-962, Dublin Embassy to State Department, 9 Feb. 1962.

31 Dáil Debates, vol. 194, col. 1418, 5 Apr. 1962.

32 NARA RG 59 Box 1651, 740a.00/4-662, Dublin Embassy to State Department, 6 Apr. 1962.

33 Joseph Morrison Skelly, *Irish Diplomacy at the United Nations, 1945–1965: National Interests and the International Order* (Dublin, 1997), p. 171

34 It is interesting to note that the files on the application to the EEC, NA, DT, S.17246A/62–W/62, reveal that Lemass's handwritten accounts were generally the line followed.

35 NARA RG 59, Office of British Commonwealth and Northern European Affairs, Alpha-Numeric files relating to Ireland, Box 1, Burke to Prince, 20 Apr. 1962.

36 Author's interview with Sir Christopher Audland, 18 Feb. 1994. Audland was First Secretary at the Brussels negotiations between Oct. 1961 and Jan. 1963 during the first British application

37 NARA RG 59 Box 1652, 740a.00(W)/1–2563, Dublin Embassy to State Department, 25 Jan. 1963.

38 Dáil Debates, vol. 299, col. 924, 5 Feb. 1963.

39 NARA RG 59 Box 3946, Pol 2–3 Ire, Dublin Embassy to State Department, 3 May 1963.

40 NARA RG 59 Box 2343, Pol 1 Ire–US, Dublin Embassy to State Department, 15 Sept. 1966.

14 'Government sources said last night . . .': The Development of the Parliamentary Press Lobby in Modern Ireland

John Horgan

The history of the parliamentary lobby, the phrase generally used to designate those political journalists with unique and privileged access to governmental sources, is one in which there are notable commonalities between the practices in Britain and Ireland. Indeed, the lobby owes its very existence to the political tension between the two islands in the 1880s, when the Fenian propensity for bombing prominent British targets, notably the Palace of Westminster, led the authorities there to restrict access by journalists and others to the precincts of the Houses of Parliament. Since 1884, in effect, this restricted list has been kept, and controlled, by the Speaker of the House of Commons.[1] Britain passed its first Official Secrets Act five years after the establishment of the first, rudimentary lobby, a successful example of closing the stable door before the horse has even thought of escaping.

The lobby, however, is effectively a list within a list. In Britain, it is comprised of a self-perpetuating elite with written rules, whose members accord government ministers and spokespersons anonymity in return for privileged access to political information. It is less a marriage of equals than, in the words of a distinguished political commentator, the creation of a new group of insiders 'to . . . exclude the public and the mass of writers of countless newsletters, pamphlet sheets and weeklies who had overcrowded the members' lobby'.[2] The same writer clearly identifies the central dilemma in any such arrangement without resolving it: 'Both government and the media are compelled by the unlimited demands of modern communications to co-operate, yet by all basic tests they are opposing and rival forces'.[3]

There have been two basic theses relevant to the lobby system in Ireland. The first, major thesis[4] is that this is a system for subverting important press freedoms, for facilitating the manipulation of information and of the media themselves by government, and has important negative consequences for the quality of democracy in those societies of which it is a feature. The minor thesis[5] suggests that the Irish and UK systems are analogous, and that the defects of one are mirrored in the other. Another commentator, Brian Farrell, argues that the Irish system, which he sees as operating on a broadly similar basis, 'creates a much more secretive form of Cabinet-media relationship, frequently characterised by leaks, often inspired and manipulated'.[6] Foley, while arguing that 'there are strong similarities in both systems', suggests that 'similarities in structures and organisation could possibly hide a system which allows a greater independent inquiry, while maintaining elements of the British lobby terms.[7]

This chapter is based to some extent on a number of participant interviews with political writers, many of them at one time – or still – members of the lobby, such as Dick Walsh, Bruce Arnold, Michael Mills, Ted Nealon and Sean Duignan. Although it is not necessary to ascribe particular views to particular individuals, the evidence they provide about the workings of the system suggests that both the major and minor theses may not hold entirely true for Ireland, or at least that the historical development of the lobby system in Ireland has diverged from that in Westminster, with important consequences both for journalists and politicians.

One way of examining the similarities and differences between the Palace of Westminster and Leinster House lobby systems is to look at the differing ways in which they have evolved and have responded to particular issues, tensions, and strains within government–media relationships.

Viewed in this context, the Westminster model has remained remarkably static. The creation of the lobby in 1884 was at first merely organisational; it developed an important professional dimension under Ramsay MacDonald, who appointed Britain's first government press secretary (although he was not described as such), George Seward. This, according to Margach, was when 'the old style competitive outsiders were organised into a fraternity of organised insiders'.[8]

It was a century after the informal creation of the lobby system that it received its first serious shock (it had, of course, grown in size along the way, but without any change of function). This was in 1986, when Margaret Thatcher was British Prime Minister and Bernard Ingham her press secretary. In that year, the newly founded London *Independent* decided that it would have no part of the lobby system. The *Guardian*, possibly somewhat upstaged on this matter of principle, decided that although it would continue to attend lobby briefings, it would henceforth refer to 'a Downing Street spokesman' or 'Mrs Thatcher's spokesman' as the source for its information. Acceptance of this practice by the lobby would have meant a change in its rule-book, which specified that all information was non-attributable. After a lengthy internal debate, the lobby decided to maintain its rules, and the *Guardian* left.[9] It was hardly a crisis, but certainly an embarrassment, and was not resolved until both Mrs Thatcher and Mr Ingham had departed, when a new regime offered both newspapers the opportunity to opt back in, encouraged by a compromise formula which allowed for minimal attribution.

Since then, controversy about the lobby and its functions has been remarkable by its absence. David Walker's derisive description of it as 'a crutch for crippled journalists',[10] like the handful of other criticisms that have been made of the system from time to time, has been greeted by a somewhat costive silence.

The development of the lobby in Ireland has been in some respects slower, in others more organic and healthy. It was slower because the initial relationships between government and media in Ireland were characterised, if not necessarily by hostility, certainly by coolness. In spite of the fact that most Irish national newspapers in 1922 supported the Free State government, their bad behaviour in insisting on reporting the civil war from a journalistic, rather than a political standpoint, engendered considerable mistrust in Government Buildings.[11]

Nor did the change in government in 1932 make things much better. The de Valera administration was viewed with a baleful eye by both *The Irish Times* and the *Irish Independent*, in a context in which the support given to him by the *Irish Press* was seen as an exercise in politics rather than an exercise in journalism.

The beginnings of a lobby system were created during the war by Seán Lemass, the long-time Minister for Industry and Commerce, who held regular briefings on the supply situation with senior journalists.[12] It grew in influence after the war was over, and became more formalised. There was at this stage relatively little specialisation; at least the current division between parliamentary journalists and political journalists was not so pronounced. The umbrella organisation for all such journalists at that time was the Parliamentary Press Gallery (which currently has as members only those journalists who report the actual proceedings of the Dáil and some parliamentary sketch writers). This was the organisation which helped to put the final nails into the coffin of the Irish News Agency, which had been founded by Seán MacBride in 1949 and which staggered on, weakened by attacks from within and without, until it received the coup de grace in 1957. There is no doubt, reading the files, that opposition to the INA by a powerful and well-organised group of Irish political journalists within the lobby was a major factor in its demise. The alacrity with which Mr de Valera jumped to pay attention to the wishes of the people who were virtually the sole conduits to the public of the proceedings of the Oireachtas and the pronouncements of governmental ministers was transparent.[13]

It is not possible to identify the point at which the lobby, as such, came formally into existence, but it is certainly possible to speak of phases in the relationship between government and media which is generally characterised by this term. The likelihood is that the lobby began to exist on a formal or semi-formal basis at some stage in the early 1950s, and retained its basic shape unchanged for about two decades. The emergence of this status quo was facilitated by continuity on both sides. On the government side, the watchful presence of Padraig Ó hAnnrachain, either as head of the Government Information Bureau or as assistant secretary of the Department of the Taoiseach, ensured that all potentially contentious matters were being dealt with by a safe pair of hands. The measure of this continuity can be gauged from the fact that Ó hAnnrachain acted in his capacity not only for de Valera, but also for Lemass and Lynch. He continued to act for Haughey but in a somewhat different role.

On the media side, the turnover was low, and it was some time before the position of political correspondent, even on a national newspaper, became a full-time one: journalists who wrote about politics were often expected to cover other high-profile areas such as industrial relations almost as a matter of course. It was before the era of specialisation, which did not dawn until the early 1960s, and indeed before political coverage as such began to account for a substantial proportion of the overall content of newspapers. Full-time or part-time political correspondents like Michael McInerney of *The Irish Times*, Arthur Noonan of the *Irish Independent* (and later of RTÉ) and Jim McGuinness and Brendan Malin of the *Irish Press* (later succeeded by Michael Mills) saw many governments come and go, and watched the transition from the de Valera to the Lemass era with a generally benign, almost in some cases avuncular, mien.

Not only was turnover low, but the personnel were also few. Mills, for example, would do double duty as political correspondent for the *Irish Press* and the *Evening Press,* using different by-lines; the same would have been true for the *Irish Independent* and the *Evening Herald.*

The political news – as opposed to features – content of the Sunday newspapers was scant enough, and frequently supplied by the same journalists who worked for the daily papers in the group concerned. There was only one broadcasting station. All in all, the lobby consisted of a small, tightly knit group of people, amounting to no more than half a dozen or so. This was in marked contrast to the press gallery – the assembly of reporters who watched and recorded the proceedings of the Dáil and Seanad – which would have comprised task forces of up to three reporters from each newspaper or media group. In such circumstances, political control of the lobby was hardly an issue, and the *esprit de corps* was strong.

Throughout this period, the actual organisation of the lobby was haphazard and reactive, rather than planned or programmed. There were no regular briefings. The job of the head of the Government Information Bureau was to provide answers from the civil service or from ministers to queries from political correspondents. Political 'exclusives' were rare. Personality politics were almost non-existent. In 1962, with the arrival of television, the number of people who were entitled to join, or wanted to join, the lobby rose, and this resulted in the provision of a special room in Leinster House in which the political correspondents all had their desks and telephones. This development, positive in itself from the lobby's point of view, had one inescapable consequence: it was possible, under these circumstances, for every political correspondent to overhear each of his colleague's telephone conversations, so that competitive journalism became even more of a rarity. If any journalist left the room in search of an exclusive or private information, the chances were that he would be rigorously interrogated by his colleagues on his return for fear that he was about to upstage them all in the following morning's newspaper. It was, perhaps to an even greater degree than its UK counterpart, an arrangement closely resembling a cartel.

It was a dynamic which was if anything reinforced by one seminal event: the journey to Japan in 1972 by Jack Lynch, then Taoiseach, to launch a new tanker for the mammoth Gulf Oil company, which was in the process of establishing a major oil terminal in Bantry, Co. Cork. Lynch was accompanied on this trip, which involved stopovers at a number of important points in the US and Australia, by the core group of political journalists of the era, and established relationships with them which were to be of considerable assistance to him and his administration in later years. This particular tour was emblematic of another development: the internationalisation of Irish politics which accompanied Irish entry to the EEC, as it then was. This process involved the Taoiseach of the day in more frequent foreign travel, and the media 'pack' accompanying him, which was largely though not completely, co-extensive with the lobby, acquired a new sense of its own importance and value in the affairs of the nation. This would be reflected, in turn, in an unwillingness to break ranks and a determination to respect confidences.

Towards the end of the Lynch era, however, a number of factors were beginning to operate which would, in turn, begin to alter the role of the lobby itself. One was the competitiveness between ministers, unknown (or at least successfully suppressed) during the de Valera era, and only in its infancy in the Lemass era.

This competitiveness reached a high point when Lemass resigned and teams of ministers operated on behalf of the two principal contenders,

Haughey and Colley, using the lobby as their primary target. The new set of relationships which this engendered would have involved principally ministers such as Charles Haughey, Brian Lenihan, Donogh O'Malley and George Colley, each of whom would have seen himself as a potential successor to Lynch. O'Malley, who died in 1968, was notable for his habit of spurning the private pleasures of the cabinet dining room, and joining the political correspondents for lunch in the communal restaurant in Leinster House.

This degree of openness and more or less overt press manipulation and leaking by ministers downgraded the importance of the lobby as a channel for news and information. This process was if anything accelerated by the substitution of Eoin Neeson for Ó hAnnrachain in 1968. Neeson, though an able journalist and historian himself, never managed to win the confidence of the lobby: 'no comment' became the standard response to many queries. In fairness to Neeson, it may be that he lacked the authority, within the system as it then existed, to bend a rather traditional and secrecy-obsessed public service to the increasingly pressing demands of the media.

This low point in the development of the lobby, and its usefulness to government, was marked in particular by the defeat of Fianna Fáil in the 1973 election. Lynch, increasingly media-conscious, hired Frank Dunlop, then an RTÉ journalist working in Belfast, as a press officer for the party in opposition. Simultaneously, the new government – the first non-Fianna Fáil administration for sixteen years – was also taking stock. It transferred responsibility for government media relations to the new Minister for Posts and Telegraphs, Conor Cruise O' Brien, and drafted in an exceptionally able young television producer, Muiris Mac Conghail, to act as the new head of a restructured government information service.

The structural changes were significant. Mac Conghail was given the rank of assistant secretary within the public service: this gave him the right to obtain information from other government departments at a senior level. He was also allowed to attend some cabinet meetings. There were regular, non-attributable briefings by Mac Conghail and by individual ministers, although the Taoiseach, Liam Cosgrave, who was publicity-shy, was conspicuous generally by his absence from these proceedings. The lobby responded positively to this acknowledgement of its status: on one occasion, at least, a non-attributable briefing by a plainly distraught (and I do not mean this as a euphemism for drunken) minister was not communicated to the public in any form because there was no way of doing so which would not have exposed the minister concerned to major, and unwelcome, political consequences. When Mac Conghail resigned in 1975 he was succeeded by a broadcast journalist, Ted Nealon, whose relationship with the lobby until the end of that government in 1977 was on the whole amiable and good tempered, although there were occasions when the journalists, sniffing a disagreement between the government partners, were visibly miffed by the spokesman's emollient approach.

When Lynch came back to power in 1977, Dunlop took over from Nealon: in 1978 he became the first person in the particular job to adopt the title of Government Press Secretary. The new title spoke of a new way of doing things, and of an increasingly political use by the government of the channels of information at its disposal. The relationship between Dunlop and Lynch's successor in 1979, Charles Haughey, was not close, however, although Dunlop remained in that role until the Fianna Fáil defeat of 1982, eventually leaving the civil service in 1986.

Changes taking place within the government press service and its relationships with the lobby were accompanied by changes within the lobby itself. For one thing, it was growing in size. Jobs which had been shared between different papers were being divided; new titles were being started up; politics was bulking ever larger on the news agenda, especially with the election of Haughey, always a controversial figure. A key date is 1980: this is the year in which Geraldine Kennedy, a young journalist from Waterford who had previously worked on the *Munster Express*, the *Cork Examiner* and *The Irish Times*, joined the newly founded *Sunday Tribune* as its political correspondent.[14] In 1982 she was to join the *Sunday Press*. Although its significance can perhaps be exaggerated, it is least noteworthy that owing to pressure on space Geraldine Kennedy was allocated her own room in a separate building, although she attended briefings by government spokesmen in the main building in the normal way. One way or another, the fierceness of her appetite for political news, especially exclusive news, upped the ante considerably for her colleagues: within government, the reaction, although unknown to most outsiders at the time, was even more marked. Alarmed and dismayed at the apparently limitless channels of information flowing between Mr Haughey's opponents in the Fianna Fáil party and Ms Kennedy, the Haughey administration even had her telephone illegally tapped.

Although she would probably disclaim any major role in what happened subsequently, Kennedy's appointment marked the beginning of a new era. She was to be joined in the political correspondents group by other formidable women journalists such as Una Claffey and Emily O' Reilly; the former cartel became infected by a new spirit of competitiveness and adventure, as government spokespersons learned, sometimes to their cost. Increasingly, unsatisfactory briefings were greeted with a chorus of disapproval or even derision. Hapless spokespersons were sent back, with their tails between their legs, to get answers from ministers to supplementary questions. On more than one occasion, some of them were seen to be close to tears. In the mid-eighties, this renewed, and more muscular, sense of professional solidarity led to the more formal creation of the Political Correspondents' Group, of which Donal Kelly of RTÉ and Chris Glennon of the *Irish Independent* became – and remain – joint chairmen. To become a member of this group, the applicant must show that he or she is a full-time journalist working exclusively on politics and for a national medium.[15] Applications for would-be members are decided on by a vote of the Group as a whole, on the grounds that only those who genuinely need this level of access should be granted it. It negotiates with the Ceann Comhairle of the day about office space and other issues affecting the working practices of its members, and now has increased substantially in size.

The 1982–87 coalition government period also saw the development of a different set of strains in relationships between government and the lobby. These strains were caused not by a conflict of personalities within government, but by political strains between that government's component parties. Such strains have been a feature of most coalition governments since that date, leading to the creation of a bifurcated, or trifurcated government information system in which the lobby is briefed independently (and sometimes, when there is conflict, differently) by a spokesperson for each of the government's component parties. This, it need hardly be added, is substantially different from the UK system. It has been in evidence during the recent series of tensions between the PDs and Fianna Fáil; but the most public manifestation was probably during the previous Fianna Fáil coalition with Labour when a row involving the party leaders and their press secretaries in 1993 about the publication of the Hamilton report on the Beef Tribunal was followed by a dispute in 1994, involving the same players, about Albert Reynolds's attempt to appoint Harry Whelehan as Attorney-General. The latter dispute is graphically depicted in Sean Duignan's diary:

4 October 1994. Albert begins writing, in his spidery scrawl, a statement for me to feed out refuting the Labour briefings or as he puts it, 'setting the record straight on Labour disinformation'. He denies trying to railroad Harry through cabinet, points to 'unrelenting briefings from certain quarters' and insists the matter must be 'resolved' as soon as possible. I tell him that Labour will see this as provocation on the eve of the first meeting between Spring and him for almost a month. Labour duly jump up and down.[16]

These developments also underlined the increasing politicisation of the role of Government Press Secretary, dating as far back as the early 1980s. In 1984 Haughey, then leader of the Opposition, took the unusual step of accusing the then incumbent, Peter Prendergast, of news management and vilification. That government, in turn, recognised the implicitly political dimension of the post by changing the rules so that all government press secretaries became, henceforth, not permanent but temporary civil servants, and had to resign their positions at the succeeding general election. Another innovation, dating from 1983, was the creation of a separate, sub-lobby system for the correspondents in Dublin of foreign media.

The lobby, it must be emphasised, was used at least as much for opposition/media relationships as for government/media relationships. The then leader of the opposition, Mr Haughey, by now had a new press spokesman, P. J. Mara, whose relationships with the lobby have been detailed to some extent in his biography.[17] Haughey's ever growing unpopularity with the media, commented on publicly by Mara in later years, spawned a tension which Mara's considerable gifts were stretched to dispel. At times, the sense of humour which he generally employed to good effect in this cause became a weapon used against him. On one occasion, it became the core of a controversy in which, for the first time, Mara was positively identified as the source of a particular statement to the lobby. This was on the occasion when, during growing internal criticism within Fianna Fáil of Haughey's leadership, Mara quoted Mussolini's famous phrase: 'uno duce, una voce'. The journalist who decided to reveal him as the source of this remark was Geraldine Kennedy, then writing for the *Sunday Press*, who argued later that she had not broken any of the conventions, and was within her rights in identifying Mara, as he could see that she had her notebook out and therefore – she presumed – accepted that what he was saying was on the record.[18] The temptation to print his name in any case must have become well-nigh irresistible as Mara, in the course of delivering this remark, put a finger across his upper lip and goose-stepped up and down the room.

In 1987 saw the return of a Fianna Fáil minority government and the appointment of P. J. Mara as Government Press Secretary. (Parenthetically, it also saw the election of Geraldine Kennedy as PD Deputy for the Dun Laoghaire constituency, until she lost her seat two years later.) Mara's relationships with the lobby were on the whole good, although he had a difficult job to do on behalf of his principal employer. At Haughey's final press conference in 1992, Mara remarked, in self-defence, that he had never told a lie to journalists on Haughey's behalf. Haughey's response was swift and, in the circumstances, more than consciously ironic: 'What was I paying you all that money for then?' This period was also notable, at least in Mara's view, for the emergence of a thinly disguised hostility towards the then leader of Fianna Fáil among lobby journalists and indeed among journalists generally, which acted as a sharp antidote to any tendencies to deference which might have existed previously. 'I find [it] quite extra-ordinary that there shouldn't be one or two or three out of twenty, thirty, forty working journalists who wouldn't have a different view of Haughey and would stand slightly apart.'[19]

Another, less commented upon feature of the operation of the lobby system at this time, however – and one which I suspect also differentiates it from the UK system – is that it became, unwittingly, part of a two-way information system. Mara was legendary for never committing anything to paper himself: his art was entirely verbal. But as far as information was concerned, he became as much hunter-gatherer as provider. As often as not, he would be sent down to the lion's den, not to put a spin on any particular government announcement or to give a briefing on future plans, but, in his employer's words, to 'find out what the fuckers are talking about'. An increasingly embattled Haughey needed information the way plants need water: information about the mood of the media, information about the moves being made by his opponents within the party, information about public concerns generally and, in this situation, the equation became not only one of an exchange of information for confidentiality, but an exchange of information for information. This trend continued under successive governments. As one former Government Press Secretary put it: 'There's a myth about politics that some political parties are media driven, and others are policy driven. We all like to think that we belong in the latter category, but the truth is that every party wants to pursue a policy line – but also wants to know how the media will react to it. The media, and especially the print media, think that they form opinion but they form opinion first within political parties, who regard them as the most critical sounding board.'[20]

The lobby in the nineties has, therefore, undergone a number of sea-changes which reflect Irish circumstances, and which differentiate itself in at least some respects from its Westminster counterpart. The most obvious difference is that it appears to be more aggressive, and less respectful, than the Westminster lobby. In one account, there were frequent and loud echoes of the complaints by political journalists about the extent to which they were manipulated by Peter Mandelson, who was leaking information on behalf of Tony Blair in the run-up to the Labour leadership election.[21] The journalists concerned were so incensed that they failed, perhaps, to realise that their complaints about the effectiveness of Mandelson's press management tactics also amounted to an admission of their own ineptness and suggestibility.

The aggressiveness of the Irish lobby was, according to a number of journalists to whom I have spoken, particularly in evidence during the many briefings which preceded and accompanied the signing of the Good Friday Agreement in Northern Ireland, and for which the Irish and UK lobby systems were, effectively, conjoined. According to these accounts, the spirit of *lèse majesté* on the part of the Irish lobby occasioned more than a little comment among their UK counterparts: the breezy way in which

Irish political journalists tackled UK, as well as their own, politicians and spokespersons, spoke of the emergence of a different tradition on this side of the Irish sea. I would not want to overstate the case, but it is at least arguable. It also seems to be the case that other democratic assemblies on these islands, free to a greater or lesser extent from Westminster tutelage, are in the process of establishing more open, and less exclusive, pathways of communication between politicians and media. The new Scottish parliament[22] sets out the principles under which journalists covering the new parliament work: there is no restricted lobby as such, and all bona-fide journalists are welcome on equal terms. Similar changes are taking place in the Welsh Assembly, whose ministers have even taken a decision to publish Cabinet minutes (subject to certain excisions) after a six-week delay.[23]

This aggressiveness among the Leinster House press corps is partly a function of the Irish lobby's increased size: over the years, the numerical balance between the two groups of reporters within parliament has swung markedly. New technology has reduced the need for the press gallery reporters to be physically present in the chamber, as has the wide availability of parliamentary proceedings on the Oireachtas website. This in return has reduced the importance of the parliamentary reporter. The lobby, however, which reports the briefings, has probably now reached critical mass, with a membership approaching two dozen. It is still tiny when compared to the UK lobby, which now numbers some 150 journalists: but perhaps, in the latter case, obesity is the problem.

The existence of a large and permanently hungry corps of political correspondents increases the need for a flow of information from government – it is hardly a coincidence that the regular five p.m. briefings are colloquially referred to as 'the feed' – and paradoxically, reduces the likelihood of politically exclusive stories emerging from this group of journalists.

This in turn has had two effects. The first is that political journalists in search of exclusives now know that they hope for them in vain from within the lobby system: they have to hunt for them elsewhere. This naturally tends to diminish the importance of the lobby as an institution in the sense that it operates on an increasingly routinised basis, in which insider status no longer confers proportionately privileged access to high-grade information.

The second, perhaps in the end more significant, is that the role of the lobby as part of a government's news management system has, if anything, diminished. There is a visibly altering government set of media priorities, with television and the main evening news bulletin at the top of every politician's list. The existing lobby system cannot always deliver the desired level and type of publicity at this level, because the briefings are non-discriminatory as between a large group of media people. In these circumstances, the lobby can find itself frequently, if subtly, downgraded by a sophisticated use of the sound-bite system in which some journalists become, in George Orwell's words, more equal than others, granted an access that is even more privileged than that accorded to other members of the political correspondents' group because they have high profile roles in particular media.

The paradox, therefore, is that the lobby is becoming of lesser importance in the overall spectrum of government/media relationships (although it was used to considerable effect during the Sheedy affair[24]) precisely because it has grown in size.

One the other hand, the very same development – the lobby's growth in size – has contributed to a much greater competitiveness among political journalists which will in the future, with luck, result in better political journalism for the benefit of the public.

There is one final point which I would make in passing and it relates to technology. The mechanics of the lobby system are essentially those of the nineteenth century: a group of reporters, a government minister or spokesman, a document or press release. Increasingly, political news is now being made in the open, on the run. And there are many sets of circumstances in which, despite all the resources at their command, political figures may be less well informed than their questioners. No politician giving a press conference, however well briefed, can expect not to be faced, towards the end of the conference, by an unexpected question from a reporter who has received additional information on his mobile phone during the press conference itself – information which may not be available to the politician. This is a trend which may in time alter, not just the modalities of the lobby system, but the modalities of political journalism itself.

NOTES

1   Michael Foley, 'The political lobby system', *Irish Communications Review* 3 (1993), 23.
2   James Margach, *Abuse of Power* (London, 1978), p. 125.
3   James Margach, *Anatomy of Power* (London, 1981), p. 129.
4   Peter Kellner, 'The lobby, official secrets and good government', *Parliamentary Affairs* 36 (1983), 275–82; Bob Franklin, *Packaging Politics: Political Communications in Britain's Media Democracy* (London, 1994), pp. 82–95
5   Foley, 'Political lobby system', 21–31
6   Brian Farrell, 'Cabinet-media relationships: approaches to a comparative typology', UCD seminar paper, 1969, cited in Foley, 'Political lobby system', 29.
7   Foley, 'Political lobby system', 29.
8   Margach, *Anatomy of Power*, p. 137.

  9 Robert Harris, *Good and Faithful Servant: The Unauthorised Biography of Bernard Ingham* (London, 1988), pp. 154–5.
 10 M. Cockerell, P. Hennessy and D. Walker, *Sources Close to the Prime Minister* (London, 1984), cited in Foley, 'Political lobby system', 29.
 11 John Horgan, 'State policy and the press', *The Crane Bag* 8 (1984), 52.
 12 John Horgan, *Sean Lemass: The Enigmatic Patriot* (Dublin, 1987), p. 107.
 13 John Horgan, 'Government, propaganda and the Irish news agency', *Irish Communications Review* 3 (1993), 31–43.
 14 Mary O'Malley, 'Geraldine Kennedy, political correspondent with *The Irish Times*', unpublished essay, MSc in Science Communication, Dublin City University, 1999.
 15 Edward Power, 'The political lobby system', seminar paper, MA in Journalism, Dublin City University, 1997.
 16 Sean Duignan, *One Spin On The Merry-Go-Round* (Dublin, 1998), p. 132.
 17 Tim Ryan, *Mara PJ* (Dublin, 1992).
 18 O'Malley, 'Kennedy', p. 4.
 19 P. J. Mara, 'More like midwives', in John Cooney and Tony McGarry (eds), *Spin-Doctors: A Threat to Democracy?* (Dublin, 1996), p. 15.
 20 Fergus Finlay, *Snakes and Ladders*, Dublin, 1998, 137.
 21 Paul Routledge, *Mandy: The Unauthorised Biography of Peter Mandelson* (London, 1999), pp. 154–82.
 22 *Report of the Expert Panel on Media Issues in the Scottish Parliament to the Consultative Steering Group of the Scottish Parliament*, Edinburgh, Scottish Parliament, MCD00105.039, 1999
 23 Geraint Talfan Davies, *Not By Bread Alone: Information, Media and the National Assembly* (Cardiff, 1999).
 24 The Sheedy affair (1999) involved the resignation of a judge who had intervened in a court case involving a Mr Sheedy in a way the Chief Justice deemed inappropriate. The judge was later nominated to a senior EU post by the Government, but withdrew from the nomination process after a lengthy controversy in the course of which media pressure on him emanated at least in part from non-attributable briefings of journalists by government sources.

15 Intelligence and the Cold War

Christopher Andrew

E very generation of historians suffers from some form of cognitive dissonance – the difficulty all of us have in grasping new concepts which disturb our existing view of the world. It is hard now to recall the extent of the historiographical shock caused by the emergence of women's history and gender studies. The challenge posed by the role of secret intelligence, however, has produced psychological denial more frequently than shock. Some major aspects of intelligence history still remain as invisible in the historiography of the Cold War as women once were in the work of male historians. Part of the explanation for this remarkable gap in the publications of many excellent historians derives from the frequent difficulty of access to intelligence archives. Academic historians have also been deterred by the crude sensationalism with which secret intelligence has frequently been treated by the media and conspiracy theorists. The root of the problem, however, is cognitive dissonance – the difficulty of adapting traditional notions of international relations and political history to take account of the information now available about the role of intelligence agencies.

One striking example of this conceptual failure concerns SIGINT (the intelligence derived from the interception and analysis of signals and other communications), a word still missing from the great majority of histories of international relations. For nearly thirty years after the Second World War almost no historian grasped even the possibility that SIGINT might have had a major influence on the War. Viewed in retrospect, however, the clues were obvious. British success in breaking German ciphers during the First World War was common knowledge; indeed, one well-publicised German decrypt produced by British codebreakers – the Zimmermann telegram – had hastened the US declaration of war on Germany in 1917. From 1945 onwards it was equally well known that American codebreakers had broken the main Japanese diplomatic cipher over a year before the attack on Pearl Harbor. But, until the revelation of the ULTRA secret in

1973, it occurred to almost no historian (save for former intelligence officers who were forbidden to mention it) that Britain might have broken German ciphers in the Second as well as the First World War.

At the end of the twentieth century, many of the historians who now acknowledge the great significance of SIGINT in the Second World War still ignore it completely in their studies of the Cold War. The sudden disappearance of SIGINT from the historical landscape immediately after VJ Day has produced a series of eccentric anomalies even in some of the leading studies of policymakers and international relations. Volumes 6 and 7 of Sir Martin Gilbert's epic biography of Winston Churchill, for example, rightly make much of his wartime passion for ULTRA. Volume 8, however, neglects entirely his interest in SIGINT as peacetime prime minister from 1951 to 1955. Nor is there a single reference to GCHQ, then as now the biggest and the most expensive of the British intelligence agencies. The reader is left to infer improbably that Churchill's enormous enthusiasm for SIGINT, which had remained constant since 1914, had inexplicably disappeared.

There are similarly startling lacunae in many of the best studies of United States policy in the early Cold War. Dwight D. Eisenhower, briefed personally by Churchill on ULTRA soon after his arrival in England in June 1942 as commander of American military forces, also became a SIGINT enthusiast. In July 1945 he declared that ULTRA had been 'of priceless value' to his conduct of the war, and sent to 'each and everyone' of the cryptanalysts at Bletchley Park 'my heartfelt admiration and sincere thanks for their very decisive contribution to the Allied war effort'. Though Ike's enthusiasm for SIGINT continued into the Cold War, there is not a single mention of it in Stephen Ambrose's otherwise excellent biography of Eisenhower as President – or in almost any other studies of his, or any succeeding, administration.[1]

The virtual exclusion of SIGINT from the history of post-war international relations has distorted understanding of the Cold War in significant ways. That point is illustrated by the very first Cold War SIGINT to be declassified: the approximately 3,000 intercepted Soviet intelligence and other telegrams (codenamed VENONA) for the period 1939 to 1948, mostly decrypted by American and British codebreakers in the late 1940s and early 1950s. The decrypts have large implications for American political history as well as for Soviet-American relations.[2] The outrageous exaggerations and inventions of Senator Joseph McCarthy's self-serving anti-Communist witch-hunt in the early 1950s made liberal opinion sceptical for the remainder of the Cold War of the significance of the Soviet intelligence offensive. The evidence of Elizabeth Bentley and Whittaker Chambers, who had worked as couriers for Soviet intelligence, was widely and mistakenly ridiculed. VENONA provides compelling corroboration for both.

For many American liberals it became an article of faith that the scientific and technological intelligence agents, Julius and Ethel Rosenberg, and the Soviet spy in the State Department, Alger Hiss, were the innocent victims of Cold War show trials. VENONA leaves no reasonable doubt that all were guilty (though that does not, of course, justify the death sentences passed on the Rosenbergs). Hiss (Agent ALES), who was a member of the US delegation at the Yalta Conference, was personally congratulated afterwards in Moscow by the Deputy Foreign Minister, Andrei Vyshinsky. Every major branch of the wartime Roosevelt administration was successfully penetrated by Soviet intelligence.[3]

By the standards of the Cold War, VENONA was a rather small-scale intelligence operation, never involving as many as a hundred people. Many much larger SIGINT operations of the 1950s remain classified. Very few decrypts from the Korean War, for example, are yet available. It is already clear, however, that the SIGINT failure at the outbreak of war was a direct consequence of the failure to learn the lessons of past mistakes. The rivalry between US service SIGINT agencies which had helped to make possible the success of the Japanese surprise attack at Pearl Harbor on 7 December 1941 reappeared in an even more confused form before the North Korean invasion of the South on 25 June 1950, once again with disastrous results.

Before Pearl Harbor the bitter turf battles between military and naval cryptanalysts had been contained, though not resolved, by an absurd compromise which gave each the right to decrypt Japanese diplomatic messages in the high-grade PURPLE cipher on alternate days. By the time of the Korean War, the number of service SIGINT agencies had doubled. The Air Force, like the Army and Navy, now had its own independent cryptanalytic agency. An interservice SIGINT body, the Armed Forces Security Agency (AFSA), set up in a vain attempt to co-ordinate the work of the three rival agencies, merely added to the confusion.

Largely as a result of the lack of co-ordination, North Korea did not become a priority SIGINT target until after it had attacked the South. Had it been targeted before the invasion began, it is difficult to believe – given the success of SIGINT operations later in the war – that no warning would have been obtained of the massing of over ninety thousand North Korean troops and 150 T-34 tanks at 'jump-off' points north of the 38th Parallel.[4] No US SIGINT unit began operating in Korea until almost four months after the outbreak of war.[5] From 1951, however, with improved co-ordination between the 'shamefaced' service agencies, SIGINT became, according to a later CIA study, 'a critically important source of information' during the Korean War.[6] A more recent study, based on the limited sources so far declassified, similarly concludes that SIGINT 'was certainly critical at the operational level after 1951 and helped the UN forces in Korea win significant battles'. Its most vital contribution was probably in the closing stages of the air war.[7]

In November 1952 US SIGINT was at last co-ordinated under the newly founded National Security Agency. NSA attracted so little attention that the few Washington insiders aware of its existence joked that the acronym stood for 'No Such Agency'. Eisenhower, however, poured into it even greater resources than those allocated to the CIA, in which he also took a close personal interest. The basement of the 1.4 million square-foot NSA headquarters at Fort Meade, completed in 1957, contained the biggest and most sophisticated computer complex in the world.[8] For most historians of the Cold War, however, NSA remains 'No Such Agency'.

Even in those Cold War crises where the significance of the role played by intelligence agencies has been widely acknowledged, such as Suez and the Cuban missile crisis, the role of SIGINT is still frequently ignored. During the 1956 Suez Crisis, the Foreign Secretary, Selwyn Lloyd, sent a personal letter to the Director of GCHQ, congratulating him on the 'volume' and 'excellence' of the decrypts it had supplied 'relating to all the countries of the Middle-East': 'I am writing to let you know how valuable we have found this material . . .'.

When historians are finally allowed access to the decrypts, they will doubtless find them valuable too. It is already clear, however, that SIGINT will force us to modify our understanding of the Suez Crisis in significant ways. Britain shared none of the Middle Eastern SIGINT generated by GCHQ with France, her co-conspirator in the Suez operation. All of it, however, was shared with the United States who was the prime mover in bringing the whole operation to an end. There are few better illustrations of the astonishing closeness of the Anglo-American intelligence alliance. Yet the 1948 UKUSA SIGINT agreement – the cornerstone of the intelligence alliance, which also involves Canada, Australia and New Zealand – rarely rates a mention in histories of Anglo-American relations. (The few studies of the Cold War which notice its existence usually date it wrongly as a 1947 accord.)[9]

Studies of the 1962 Cuban missile crisis invariably mention the crucial role of US imagery intelligence (IMINT) in revealing the existence of the missile sites during the course of their instruction. Once again, SIGINT is usually ignored. NSA, however, provided important intelligence on the build-up of Soviet Bloc arms in Cuba during the two years before the crisis began. During the late summer of 1962, SIGINT, on the Soviet construction of a new Cuban air defence system designed to prevent overflight by U-2 spy-planes, prompted the Director of Central Intelligence, John McCone, to ask what the Soviet Union was so anxious to hide – and to consider the possibility (subsequently confirmed by IMINT) that it was constructing offensive missile sites.[10]

SIGINT in the Soviet Bloc has received even less attention from historians of the Cold War than the operations of the NSA and GCHQ. The Soviet Union, however, put even more resources (though less advanced computer technology) than the West into SIGINT operations, which were conducted on a massive scale by both the KGB and GRU. By the Gorbachev era the Red Army had 40 SIGINT regiments, 170 battalions, and over 700 companies. Since the launch of *Kosmos 189* in 1967, the GRU Space Intelligence Directorate had put over 130 SIGINT satellites into orbit. More than 60 Soviet surface ships and over 20 different types of aircraft were used for SIGINT collection. The GRU and KGB had between them over 500 SIGINT ground stations in the Soviet Union and around the world. In all, the GRU and KGB SIGINT network probably employed about 350,000 intercept operators, processors, cryptanalysts and other technical specialists, a majority of them military personnel – about five times as many as the NSA and US service cryptological authorities, which together had an estimated 60,000 to 70,000 personnel.[11]

Though the highest-grade cipher systems of the Cold War were less vulnerable than those of the Second World War, the total volume of SIGINT greatly increased in both East and West. There was probably never a year during the Cold War, at least from the 1950s onwards, when the KGB sent fewer than 100,000 diplomatic decrypts to the Central Committee (chiefly, no doubt, to its International Department). By 1967 the KGB was able to decrypt 152 cipher systems employed by a total of 72 states.[12]

The KGB owed much of its SIGINT success to penetration of Western embassies in Moscow and to the recruitment of cipher clerks and other personnel in Western foreign ministries. Few, if any, Moscow embassies escaped some degree of KGB penetration. The US embassy was penetrated virtually continuously from the beginning of Soviet-American diplomatic relations in 1933 until at least the mid-1960s. In 1952 the new American Ambassador, George Kennan, ordered a thorough search of both the embassy and his own residence. The security experts sent from Washington asked him to dictate the text of an old diplomatic despatch in his study in order to help them discover any voice-activated listening device. As he continued his dictation, one of the experts suddenly began hacking away at the wall behind a wooden replica of the Great Seal of the United States. Finding nothing in the wall, he then attacked the Seal itself with a mason's hammer and triumphantly extracted from it a pencil-shaped bug which had been relaying Kennan's every word (and no doubt those of previous ambassadors) to Soviet eavesdroppers.

In 1953 work began on a new US embassy in Tchaikovsky Street. During its construction American security personnel stood guard each day to prevent the installation of listening devices. The day-long security vigil, however, served little purpose since the guards were withdrawn at night, thus allowing KGB personnel ample opportunity to bug the embassy. During a heated discussion with US Ambassador Foy Kohler in 1962, Khrushchev made clear – to the dismay of the KGB – that he knew the Ambassador had personally opposed the supply of steel tubing manufactured in the West for the construction of natural gas pipelines in the Soviet Union. Though Kohler probably deduced that Khrushchev knew the contents of some of his cables to Washington, he seems not to have realised that the information came from the bugging of his own embassy. In 1964, however, acting on intelligence from the KGB defector, Yuri Nosenko, the embassy discovered over forty bugs concealed in bamboo tubes built into the walls behind the radiators in order to shield them from metal detectors.[13] Remarkably, most studies of US-Soviet relations continue to take no account of the almost continuous haemorrhage of diplomatic secrets from the Moscow embassy for more than thirty years.

Though security at the US embassy subsequently improved, that at many other embassies did not. According to Admiral Fulvio Martini, head of SISMI (Italian foreign intelligence) from 1984 to 1991, the attitude to security in Italian embassies in the Soviet Bloc frequently continued to be characterised by 'leggerezza e superficilità'.[14] Soviet SIGINT throughout the Cold War was also greatly assisted by the penetration of a number of Western foreign ministries. In 1945 the KGB's Paris residency recruited a twenty-three-year-old cipher officer, codenamed JOUR, in the Quai d'Orsay who for the next forty years became probably the KGB's most valuable French agent. The large amount of French diplomatic documents and cipher material supplied by JOUR were regularly despatched to Moscow in what JOUR's file describes as 'a special container'. He also talent-spotted other Quai d'Orsay cipher and secretarial staff. In 1957 JOUR was secretly awarded the Order of the Red Star. A quarter of a century later he was awarded the Order of the Friendship of Peoples for his 'long and fruitful co-operation'. DARIO in the Italian Foreign Ministry had an equally long career as both KGB agent and talent-spotter, and for most of the Cold War was probably the most important agent run by the Rome residency.[15]

The incomplete evidence currently available suggests that, at a number of periods during the Cold War, France and Italy were conducting towards the Soviet Union something akin to open diplomacy. In 1983, for example, the French embassy in Moscow discovered that bugs in its teleprinters had been relaying all incoming and outgoing telegrams to the KGB for the past six years. According to Viktor Makarov, who served in the KGB Sixteenth (SIGINT) Directorate from 1980 to 1986, the European states whose diplomatic traffic was decrypted with varying frequency during these years included Denmark, Finland, France, Greece, Italy, Sweden, Switzerland and West Germany.[16]

An inner circle within the Politburo – consisting, in 1980, of Brezhnev, Andropov, Gromyko, Kirilenko, Suslov and Ustinov – were sent a daily selection of the most important intercepts. A larger selection was forwarded each day to the heads of the KGB First and Second Chief Directorates.[17] Though neither selection is yet available for research, both will one day be sources of major importance for historians of Soviet foreign policy. In the meantime, though there are some excellent histories of the Soviet Union, it is difficult to think of a single one which devotes as much as a sentence to the enormous volume of SIGINT generated by the KGB and GRU.

Those who research the history of the Cold War now face an interesting but difficult challenge which some will probably continue to ignore: either to seek to take account of the role of SIGINT or to explain why they consider it unnecessary to do so.

The role of intelligence during the Cold War has frequently been mis-understood as well as underestimated. It has often been wrongly supposed that there was an approximate symmetry between the intelligence operations conducted by the two opposing blocs. There were, of course, similarities in the operational techniques employed by intelligence agencies in East and West, as well as in the importance which each side attached to the other as an intelligence target. The fundamental difference between the Soviet one-party state and the Western democracies, however, was reflected in fundamental differences between their intelligence operations abroad as well as at home.[18]

In the early years of the Cold War Stalin was probably as obsessed with hunting down often imaginary Titoists and Zionists in the Soviet Bloc as he was with the supposed and actual machinations of the West. His chief foreign policy objective at the end of his life may well have been the plan for a KGB illegal to assassinate Marshal Tito, who had succeeded Trotsky as the leading heretic of the Soviet Bloc. Stalin once called Lavrenti Beria, the most powerful of his intelligence chiefs, 'my Himmler'. But there was no Western intelligence chief with whom Beria – or Himmler, the head of the SS – could be credibly compared.[19]

Even after Stalin's death and Beria's execution in 1953, there remained basic differences between intelligence priorities in East and West. Perhaps the simplest way of judging whether any intelligence report is of critical importance is to ask the question: If it arrives in the middle of the night would you wake the relevant government minister? The answer to that question in Moscow was often quite different from that in Western capitals. On 27 October 1978, for example, the KGB resident in Oslo, Leonid Makarov, rang Mikhail Suslov, the member of the Politburo chiefly responsible for ideological purity, in the early hours. Why? Not to tell him that some great international crisis was about to break out, but to report that the Russian dissident Yuri Orlov had failed to win the Nobel Peace Prize. The Oslo residency was warmly congratulated for its supposed 'operational effectiveness' in achieving this entirely predictable result.[20] It is simply not possible to imagine any Western minister being woken for any comparable reason.

The priority given by the KGB to maintaining the ideological orthodoxy of the Soviet Bloc was reflected by the fact that it deployed more of its elite group of illegals to Czechoslovakia during the Prague Spring of 1968 than, so far as is known, were ever used in any operation against a Western target. Its obsession with the detection and suppression of 'ideological subversion' spilled over into its operations in the West. The KGB sought to impress the Party leadership by its zeal in discrediting dissidents abroad as well as at home. In the summer of 1978 the KGB First Chief (Foreign Intelligence) and Fifth (Ideological Subversion) Directorates jointly arranged the secret screening in Moscow to an audience of KGB and Party notables of the 'commencement' (graduation) address by the dissident writer Aleksandr Solzhenitsyn at Harvard University. The purpose of this extraordinary evening was to seek to demonstrate that, thanks to the efforts of the KGB, Solzhenitsyn was now a largely discredited figure in the United States. The KGB's mission to discredit dissidents who had emigrated to the West extended even to dissident ballet dancers, musicians and chess players.[21]

The KGB and its allies were central to the functioning of Communist one-party states in ways that intelligence communities never were to the government of Western states. After the Second World War the NKVD and MGB (predecessors of the KGB) played a central role in the creation of the new Soviet Bloc in eastern and central Europe. Their role, according to a sanctimonious Soviet official history, was to 'help the people of liberated countries in establishing and strengthening a free domestic form of government'[22] – in other words, to construct a series of obedient one-party states along the Soviet Union's western borders. Throughout the Soviet Bloc, security and intelligence services, newly created in the image of the MGB, played a crucial part in the imposition of Stalinist regimes. Informers in the German Democratic Republic were seven times more numerous even than in Nazi Germany.[23]

The KGB's most effective methods of social control were the immensely labour-intensive techniques of ubiquitous surveillance and intimidation of dissidents. Yuri Andropov's first-hand experience of the Hungarian Uprising as Ambassador in Budapest in 1956, reinforced by the challenge of the Prague Spring during his first year as KGB Chairman, convinced him that the KGB could not afford to overlook a single instance of 'ideological subversion'. 'Every such act', he insisted, 'represents a danger'.[24] None was too trivial to attract the attention of the KGB. The effort and resources employed to track down each and every author of an anonymous letter or seditious graffito criticising the Soviet system frequently exceeded those devoted in the West to a major murder enquiry.

Among the many successful operations against such authors which were celebrated in the classified in-house journal, *KGB Sbornik*, was the hunt for a subversive codenamed KHUDOZHNIK ('Artist'), who in July 1971 began sending anonymous letters attacking Marxism–Leninism and various Party functionaries to CPSU and Komsomol committees. The letters were written in ballpoint pen and signed 'Central Committee of the Freedom Party'. Forensic examination revealed barely detectable traces on the back of some of the letters of pencil drawings – hence the codename KHUDOZHNIK and the hypothesis that he had studied at art school. The fact that some of the letters were sent to military Komsomols led to an immense trawl through the records of people dismissed from military training establishments and the files of reserve officers. The search for KHUDOZHNIK was concentrated in Moscow, Yaroslavl, Rostov and Gavrilov-Yam, where his letters were posted. In all four places the Postal Censorship Service searched for many months for handwriting similar to KHUDOZHNIK's; numerous KGB agents and co-optees were also shown samples of his writing and given his supposed psychological profile. An enormous research exercise was undertaken to identify and scrutinise official forms which KHUDOZHNIK might have filled in. Eventually, after a hunt lasting almost three years, his writing was found on an application to the Rostov City Housing Commission. In 1974 KHUDOZHNIK was unmasked as the Chairman of a Rostov Street Committee named Korobov. After a brief period under surveillance, he was arrested, tried and imprisoned. As in many similar cases, the triumphalist KGB report on the lengthy operation to track down KHUDOZHNIK showed no sense of the absurdity of devoting huge resources to the hunt for an author of 'libels against Soviet reality', none of which ever became public. The whole exercise was, on the contrary, presented as a model of its kind.[25]

It was chiefly because of the immense time and effort expended in the war on all fronts against ideological subversion that the KGB was many times larger than any Western intelligence or security service. One example of the overwhelming concentration by provincial KGBs on cases of ideological subversion is provided by the classified report for 1970 by the KGB Directorate for Leningrad and Leningrad Oblast. Not a single case had been discovered of either espionage or terrorism. By contrast, 502 people were given 'prophylactic briefings' (warnings) over their involvement in 'politically harmful incidents'. Forty-one were prosecuted for committing or attempting to commit State crimes (most almost certainly involving ideological subversion). Thirty-four Soviet citizens were caught trying to cross the frontier. Extensive work was carried out in institutes of higher education 'to prevent hostile incidents'. The postal censorship service intercepted about 25,000 documents with 'ideologically harmful contents'; a further 19,000 documents were confiscated at the frontier. One hundred and nine individuals (as compared with 99 in 1969) were identified as distributing subversive leaflets and sending anonymous letters; twenty-seven of the culprits were tracked down. The KGB's huge agent network was reported to have grown by another 17.3 per cent over the previous year. On the debit side the KGB surveillance service was reported to have crashed twenty-seven cars in the course of its operations.[26]

As head of the KGB, Andropov sought to keep ideological subversion at the forefront of the leadership's preoccupations. Issues as trivial (by Western standards) as the activities of a small group of Jehovah's Witnesses in the depths of Siberia or the unauthorised publication in Paris of a short story by a Soviet author were liable to reach not merely Andropov's desk but also, on occasion, the Politburo. Though even the leading dissidents had little resonance with the rest of the Soviet population, at least until the Gorbachev era, they occupied many hours of Politburo discussions. Early in 1977 a total of thirty-two 'active measures' operations against the leading dissident, Andrei Sakharov, denounced by Andropov as 'Public Enemy Number One', were either in progress or about to commence both within the Soviet Union and abroad.[27]

No group of Soviet dissidents during the Cold War could long avoid being penetrated by one or more of the KGB's several million agents and co-optees. Their capacity to make a public protest was limited to the ability to circulate secretly samizdat pamphlets or unfurl banners briefly in Red Square before they were torn down by plain-clothes KGB men. The KGB and its Soviet Bloc allies succeeded in making the notion of serious political change appear an impossible dream. It simply did not occur to the vast majority of the Russian people that there was any alternative to the Soviet system. Their almost unquestioning acceptance of the status quo had a profound effect on attitudes in the West. During the Cold War, most Western observers reluctantly assumed that the Soviet system would continue indefinitely. Hence the general sense of shock as well as of surprise when the Communist order in Eastern Europe crumbled so swiftly in the final months of 1989, followed two years later by the almost equally rapid disintegration of the Soviet one-party state. Henry Kissinger claimed in 1992, 'I knew no-one . . . who had predicted the evolution in the Soviet Union'.[28]

The new freedoms of the Gorbachev era went far to justifying the KGB's earlier fears of the potential damage to the Soviet regime if political dissidents were allowed to proceed with their 'ideological subversion'. The partial dismantling of the great edifice of KGB social control was an essential precondition of political change. In 1989, less than three years after Sakharov was freed from internal exile and allowed to return to Moscow, he established himself, as – in Gorbachev's words – 'unquestionably the outstanding personality' in the Congress of People's Deputies. Almost all the main dissident demands of the early 1970s were now firmly placed on the political agenda. One of the most striking visual images of the crumbling of the Soviet system, which deserves to be as well known as the destruction of the Berlin Wall, is of Gorbachev and other members of the Politburo standing bareheaded by Sakharov's open coffin after his sudden death in December 1989.

The manifesto of the hardline leaders of the August 1991 coup, led by the KGB Chairman, Vladimir Kryuchkov, which attempted to overthrow Gorbachev, implicitly acknowledged that the relaxation of the KGB campaign against ideological subversion had shaken the foundations of the one-party state: 'Authority at all levels has lost the confidence of the population . . . . Malicious mockery of all the institutions of state is being implanted. The country has in effect become ungovernable.'[29] What the plotters failed to realise was that it was too late to turn back the clock. 'If the *coup d'état* had happened a year and a half or two years earlier', wrote Gorbachev afterwards, 'it might, presumably, have succeeded. But now society was completely changed.'[30] Crucial to the change of mood was declining respect for the intimidatory power of the KGB, which had hitherto been able to strangle any Moscow demonstration at birth. Large crowds, which a few years earlier could never have been assembled, gathered outside Yeltsin's headquarters in the Moscow White House to protect it from attack, and later circled the KGB's own headquarters in the Lubyanka, cheering enthusiastically as the giant statue of the founder of the Cheka (the forefather of the KGB), Feliks Dzerzhinsky, was toppled from its plinth.

What now seems most remarkable is less the sudden death of the Communist regime at the end of 1991 than its survival for almost seventy-five years. Without the systems of surveillance and repression pioneered by Lenin and Dzerzhinsky, without the KGB's immense Cold War campaign against ideological subversion, the Soviet experience would have been much briefer. The KGB's most enduring achievement was to sustain the longest-lasting one-party state of the twentieth century.

NOTES

1 Christopher Andrew, 'Intelligence and international relations in the early Cold War', *Review of International Studies* 24 (1998), 321–2.

2 Though declassification of the VENONA decrypts began only in 1995, their existence had been known since the early 1980s and some of their contents had leaked out during that decade. VENONA was, however, ignored by most US historians until the late 1990s.

3 The growing literature on VENONA includes: Daniel Patrick Moynihan, *Secrecy: the American Experience* (New Haven CT, 1998); Allen Weinstein and Alexander Vassiliev, *The Haunted Wood: Soviet Espionage in America – the Stalin Era* (New York, 1999); John Earl Haynes and Harvey Klehr, *VENONA: Decoding Soviet Espionage in America* (New Haven CT, 1999); Christopher Andrew, 'The Venona secret', in K. G. Robertson (ed.), *War, Resistance and Intelligence: Essays in Honour of M. R. D. Foot* (Barnsley, 1999).

4 Christopher Andrew, *For the President's Eyes Only: Secret Intelligence and the American Presidency from Washington to Bush* (London, 1995), chs 5 and 6.

5 Matthew M. Aid, 'US Humint and Comint in the Korean War: from the approach of war to the Chinese intervention', *Intelligence and National Security* 14 (1999), 53–5.

6 Andrew, *For the President's Eyes Only*, p. 187.

7 Matthew M. Aid, 'American Comint in the Korean War (Part II): from the Chinese intervention to the armistice', *Intelligence and National Security* 15 (2000), 14.

8 Andrew, *For the President's Eyes Only*, pp. 194–7, 215–20.

9 *Ibid.*, p. 218; Andrew, 'Intelligence and international relations in the early Cold War', pp. 329–30.

10 Declassified decrypts relevant to the Cuban missile crisis are accessible on the NSA website: http://www.nsa.gov.docs.cuba. See also: David Alvarez, 'American signals intelligence and the Cuban missile crisis', *Intelligence and National Security* 15 (2000).

11 Desmond Ball, *Soviet Signals Intelligence (SIGINT)* (Canberra, 1989); Desmond Ball and Robert Windren, 'Soviet signals intelligence (Sigint): organisation and management', *Intelligence and National Security* 4 (1989).

12 Raymond L. Garthoff, 'The KGB Reports to Gorbachev', *Intelligence and National Security* 11 (1996), 228.

13 Christopher Andrew and Vasili Mitrokhin, *The Mitrokhin Archive: The KGB in Europe and the West* (London, 1999), ch. 21.

14 Admiral Fulvio Martini, *Nome in codice: ULISSE* (Milan: Rizzoli, 1999), pp.19–20.

15 Andrew and Mitrokhin, *The Mitrokhin Archive*, pp. 200, 361–2, 459, 601, 603, 608–9, 621, 628, 630, 718. On DARIO, see the additional information in the Italian edition, *L'Archivio Mitrokhin* (Milan, 1999), pp. 693–4.

16 Andrew and Mitrokhin, *The Mitrokhin Archive*, pp. 458–9, 625–6.

17 David Kahn, 'Soviet Comint in the Cold War', *Cryptologia* 22 (1998).

18 The Cold War was not a zero-sum game. Criticism of one side's intelligence agencies does not, of course, necessarily imply eulogy of the other's.

19 Andrew and Mitrokhin, *The Mitrokhin Archive*, pp. 2, 322–3, 464–6.

20 *Ibid.*, pp. 429–30.

21 *Ibid.*, pp. 418–19, 727–8.

22 Sergei Z. Ostryakov, *Voyennye Chekisty* (Moscow, 1979), p. 258.

23 David Childs and Richard Popplewell, *The Stasi: The East German Intelligence and Security Service* (London, 1996).

24 Andrew and Mitrokhin, *The Mitrokhin Archive*, pp. 430–1.
25 *Ibid.* p. 711.
26 *Ibid.*, pp. 713–14.
27 *Ibid.*, chs 19, 20 and 28.
28 Kissinger subsequently acknowledged that Senator Pat Moynihan had been an exception. 'Your crystal ball', he told him, 'was better than mine'. Moynihan, *Secrecy*, p. 6.
29 The text of the appeal of the 'State Committee for the State of Emergency', dated 18 August 1991, was published in *The Times*, 19 Aug. 1991.
30 Mikhail Gorbachev, *The August Coup: The Truth and the Lessons* (London, 1991), p. 31.

16 Communication and Political Power in the Thought of Jürgen Habermas

Allen Bass

Jürgen Habermas (b. 1929) is today widely acknowledged to be one of the world's leading socio-political thinkers. He is arguably one of the most wide ranging, innovative, and profound social theorists of our time. In this chapter I shall attempt to give a concise, clarifying overview of Habermas's extensive and complex recent work on the relation of communication to political power and democracy. I shall do this in part by comparing his ideas to those of Hannah Arendt, a political thinker who was one of the formative influences on Habermas, but from whose ideas he came to diverge significantly.

Over the last four decades, Habermas has been trying to construct a *comprehensive theory* of society and politics – a theory both philosophically grounded and empirically verified. He has been striving, with considerable resourcefulness and intellectual agility, to combine the insights of rational reflection and concrete experience, of the philosophical tradition and the social sciences. In this way he has been seeking to achieve a critical, though balanced, understanding of modern Western societies – and, by extension, of all modern or modernising societies.[1]

As the outcome of these efforts, Habermas has concluded, in general, that it is only by working from a general concept of *intersubjective* – which is to say *communicative* – reason that it is possible to build and maintain a truly democratic and humane socio-political order. This position has put him at odds with other strong tendencies in contemporary social thought – most notably, with the outlook of 'postmodernism' in the work of such thinkers as Lyotard, Derrida and Foucault.[2]

The core idea and distinctive flavour of Habermas's innovative use of the concept of *communication* to establish a *rational basis* for political discourse and power legitimation in democratic states appear clearly in the following passage:

No matter how the intersubjectivity of mutual understanding may be deformed, the *design* of an ideal speech situation is necessarily implied in the structure of potential speech, since all speech, even of intentional deception, is oriented towards the idea of truth. This idea can only be analysed with regard to a consensus achieved in unrestrained and universal discourse. Insofar as we master the means for the construction of an ideal speech situation, we can conceive the ideas of truth, freedom and justice.[3]

The strong intellectual-political appeal of such a position has been noted astutely by the eminent Arendt scholar Margaret Canovan:

Habermas's theory has caused great excitement because it appears to promise an escape from the subjectivism characteristic of modern thought. He seems to give grounds for the hope that disputes even about intractable matters such as morality and politics can be settled by rational discourse, provided that the discourse is not blocked by the distortions induced by domination, ideology, and repression.[4]

More specifically, Habermas's approach seems to hold out the prospect of reconciling diversity of individual opinions with an objective standard of rationally grounded truth. Indeed, Habermas discerns an inherent tendency in free political discourse to approximate closer and closer to such rationally grounded truth. As Canovan puts it:

He points out that our capacity to engage in rational discourse shows that we can in fact correct our individual views and advance from opinion to truth, which is the rational consensus reached among individuals in unconstrained discourse. The great attraction of the theory is that it appears to hold together in a dialectical unity two previously opposed notions: on the one hand, a recognition of the plurality and diversity of minds, and on the other an ideal of a single, objective truth.[5]

In the last decade, Habermas has turned his attention to more specifically *political* and *legal* issues. The result is *Between Facts and Norms*, a wide-ranging exploration of the nature and structure of the modern constitutional, democratic state.[6] In this study, Habermas explores in great detail the potential of contemporary law and legal institutions for grounding democracy and democratic legitimacy on a *communicative* basis.

For Habermas, law provides an institutionalised form of discourse through which communicative action can perform its primary function more effectively: namely, the further integration and rationalisation of society through consensus and solidarity built on free, rational discussion. This is central to Habermas's ongoing theoretical effort to redeem the promise of substantive socio-political progress that he believes to lie deeply embedded – though dormant – in the *formal* legal and political institutions of constitutional states.

More generally, in Habermas's socio-political thought, both concepts of *reason/rationalisation*, and (even more centrally) concepts of *communication*, play the key roles. The link connecting them is 'the rational potential intrinsic in everyday communicative practices'.[7]

As for the centrality of communication to democratic politics, Habermas asserts bluntly, in his most recent discussion of the subject: 'Only a democracy that is understood in terms of communications theory is feasible under the conditions of complex societies'.[8]

In fact, not only Habermas's most recent, but also his earliest major work, *The Structural Transformation of the Public Sphere*, focused on this central socio-political role of communication.[9] *Structural Transformation* was a study of the origins, growth and decay of a 'bourgeois public sphere' in western Europe between the late seventeenth and the twentieth centuries. In this study, Habermas began his still ongoing effort to define and to understand the relation between *communication*, on the one hand, and *political power*, on the other.

Structural Transformation is the most historically oriented of all Habermas's major studies. In it he traces the gradual formation of a politically potent 'bourgeois public sphere', mainly in England, France and parts of Germany. Habermas has described this sphere succunctly as the 'sphere of private persons come together as a public'.[10] This public sphere evolved (in his view) out of the robust social and intellectual life of a multiplicity of private persons and private associations in civil society.[11]

The emergence of this new public sphere was crucially dependent on the growth both of new social *fora* – such as coffee houses (in England), *salons* (in France), and reading circles (in Germany) – and also on the growth of book- and periodical-publishing for an unprecedentedly wide middle-class market.[12] According to Habermas's analysis (in the revised 1990 edition of *Structural Transformation*), 'the French Revolution eventually triggered a movement toward the politicization of a public sphere that at first revolved around literature and art criticism. . . . [T]he rise of a partisan press, the fight against censorship and for freedom of opinion [marked] the change in function of the expanding network of public communication up to the middle of the nineteenth century'.[13]

In fact, from its first formulation in 1962, Habermas's basic concept of a communicatively based 'public sphere' has been heavily dependent precisely on a relatively unfettered *freedom of communication*. For Habermas, this essential 'communicative freedom' means an array of communicative sites and media that are substantially unhindered both by official censorship, and by other, more subtle forms of external constraint or systemic distortion.[14]

In studying historically the gradual emergence of the 'bourgeois public sphere', and in defining its structure, Habermas used England as his main paradigm. It was in England (in his view) that the ending of formal, official pre-censorship of publications (in the late seventeenth century) began a more advanced phase in the evolution of public discourse. The elimination of pre-censorship of publications helped make possible that open access to information and that free articulation of opinions by private citizens without which the public sphere simply could not exist as the site for rational, critical, and – ultimately – for consensus-building discourses. For the first time, it now became possible for the public to form its own rational, informed opinions on issues of common interest.[15]

For Habermas, the existence of this epoch-making 'public sphere' (in German: *die Öffentlichkeit*) does not depend upon institutional forms. Instead, he conceives it as 'a network for communicating information and points of view . . . ; the streams of communication are, in the process, filtered and synthesized in such a way that they coalesce into bundles of *topically specified* public *opinions*'.[16] Or, as he elsewhere expresses it: 'In the simultaneously decentered and porous structures of the public sphere, the scattered critical potential [of society] is collected, activated, and bundled together.'[17] In more concrete terms, the *contemporary* public sphere (as Habermas conceptualises it) includes many diverse social elements. These range from schools, churches, cultural associations, universities, the various mass media, sports and hobby clubs, through 'grass-roots' movements and special-interest advocacy groups, to labour unions, professional groups, and political parties.[18]

According to Habermas's analysis, the *original* bourgeois public sphere, which emerged fully in the eighteenth century, was constituted in a way that was strikingly similar to this contemporary public sphere. It functioned as a multiform and widely dispersed complex of sites for a critical *public opinion of a new type*. This public opinion was, for the most part, independent of state power and of state organisations, and it was therefore able to effectively criticise and evaluate state policies 'from the outside'. It acted with real freedom, and was able to apply an informed and rational critique to the policies and powers of government.[19]

Habermas contends that this original, autonomous, and (above all) '*rational-critical*' type of public opinion grew out of substantially free and undistorted communication among relatively informed, independent citizens. But in the twentieth century, by a gradual process foreshadowed earlier, this *critical* type of public opinion, shaping itself through *rational communication*, has been hollowed out and degraded into a *manipulated* public sphere. In part, this has resulted from the fact that, in the media, 'there are . . . structures that . . . make the isolated and privatized viewers susceptible to an incapacitating collectivization of their conceptual worlds. Such shaped public spheres . . . serve as forums for legitimation by plebiscite'. As such they differ radically from the original *rational-critical* public sphere.[20]

Moreover, according to this analysis, the public sphere has been subject also to organised publicity and mass propaganda, and to the pressures of large-scale, wealthy, and powerful interest groups. 'In the course of our century, the bourgeois forms of sociability have found substitutes that have one tendency in common despite their regional and national diversity: abstinence from literary and political debate. . . . The leisure activities of the culture-consuming public . . . themselves take place within a social climate, and they do not require any further discussions.' [21]

Under these changed circumstances, free and undeformed public communication becomes (in Habermas's view) harder and harder to sustain, and the originally '*rational-critical*' public sphere tends to degenerate into a profoundly *uncritical* one. It becomes increasingly a sphere not of real *communication*, but of mere *publicity*. As Habermas remarks trenchantly: '[t]he world fashioned by the mass media is a public sphere *in appearance only*'.[22]

More recently, however, Habermas has changed his position on this. In 1990, almost thirty years after the first publication of *Structural Transformation*, Habermas (in his introduction to the new German edition) retreated dramatically from his originally harsh critique of the twentieth-century public sphere. He wrote: 'My diagnosis of a unilinear development from a politically active public to one withdrawn into bad privacy, from a "culture-debating to a culture-consuming public", is too simplistic. . . . I was too pessimistic about the resisting power and the . . . critical potential of a pluralistic, internally . . . differentiated mass public'. [23]

Already, a decade earlier, in his 1981 *Theory of Communicative Action* (vol. II), Habermas had begun to revise radically his negative assessment of the relation between the mass media and the public sphere. 'The mass media [he then observed] . . . free communication processes from the provinciality of spatiotemporally restricted contexts, and they permit public spheres to emerge, through establishing the abstract simultaneity of a virtually present network of communication contents far removed in space and time, and [also] through keeping messages available for manifold contexts'.[24]

These [mass] media [Habermas argued] . . . both *hierarchize*, and at the same time, *remove restrictions* on the horizon of possible communication. The one aspect cannot be separated from the other – and therein lies their *ambivalent potential.* Insofar as mass media one-sidedly channel communication flows in a centralized network – from the center to the periphery or from above to below – they considerably strengthen the efficacy of social controls. But tapping this *authoritarian potential* is always precarious, because there is a counterweight of *emancipatory potential* [that is] built into communication structures themselves.[25]

More recently, Habermas has re-emphasised the negative political potential of the mass media as power centres in their own right. He argues that 'journalists [and] publicity agents . . . to a certain extent control the entry of topics, contributions and authors into the mass-media-dominated public sphere. As the mass media become more complex and more expensive, the effective channels of communication become more centralized'.[26]

To understand more clearly what Habermas means by the *ambivalent potential* of the mass media, it is useful to consider briefly one of the specific examples that he offers: the medium of television. Habermas illustrates the *ambivalent communicative-political potential* of this key contemporary medium by citing with approval 'Stuart Hall's distinction between three different interpretive strategies on the part of [television] spectators. [These may] either submit to the structure of what is being offered, [or] take an oppositional stance, [or] synthesize it with their own interpretations.' [27] In sum, as Habermas sees it, recent 'research on effect and reception has at least done away with the passive image of "cultural dopes" who are manipulated by the programs offered to them'.[28]

More recently still, Habermas has turned his attention to the *boundary-dissolving power* of contemporary communications, a development accelerated still further by the proliferating use of the Internet, and by the increasing globalisation of financial and corporate activity that parallels it, and is, in large part, based on it. He observes that '[w]orldwide physical, social, and symbolic contacts are produced via space-spanning, accelerated connections, chiefly electronic. These communications . . . promote the expansion of the consciousness of the actors'. [29]

But in Habermas's view this exuberant proliferation of worldwide communications is clouded by a profoundly *ambivalent potential*: it can, in short, produce *negative* as well as *positive* socio-political results. Besides expanding individual consciousness, the revolution in communications has promoted 'the branching out, extension, and connection of systems, networks, and organisations'.[30] From this seemingly *boundless differentiation* of communications, there springs a *contrary tendency* that impinges constrictingly on the development of the nascent global public sphere. This is a tendency to '*fragmentation* of the consciousness of planning subjects who are communicating and acting with one another'.[31] From this, Habermas fears a possible negative outcome for the future of the emerging global public sphere – but an outcome which may yet, with effort, be averted. The danger is, in his view, that 'the manifold forms of communication [will] spread out centrifugally and be lost in [isolated] global villages'.[32]

As a result of this accelerating globalisation of communications, Habermas observes that we now confront a structure of the public sphere that is being *transformed fundamentally*. Technological and economic imperatives are expanding the *original* public sphere, born in the late seventeenth and eighteenth centuries, into an increasingly *global* communicative structure. It is a structure that can no longer be confined (as it still was in Habermas's 1962 study) by the traditional political borders of nation states. Habermas sums up these continuing and crucial developments in this way:

the different tendencies toward the globalization of every kind of interchange and communication, economic production and its financing, transfers of technology and weaponry, the drug trade and criminality, and especially strategic and ecological dangers, confront us with problems that can no longer be solved within the framework of the nation-state. The hollowing-out of the sovereignty of the nation-state will continue, and require us to develop capacities for political action on a supernational basis.[33]

This analysis raises the urgent practical question of how both formal political structures and the public sphere itself might be reconfigured so that instantaneous global communications can help us to bring under *democratic control* the new global economic and political order that they have helped to create. In Habermas's view, this problem is particularly urgent in the context of European integration. 'Before a European constitution can take hold, a public sphere extending throughout Europe must be formed, which will allow its citizens, and not just its governments, to take part in a common process of shaping a political will.'[34] What is needed, Habermas believes, is a concerted effort to 'foster a focussed process of shaping will and opinion'. In short, *transnational* 'public spheres must now be created' by conscious effort and rational planning.[35]

Seen from these varying angles, the complex, still-evolving concept of the 'public sphere' provides Habermas with the essential basis for his continuing exploration of the role of communication in the political life of contemporary Western societies. The core of his most recent conclusions on the relationship between *communication* and *political power* depends directly on the way he has extended and refined his originally *sociological* concept of the public sphere to make it a useful tool for a more specifically *political* analysis.

In his most recent major work, *Between Facts and Norms* (1992), Habermas has come to refocus his attention precisely on the *political and legal structures* of the contemporary constitutional, democratic state.[36] More particularly, he has directed his efforts at understanding and, if possible, defining, the basis of democratic legitimacy. In essence, he has discovered that basis in the same communicative activities which he had conceptualised, in his earlier works, as the 'public sphere'.

Habermas argues that public communication, in its various forms, provides the *essential foundation* for all legitimate political power and for all 'legitimate law' in a democratic (or constitutional) state (in German: *der*

Rechtsstaat). Public, political communication, in order to function in this positive and legitimating way, must (Habermas believes) operate on *two very different levels of discourse*. Both of these levels of public discourse are absolutely necessary for the effective functioning of what Habermas now terms 'the discourse concept of democracy'.[37] The first level of discourse is an *informal, diffuse, multiform, multi-layered complex* of discursive activities and arrangements, an array of discourses spread out randomly through society at large. These diverse sites of public communication *discover or originate* social concerns, and then *shape in a preliminary way* the newly emerging social problems into *political issues*.[38] The second level of public discourse consists of the formally organised and legally binding framework of parliamentary and judicial institutions. In Habermas's analysis, the newly emergent political issues, first identified and formulated by the *informal* communicative complex of the public sphere, are then further focused and – in the end – legally decided by the *formal constitutional structures* of the democratic state.[39]

To provide a more concrete understanding of what these rather abstract ideas might mean in practice, Habermas illustrates them with two examples:

Because the . . . public sphere is 'unconstrained', in the sense that its channels of communication are not regulated by procedures, it is better suited [than parliamentary bodies] for the 'struggle over needs' and their interpretation. Whether it is the question of spousal abuse or the question of day-care facilities for the children of working parents, it is usually a long road, involving dogged efforts at staging public 'actions', before such initially 'private' matters even begin to acquire the status of recognized political issues. . . . Only after [such] a public 'struggle for recognition', can the contested interest positions be . . . put on the parliamentary agenda, discussed, and . . . worked into legislative proposals and binding decisions.[40]

For these reasons, the *informal* communicative network of the public sphere is absolutely essential, in Habermas's view, for providing the *initial and most widely based* phase of the process by which, in a secular, post-traditional society, law and political power are both *created* and *legitimised*. Parliamentary bodies, by enacting laws, then complete the conversion of what Habermas terms '*communicative power*' into '*administrative power*'.

Just what is 'communicative power'? Habermas describes its emergence in the following way:

Communicative power can be formed only in public spheres that produce intersubjective relationships on the basis of reciprocal recognition and make it possible to use communicative freedoms; that is, to take spontaneous positive or negative positions with regard to free-floating themes, grounds, and information.[41]

According to Habermas's analysis, administrative power is perceived as *legitimate* in the wider society precisely because it is *communicatively* based – in other words, because it is the end product of such a free and open process of articulation and discussion of issues. It is a process that must begin (as we have seen) in the diverse and widely scattered communicative spaces of the *informal* public sphere. In Habermas's view, an 'administrative power' established in this way can gain *legitimacy* – and hence stability and continuity – in so far as it reflects a consensus freely achieved on the basis of *intersubjective communication.*

At this point, it may be useful to restate succinctly Habermas's basic thesis. In essence, it is that in highly pluralistic, post-traditional Western societies, the work of achieving social solidarity and consensual cohesion is done *both* by the informal public sphere *and* by the formal structures of 'legitimate lawmaking'. These constitutional structures filter, focus and enact as formal law the widely dispersed issues and concerns that first emerged from the informal network of diverse communicative sites that constitute the public sphere.

Looked at from a somewhat different perspective, Habermas's theory radically reconfigures the older, ultimately Rousseauan, concept of 'popular sovereignty'. As Habermas expresses it: 'If there is still to be a realistic application of the idea of the sovereignty of the people to highly complex societies, it must be uncoupled from the concrete understanding of its embodiment in physically present, participating . . . members of a collectivity.'[42]

To replace this traditional concept of popular sovereignty, Habermas relies on his central concept of *communicative action.* A discursive or deliberative model replaces the contract model: 'the expectation deriving from a discourse-centred theoretical approach, that rational results will obtain, is based on the interplay between a constitutionally instituted formation of the political will and the spontaneous flow of communication unsubverted by power, within a public sphere that is not geared toward decision-making but toward discovery and problem resolution and in that sense is *nonorganised* '.[43] What results is a consensual agreement reached through free and rational discourse – and this, in turn, depends on the functioning of the diverse and complex array of communicative activities that are dispersed widely through the public sphere. As Habermas puts it:

According to the discourse-theoretic conception of government by law, popular sovereignty is no longer embodied in visibly identifiable gathering of autonomous citizens. [Instead,] it pulls back into the . . . 'subjectless' forms of communication circulating through forums and legislative bodies. Only in this anonymous form can its communicatively fluid power bind the administrative power of the state apparatus to the will of the citizens.[44]

A key aspect of Habermas's theory is its premise that a system of *individual legal rights* furnishes the essential *political medium* by which the forms of communication that are required by the theory of 'discursive democracy' can be realised in practice. In the Habermasian model of discursive democracy, the existence of strong individual civic rights makes possible the *communicative generation of law* which is at the heart of this model. In Habermas's words: 'legitimate law is generated from communicative power and the latter in turn is converted into administrative power via legitimately enacted law'.[45]

More specifically, Habermas provides the following account of the process by which *communicative* power can be converted into an *administrative* power that will be 'democratically legitimate':

> Laws [he argues] can regulate the transformation of communicative into administrative power inasmuch as they come about according to a democratic procedure, ground a legal protection guaranteed by impartially judging courts, and *shield* from the implementing administration the sorts of reasons that support legislative and judicial decision making. These normative reasons belong to a universe within which legislature and judiciary share the work of justifying and applying norms.[46]

The sphere of action of the executive, on the other hand, should be much narrower:

> An administration limited to pragmatic discourses must not change anything in this universe by its contributions; at the same time, it draws therefrom the normative premises that have to underlie its own empirically informed, purposive-rational decision-making.[47]

Some of the roots of Habermas's key concept of 'communicative action' can be traced back to the political philosophy of another eminent twentieth-century political thinker, Hannah Arendt.[48] There are, however, a number of crucial differences between them. To mention the most obvious: Habermas's theory rejects decisively Arendt's underlying 'communitarian' or 'republican' standpoint – a standpoint reflecting her idealised image of direct democracy and cultural unity in the classical Greek city-state. The classical Greek inspiration of Arendt's political vision can perhaps be seen most clearly in *The Human Condition*.[49] As Seyla Benhabib comments: 'at one level Arendt's text is a panegyric to the agonistic political space of the Greek *polis*'.[50]

For this reason Arendt's political outlook has sometimes been dismissed as an exercise in political nostalgia that is fundamentally irrelevant to contemporary mass societies. To a degree, Habermas shares this view. Extending this critique to the level of abstract thought, he attributes the 'weaknesses' of Arendt's political theory to 'the fact that [she] remains bound to the historical and conceptual constellation of classical Greek philosophy'.[51] In particular, he believes she is bound to certain (in Habermas's view, highly rigid and misleading) Aristotelian definitions and categories.

These have the effect, in Habermas's analysis, of barring from the sphere of politics both 'strategic' considerations relating to the pursuit and allocation of power, and also any intervention in or management of socio-economic issues.

Arendt herself at times has appeared to confirm the critical view that sees her stance as incorrigibly and unrealistically classicising and nostalgic. This has been the case particularly with some of her unqualified assertions of the primacy of the classical Greek conception of political life. For example, she has asserted baldly that 'city-states have remained paradigmatic for all Western political organisation'.[52]

The most basic difference, however, between Habermas and Arendt is that Arendt is concerned primarily with the lived, practical experience of political activity in a particular society (a phenomenology of power, as it were). Habermas is operating on a more abstract, theoretical level: he is concerned less with the subjectively experienced quality of political activity, and more with providing a fully worked out, theoretical explication of the inner nature of all human communication in its relation to political power and democratic legitimacy.

But however significant the differences between the perspectives of Habermas and Arendt, we must be clear that Habermas himself sees, above all, a *fundamental convergence* between his own position and Arendt's on the *essential nature and genesis* of political power. In fact, he claims to have found the inspiration for his own concept of the relation of public communication to political power precisely in Arendt's ideas. His acknowledgement of this intellectual debt could not be fuller or more emphatic: 'I have learned', he writes, 'from H. Arendt how to approach a theory of communicative action'.[53] And communicative action is, of course, the central element of Habermas's whole socio-philosophical project.[54]

More particularly, Habermas has been influenced deeply by Arendt's 'concept of action as "praxis" which articulates the historical experiences and the normative perspectives of what we today call participatory democracy'.[55] Indeed, we can see from Habermas's sympathetic summary of Arendt's conceptualisation of power that his own developed concepts of 'communicative action' and 'discursive democracy' grew out of Arendt's earlier formulation of the nature and genesis of political power. Habermas himself sums up Arendt's concept of political power in this way: 'The fundamental phenomenon of power is not the instrumentalisation of *another's* will, but the formation of a common will'.[56] For Arendt, in other words, power that is *genuinely political* (as opposed to merely oppressive *violence* or coercive *force*) arises out of the willing co-operation of a multitude of individuals on a common project or action, a co-operation founded ultimately on *shared opinion*. This shared opinion is itself shaped by political leaders using the means of verbal persuasion – a specifically political form of *communication* – in the public forum. These ideas emerge clearly from several key Arendtian passages:

Power corresponds to the human ability not just to act, but to act in concert. Power is never the property of an individual: it belongs to a group and remains in existence only so long as the group keeps together. When we say of somebody that he is 'in power' we actually refer to his being empowered by a certain number of people to act in their name.[57]

power springs up between men when they act together and vanishes the moment they disperse.[58]

It is the people's support that lends power to the institutions of a country, and this support is but the continuation of the consent that brought the laws into existence to begin with[59]

power [is] generated when people gather together and 'act in concert'[60]

power [is] this potentiality in being together, . . . dependent upon the unreliable and only temporary agreement of many wills and intentions[61]

The essence of the matter is that, for Arendt, all genuinely political power always grows out of 'an opinion upon which many are in agreement'.[62] Or, as Habermas reconstructs her view, Arendt sees the essential nature of political power as 'the formation of a *common* will in a communication directed to reaching agreement'.[63] For Arendt (as Habermas also restates her view), politics may be defined as 'the praxis of those who talk together in order to act in common'.[64] Habermas, moreover, understands Arendt's concept that *opinion-formation is the basis of power* in terms of communicative *freedom*. He claims that Arendt 'attempts to derive from the structures of *unimpaired intersubjectivity* the conditions of the public-political realm that must be met if power is to be communicatively engendered or expanded'.[65] More concisely, he observes that 'power can, on her assumption, arise only in the structures of *unconstrained* communication'.[66] Habermas argues that the achievement of the 'agreed opinion' that Arendt makes the basis of all true political power itself depends on *free and rational* communication. Only by this means is genuine 'conviction' attainable – what Habermas calls 'that peculiarly forceless force with which insights assert themselves'.[67] Ultimately, the basis of all such consensus achieved by discourse is, in Habermas's view – though not unambiguously in Arendt's – 'the *rational claim* immanent in speech'.[68]

Habermas has been severely criticised for his alleged distortion and misreading of Arendt's concept of power.[69] More specifically, it has been argued that while Arendt actually defines the genesis of political power in terms of common *action*, Habermas twists her thought to suit his own pre-conceptions by making her define power, instead, in terms of intersubjective *speech* or *communication*. He thus (according to the critics) imposes his own central idea of 'communicative action' in the guise of restating Arendt's very different concept.[70] This line of criticism is perhaps best summed up by Canovan, when she remarks: 'His account is dominated by his over-riding interest in communication and rational agreement, which elbows out Arendt's own concern with political action and worldly institutions'.[71]

But how cogent is this critique? More specifically, how persuasive is the alleged opposition between Arendtian 'action', on the one hand, and Habermasian 'speech' or 'communication', on the other? I would argue that a closer examination of Arendt's own words shows that, in her mind at least, the two concepts merge into one another: in fact, the former *requires* the latter as one of the means essential for its realisation. As Arendt somewhat elliptically puts it: 'many, and even most [political] acts, are performed in the manner of speech'.[72]

That this interpretation of Arendt is the correct one seems to emerge clearly from a close reading of the passages already cited on p. 296, and also from Arendt's initial definition of what she calls the *space of appearance*. This is the public space where, according to her, all genuine political power is generated:

The space of appearance [she writes] comes into being wherever men are together in the manner of speech and action. . . . [T]he public realm, . . . ultimately resides on action and speech[73]

And again, clearly implying the centrality of sincere and undistorted public 'speech' as an essential genetic element in all political 'action':

Power is actualised only where word and deed have not parted company, where words are not empty and deeds not brutal, where words are not used to veil intentions but to disclose realities[74]

The centrality of public speech to Arendt's vision of politics is implied also when she writes: 'power is what keeps the public realm, the potential space of appearance between acting and *speaking* men, in existence'.[75] Here (as in the two preceding citations) action and speech are given equal weight in the generation of political power. And Arendt's stress on the role of 'opinion' as the ultimate foundation of all governmental power points in the same direction. In this vein, Arendt cites approvingly the dictum of James Madison that 'all government rests on opinion'; it is, she asserts, 'a word no less true for the various forms of monarchy than for democracies'.[76] Clearly, to say that *opinion* is the basis of all political power is also to say that *public discussion and debate*, in which opinion is necessarily *formed* or *changed*, is also central to the generation of political power. Once this is recognised, Habermas's attribution to Arendt's thought of the essential origins of his own central concept of 'communicative action' seems substantially justified.

We shall now consider in more detail the ways in which Habermas's concept of political power, for all these affinities, yet departs in important ways from Arendt's. Most fundamentally, Habermas utterly rejects Arendt's attempt to exclude from the sphere of truly 'political' concerns the whole area of socio-economic activity in modern societies. As he writes:

Arendt stylizes the image she has of the Greek polis to the essence of politics as such. This is the background to her favored conceptual dichotomies between the public and the private, between state and economy, freedom and welfare, political-practical activity and production – rigid dichotomies which modern . . . society and the modern state, however, escape.[77]

Habermas argues that, on a basic methodological level, Arendt has gone badly astray. In his view, her theoretical extrusion of the socio-economic realm from the sphere of politics grew, somewhat arbitrarily, out of philosophical abstractions. It lacked any concrete basis in sociological investigation and contemporary human experience.[78] As a result, Arendt 'becomes the victim of a concept of politics that is inapplicable to modern conditions'.[79] Habermas is scathingly critical of Arendt's sweeping rejection of the political legitimacy of the whole sphere of social and economic policy, her scornful dismissal of the very notion that government should take active measures to promote the material well-being of the great majority of the population. With lapidary conciseness, and more than a hint of impatience, Habermas sums up and decisively rejects Arendt's highly restrictive definition of politics as excluding the whole material and social life of the society being governed:

a state which is relieved of the administrative processing of social problems; a politics which is cleansed of socio-economic issues; an institutionalization of public liberty which is independent of the organization of public wealth; a radical democracy which inhibits its liberating efficacy just at the boundaries where political oppression ceases and social repression begins – this path is unimaginable for any modern society.[80]

Habermas could not be more emphatic in rejecting such a definition of the true sphere of the 'political'. Arendt's rigid separation of political activity from socio-economic concerns is, he concludes, 'a conception of politics which, when applied to modern societies, leads to absurdities'.[81]

Despite these important criticisms, Habermas uses his interpretation – or what we may perhaps call his *communicative reconstruction* – of Arendt's views to develop his *own* central concept of the relation between communication and political power. As he puts it: 'Arendt rightly urges that strategic contests for political power neither call forth nor maintain those institutions in which that power is anchored. Political institutions live not from force but from recognition. . . . Legitimate power *arises* only among those who form common convictions in unconstrained communication.'[82]

But – as Habermas points out – Arendt's original and brilliant insight into the essential nature of 'communicative power' left some of the main elements of our *actual* contemporary political life outside its bounds. This narrowness of focus arose (he believes) because Arendt

conceives political power neither as a potential for asserting one's own interests or for realizing collective goals, nor as the administrative power to implement collectively binding decisions, but rather as an authorizing force expressed in 'jurisgenesis' – the creation of legitimate law – and in the founding of institutions. It manifests itself in orders that protect political liberty; in resistance against the forms of repression that threaten political liberty . . . ; and above all in the freedom-founding acts that bring new institutions and laws 'into existence'.[83]

But in Habermas's view such a definition of the political is much too narrow. He insists that 'the concept of the political must extend to the strategic competition for political power and to the employment of power within the political system'.[84] Arendt, in his view, is making a fundamental, if empathetic, mistake in *restricting* the concept of the truly political to 'the praxis of those who talk together in order to act in common'.[85]

There is another major area in which some recent commentators have discovered a fundamental opposition between the perspectives of Habermas and Arendt on communication and political power. Unfortunately, the polarity of this alleged opposition reverses itself totally, depending on which commentator we choose to follow.

To put the matter simply: one school of interpretation sees Habermas as advancing the concept of power as a unitary political will formed by rational discussion leading to a unanimous and intellectually compelling conclusion, while Arendt (in this interpretation) supposedly defines power as a shifting and unstable set of relations between irreducibly plural individuals.[86] On the other hand, in an opposing interpretation, it is *Arendt* (reflecting in this the moral unity of her 'republican' or 'communitarian' outlook) who postulates a unitary political will, while Habermas defines power as a complex array of issue-specific agreements, each arising from the exercise of unfettered discourse in a multiplicity of social, political and cultural fora.

The second of these interpretations perhaps can be seen most clearly in the commentary of Baynes.[87] He argues that Habermas, in contrast to Arendt, does not conceive communicative power in a *substantive* way – as the '(more or less spontaneous) expression of a common will'.[88] Rather, Baynes interprets Habermas's 'communicative power' as the ever-shifting outcome of a continuing interplay and interweaving of diverse kinds of public discourse.[89] According to this view, Habermas's version of communicative power does *not* require a 'shared ethical-political self-understanding'[90] of the type supposedly assumed by communitarian / republican thinkers like Arendt. Habermas's communicative power, on the contrary, 'is identified with the realization of a rational public opinion formation and will formation in a process of lawmaking that comprises a complex network of . . . [methods] of reaching understanding *and* bargaining'.[91]

This is Baynes's interpretation, and – so far as Habermas's position is concerned at least – it seems (as we shall see) on the whole to be well founded. But other commentators, best represented by Canovan, confidently characterise the positions of both Habermas and Arendt in essentially the *opposite* way.[92] For Canovan,

Habermas appears to believe that free politics is a matter of citizens first of all talking, and then, after they have all formed a common conviction and will, proceeding to act as one. . . . But Arendt thought . . . that the whole notion of getting individuals to act as one was a dangerous illusion. What she . . . stressed was the inescapable plurality of men, not just in the early stages of discussion, but in action.[93]

But how, if plurality remains the central fact *even in action*, is any effective public action possible at all? This conundrum is only deepened by Canovan's attempt to explicate further the Arendtian concept of action:

men can certainly act together, but not out of anything as stable as a common will based on rational consensus. Instead, human plurality means that action is always a web of intersecting actions with no common goal or definite consummation.[94]

There is a crucial difference between (on the one hand) the concept of a unitary, all-powerful will (as mythologised, for example, by Rousseau in his concept of the 'General Will'), which Arendt surely rejects, and (on the other hand) a series of piecemeal, incomplete, but politically potent consensuses on specific issues for a limited time, leading to effective (though always in principle contestable) common action. The first it seems to me is *rejected* by *both* Arendt and Habermas; the second is, equally, *accepted* by *both* of them. This crucial convergence is, I believe, made clear in the following passages:

Habermas

The public sphere can best be described as a network for communicating information and points of view . . . ; the streams of communication are, in the process, filtered and synthesized in such a way that they coalesce into bundles of *topically specified* public *opinions*.[95]

Stability and absence of ambiguity are rather the exception in . . . communicative practice. . . . A more realistic picture is that . . . of a diffuse, fragile, continuously revised and only momentarily successful communication in which participants . . . feel their way from one *occasional commonalty* to the next.[96]

This [communication] model takes a *structuralist approach* to the manner in which institutionalized opinion- and will-formation is linked with informal opinion building in culturally mobilized public spheres. This linkage is made possible neither by the homogeneity of the people and the identity of the popular will, nor by the identity of a reason that is supposedly able simply to *discover* an underlying homogeneous general interest.[97]

Discourse theory has the success of deliberative politics depend not on a collectively acting citizenry but rather on the institutionalization of . . . procedures and conditions of communication.[98]

Arendt

power [is] . . . dependent upon the unreliable and only temporary agreement of many wills and intentions.

Sovereignty, which is always spurious if claimed by an isolated single entity, be it the individual entity of the person or the collective entity of a nation, assumes, in the case of many men mutually bound by promises, a certain limited reality. . . . [This is] the sovereignty of a body of people bound and kept together, not by an identical will which somehow magically inspires them all, but by an agreed purpose for which alone the promises are valid and binding.[100]

The danger and the advantage inherent in all bodies politic that rely on contracts and treaties is that they, unlike those that rely on rule and sovereignty, leave the unpredictability of human affairs and the unreliability of men as they are, using them merely as the medium . . . into which certain islands of predictability are thrown and in which certain guideposts of reliability are erected.[101]

There is, therefore, as these passages show, a *fundamental convergence* between Habermas and Arendt on the essential nature of public opinion and will formation in political life. But Habermas takes Arendt's highly original position as the basis for a more comprehensive and (it seems to me) a more realistic view of the scope of politics in the modern state. He develops and extends the scope of Arendt's innovative concept of the genesis of political power, which (as we have seen) is, in essence, 'an opinion upon which many publicly are in agreement'.[102] Habermas assigns power that is genuinely political a key role *not only* (as Arendt does) in the founding of free political institutions, *but also* in the day-to-day operation of government and administration. 'The concept of communicative power requires a differentiation in the concept of political power.'[103] It is true, he concedes, that Arendt was right to stress that 'the exercise of political autonomy implies the discursive formation of a common will'.[104] But 'the concept of the political in its full sense also includes the *use of administrative power* within the political system, as well as the *competition for access* to that system'.[105]

Habermas himself, as we have seen,[106] is well aware of the strong affinity between Arendt's central concepts and his own understanding of the relationship between communication and power. Indeed, he makes this fundamentally Arendtian relationship the cornerstone of his whole theory of the democratic constitutional state. As he explains:

The discursive character of opinion- and will-formation in the political public sphere and in parliamentary bodies . . . [establishes] relations of mutual understanding that are 'violence-free' in Arendt's sense and that unleash the generative force of communicative freedom. The communicative power of shared convictions issues only from structures of unimpaired intersubjectivity. This [means an] interpenetration of *discursive lawmaking and communicative power formation*.[107]

Habermas goes on to emphasise Arendt's pioneering role in explicating this crucial relation between communicative activity and political power. He agrees strongly with Arendt that communicative power has its source in 'an opinion upon which many publicly are in agreement'.[108] As he sees it: 'Hannah Arendt disconnects the concept of power from the teleological model: power is built up in communicative action; it is a collective effect of speech'.[109] Habermas quotes directly and fully endorses Arendt's seminal observation: 'power springs up between men when they act together and vanishes the moment they disperse'.[110] He argues that for Arendt 'the fundamental phenomenon of power is not the instrumentalisation of *another's* will, but the formation of a *common* will in a communication directed to reaching agreement'.[111]

This leads Habermas to one of his most important and original concepts regarding the function of *law* in contemporary, post-traditional societies. He contends that 'we [should] view law as the *medium* through which *communicative* power is translated into administrative power. [This] . . . transformation of communicative power into *administrative* [power] has the character of an *empowerment* within the framework of statutory authorisation'.[112]

Starting from this basic principle, Habermas develops further, on a communicative basis, his general theory of the *modern constitutional state*:

the institutional differentiation displayed in the separate branches of government has the purpose of binding the use of administrative power to democratically enacted law in such a way that administrative power regenerates itself solely from the communicative power that citizens engender in common.[113]

In his 'Postscript' to the English translation of *Between Facts and Norms* [1994], Habermas summarises concisely the core of his analysis of the relationship between *communication* or *discourse* (on the one hand) and law and the *constitutional state* (on the other). He starts out from the fundamental premise that, in a secular, post-traditional society, '*positive* law [i.e. the law enacted by the State] can no longer derive its legitimacy from a higher-ranking *moral* law'.[114] From what, then, can its legitimacy derive? Habermas argues that the legitimacy of the legal order in a contemporary democratic state can derive *only* from 'a procedure of presumptively rational opinion- and will-formation'.[115] In Habermas's view, only such an open and fair communicative process, or (in his own terms) such a discursive democratic procedure, can give 'legitimating force to lawmaking under conditions of social and ideological pluralism'.[116]

Looking more closely at Habermas's theory, it seems clear that the *point of departure* for his whole discursive democratic procedure is (in his own words) the 'principle . . . that the only regulations and ways of acting that may claim legitimacy are those to which all who are possibly affected could assent as participants in rational discourses.'[117]

Habermas goes on to explain that it is on the basis of this fundamental 'discourse principle' that 'citizens test which rights they should mutually accord each other'.[118] And he has no doubt about the *wide scope* of the individual rights and liberties that will, in fact, be established by such a discursive procedure founded on rational discourse that is open to all equally. As Habermas puts it: the citizens 'must legally institutionalize those communicative presuppositions and procedures of a political opinion- and will-formation . . . [by which] the discourse principle is applied' in a post-traditional, pluralistic society.[119]

And Habermas's whole analysis culminates in the sweeping assertion of the central *political relevance* of this discourse principle. This principle (besides the other functions already cited) is particularly important for both establishing and *legitimating individual rights and liberties* in a contemporary legal order.

The fundamental principle of democratic political power at the beginning of the twenty-first century is, for Habermas, that 'just those norms deserve to be valid that could meet with the approval of those potentially affected, insofar as the latter participate in rational discourses'.[120] This view has recently been endorsed from a feminist perspective by Seyla Benhabib, in her discussion of models of 'public space'. She argues that Habermas's 'discourse model is the only one which is compatible both with the general social trends of our societies and with the emancipatory aspirations of new social phenomena like the women's movement'.[121]

I shall conclude with Habermas's own sweeping conclusion, in which we find encapsulated the essence of his mature thought on the relation of communication to political power: 'the establishment of the legal code, which is undertaken with the help of the universal right to equal individual liberties, must be *completed* through communicative and participatory rights that guarantee equal opportunities for the *public use* of communicative liberties. In this way, the discourse principle acquires the legal shape of a democratic principle'.[122]

NOTES

1 For lucid and well-balanced introductions to the overall shape of Habermas's project, with helpful bibliographies, see in particular Stephen K. White, *The Recent Work of Jürgen Habermas* (Cambridge, 1988); Mathieu Deflem, *Habermas, Modernity and Law* (London, 1996); Stephen K. White (ed.), *The Cambridge Companion to Habermas* (Cambridge, 1995).

2 For Habermas's continuing debate with the postmodernists, see, in general, Jürgen Habermas, *Der philosophische Diskurs der Moderne. Zwölf Vorlesungen* (Frankfurt am Main, 1985); English translation: *The Philosophical Discourse of Modernity*, trans. F. Lawrence, (Cambridge, 1987); Habermas, 'Modernity versus postmodernity', *New German Critique* 22 (1981), 3–14; Maurizio Passerin D'Entrèves and Seyla Benhabib (eds), *Habermas and the Unfinished Project of Modernity* (Cambridge, 1996); H. Stuart Hall, D. Held, and T. McGrew (eds), *Modernity and its Futures* (Cambridge, 1992), ch. 7; Richard Rorty, 'Habermas and Lyotard on postmodernity', in R. J. Bernstein (ed.), *Habermas and Modernity* (Cambridge, 1985), pp. 161–75.

3 Habermas, 'Towards a theory of communicative competence', *Inquiry* 13 (1970), p. 372

4 Margaret Canovan, 'A case of distorted communication: a note on Habermas and Arendt', *Political Theory* 11 (1983), 105

5 Canovan, 'Distorted communication', p. 106

6 *Faktizität und Geltung. Beiträge zur Discurstheorie des Rechts und des demokratischen Rechtsstaats* (Frankfurt am Main, 1992); English translation: *Between Facts and Norms: Contributions to a Discourse Theory of Law and Democracy*, trans. W. Rehg (Cambridge, MA, 1994).

7 J. Habermas, 'Further reflections on the public sphere', in Craig Calhoun (eds), *Habermas and the Public Sphere* (Cambridge, MA, 1992), p. 442.

8 J. Habermas, *A Berlin Republic: Writings on Germany* (Cambridge, 1998), p. 133.

9 J. Habermas, *Strukturwandel der Öffentlicheit* (Darmstadt and Neuwied, 1962); English translation: *The Structural Transformation of the Public Sphere*, trans. T. Burger (Cambridge, 1992).

10 Habermas, *Facts and Norms*, p. 366

11 Habermas, *Structural Transformation*, pp. 57-88.

12 *Ibid.*, pp. 41ff, 72–3.

13 *Ibid.*

14 Habermas, *Facts and Norms*, p. 147.

15 Habermas, *Structural Transformation*, pp. 57–73.

16 Habermas, *Facts and Norms*, p. 360.

17 Habermas, *Berlin Republic*, p. 144.

18 Habermas, 'Further reflections', pp. 453–4.

19 This summarises the central theme of Habermas, *Structural Transformation*, ch. 3, 'Political functions of the public sphere', pp. 56–88

20 Habermas, *Berlin Republic*, p. 144.

21 Habermas, *Structural Transformation*, p. 163.
22 *Ibid.*, p. 171; emphasis added.
23 An English version of this introduction, entitled 'Further reflections on the public sphere', appears in Calhoun (ed.), *Habermas and the Public Sphere*, pp. 421–61.
24 J. Habermas, *The Theory of Communicative Action*, II (Cambridge, 1995), p. 390.
25 Habermas, *Communicative Action*, II, p. 390; emphasis added; cf. Habermas's remark in 'A Conversation about questions of political theory', *Berlin Republic*, p. 144: 'In the public sphere of the media . . . there are still structures that block a horizontal exchange of spontaneously taken positions – that is, the use of communicative freedoms'.
26 Habermas, *Facts and Norms*, p. 376.
27 Habermas, 'Further reflections', p. 439.
28 Habermas, *Facts and Norms*, p. 377.
29 Habermas, *Berlin Republic*, p. 176.
30 *Ibid.*, p. 176.
31 *Ibid.*, p.177.
32 *Ibid.*, p. 177.
33 Habermas, '1989 in the shadow of 1945: on the normality of a future Berlin republic', in *Berlin Republic*, p. 168.
34 Habermas, *Berlin Republic*, p. 176.
35 *Ibid.*, p.177.
36 Habermas, *Facts and Norms*, esp. chs 3, 4, 7.
37 *Ibid.*, p. 302.
38 *Ibid.*, pp. 307–8, 314
39 *Ibid.*, p. 371.
40 *Ibid.*, p. 314.
41 Habermas, *Berlin Republic*, p. 143.
42 Habermas, 'Further reflections', p. 451.
43 *Ibid.*, p. 451.
44 Habermas, *Facts and Norms*, pp. 135-6.
45 *Ibid.*, p. 169.
46 *Ibid.*, p.192.
47 *Ibid.*, p. 192.
48 For an exceptionally clear, thoughtful and well-written introduction to Arendt's thought, see Margaret Canovan, *Hannah Arendt: A Reinterpretation of her Political Thought* (Cambridge, 1992), which also includes a good bibliography. For a wide range of interpretation, see Lewis P. Hinchman and Sandra K. Hinchman (eds), *Hannah Arendt: Critical Essays* (Albany, NY, 1994).
49 Arendt, *Human Condition*, esp. pp. 196–207.
50 Seyla Benhabib, 'Models of public space: Hannah Arendt, the Liberal Tradition, and Jürgen Habermas', in Calhoun (ed.), *Habermas and the Public Sphere*, p. 75.
51 Habermas, 'Arendt's communications concept', p. 214.
52 Arendt, *Human Condition*, p. 201.
53 Jürgen Habermas, 'On the German-Jewish heritage', *Telos* 44 (1980), 128–9; see also his earlier testimonial to Arendt's influence on his understanding of political praxis in *Theory and Practice* (London, 1974), p. 286.
54 For Habermas's extended development of the theory, largely in terms of a complex dialogue with earlier socio-political theories, see Habermas, *Theory of Communicative Action, passim*.
55 Habermas, 'German-Jewish heritage', p. 128.

56 Habermas, 'Arendt's communications concept', p. 212.
57 Hannah Arendt, *On Violence* (New York, 1970), p. 44.
58 Hannah Arendt, *The Human Condition* (Chicago, 1958), p. 200.
59 Arendt, *On Violence*, p. 41.
60 Arendt, *Human Condition*, p. 244.
61 *Ibid.*, p. 201.
62 Arendt, *On Revolution* , p. 71
63 Jürgen Habermas, 'Hannah Arendt's communications concept of power', in Lewis P. Hinchman and Sandra K. Hinchman (eds), *Hannah Arendt: Critical Essays* (Albany, NY, 1994), p. 212.
64 Habermas, 'Arendt's communications concept', p. 224.
65 *Ibid.*, p. 224; emphasis added.
66 *Ibid.*, p. 223; emphasis added.
67 *Ibid.*, p. 213.
68 Jürgen Habermas, *The Past as Future*, trans. Max Pensky (Lincoln, Nebraska, 1994), p. xviii.
69 In particular, see two trenchant critiques: David Luban, 'Habermas on Arendt on power', *Philosophy and Social Criticism* 6 (1979), 81–93, and Margaret Canovan, 'A case of distorted communication: a note on Habermas and Arendt', *Political Theory* 11 (1983), 105–16; see also, in general, Benhabib, 'Models of public space', pp. 73–98.
70 Luban, 'Habermas on Arendt', pp. 86–7; Canovan, 'Distorted communication', pp. 107–12.
71 Canovan, 'Distorted communication', p. 108. In a similar vein, Luban comments: 'Habermas's reconstruction of the communications concept of power contains . . . more Habermas than Arendt.' Luban, 'Habermas on Arendt', pp. 81–2.
72 Arendt, *Human Condition*, p. 178.
73 *Ibid.*, pp. 199–200.
74 *Ibid.*, p. 200.
75 *Ibid.*, p. 200; emphasis added.
76 Arendt, *On Violence*, p. 41.
77 Habermas, 'Arendt's communications concept', p. 219.
78 *Ibid.*, p. 218.
79 *Ibid.*, p. 219.
80 *Ibid.*, pp. 219–20.
81 *Ibid.*, p. 220.
82 *Ibid.*, p. 222.
83 Habermas, *Facts and Norms*, p. 148.
84 Habermas, 'Arendt's communications concept', p. 224.
85 *Ibid.*, p. 224.
86 Canovan, 'Distorted communication', pp. 108–12; Luban, 'Habermas and Arendt', pp. 88–9.
87 Kenneth Baynes, 'Democracy and the Rechtsstaat: Habermas's *Faktizität und Geltung*', in White (ed.), *Cambridge Companion to Habermas*, pp. 201–32.
88 Baynes, 'Democracy and the Rechtsstaat', p. 213.
89 *Ibid.*, p. 213.
90 *Ibid.*, p. 213.
91 *Ibid.*, p. 213.
92 Canovan, 'Distorted communication', pp. 108–12.
93 *Ibid.*, pp. 109–10.
94 *Ibid.*, p. 110.

95 Habermas, *Facts and Norms*, p. 360; emphasis altered.
96 Habermas, *Communicative Action*, I, pp. 100–1; emphasis added.
97 Habermas, *Facts and Norms*, p. 185.
98 Habermas, *Faktizität und Geltung*, pp. 361–2; emphasis added; as cited in Baynes, 'Democracy and the Rechtsstaat', p. 215.
99 Arendt, *Human Condition*, p. 201.
100 Arendt, *Human Condition*, p. 245.
101 Arendt, *Human Condition*, p. 244.
102 Arendt, *On Revolution*, p. 71.
103 Habermas, *Facts and Norms*, p. 150
104 *Ibid.*, p. 150.
105 *Ibid.*, p.150; emphasis added.
106 See above, pp. 294–300.
107 Habermas, *Facts and Norms*, p. 151.
108 Arendt, *On Revolution*, p. 71.
109 Habermas, 'Arendt's communications concept', p. 213.
110 Arendt, *Human Condition*, p. 200.
111 Habermas, 'Arendt's communications concept', p. 212.
112 Habermas, *Facts and Norms*, p. 150; emphasis added.
113 *Ibid.*, p. 173.
114 *Ibid.*, p. 457.
115 *Ibid.*, p. 457.
116 *Ibid.*, p. 458.
117 *Ibid.*, p. 458.
118 *Ibid.*, p. 458.
119 *Ibid.*, p. 458.
120 *Ibid.*, p. 127.
121 Seyla Benhabib, *Situating the Self: Gender, Community, and Postmodernism in Contemporary Ethics* (London, 1992), p. 113.
122 Habermas, *Facts and Norms*, p. 458

Contributors to this Volume

Christopher Andrew is Professor of Modern and Contemporary History, and Chair of the History Faculty at the University of Cambridge. His most recent books include *For The President's Eyes Only: Secret Intelligence and the American Presidency from Washington to Bush*, and *The Mitrokhin Archive: The KGB in Europe and the West* (with Vasili Mitrokhin).

Tony Ballantyne taught at the National University of Ireland, Galway before taking up his current position in the Department of History at the University of Illinois, Urbana-Champaign. His research focuses on the British Empire as an agent of cultural globalisation, a theme explored in his *An Aryan Empire? Orientalism, History and Identity in Colonial India and the Pacific* (forthcoming, Macmillan, 2001).

Thomas Bartlett is Professor of Modern Irish History at University College Dublin. His recent publications include an edited and restored *Life of Theobald Wolfe Tone* (Dublin, 1998).

Allen Bass lectures in history at University College Cork. He is a specialist in the history of political ideas. Recent publications include 'The metaphor of the human body in the political theory of John of Salisbury', in D. Steuer and B. Debattin (eds), *Metaphor and Rational Discourse* (Tübingen, 1997) and 'Early Germanic Experience and the origins of representation', *Parliaments, Estates and Representation*, 15 (1995).

C. A. Bayly is Vere Harmsworth Professor of Imperial and Naval History at the University of Cambridge. His books include *Imperial Meridian: The British Empire and the World* (1989), and *Empire and Information: Intelligence Gathering and Social Communication in India 1780–1870* (1996).

Guy Beiner is currently completing a PhD at the Department of Irish History in University College Dublin. His main fields of interest at present relate to the use of folklore sources in the study of modern Irish history.

Anthony G. Corbett works in the Department of English at University College Cork, and wrote his PhD on alternative modes of communication in late medieval religious theatre. He is completing two books, the first on structures in the York cycle, and the second on the audience for medieval theatre, provisionally entitled *Drama and Belonging*. He has previously published in *Medieval English Theatre, Formes Teatrals de la Tradició Medieval* and *Research Opportunities in Renaissance Drama*.

John Horgan is Professor of Journalism at Dublin City University. He is the author of two recent biographies of Sean Lemass and of Noel Browne, and of the forthcoming *A Critical History of Irish Media 1922–2000* (Routledge).

Yrjö Kaukiainen is Professor of European History at the University of Helsinki. He has published on maritime history, demographic history and economic and social history, mainly of the eighteenth and nineteenth centuries. His recent books include *Sailing into Twilight: Finnish Shipping in an Age of Transport Revolution, 1860–1914* (Helsinki, 1991) and *A History of Finnish Shipping* (London, 1993).

Ralph Kingston graduated from Trinity College, Dublin in 1997. He is currently at University College London, writing up his doctoral thesis. His work on bureaucracy plays a central part in this wider project, investigating the consolidation of bourgeois culture in early-nineteenth-century France.

Sian Lewis is the author of *News and Society in the Greek Polis* (London 1996). She completed her DPhil on information in the classical world at the University of Oxford in 1993, and is now Lecturer in Ancient History at the University of Wales, Cardiff. She is currently working on a study of female iconography in classical Greek art.

Charles C. Ludington is a doctoral candidate in history at Columbia University. He has published articles on Huguenot settlements in County Tyrone, the treatment of Huguenots in Irish historiography and on British and Irish political thought. He is currently completing his dissertation on the politics of wine in Britain and Ireland, 1660–1860.

Brian McGing is a Fellow of Trinity College, Dublin, where he is Professor in the Department of Classics. His research interests and publications centre largely on the Hellenistic world of the eastern Mediterranean – Asia Minor, Judaea and Egypt. He is at present editing a collection of second-century BC Greek papyrological texts from the Egyptian city of Lycopolis held in the Library of Trinity College.

Hiram Morgan teaches Renaissance and Reformation history at University College Cork. He has authored *Tyrone's Rebellion* (1993) and edited *Political Ideology in Ireland, 1541–1641* (1999). He is joint-editor of *History Ireland*, an illustrated quarterly magazine.

Gary Murphy lectures in Government at Dublin City University Business School. He has published numerous articles on the history of the Irish state and is currently working on a biography of the Fianna Fáil politician Sean MacEntee and an edited volume of essays on the Sean Lemass era.

Alan O'Day has taught for American, British, Canadian and German universities and is now a Visiting Fellow, Mansfield College, Oxford. His publications include, *The English Face of Irish Nationalism* (1977), *Parnell and the First Home Rule Episode* (1986), *Irish Home Rule 1867–1921* (1998) and *Charles Stewart Parnell* (1998).

Thomas O'Loughlin was born in Dublin and is now Senior Lecturer in Theology in the University of Wales, Lampeter. He is a specialist in the history of ideas in the Latin West in the late classical and early medieval periods, and over the years has given particular consideration to the history of ideas in the insular region. His major study of the transmission of ideas in the period was published in 1999: *Teachers and Code-Breakers: The Latin Genesis Tradition, 430–800* [*Instrumenta Patristica* 35].

Index